The Legacy of Liberal Judaism

The Legacy of Liberal Judaism

Ernst Cassirer and Hannah Arendt's Hidden Conversation

❋

Ned Curthoys

berghahn
NEW YORK · OXFORD
www.berghahnbooks.com

Published in 2013 by
Berghahn Books
www.berghahnbooks.com

© 2013, 2016 Ned Curthoys
First paperback edition published in 2016

Library of Congress Cataloging-in-Publication Data

Curthoys, Ned.
The legacy of liberal Judaism: Ernst Cassirer and Hannah Arendt's hidden
conversation / Ned Curthoys. -- First edition.
    pages cm
Includes bibliographical references and index.
ISBN 978-1-78238-007-8 (hardback) -- ISBN 978-1-78533-216-6
(paperback) -- ISBN 978-1-78238-008-5 (ebook)
1. Reform Judaism--Philosophy. 2. Jewish philosophy--20th century.
3. Cassirer, Ernst, 1874-1945--Religion. 4. Arendt, Hannah, 1906-1975--
Religion. I. Title.
 BM197.C87 2013
 296.8'34--dc23
                                                    2013005571

British Library Cataloguing in Publication Data
A catalogue record for this book is available from the British Library

ISBN 978-1-78238-007-8 (hardback)
ISBN 978-1-78533-216-6 (paperback)
ISBN 978-1-78238-008-5 (ebook)

To my parents,
Ann Curthoys and John Docker

Contents

❄

Acknowledgements

❄

This book has been made possible by the assistance and advice of organizations, institutions, and valued friends and colleagues. Most of the research for this book was conducted under the auspices of an Australian Research Council Australian Postdoctoral Fellowship. I was able to conduct research in the United Kingdom thanks to funds from the Research School of Humanities and the Arts at the Australian National University. I am also grateful to the Australian Academy of the Humanities for providing a Humanities Fieldwork Fellowship allowing me to travel to the United States and conduct invaluable research at the Hannah Arendt Archives at the Library of Congress. I am grateful to staff and colleagues at the former Centre for Cross-Cultural Research and the School of Cultural Inquiry. I would like to acknowledge the assistance of staff at the Chifley and Menzies Libraries of the Australian National University.

I have many family members, friends, and colleagues to thank for their support and helpful advice. I would like to thank Debjani Ganguly for her friendship, guidance, and continuing support. For their generosity in conversation and in reading and commenting on parts of the book, I thank Alex Cook, Willi Goetschel, Richard King, Dirk Moses, Andy Schaap, and Dan Stone. I am especially grateful to Ann Curthoys and John Docker for reading the entire manuscript and offering invaluable advice and guidance. I could not have undertaken this project without their extraordinary efforts, and their generous and unstinting support. My most heartfelt gratitude goes to my partner Shino Konishi who has provided wonderful feedback, loving support, and expert help. This book could not have been written without you. My thanks also to Glenys Holley and the Holley family for their love and support. My son Leo is my greatest inspiration.

I dedicate this book to my parents.

Earlier versions of Chapters 1 and 8 appeared, respectively, as 'A Diasporic Reading of *Nathan the Wise*', in *Comparative Literature Studies* 47(1) (2010), 70–95, and 'Hannah Arendt: A Question of Character', in *New Formations* 71 (2011), 58–78.

Introduction

❋

This book is an attempt to historicize the so-called 'Jewish writings' of Hannah Arendt but it is also a reconstruction of an important tradition of Jewish thought and politics, one that is continually being renewed in the face of contemporary challenges. For some time I have felt that despite the veritable critical industry that has grown up around Arendt as a political theorist and philosopher, the specific intellectual and ethical background to her writings on Jewish issues has yet to be sufficiently illuminated. In *The Legacy of Liberal Judaism: Ernst Cassirer and Hannah Arendt's Hidden Conversation* I suggest that Arendt's desire for a progressive or 'worldly' Judaism that eagerly participates in contemporary culture is informed by a vital legacy of liberal Jewish political advocacy, ethical idealism, and refractory historical consciousness. It was a legacy forged by luminaries of German Jewish letters such as Moses Mendelssohn, Leopold Zunz, Abraham Geiger, Heinrich Graetz, Heinrich Heine, Hermann Cohen, and Ernst Cassirer.

By the rubric 'liberal Judaism' I have in mind a progressive conception of Jewish culture and history that arose after the German Jewish Enlightenment or *Haskalah* in the late eighteenth century and maintained a powerful influence on German Jewry until the demise of that community beginning in 1933. I interpret liberal Judaism as an energetic worldview which seeks to accommodate the vitality and evolving nature of Jewish life in diaspora by emphasizing that in preserving the ethical kernel of genuine monotheism, Jews have an exemplary role to play in world history. Liberal Jewish thought emphasizes the importance of post-exilic Jewish history in shaping modern Jewish identity and points to the variety of religious, literary, and historical sources informing contemporary Judaism. Liberal Jewish intellectuals from Moses Mendelssohn onwards have taken particular pride in Jewish traditions of philosophical rationalism which articulate an ethical interpretation of Judaism. Maimonides stands at the pinnacle of this tradition because of his ethically motivated and idealistically inclined interpretation of the significance of Jewish monotheism and Jewish Law.

Liberal Judaism is also notable for its inclusive conception of Judaism and the keen interest it displays in 'non-Jewish Jews', those liminally situated and heterodox Jews who have been expelled from or have left the Jewish community such as, for example, Baruch Spinoza and Heinrich Heine. Interested in the creative adaptability of Judaism under diasporic conditions, liberal Jewish thinkers extol the formative influence of non-Jewish cultural milieux such as Andalusian Spain or republican Holland in the seventeenth century on the flourishing of Jewish philosophy, literature, and biblical hermeneutics. Wary of ethnocentric and normative conceptions of Jewish belief and identity, liberal Jewish thought displays a constant willingness to incorporate the ideas of non-Jewish thinkers, such as the cosmopolitan philosophies of Lessing and Kant, into Jewish philosophy and theology. Liberal Judaism encourages an active and alert historical consciousness and a cautiously optimistic interpretation of the unfolding history of the Jewish people that is suspicious of the 'lachrymose' narrative of Jewish history as a story of perpetual suffering and martyrdom, a history that can only be redeemed by the ingathering of the Jewish people and the end of exile or *Galut*.

Liberal Jewish thought pays very close attention to the political affairs, social attitudes, and scholarly tendencies of the non-Jewish world and interprets Jewish advocacy as intervening in and attempting to progressively transform the host society's self-conception and formative historical narratives. From Moses Mendelssohn onwards, liberal Jewish intellectuals and political advocates assume that the fate of Jews and Judaism is closely tied to the broader achievement of social justice, and to the decoupling of state and nationality. As a reformist ethos, liberal Judaism promotes a secularized and pluralist conception of Jewish identity which is attentive to the polyglot nature of the diaspora. Impressed by the extraordinary intellectual and creative achievements of recent diaspora history, liberal Jewish thought is interested in the exemplary character, sensibility, and art of living of Jewish individuals throughout history. Liberal Jewish thinkers often suggest that the worldly Jewish characteristics they prize are more luminously disclosed through interaction with the non-Jewish world. Liberal Judaism urges an ethos of cosmopolitanism and humanism that is strongly opposed to Jewish nationalism and exclusivism. It regards Judaism as a religious and ethical impulse, a spiritual power or 'energy' that manifests itself immanently in world affairs while striving idealistically towards a redemptive or 'messianic' future that will unify humanity. Ecumenically inclined, the liberal Jewish thinkers I discuss have an abiding concern with the historical importance and ethical potential of cross-cultural friendship and sociability, inspired by the epochal friendship of Moses Mendelssohn and Gotthold Ephraim Lessing, discussed in the first chapter. Many German Jews celebrated and commemorated their legendary friendship and intellectual collaboration as an exemplary instance of the fertile participation of Jews in modern culture as long as their difference and distinctiveness are fully acknowledged.

The Legacy of Liberal Judaism argues against the critical consensus that Hannah Arendt's Jewish politics and historical consciousness were forged as a response to anti-Semitism and Nazism. I suggest that Arendt's stance – that the Jewish people should be at the vanguard of history in demonstrating the ethical nullity of the ethnic majority nation state – is distinctly redolent of a liberal Jewish articulation of Jews as vessels of ethical idealism and bearers of innovation and progress in a world blighted by parochialism and sectarianism. Arendt's sympathy for Jewish outsider figures, memorably epitomized in her praise for the rebellious figure of the Jewish 'pariah', resonates with the 'Prophetic' tradition of Judaism espoused *inter alia* by Abraham Geiger, Hermann Cohen, and Ernst Cassirer, which acknowledged the searing internal criticism of the Jewish Prophets as a crucial and exemplary chapter in the religious evolution of Judaism. Arendt's famous suggestion that the pariah, as a particular Jewish 'type', evokes a 'hidden tradition' of Jewish historical agency under diasporic conditions recalls liberal Jewish attempts to read Jewish history against the grain and to articulate the fecundity of Judaism's post-biblical history. I also suggest that when Arendt interpreted anti-Semitism historically as a contingent modern ideology that could be overcome, thus repudiating the fatalistic Zionist conception of an 'eternal anti-Semitism', a rationale for the inevitable failure of the Jewish diaspora, she was reprising liberal Jewish challenges to Zionism's lachrymose historical consciousness and primordial conception of Jewish identity, challenges that had previously been voiced by Abraham Geiger and Hermann Cohen among others. Arendt's Jewish thought reprises liberal Judaism in that it is focused on possibilities for secular Jewish agency under diasporic conditions and thus motivated by hope for the future rather than by a fatalistic and paradigmatically inclined interpretation of the cyclical and ever recurring historical suffering of the Jewish people.

All of this suggests that there are heuristic benefits in comparing Arendt to paragons of liberal Jewish thought such as Abraham Geiger, Hermann Cohen, and Ernst Cassirer, public intellectuals who articulated the vibrancy of Jewish diasporic life and expressed pride in the manifold contributions Jews have made to Western ethics and philosophy. Yet given the almost total absence of such a genealogical and comparative focus in Arendt studies to date, we need to explore why scholars of Arendt have been reluctant to locate the sources of her Jewish self-conception and ethical sensibility in post-Enlightenment liberal Judaism. It is a curious fact, and one in need of explanation, that Arendt has not been compared in any sustained fashion to prominent German Jewish philosophers such as Hermann Cohen (1842–1918) and his great student, Ernst Cassirer (1872–1945), justly famous philosophers of whom she would surely have been aware as a young philosophically inclined German Jewish intellectual in the 1920s. The records of the Hannah Arendt collection at the Bard college library show, for example, that Arendt possessed a significant collection of Cassirer's works, some with marginalia and underlining, Cohen's three-volume *Jüdische Schriften* (Jewish Writings), as well as the collected edition of Kant's writings published by Bruno Cassirer (1922–1923) that Cassirer edited with Hermann Cohen.[1]

One of the obstacles to sourcing Arendt's ideas in nineteenth-century German Jewish liberal traditions has been a strong tendency in Arendt scholarship to take her at her word; that is, to judge Arendt as a quintessentially modern theorist who broke with the authority of tradition and invented a mode of philosophizing and judging 'without banisters', in other words, without meaningful precedents. Arendt's thought is often adjudged to be virtually *sui generis* because it is formed by, and an engaged reflection on, very recent experiences. These include Arendt's experiences of anti-Semitism in Germany in the 1920s and 1930s, her subsequent lengthy period as an endangered stateless refugee until her arrival in the United States in 1941, and later her reportage on the Eichmann trial for the *New Yorker* that (in)famously produced her controversial theory of the 'banality of evil'. Arendt studies have tended to agree with her self-perception as a theorist of modernity, and privilege her as one of the foremost participant-cum-theorists of the twentieth century. As we shall see, this presentism extends to discussions of Arendt's Jewish writings and activism, which are often interpreted as ascribable to her belated discovery of the 'Jewish question' under historical pressure and in scathing reaction to a baleful history of German Jewish assimilation.

In one of the most recent volumes dedicated to Arendt's ethics and politics, *Thinking in Dark Times* (2010), Jerome Kohn contends that Arendt not only wrote on Jews and Jewish affairs over four decades, from the 1930s to the 1960s, but that her 'political thought in general is anchored in her experience as a Jew . . . her Jewish experience is literally the foundation of her thought'.[2] Kohn reads Arendt's 'Jewish experience' as negatively forged by her reaction against the 'assimilation of Jews into German society'. That assimilation and the 'lack of responsible political action' by German Jews are the 'kernels' that engendered Arendt's well known distinction between social and political life, marking 'the beginning of her career as a conscious pariah among her own people'.[3] Another prominent interpreter of Arendt's Jewish thought, Ron Feldman, argues in the same volume that Arendt's Jewishness was adamantly secular and political, thus in elective affinity to the Zionist response to Jewish modernity. As for so many German Jews, 'its significance was thrust upon her by the rise of Nazism'.[4] Despite Arendt's critique of Theodor Herzl's Zionist philosophy, her 'personal transformation into a Zionist bears many similarities to that of political Zionism's founder'. For both Arendt and Herzl, Feldman suggests, their 'German cultural education was more significant than their Jewish education', nor did either take any particular interest in 'Judaism'. After becoming politicized in the face of growing anti-Semitism, neither Arendt nor Herzl displayed any real personal interest in Jewish religion, philosophy, or literature, but were instead 'focused on political and historical issues'.[5]

I would dispute Kohn and Feldman's presentist assumption that Arendt's political theory and Jewish commitments can be experientially derived from her belated awakening to contemporary circumstances, rather than from an interpretation of Jewish identity, philosophy, and history with profound moorings in German Jewish letters.[6] If we accept, as the scholarship does, that Arendt was strongly influenced by what she took to be the critical realism of the German Zionist movement, led by her friend Kurt Blumenfeld, a movement which, given its hopes for a Jewish cultural renaissance, can hardly be reduced to an epiphenomenon of anti-Semitism, it follows that the non-Zionist aspects of her thinking, particularly apparent from the 1940s, may have been influenced by other Jewish philosophical and ethical traditions intrinsic to her German Jewish background.

Where Feldman and Kohn argue, conventionally, for an interpretation of Arendt's Jewishness as a belated conversion to political Zionism after she became alert to the threat of anti-Semitism in Germany, recent scholarship interested in Arendt as a 'post-Zionist' *avant la lettre* has also contributed to the tendency to derive Arendt's Jewish worldview from her contemporaneous experience and political engagements. Moshe Zimmerman, for example, in seeking to explain Arendt's growing concern during the 1940s at the prospect of a sovereign Jewish state with a Palestinian Arab minority, suggests that the 'European experience taught Hannah Arendt to doubt minority agreements of any kind in the search for a solution to the Middle Eastern problem'.[7] While this statement and others quoted above are largely correct, they typify an approach that rarely asks after the possible 'Jewish sources' of Arendt's critique of the ethnocentric nation state. Such an approach, while interested in Arendt's non-Zionism or idiosyncratic cultural Zionism, fails to recognize how closely Arendt's desire to defend the wide spectrum of contemporary Jewish life against Zionism's often aggressive critique of the alienated condition of the diaspora echoes Hermann Cohen's defence of diasporic Judaism in his 1916 debate with the cultural Zionist Martin Buber, discussed in Chapter 4. In his introduction to the volume *Hannah Arendt in Jerusalem*, Steven Aschheim quotes Arendt as reminding her friend Karl Jaspers that 'the state of Israel . . . in no way arose exclusively from . . . necessity'.[8] Perhaps Arendt was also obliquely referring to her own heterodox position on Jewish issues, indicating that her ideas were by no means simply a response to being, in her words 'hit over the head by History', or motivated by the perception that the 'modern European Jewish project of assimilation was a complete disaster'.[9] After all, both liberal Judaism and Zionism are different responses to anti-Semitism and cannot simply be derived from experience or personal predilection. Ideas, particularly ones that attempt to express or enact political emotions, rarely can.

However, if many of Arendt's ideas about Jews and Judaism are attributable to the influence of the liberal Jewish ethos, with its proud defence of the creative individuality of Jewish individuals, this genealogy has been occluded by the commonplace that Arendt's Jewish commitments represent a sharp reaction to her German Jewish heritage.

Arendt as a German Jew

The persistent failure of Arendt studies to analyse her affiliations with liberal German Jewish thought – an affinity that would illuminate her heterodox approach to Jewish history, politics, and culture – is attributable, I argue, to the assumption that much of the German Jewish response to modernity can be safely dismissed as 'assimilationist'. As we have seen, there is a marked tendency in Arendt scholarship to interpret her politicized and performative conception of Jewish identity as a vigorous rejection of the assimilationist posture of her bourgeois German Jewish forebears. Analysing the famous disagreement between Arendt and Gershom Scholem, David Suchoff, for example, points to their dispute over Jewish identity as a kind of family quarrel. He argues that since both Arendt and Scholem sought to highlight the 'scandal Jewish particularity signified to the German cultural tradition', their work has a deeper affinity as a 'Jewish critique of German culture'.[10] Where Arendt faulted German Jews as careerist 'parvenus', Scholem bitterly attacked them for a self-deceptive belief in universalism that hid the particularities of the Jewish situation in Europe.[11] Steven Aschheim agrees with Suchoff's assessment, arguing that both Arendt and Scholem 'exemplified the radical revolt against German Jewish bourgeois modes of assimilation'.[12]

Underlying many of the assessments of Arendt's Judaism is the tacit consensus that, in the words of Anson Rabinbach, Arendt articulates a 'new Jewish *ethos*' which above all 'refused to accept . . . the optimism of the generation of German Jews nurtured on the concept of *Bildung* as the German Jewish mystique'.[13] The 'modern Jewish type', Rabinbach argues, 'emerges as the negative image of the assimilated German Jew'.[14] Significantly, Rabinbach establishes Hermann Cohen's 'unproblematic interpretation of Judaism as "the religion of reason"' as the generational foil of this 'new' Jewish sensibility. Cohen, according to Rabinbach, epitomizes the 'rationalism of Wilhelminian Jewish intellectuals', displaying a lamentably naive faith in a symbiosis of German and Jewish identities 'which only in retrospect appears to us as a fatal blindness'.[15] Rabinbach's jaundiced generational thesis is clearly influenced by the great social historian George Mosse's famous critique of the German Jewish embrace of *Bildung* or autonomous self-formation through acculturation, in which the German Jewish acquisition of classical learning, aesthetic sensitivity, and norms of social respectability were considered 'entry tickets to German society', signifying 'membership in the bourgeoisie'.[16] That the German Jewish strategy of embourgeoisement proved a lamentable failure in protecting Jews from anti-Semitism has become a commonplace of German Jewish historiography.[17] As Dirk Moses has recently argued, however, in a revisionist critique of some of the guiding assumptions of German Jewish studies, the tendency to 'posit Germans and Jews as ontologically distinct categories' leads to a 'zero-sum game of interaction in which a cultural adaptation, layered or co-mingled identity is coded as a loss or gain for a minority or majority', subtending an interpretation of Jewish emancipation in Germany as amounting to assimilation and the decline of 'Jewish strength and vitality'.[18] This zero-sum game is clearly evidenced in the broad assumption that Arendt's Jewish identity was a revolt against her 'German cultural education' and Enlightenment background, yet is nevertheless ironic given Arendt's complaint against the Zionist division of Jews and non-Jews into two warring 'natural substances'.[19]

This brings us to the continuing elision of Ernst Cassirer from Arendt studies. It is regrettable that in his recent intellectual biography of Ernst Cassirer, Edward Skidelsky recapitulates the thesis of a potent Jewish generational divide separating the dated German Jewish rationalist from the vigorous 'new Jew'. In *Ernst Cassirer: the Last Philosopher of Culture* (2008), Skidelsky sheds doubt as to whether a classic product of the cultured, rationalist German Jewish *Bildungsbürgertum* like Ernst Cassirer can still speak to modern audiences. He laments, while also affirming as necessary, that we moderns remain, in Richard Wolin's terms, 'Heidegger's children'. Denying that Cassirer's philosophy of symbolic forms possesses a coherent ethics and politics, Skidelsky suggests that 'Cassirer, for all his decency – indeed precisely *because* of his decency – did not see what Heidegger and many others saw so clearly: that the secular idols of humanity and progress were dead.'[20]

I will be engaging with Skidelsky's critique of Cassirer as an apolitical Wilhelminian German Jew in Chapter 5, but I mention his reprise of the generational argument to illustrate how contemporary scholarship has worked very effectively to categorize Arendt, but not overlapping contemporaries such as Ernst Cassirer and the later Hermann Cohen, as a vigorous participant in the 'Jewish Renaissance'. This was a movement of German and central European Jews after the First World War which critiqued the assimilationism and embourgeoisement of their parents' generation and sought to prioritize their Jewish identity, often by looking to the example of East European Jewry and the revivalist 'Hebrew humanism' of cultural Zionists such as Martin Buber. Many scholars hold that there is a distinct generational and attitudinal divide between, on the one hand, Weimar era thinkers such as Hannah Arendt, Gershom Scholem, Franz Rosenzweig, and Walter Benjamin who articulate different forms of Jewish modernity and, on the other, those German Jews, like Cassirer, whom they characterize as bourgeois, rationalist, and ultimately deluded by their faith in the salutary power of German culture. Wilhelmine era Jews are held to have naively underestimated the threat of anti-Semitism, and are condemned as part of a liberal Jewish community that transformed Judaism into a voluntaristic confessional faith rather than an encompassing cultural and spiritual identity. The interpretation of Arendt as a quintessentially modern and secular thinker who rejected the thin universalism of the Enlightenment, thus a student ('child') of Heidegger, has also contributed to the perception that she represents a completely different era from the now passé neo-Kantian idealism of thinkers like Hermann Cohen and Ernst Cassirer.

In *The Legacy of Liberal Judaism: Ernst Cassirer and Hannah Arendt's Hidden Conversation* I attempt to break down this highly influential generational thesis which has tended to discourage genealogical investigations of Arendt's relationship to liberal and progressive strands of German Jewish thought or to resemblances between Arendt's activity as a Jewish public intellectual and earlier eras of German Jewish advocacy. We can see the efficacy of the putative generational divide between the radical 'new Jew' and the bourgeois and quietist German Jew when we consider that there are few if any comparisons of the philosophy and Jewish writings of Arendt and Ernst Cassirer. This is peculiar when we remember that Cassirer was a leading interpreter of Kant who anticipated Arendt in taking great interest in Kant's Enlightenment context, including his enthusiasm for the French Revolution, his cosmopolitan political theory and philosophy of history, and his humanist desire to engage a broader public. As Arendt would in the 1950s, as early as the 1920s Cassirer extolled the epochal significance of Lessing's dynamic conception of reason and enthused over Lessing as one of the great representatives of the 'religious Enlightenment'. Like Arendt, Cassirer was critical of a particularist conception of Judaism focused on territorial sovereignty and the priority of Jewish survival. Responding to the injunction of his friend and mentor Hermann Cohen, Cassirer theorized an ethically inspired 'Prophetic Judaism' that promotes diaspora Judaism's ongoing world-historical task to articulate the ethical principles of monotheism and its correlative conception of a unified humanity.

While commentators seem to remember well Arendt's caustic – one might say parricidal – critique of German Jewish responses to the post-emancipation era, a critique that is certainly comparable to Gershom Scholem's in its intensity, they tend to pay far less attention to the thematic significance of Arendt's post-war writings, which provide abundant evidence of a reconciliation with many aspects of liberal German Jewish thought. I have in mind Arendt's increasing sympathy for the German *Aufklärung*, evoked by her mature enthusiasm for Lessing and Kant, her growing interest in the redemptive political potential of friendships between Germans and Jews, and her evocation of the exemplary qualities of rebellious Jewish character types in recent Jewish history. I think too of Arendt's sympathetic focus on those diasporic Jewish 'worlds', such as the Polish-Jewish milieu of Rosa Luxemburg, that have nourished political agency and relational sensibilities; of great significance in this regard is Arendt's mature 'Prophetic' willingness to be an outsider to or rebel within the Jewish community.

In a very interesting aperçu that questions the notion of Arendt's Jewishness as a purely secular phenomenon divorced from historical Judaism, the late Elisabeth Young-Bruehl recently affirmed the influence of the Prophetic tradition of Judaism on Arendt's historical consciousness. She maintains that it was 'Arendt's Jewish identity – not just the identity she asserted in defending herself as a Jew when attacked as one, but more deeply her connection to the Axial Age prophetic tradition – that made her the cosmopolitan she was'. Young-Bruehl suggests that in the anti-Semitism section of *The Origins of Totalitarianism* and throughout her writings on 'the Jewish question', Arendt invokes the 'cosmopolitan tradition that was established for the Jews by their Axial Age prophets' as an antidote to 'tribalist Jewish thinking, parochial and governed by mythic notions about the Jews as a chosen people ... transcendently oriented rather than in and of this world and its interrelated peoples'.[21] Susannah Young-ah Gottlieb has also recently renewed interest in a post-secular Arendt by arguing suggestively that 'Arendt's use of messianic language [Gottlieb refers to Arendt's analysis of the 'fact of human natality' in *The Human Condition* as that 'miracle' which expresses 'faith in and hope for the world'] and redemptive motifs has a long and distinguished tradition in German Jewish scholarship', articulated in Arendt's work as the 'weak [because non-sovereign] redemptive power of action'.[22]

Young-Bruehl and Gottlieb's 'post-secularist' approach to the sources of Arendt's Jewish thought is immensely valuable, particularly as both stress that Arendt draws on a tradition of German Jewish religious thought which is emphatically non-eschatological in that it expresses hope for, rather than flight from, the world. Following Young-Bruehl, *The Legacy of Liberal Judaism: Ernst Cassirer and Hannah Arendt's Hidden Conversation* explores the continuity and expressive power of the ideals of Prophetic Judaism, an influential German Jewish discourse throughout the nineteenth century, which arguably culminated in Hermann Cohen's *Religion of Reason from the Sources of Judaism* (1919) and was a source of inspiration for Ernst Cassirer's philosophical anthropology.

Prophetic Judaism, I argue, was less a purely religious teaching than a way of modelling Jewish cultural identity in the present: defending, for example, the role of the creative outsider and internal critic of the Jewish community, and establishing the historical importance of a visionary and reformist stream of Jewish philosophical and literary creativity. Rather than illuminating Arendt's Jewish writings against an antithetical German Jewish background, I point to the fecundity and adaptability of liberal Jewish thought, which, like Arendt's Lessing in *Men in Dark Times*, defends Judaism's 'position in the world' while never losing sight of the richness of its historical sources. The reconstruction of liberal Jewish thought I undertake here suggests, as does Elisabeth Young-Bruehl, that Arendt's willingness to relationally perform her Jewishness in response to an oppressive environment, and her espousal of a refractory, cosmopolitan historical consciousness that challenges official histories, situate her as a proponent of the Prophetic tradition of Jewish ethics. Arendt's relationship to Prophetic Judaism can only be illuminated, however, by acknowledging her contribution to a tradition of liberal Jewish thought stretching back some two and half centuries. Methodologically, such an investigation cannot remain content with rehearsing Arendt's explicit distaste, predicated on a distorted and jaundiced interpretation, for German Jewish forebears such as Moses Mendelssohn, the Jewish philosopher and political advocate. Despite her antipathy to Mendelssohn's alleged quietism and ahistorical emphasis on individual *Bildung*, Arendt's celebration of a Jewish sensibility synonymous with a humane sympathy for outsiders and heretics, her belief that overarching historical philosophies diminish the intellectual independence of the individual, her sympathy for the dialogical philosophizing of Socrates, and her vigorous defence of Judaism's contribution to human progress, can all be traced back to Mendelssohn, her putative nemesis.

In Chapter 1 I resituate the oft maligned Moses Mendelssohn as a 'world thinker', a cosmopolitan liberal thinker and public-intellectual who established a number of influential strategies for combating anti-Jewish sentiment and Christian hubris. These discursive stratagems included alerting Christians to the greater tolerance of the Muslim world towards Jews and providing a 'counter-historical' critique of Christianity as historically persecutory and theologically dogmatic. In Chapter 2 I discuss the famous *Wissenschaft des Judentums* movement that arose in the second decade of the nineteenth century. I argue that scholars and writers working under its aegis, such as Leopold Zunz, Heinrich Heine, and Heinrich Graetz, were, in the words of Ismar Schorsch, 'confrontational' in their emancipative politics and 'counter-historical' methodologies, their challenge to the normative conceptions and collective memory of the Christian majority.[23] Chapter 3 explores the efflorescence of Jewish historical consciousness in the passionate and polemical writings of Abraham Geiger, the great theorist of Reform and Liberal Judaism. I discuss Geiger's attempts to reinvigorate Jewish history and identity by evoking Judaism's interpretive creativity and 'Prophetic' orientation to the future as key elements of Judaism's congenial relationship to 'new cultures'.

Chapter 4 queries an influential critique of Hermann Cohen as advocating a 'Protestantized Judaism' that naively stresses the compatibility of Judaism and *Deutschtum*. I suggest that Cohen's invocation of Germany's 'better self', that is, its fostering of the individual conscience, was a counter-historical stratagem cautioning against the rise of Romantic irrationalism in Germany. Influenced by Abraham Geiger, Cohen celebrated the diversity of Jewish diasporic history, particularly its 'golden age' in Andalusian Spain. In Chapter 5 I argue for Cassirer as a 'Jewish' thinker in the liberal Jewish tradition, suggesting, through a reading of Toni Cassirer's memoir of her life with Ernst Cassirer, that Cassirer was not naïve or delusional but an engaged advocate of the German Jewish community who did his utmost to warn Germany of the looming catastrophe. I suggest that Cassirer's philosophy of symbolic forms was informed by his liberal Jewish ethics and specifically his Prophetic monotheism. Cassirer's emphasis on the mediated and symbolic dimension of human perception and expression, in which human beings transcend their immediate environment and biological facticity, is closely cathected to his frequent invocations of the Jewish Prophets. In Cassirer's reading, the monotheism of the Jewish Prophets represents the overcoming of the ancestral cosmologies and object fetishism of myth in the vision of a 'new heaven and a new earth', an ethical and religious interpretation of life. Cassirer's evocation of Prophetic ethics throughout his writing works in tandem with the liberal Jewish argument that Judaism is the most demythified monotheistic religion and that its ideal tendency, still historically evolving, is to overcome its own residual mythic elements, including biblical literalism and ethnocentrism, through semiotic reflexivity and the ethical interpretation of Jewish sources.

In Chapter 6 I turn to Cassirer's liberal Jewish enthusiasm for the European Enlightenment and the German *Aufklärung* in particular. Cassirer was an active contributor to the important 200th anniversary commemoration of the birth of Mendelssohn in 1929, and he used that occasion to speak to Jewish and non-Jewish German audiences about Mendelssohn's formative contribution to Germany's intellectual heritage, and the profound significance of the Mendelssohn/Lessing friendship. From 1928 onwards, Cassirer invoked the Enlightenment as a challenge to German nationalist exceptionalism, evoking its sociably engaged conception of critique as a valuable antidote to the philosophical fatalism of Heidegger and Spengler and to the 'co-ordination' of many German academics with the Nazi worldview.

In Chapter 7 I grapple with the complex issue of Arendt's relationship to liberal Jewish thought. I point to a peripeteia or 'turn' in Arendt's thinking in the late 1930s, in which she moves from a harsh critique of the baleful effect of the Enlightenment on Jewish solidarity and political agency, towards a growing appreciation of the Enlightenment's emphasis on independent thought as a valuable ethical alternative to the historical meta-narratives of

Hegel and Marx. In a near-complete reversal of her earlier critique of the Enlightenment, Arendt drew on Lessing and Kant's ethic of *Selbsdenken* (thinking for oneself) and more obliquely upon Mendelssohn's ethos of *Bildung* in order to articulate a robustly relational and humanist conception of Jewish ethics that memorably clashed with the ethnocentrism of Gershom Scholem.

In Chapter 8 I discuss Arendt's post-war interest in questions of moral 'character' and 'personality'. Analysing Arendt's discursive conception of character as emerging from the inner dialogue of consciousness/conscience, I argue that Arendt's idealization of the relational energies of a particular Jewish 'type' – the Jewish pariah – resonates with liberal Jewish sympathies for the Jewish outsider who maintained their Jewish distinctiveness while energetically contributing to world literature and world culture. In the postscript I gesture tentatively towards the legacy of liberal Jewish thought in contemporary Jewish theories of diaspora and post-Zionist historiography and Jewish cultural studies, and I suggest ways in which reconstructing liberal Judaism can help us to think about some of the preoccupations and 'counter-historical' tendencies of recent Jewish scholarship.

Notes

1 See 'The Hannah Arendt Collection' [online], 2009. Stevenson Library, Bard College. Available at http://www.bard.edu/arendtcollection/, accessed 4 May 2011.

2 J. Kohn. 2010. 'Hannah Arendt's Jewish Experience: Thinking, Acting, Judging', in R. Berkowitz, J. Katz, and T. Keenan (eds), *Thinking in Dark Times, Hannah Arendt on Ethics and Politics*, New York: Fordham University Press, 187–188.

3 Kohn, 'Hannah Arendt's Jewish Experience', 184. Kohn's analysis of the German Jewish matrix determining Arendt's separation of 'social' and 'political' questions and values is probably indebted to Dagmar Barnouw's seminal study of the relationship between Arendt's Jewish identity and her political thought, D. Barnouw. 1990. *Visible Spaces: Hannah Arendt and the German-Jewish Experience*, Baltimore and London: Johns Hopkins University Press. Barnouw argues there that Arendt's critique of Jewish assimilation leading to 'parvenuism' acknowledged the 'co-responsibility of Jews because, like most Germans, herself included, they had been excellent Germans and mediocre citizens'. Kohn, 'Hannah Arendt's Jewish Experience', 83.

4 R.H. Feldman. 2010. 'The Pariah as Rebel, Hannah Arendt's Jewish Writings', in R. Berkowitz, J. Katz, and T. Keenan (eds), *Thinking in Dark Times, Hannah Arendt on Ethics and Politics*, New York: Fordham University Press, 198.

5 Feldman, 'The Pariah as Rebel, Hannah Arendt's Jewish Writings', 199. Natan Sznaider's recent and suggestive analysis of Arendt's 'rooted cosmopolitanism' nevertheless rehearses the accepted wisdom that Arendt's principal interlocutor in the formation of her Jewish identity was Zionism: 'For Arendt, being a Jew was first of all a political stance, one that she developed while still in Germany through her

intellectual connections with Zionism'. See N. Sznaider. 2011. *Jewish Memory and the Cosmopolitan Order*, Cambridge, UK: Polity, 18.

6 Richard J. Bernstein's influential book *Hannah Arendt and the Jewish Question* has helped to catalyse the notion that Arendt's Jewish identity, because secular and a single generation removed from the assimilationist 'liberal Jewish community', was thin and deracinated: 'It was not any religious, spiritual, or even deeply emotional experiences that attracted [Arendt] to Zionism . . . It was politics – the need for a Jewish politics – that led her to Zionism'. See R.J. Bernstein. 1996. *Hannah Arendt and the Jewish Question*, Cambridge, Mass.: MIT Press, 102.

7 M. Zimmerman. 2001. 'Hannah Arendt, the Early "Post-Zionist"', in S.E. Aschheim (ed.), *Hannah Arendt in Jerusalem*, Berkeley: University of California Press, 186.

8 S. Aschheim. 2001. 'Introduction', in S.E. Aschheim (ed.), *Hannah Arendt in Jerusalem*, Berkeley: University of California Press, 14.

9 Bernstein, *Hannah Arendt and the Jewish Question*, 103.

10 D. Suchoff. 1997. 'Gershom Scholem, Hannah Arendt, and the Scandal of Jewish Particularity', *The Germanic Review* 72(1), 59.

11 Suchoff, 'Gershom Scholem, Hannah Arendt', 70.

12 Aschheim, 'Introduction', 10.

13 A. Rabinbach. 1985. 'Between Enlightenment and Apocalypse: Benjamin, Bloch and Modern German Jewish Messianism', *New German Critique* 34, 78.

14 Rabinbach, 'Between Enlightenment and Apocalypse', 79–80.

15 Rabinbach, 'Between Enlightenment and Apocalypse', 78–79.

16 G.L. Mosse. 1985. 'Jewish Emancipation, Between *Bildung* and Respectability', in J. Reinharz and W. Schatzberg (eds), *The Jewish Response to German Culture*, Hanover and London: University Press of New England, 2.

17 Paul Mendes-Flohr, a prominent theorist of the German Jewish legacy, argues that 'The very Bildung that promised to integrate the Jews into the common fabric of humanity left them in the end virtually isolated within a German society overtaken by nationalism and its invidious myths and symbols'. See P. Mendes-Flohr. 1999. *German Jews: a Dual Identity*, New Haven: Yale University Press, 41.

18 A.D. Moses. 2009. 'The Contradictory Legacies of German-Jewry', *The Leo Baeck Institute Yearbook* 54, 37.

19 H. Arendt. 2007. *The Jewish Writings*, J. Kohn and R.H. Feldman (eds), New York: Schocken Books, 50.

20 E. Skidelsky. 2008. *Ernst Cassirer: The Last Philosopher of Culture*, Princeton: Princeton University Press, 8.

21 E. Young-Bruehl. 2010. 'Hannah Arendt's Jewish Identity', in R. Berkowitz, J. Katz, and T. Keenan (eds), *Thinking in Dark Times, Hannah Arendt on Ethics and Politics*, New York: Fordham University Press, 208.

22 S. Young-ah Gottlieb. 2003. *Regions of Sorrow: Anxiety and Messianism in Hannah Arendt and W.H. Auden*, Stanford: Stanford University Press, 22–23.

23 See I. Schorsch. 1994. *From Text to Context: The Turn to History in Modern Judaism*, Waltham, Mass.: Brandeis University Press.

CHAPTER 1

'This Man of Our Destiny'

Moses Mendelssohn, *Nathan the Wise* and the Emergence of a Liberal Jewish Ethos

While most foundation myths centred on the heroic achievements of individuals require sober appraisal, it is difficult to overestimate the unique significance of one man, Moses Mendelssohn (1729–1786), for the emergence of a liberal Jewish philosophical tradition in Germany. Even liberal German Jewish thinkers such as Hermann Cohen and Ernst Cassirer, who demurred at Mendelssohn's critique of Lessing's philosophy of human progress, remained faithful to his reconciliation of Judaism and reason and his pride in Judaism's ethical monotheism. For liberal Jewish intellectuals and for much of the German Jewish community up until 1933, the legendary character of Mendelssohn, his capacity for cross-cultural friendship and his aptitude for kindling ecumenical dialogue, transforming anti-Jewish hostility into admiration and respect for his extraordinary talents, helped to efface the image of Jews as permanent outsiders to European civilization. Mendelssohn promised German Jews a dignified future as creative agents in a culturally progressive, secularizing European modernity.[1]

Mendelssohn's importance for nineteenth-century liberal Jewish thought, which was acutely aware of its relationship to the history of Judaism and the Jewish people, is only comprehensible, I would suggest, if we move beyond the trite image of Mendelssohn as a classic Enlightenment rationalist, a disciple of Christian Wolff with little regard for the formative power of history and tradition. I think it much more rewarding to situate Mendelssohn as a 'world-thinker', someone who, according to Edward Said, is an 'overturner and a re-mapper of accepted or settled geographies and genealogies'.[2] Mendelssohn's desire for a renaissance in Hebrew culture, his attempt to revive philosophy and Biblical exegesis in Hebrew, reflects Sutcliffe and Brann's argument that in periods of transition and transformation for Judaism Jewish intellectuals have actively 'refashioned their relationship to the Jewish past and its available canon of cultural ideals'.[3] As David Sorkin argues, Mendelssohn was one of the foremost representatives of the *Haskalah*, or Jewish Enlightenment, which originated as an 'indigenous effort to correct the historical anomaly of a Judaism out of touch with central aspects of its textual heritage and the larger culture'.[4] Following Shmuel Feiner, we should be mindful that every social, cultural, and political trend in modern Jewish history has been accompanied by a 'distinctive sense of the past', a caution that we should not take Mendelssohn's seeming indifference to history at face value.[5] If Mendelssohn's character and worldview resonated with many German Jewish intellectuals in the nineteenth and early twentieth centuries, it may be because he fashioned the possibility of a diasporic and syncretic Judaism in continuing conversation and cross-fertilization with other cultures. Mendelssohn re-imagines a Judaism that is not culturally isolated or insular, but outwardly directed and relational, thus open to transformation and renewal.

There could be no more salient representation of a modern Jewish individual as a creative 'world-thinker' disrupting normative identities and bringing warring cultures into dialogue than Gotthold Ephraim Lessing's epochal 1779 drama *Nathan der Weise* (Nathan the Wise). Its chief protagonist, the noble and wise Jewish merchant Nathan, is almost universally acknowledged as inspired by Lessing's friend and critical collaborator, Moses Mendelssohn. Given the degree of recent critical opprobrium towards the play and the character of Nathan, now disdained as an innocuous exemplar of 'humanity' who lacks Jewish attributes, I wish to reconstruct the appeal of Nathan's character and Lessing's play, which was extolled by the predominantly liberal German Jewish community throughout the nineteenth and early twentieth centuries.[6] Before discussing the play and its historical significance as a text of the philosemitic radical Enlightenment, it is important to reflect on why the character of Nathan, and his putative historical model Moses Mendelssohn, have become such controversial representatives of Judaism for twentieth-century criticism, particularly since the Holocaust; namely because of a withering social historical critique concerned to identify and repudiate the failed German Jewish strategy of assimilation as an archetype of diasporic Jewish passivity and bad faith. This influential genre of critique has been hostile to Mendelssohn, now held responsible for the erosion and atomization of Jewish identity. David Sorkin points out, for example, that whereas the Jewish rabbi and historian Meyer Kayserling could celebrate Mendelssohn in 1862 as a 'sincere religious Jew and a German writer', as a 'noble model for posterity', since the late nineteenth century there has been a contrary tendency to judge Mendelssohn caustically as the 'false prophet of assimilation and de-nationalization'.[7]

The Anti-assimilationist Critique of Moses Mendelssohn and Nathan the Wise

The biographer of the German Jewish poet and essayist Heinrich Heine, Jeffrey Sammons, has argued against the 'condescension toward if not condemnation of German Jews that has become a conspicuous feature of post-Holocaust discourse and, in the interest of justice and equity, is much in need of readjustment'.[8] There are a number of reasons for this condescension, including Zionist influenced hostility towards the supposed assimilationist tendencies of German Jews, and a deeply rooted hermeneutic suspicion of the Enlightenment as an arrogant ideological project that attacked traditions and cultures that did not live up to rational norms, a project perceived as particularly inimical to the alleged backwardness, obduracy, and sectarian exclusivity of the Jews.[9]

Criticism of *Nathan the Wise* has been profoundly affected by the near universal critical consensus that Lessing based the humane and wise character of Nathan on his dear friend the philosopher Moses Mendelssohn, the first German Jewish public intellectual, of great repute in both the German and German Jewish communities, and throughout Europe, for his writings on metaphysics, aesthetics, political theory, and in his mature years, Judaism.[10] Mendelssohn was one of the chief promulgators of the German Enlightenment or *Aufklärung* and its core values of religious and ethnic tolerance, humanism, and rationality. He is also considered the progenitor of the *Haskalah*, the German Jewish Enlightenment, which encouraged Jews to enter secular studies such as science, history, and languages, often deplored the intolerance, insularity, and parochialism of orthodox rabbis, and reconceived Judaism in less exclusive and more universalist terms as a faith compatible with reason and the progressive tendencies of world history.

Debate still rages over Moses Mendelssohn as a figure of Jewish modernity and over the effect of his legacy on Judaism. The prominent historian of the German Jewish encounter with modernity, Michael Meyer, articulates the continuing anxieties catalysed by Mendelssohn's philosophical idealization of Judaism as a rational and inclusive religious faith, when he describes emancipation and the Enlightenment as 'seductive' for the Jews, an era that called into question the 'viability of Judaism and [undermined] Jewish solidarity'.[11] Mendelssohn's insistence on a 'tolerant Judaism' that was more a matter of individual faith than a cohesive community of observance created, Meyer argues, a 'subjectivized' Judaism that 'entered the modern world without clear norms and uncertain of its future'.[12] Thus the question as to whether Mendelssohn is a Jewish hero inaugurating the cultural efflorescence of Judaism after emancipation, or a catalyst for the destruction of Judaism by the forces unleashed by a homogenizing modernity, is at the very heart of post-war *Nathan the Wise* criticism. The historian George Mosse's pointed question in *German Jews beyond Judaism* – 'what, after all, was Jewish about Nathan?' – lingers on. The question was first articulated by a generation of German Jews in the vanguard of the Jewish Renaissance in the Weimar Republic, who rejected the bourgeois assimilation of their parent's generation, critiqued the political inertia of German Jewish history, and sought to articulate a more vital and distinctive conception of Jewish identity that proudly acknowledged Jewish difference.[13]

One such prominent figure of the post-assimilationist Jewish Renaissance was the German Jewish philosopher Franz Rosenzweig, who, in a 1919 lecture on *Nathan the Wise*, responded with irritation and bemusement to Nathan's famous declaration to the hostile Knight Templar: 'Are Christian and Jew sooner Christian and Jew than human being?' Rosenzweig exclaimed in his notes, 'how empty is this presupposition of humanity, if men do not want it'.[14] In contrast to the play's enthusiasm for the 'unhoused' human being as revealed in the play's 'anemic' fifth act, Rosenzweig commends Zionism for recognizing that, in light of contemporary circumstances, 'the Jewish human being has the power of a fact'; for today, muses Rosenzweig, we German Jews can no longer wish to remain 'naked human beings'.[15] Rosenzweig also laments the mesmerizing appeal of the Mendelssohn/Lessing friendship on which the play was supposedly based, a friendship, he suggests, that was not really the meeting across difference of Christian and Jew but rather of two men who 'found themselves in the common abstraction of their positive religions'.[16] Rosenzweig regards the Lessing/Mendelssohn friendship as only possible in an age, that of the Enlightenment, that 'lacked the blood of the present time'.[17] Indeed, laments Rosenzweig, the space of co-existence and mutual dialogue envisioned by *Nathan the Wise* is today devoid of even 'the best Christians'.[18]

Perhaps the most problematic aspect of *Nathan the Wise* for Rosenzweig is the legacy of Mendelssohn himself, that 'man of our destiny' who was a Jew but also 'covered up the fact', a reference to Mendelssohn's many Gentile friends and his initial reluctance to become involved in religious controversy.[19] Ten years later, in 1929, in his 'Pronouncement for a Celebration of Mendelssohn' upon the bicentennial of his birth, Rosenzweig ambivalently refers to Mendelssohn as the 'first German Jew' but one who 'has not been able to bequeath to us the protection under which he himself effected the new combination'. Rosenzweig laments Mendelssohn's heirs, many of whom were converts to Christianity (such as the famous composer Felix Mendelssohn Bartholdy), as a 'symbol of the menace into which he led the existence of our, his, spiritual descendants'. Mendelssohn, complains Rosenzweig, 'led us defenseless into this danger', the danger of an anti-Semitism that no longer accepted converted or assimilated Jews. For Mendelssohn's own protection was the 'worldview of his century', an ephemeral phase of German history that believed in the unifying power of ahistorical ideals such as humanity, tolerance, and truth.[20]

Hannah Arendt

From the early 1930s the political theorist Hannah Arendt, energized by the Zionist critique of Jewish assimilation, endorsed Rosenzweig's sentiments, interpreting Mendelssohn as prefiguring all those educated and secularized German Jews who sought to assimilate to German culture, neglecting solidarity with their more downtrodden co-religionists. Arendt's most scathing depiction of Mendelssohn is in *Rahel Varnhagen: The Life of a Jewess* which was begun in 1929, completed in draft form in the fateful year of 1933, but only published, in English, in 1957. Arendt writes of Mendelssohn that his lack of civil rights 'hardly troubled him', that he only took a very incidental interest in social inclusion, and that he was satisfied to be the 'least inhabitant', protected but without equal rights, of the Prussia of the enlightened absolutist ruler Frederick II.[21] Arendt's distaste for Mendelssohn's alleged assimilationist quietism is historically dubious. As Willi Goetschel explains, Mendelssohn was a bold political philosopher who argued for the unconditional acceptance of Jews and the Jewish faith within the German polity, vigorously disagreeing with the civil rights in exchange for moral regeneration paradigm favoured by Christian Wilhelm Dohm, the first Prussian political figure to famously call for the civic equality of the Jews in Germany.[22] Mendelssohn was also a prominent public figure or *shtadlan,* an advocate and spokesperson on behalf of German and European Jewish communities experiencing discrimination and occasional orders of expulsion. As Goetschel writes, 'Mendelssohn's international stature and his irrefutable integrity made him one of the most prominent and effective advocates and representatives of Jewry in his time'.[23]

Arendt's hostility towards Mendelssohn is more explicable if we look at another contemporaneous analysis of hers, 'The Enlightenment and the Jewish Question' (1932), where it is clear that she repudiates Mendelssohn's conduct for reasons that resonate with Rosenzweig's *J'accuse.* Here Arendt analyses Mendelssohn as a prototype of the educated, secularized German Jew who readily falls for the seductive appeal of the rationalizing forces of modernity, heedless of their baleful effects on Jewish communal solidarity and historical consciousness in subsequent generations. Arendt reserves her sharpest criticisms for Mendelssohn's famous defence of Judaism in a book which ensured his lasting legacy as a religious and political thinker, *Jerusalem* (1783). According to Arendt, in *Jerusalem* Mendelssohn attempted to salvage the Jewish religion on the basis of its rational 'eternal content', rather than its historical attestation as a revealed religion preserved, in the face of tremendous odds, by a people in dispersion for nearly two thousand years.[24] Arendt makes it clear that she sees Mendelssohn as a typically anti-historical representative of the Enlightenment who assumed that reason and truth are antithetical to the chaotic fluctuations of history and the superstitions and prejudices bequeathed by tradition. For Arendt, Mendelssohn's pursuit of rational inquiry and dedication to the autochthonous pedagogical ethos of self-cultivation or *Bildung* removed him from history, the very key to understanding the 'factual position of the Jew in the world'. With biting irony, Arendt portrays Mendelssohn as the archetypal '"educated [*gebildet*]" Jew' who 'continues to regard the historical world with the same indifference felt by the oppressed Jew in the ghetto'.[25]

Doubtless with Mendelssohn in mind, Arendt endorses Herder's argument that in the character of Nathan the Wise, Lessing accurately portrayed the lack of prejudice in educated Jews of the Enlightenment era, that is, individuals who were 'not connected to any sort of historical content' in the manner of the non-Jewish world.[26] Like Rosenzweig, Arendt suggests that Mendelssohn's emphasis on a forward looking, autonomously conceived process of self-education, or *Bildung*, left the Jews as isolated human beings rather than a proud and politically active community, thus merely perpetuating the ongoing 'failure of Jews to appreciate history'. Arendt reads the trajectory of Jewish emancipation in Germany as stemming from the generation of assimilationists who followed Mendelssohn, typified by social climbing rationalists such as David Friedländer, men who 'denied their own history and regarded everything particular about themselves as an impediment to their integration, to becoming full human beings'.[27] Arendt implicitly blames Mendelssohn for the bitterly ironic aftermath of the initial hopes of the emancipation era, where Jewish emancipation seemed increasingly to signify emancipation from the onerous stigma of Jewish identity and history, regarded as inhibiting social advancement. Like Rosenzweig, Arendt felt that Mendelssohn's rationalist apologetics for Judaism were only conceivable in the deceptively benign intellectual climate of the Enlightenment, an era which left the newly isolated German Jew defenceless against the rise of German nationalism and organized political anti-Semitism.[28]

Gershom Scholem's Construction of the Self-Negating German Jew

Perhaps the most influential critic of the Enlightenment's influence on the course of German Jewish history has been Gershom Scholem, who set the tone for the post-war repudiation of the assimilationist tendencies of educated

German Jews in his polemical essay 'Against the Myth of the German-Jewish Dialogue', written in Israel in 1964. Scholem begins by refusing the seemingly self-exculpatory German invitation to celebrate a 'German-Jewish symbiosis', a hybrid form of 'German-Judaism' tragically interrupted by Nazism. Scholem considers the notion of such a symbiosis to be illusory and mystifying, arguing that there never was a German Jewish dialogue, indeed that it 'died at its very start and never took place'. This is because while Jews in Germany 'put their own creativity' at the disposal of German culture, even their most humane German interlocutors never addressed them in regard to 'what they had *to give* as Jews', but only in terms of 'what they had to *give up* as Jews' in order to participate in German culture as equal citizens.[29]

Scholem explores the abortive emancipation of Jews in the late eighteenth and early nineteenth centuries, noting that even liberal Germans, including passionate advocates of Jewish emancipation and civil rights such as Wilhelm von Humboldt, demanded a 'resolute disavowal of Jewish nationality', a price that the leading spokespeople and writers of the Jewish avant-garde 'were only too happy to pay'.[30] Scholem laments the 'tragedy' that German Jews struggled for emancipation not for the sake of their rights as a people but rather for the sake of 'assimilating themselves to the peoples among whom they lived'. Losing their confidence as a people, as an integral nation with a transmissible tradition, many German Jews were 'disordered' by the deep insecurity that began to hound them upon leaving the ghetto.[31] The German rejection of the Jews as a people intensified the progressive 'atomization of the Jews as a *community*', a 'process accelerated by individual Jews attempting to ingratiate themselves with a German, Christian culture.[32]

Some of Scholem's most pointed criticisms are reserved for the German Jewish Enlightenment, the *Haskalah*, and the proponents of Jewish reform and secular education, the *Maskilim*, whose most famous early proponent and icon of German Jewish bi-cultural achievement was Moses Mendelssohn. With Mendelssohn, and above all with the school of Enlightenment reformers of Judaism he inspired, there began, in Scholem's view, a fateful process of 'turning towards the Germans', leading to a propaganda campaign by 'enlightened' modernizing Jews for the Jews' resolute absorption by German culture and, shortly thereafter, by the German people itself.[33] The era of German Jewish entreaties to become active participants in German culture, continually stonewalled by the anti-Semitic suspicions of German society, should now be read, according to Scholem, as a process of self-estrangement and increasing neurosis, of a 'decay in the Jewish tradition and in Jewish self-consciousness'.[34]

More recently, Sander Gilman's reading of German Jewish identity as it was shaped by the *Aufklärung*, the era of Jewish emancipation, also shares a Zionist proclivity to pathologize and repudiate the Jewish response to German culture that was inaugurated by Moses Mendelssohn. In his revealingly titled 1986 book *Jewish Self-Hatred*, Gilman reads Mendelssohn's desire to fully participate in the philosophical and cultural debates of his times as assimilationist and self-abandoning, as an attempt to seek out and then imitate the 'life and learning of the Christian world'.[35] Gilman regards Mendelssohn as an upwardly mobile parvenu who ingratiates himself as an acceptable model of the 'Good Jew', the exceptional Jew tolerable to Christian Germans. In Gilman's doleful narrative, strongly redolent of Arendt's suspicion of Mendelssohn's quietism, Mendelssohn abandons his Jewish mien for the sake of participating in a small clique of Enlightenment thinkers in Berlin from the 1750s, notably including his close friend and intellectual companion, Gotthold Ephraim Lessing.[36] Mendelssohn, according to Gilman, fashioned himself in the role of the inconspicuous, culturally odourless Court protected elite Jew, an assimilated Jew who speaks Prussian German rather than East European Yiddish, and is polite and decorous rather than argumentative in the rabbinic, Talmudic mode: 'Mendelssohn's creation of an image of the nondisputive, rational, German-speaking Jew using tools of Western rhetoric and logic was in fulfilment of the cultural demands of Christian, capitalistic society.'[37]

Echoing Mosse's suspicion of Nathan's Judaism, Gilman notes that the perfect German of the character of Nathan in Lessing's *Nathan der Weise* was not at all typical of German Jews of that era, but rather conformed to an Enlightenment version of toleration that 'draws the line at language difference'.[38] Gilman reads Lessing's play as a metonym for the Enlightenment itself, a normative project that was only capable of acknowledging Mendelssohn/ Nathan as an extraordinary Jew, an exception to the norm of Jewish dishonesty, corruption, and greed.[39]

Disdainful of the putatively ahistorical humanism of Enlightenment influenced German Jews, a humanist orientation now read as naïve and ineffective in combatting the looming crisis of anti-Semitism, the widely accepted critique of German Jewish assimilation articulated by Rosenzweig, Arendt, Scholem, and Gilman ignores or elides the agency of German Jewish intellectuals from the age of emancipation until the twentieth century in creating their own, diasporic image of Jewish identity and Jewish history.[40] Contrary to the teleological critique that I have discussed, which seeks reasons for the demise of German and European Jewry in diasporic Jewish conduct towards the Gentile world, and which tends to anachronistically dichotomize German and Jew, in general the German Jewish community up until 1933 celebrated Mendelssohn and his representation in *Nathan der Weise* with great enthusiasm. They interpreted the play as fashioning a historically accurate portrayal of a diasporic Jew at ease in a variety of cultural spheres. Many Jews found in Nathan/Mendelssohn an exemplary character that symbolized their own aspirations for creative participation as Jews in the non-Jewish cultures in which they found themselves.[41]

I would suggest that for many German Jews Moses Mendelssohn and his dramatic avatar, Lessing's memorable character of Nathan the Wise, evoked an appreciation, originating in the German Jewish Enlightenment, for the cultural and philosophical heritage of Levantine and Sephardic Jews – the so called 'Sephardic Mystique'. This rich medieval Judeo-Arab heritage includes the ninth- and tenth-century CE Egyptian born Jewish philosopher, grammarian, and exegete Saadia Gaon who translated the Bible into Arabic; the brilliant Andalusian lyrical poet and philosophical defender of Judaism Judah Halevi, author of the theological dialogue, the *Kuzari*, also written in Arabic; and the great twelfth-century CE Jewish philosopher and physician Maimonides who originally wrote his famous *Guide for the Perplexed* in Arabic.

The 'Sephardic mystique', now accepted as an enduring facet of the German Jewish imaginary up until 1933, suggests an enthusiasm for a diasporic Jewish heritage that was highly acculturated and receptive to diverse creative and philosophical influences, polymathic in spirit, and linguistically polyglot. In the last decades of the eighteenth century, the proponents of the Jewish Enlightenment extolled Andalusian Jews such as Maimonides as exemplars of the possible achievements of Jews in less restrictive and discriminatory cultural contexts than Christian Europe. As Dirk Westerkamp points out, the *Maskilim* were participants in an emerging eighteenth-century Enlightenment historiography in Germany that was showing a deepening interest in Jewish and Arabic thought and philosophy, and that viewed Islamic and Judaic philosophical traditions as closely related.[42] As Feiner argues, many eighteenth-century thinkers and historians were struggling against 'Christian' versions of history, and were practicing forms of history that would offer both pragmatic benefit for their community in a transitional age and exemplary illustration of desirable character traits.[43]

The *Maskilim* were participants in this historiographical shift towards the concrete exemplification of mores and virtues. They extolled a version of Jewish history that illuminated exemplary Jewish lives such as that of Maimonides, who was held to demonstrate the importance of philosophical virtues such as humanism, morality, and wisdom. In the words of Feiner, Maimonides 'exemplified the breakthrough into the world of external culture'.[44] As he points out, it was not simply actual Jewish individuals who took on exemplary status for the *Maskilim* but also the syncretic cultural contexts in which such individuals were able to flourish, such as the Muslim Spain of the eleventh century CE from where Maimonides originated. It was in the so-called golden age of Andalusian Spain that flourishing arts, sciences, advanced linguistic and grammatical studies, a high level of education amongst the inhabitants, and renowned universities and academies of learning created the circumstances that contributed to Maimonides' exceptional erudition, his unparalleled knowledge of the Torah, and exemplary human qualities.[45] In the following chapters, we shall discuss how the *Haskalah* endorsement of the Levantine and Sephardic Jewish legacy profoundly influenced the historical consciousness of the prominent nineteenth-century German Jewish historians Heinrich Graetz and Abraham Geiger.

Mendelssohn/Nathan's Spinozism

What elements of Mendelssohn's contemporary reputation, philosophical outlook, and political philosophy – and what aspects of the character of Nathan the Wise – allow us to read both Mendelssohn and Nathan as imbued with the 'Sephardic mystique' and the rich Judeo-Arabic cultural heritage it invokes? Alexander Altmann's monumental biography of Mendelssohn is helpful in this regard, noting that Mendelssohn was one of the first eighteenth-century thinkers to rehabilitate the controversial, heretical, ex-communicated philosopher Spinoza (1632–1677). Mendelssohn introduced Lessing to Spinoza's writings in the 1750s and thereby helped to catalyse the Spinozist renaissance which had a dramatic impact upon the thought of Lessing, Herder, and Goethe amongst others, and was a pervasive if subterranean influence on the eighteenth-century Enlightenment.[46]

Altmann suggests that Spinoza had a 'special fascination' for Mendelssohn, for like Spinoza, born in Amsterdam of an emigrant Portuguese Marrano family (Christian converts who secretly practised an adapted form of Judaism in post-Inquisition Spain and Portugal), Mendelssohn was also an emigrant Jew (born in Dessau, he came to Berlin as a fourteen-year-old) trained in medieval Jewish philosophy, principally the Aristotelian influenced philosophy and rationalist hermeneutics of Maimonides. Mendelssohn identified with the philosophical adventurousness of Spinoza and felt that despite his 'speculative doctrine' he could have remained an Orthodox Jew if he had not so drastically renounced Jewish Law.[47] Not only did Mendelssohn vigorously criticize the conventional denunciation of Spinoza as an outcast, heretic, blasphemer, and scandalous atheist, but also, according to Altmann, he was 'attracted to [Spinoza]' and may even have dreamt of becoming a 'second Spinoza'. In the early stages of their enthusiastic friendship, in the autumn of 1754, Lessing captured Mendelssohn's desire to emulate Spinoza when he suggested of Mendelssohn that 'his honesty and his philosophical mind make me anticipate in him a second Spinoza equal to the first in all but . . . his errors'.[48]

With surprising audacity for an alleged assimilationist, Mendelssohn defended the honour of the Marrano Sephardic Dutch Jew and secular philosopher, who, Mendelssohn argued, 'lived moderately, withdrawn, and blamelessly', denying himself 'all human pleasures' in a life 'devoted to contemplation'. As Adam Sutcliffe writes, the Sephardic Spinoza was a source of 'confused fascination' for emancipated Jews who sought historical models for mediation between Jewish and non-Jewish worlds.[49] Sutcliffe points out that a rival interpretive tradition eulogizing Spinoza as a kind of 'philosopher-hero', a tireless seeker after truth and a paragon of virtues such as modesty, moderation, and moral seriousness, had sprung up within a year of his death. This biographical tradition, which admired Spinoza for standing outside conventional social categories, was espoused by members of Spinoza's circle such as Jean Maximilien Lucas, a French Huguenot resident of the Netherlands, and somewhat later by Johannes Colerus, a German minister of the Lutheran Church at The Hague, who discovered that his own home had recently housed Spinoza.[50] While influentially indicting Spinoza's philosophy, Pierre Bayle in his *Dictionnaire Historique et Critique* (1697) drew heavily on Lucas in fashioning an image of Spinoza, as, in Sutcliffe's words, 'the quintessential virtuous atheist', sociable, honest, affable, and obliging. This was a dissonant but fascinating image of the philosophical life, forged across confessional divides, which, Sutcliffe suggests, helped to expose the inadequacy and potential hypocrisy of mere piety, and pointed the way towards attempts to develop a more rationalist and secular ethic.[51] Up until his final writings Mendelssohn continued his fulsome praise of Spinoza's sociable relationships with Gentile scholars and acquaintances throughout Europe, thereby subtly recovering the intercultural milieu which gave rise to the legend of his unblemished philosophical life: 'Who would not be delighted to have had Spinoza as a friend . . . who would refuse to give Spinoza's genius and excellent character their due?'[52]

A continuing thread in Mendelssohn's philosophy, from his *Philosophische Gespräche* (Philosophical Dialogues, 1755) to his *An die Freunde Lessings* ('To the Friends of Lessing', 1786), is his effort to prove that Spinoza's doctrine is 'consistent with reason and religion'.[53] Responding to Lessing's own estimation of him as a 'second Spinoza', both an exemplar of Jewish intellectual vitality and a rebel against the parochialism of many orthodox rabbis, Mendelssohn celebrated Spinoza as an acculturated Sephardic Jew whose breadth of knowledge and virtuous conduct were more significant than adherence to any dogma or orthodoxy. In Mendelssohn's 'Dialogues', a revised version of which appeared in his *Philosophische Schriften* (Philosophical Writings, 1761), his interlocutors Neophil and Philopon rehabilitate the character and philosophical significance of Spinoza as a catalyst for the philosophical republic of letters, interrupting the complacent image of philosophy as a Western, and, at that time, Christian inspired achievement:

Neophil: Let us acknowledge that even someone other than a German, I add further, someone other than a Christian, namely, Spinoza, has participated immensely in the work of bettering philosophy . . . Without him, philosophy would never have been able to extend its borders so far.[54]

Mendelssohn's Spinoza is a figure who unsettles a well-established narrative of human cultural and philosophical development, exemplified in the preface to Leibniz's *Theodicy* (1710). In this work Leibniz compared pagan thought to the period of childhood, Judaic thought to the juvenile period, and Christian thought to the adulthood of humankind, a narrative of human evolution later echoed in Kant's dismissal of Judaism as a form of heteronomous legalism incapable of serving the needs of an inward, spiritual, and critically autonomous 'rational religion'.[55]

In 1783, Mendelssohn translated and wrote a preface to the *Vindiciae Judaeorum* (1656), by the ecumenically inclined Amsterdam Jewish community leader and Portuguese-Jewish Rabbi, Menasseh Ben Israel (1604–1657), who was thought to have taught Spinoza. The *Vindiciae Judaeorum* (Vindication of the Jews) was written in order to facilitate the return of the Jews to England by refuting the many calumnies being made against them. In the preface, Mendelssohn upholds seventeenth-century Holland, from which Ben Israel emerged as a Jewish advocate confident in his cross-cultural acumen, as an astonishing model of prosperity and achievement in industry and the arts. In terms redolent of Spinoza's own political theory, Mendelssohn argues that this happy state of affairs is due to its freedom, benevolent government, just laws, and the open arms with which it received and protected peoples of all kinds, opinions, outer appearance, mores, customs, and religious beliefs, allowing free reign to their creative energies.[56]

While Mendelssohn appropriated a dissident and cosmopolitan ethical tradition of Spinoza appreciation, which he politicized, Sutcliffe argues that Spinoza's complex relationship to Judaism and exemplary life of philosophical contemplation were at least as interesting to Lessing as his humane philosophy, suggesting that for both Mendelssohn and Lessing common humanity and virtuous character transcend theological and sectarian differences. Following Sutcliffe and Goetschel, I think it more than likely that Spinoza himself was an inspiration for Lessing's two philo-Jewish plays *The Jews* (1749) and *Nathan the Wise* (1779).[57]

Many of Spinoza's philosophical and religious precepts appealed greatly to both Mendelssohn and Lessing, stimulating, for example, their rational, ethical and inclusive conception of God, a pluralistic theism suspicious of the exclusive and violent claims to a single and unrepeatable Revelation on which the Mosaic distinction between true and false religions is predicated. Spinoza postulated, for example, that God takes account of the whole of Nature and not merely of the human race alone. God is not an anthropomorphic being that plans and acts purposively, who punishes and rewards, and who therefore needs to be obeyed, feared, and placated by the intercessions of a priestly caste.[58] As Steven Nadler argues, Spinoza's God 'does not "do" things for the sake of anything else . . . All talk of God's purposes, intentions, goals, preferences, or aims is just an anthropomorphizing fiction'.[59] Nor does Spinoza's God perform miracles since there are no departures possible from the necessary course of nature; indeed Spinoza believed that the retreat to superstition was the 'bitter enemy of all true knowledge and true morality'. Spinoza's philosophy is a form of religious humanism characterized by an intellectual love of God and the desire for an immanent knowledge of the world God has created.

Spinoza argued that the Supreme Being desires only practical virtues such as love of one's neighbour rather than inflexible dogmas or sectarian devotion. True faith in God does not involve metaphysical doctrines or anything contrary to our understanding of the natural world, but is best represented by a 'simple idea of the Divine mind', namely that obedience to God involves the 'practice of justice and charity'.[60] Therefore Spinoza held that familiarity with Scripture or other holy texts is not necessary for a blessed condition, since the loving message of Scripture is in fact available to our rational faculties alone. Spinoza's religious humanism and rationalism, which denounced clerical demagoguery, the superstitions of the multitude, and the hubris of invoking God as somehow on the side of a particular people, greatly appealed to Lessing and Mendelssohn as they attempted to articulate the ethical and edifying rather than exclusive and violent tenets of their respective religions.[61]

Is Nathan a Spinozist?

Nathan the Wise offers many clues that its hero, Nathan, is not a representative 'Jew' whose humanity demands our tolerance and sympathy. He can be read in a more specific sense as a polyvalent Spinozist, a perpetual outsider figure and philosophical sceptic, both Jew and heretic, inside and outside Judaism, neither a 'housed' nor abstractly 'unhoused' human being. A Jew who is prospering in the medieval Islamic world that stretched from the Middle East to Moorish Spain, Nathan is a world-thinker conversant with a variety of religions and cultures, analysing human beliefs and folly with a degree of sympathetic detachment. In the play's second scene Nathan has returned from his merchant travels to Baghdad, the seat of the Islamic empire, and elsewhere in the Levant, only to find his adopted daughter Recha inflamed with pious enthusiasm for an 'angel', in fact the Christian Knight Templar, who has miraculously saved her from a house fire.

Recha: Let us now rejoice
And praise our God. He surely bore you and

Your boat on wings of his unseen angels
Across the treacherous streams. And it was God
Who beckoned to my angel to be seen,
Carrying me through the flames on his white wings.

Nathan: sotto voce: (On his white wings – of course! That must have been
The Templar's white and outspread cloak) (86–93.)[62]

Nathan's rational substitution of a natural phenomenon, the Knight Templar's flowing cloak, for Recha's impression of an angel saviour, is distinctly reminiscent of Spinoza's philological method of analysis in his *Theologico-Political Treatise,* in which biblically attested miracles are re-described in the light of their 'immediate natural causes'.[63]

Nathan's rationalist, Spinozist suspicion of miraculous occurrences and the contagious religious enthusiasm they generate (such enthusiasm was usually termed *Schwärmerei* in eighteenth-century Germany and was vigorously opposed by *Aufklärers* such as Mendelssohn and Lessing) has an ethical justification, a warning against the camouflaged hubris implied by the belief that God is capriciously revealed to particular individuals or communities. Responding to the naïve and enthusiastic Christian zealotry of Recha's woman companion Daja, who suggests that there is no harm in Recha thinking that she has been saved by an angel rather than a human being, Nathan denounces this narcissistic belief in an anthropomorphic God.

Nathan: Pride! Nothing but pride! The iron pot
Wants to be lifted from the fire with silver
Tongs, in order to imagine it's a pot
Of silver . . . your 'Feeling so much nearer to God'
Is either nonsense or else blasphemy.
And there *is* harm in it, there really is. (292–300)

We should not, however, mistake Nathan's Spinozist scepticism for a disenchanted and purely materialist interpretation of nature and history. In *The Origins of Violence* (2008) John Docker stresses that Spinoza did not believe in the hubris of a reason that masters and controls the world, indeed Spinoza confessed limitations to human knowledge; he did not believe that Nature was so limited that 'man' is its chief part. Spinoza rejected the idea that a wisely conducted life should accept nothing as true that could not be called into doubt, for most of our actions, he wrote, are fraught with 'uncertainty and hazard'.[64] Spinoza believed that the universe is governed by a single substance (God, Nature) which has no final cause or telos, natural end or aims, 'permitting the flourishing of difference, diversity, and experimentation'.[65]

Spinoza did not believe in a strict mind/body dualism, arguing for the mind as the 'idea' of the body in all its intersubjective desires and unpredictable encounters. For Spinoza, the highest form of knowledge is not obtainable by apodictic reason or the ascetic denial of the senses, but by reason working with intuition, imagination, and emotion (love) in order to enable us to be active and autonomous beings.[66]

It is in a Spinozist fashion, then, that Nathan points out to Recha that the workings of Providence are all the more extraordinary, unpredictable, and enchanting when it comes to embodied human beings, where even the most embedded prejudices against other races and religions, such as the Knight Templar's initial enmity towards Jews and Muslims, dissolve in the face of his salvation by Saladin and his amorous desire for the charming Recha. This is especially true when the Knight Templar is confronted by the disarmingly genial, sentimental Nathan, whose cleansing teardrop on the Templar's cloak marks the beginning of an improbable friendship:

Nathan: It might sound natural and commonplace
If he who saved you were a real Templar
Knight; but surely that would be no less a Miracle! – The greatest miracle
is that those miracles which are both real and true
Can and do become so commonplace to us.[67]
… No thinking person would call miracles
Those things which only seem so to a child,
Who stares at and pursues the strangest things,
Struck only by their novelty. (213–223)

Although he adheres to Mosaic Laws, such as the principle of charity and alms, Nathan, it is claimed, has brought up Recha in 'no faith at all, and taught her neither more nor less of God than reason finds sufficient' (2555–2558). In conversation with Daja, who is deeply distressed that the baptized Recha has yet to return to the Christian fold, Recha confirms that her upbringing by Nathan has been purely in the sublime spirit of religious humanism rather than a distinct creed based on Revelation:

Recha: To whom does God belong? What sort of God
Belongs to just one person? One who needs
People to fight for him? (1555–1558)

What has [Nathan] done to make you want to mix
The seed of pure reason, which he planted
In my soul, with weeds or flowers of
Your homeland? (1564–1567)

What I found more consoling was
The lesson that devotedness to God
Does not wholly depend on what
We speculate about him. Dear Daja,
My father has so often told us that. (1589–1593)

Nathan's religious humanism, alive to the uncertainty and future possibilities of God's Providence rather than assured of God's plan as determined by a unique historical event and its concomitant testament, stands in strong contrast to the vengeful eschatology of hateful bigots such as the senior Christian in Jerusalem, the Patriarch, who upon hearing that Nathan has brought up a baptized Christian girl declaims ominously, 'The Jew shall burn' (*Der Jude wird verbrannt*) (2559).

Nathan's Philosemitism

As a Spinozist Nathan is not just the protagonist of a rational and humane philosophy; the Marrano Spinoza reprises leading figures of the medieval Judeo-Islamic world such as the Jewish Maimonides and the great Islamic philosopher Averroes. As Adam Sutcliffe has argued, Spinoza, well versed in medieval Jewish and Arabic philosophy and influenced by Maimonides' Aristotelian rationalism and refined conception of God, was an 'intellectual bridge between the secular Enlightenment and medieval Andalusia'.[68] Mendelssohn was a close student of Maimonides' writings and published a commentary on Maimonides' *Logical Terms* in 1761.[69] Indeed Spinoza's intellectual independence, his anti-clerical attitudes, and critique of the Mosaic Distinction, encouraged those strands of what Jonathan Israel has called the 'radical Enlightenment' which were cosmopolitan and distinctly philosemitic in the broadest sense, embracing the wisdom of Arabic and Jewish religion and culture and criticizing Christianity's supercessionist claim to be the one true faith at the vanguard of historical progress.[70]

A prominent example of the Spinozist influenced radical Enlightenment in the eighteenth century was the free thinker and pantheist John Toland, an Egyptophile who believed the Egyptians were the 'wisest of mortals' because they secretly encoded their esoteric religious knowledge in hieroglyphic form. Toland loved the Greek philosophers and Confucius for their wise teachings and virtuous actions.[71] In his remarkably syncretic *Nazarenus: Or, Jewish, Gentile, and Mahometan Christianity* (1718), Toland claimed to have exhumed a 'Mahometan Gospel' unknown to any Christians, which observes the 'true and original plan of Christianity', that is, the encouragement of a diversity of observances and ceremonies, a pluralism of worship bitterly opposed by Paul, who lamentably expelled the first Jewish Christians.[72] In praising the multi-religious space of the Ottoman Middle East, Toland thought that Muslims and their mosques should be tolerated as much in Amsterdam and London as Christians of every kind are in Constantinople.[73]

Toland's heterodox appreciation of Islam conversed with Unitarians such as Stephen Nye, who thought that the ancient Nazarene faith in the unity of God had been corrupted by institutional Christianity but preserved in Turkish and other Muslim dominions, and Montesquieu's satirical *Persian Letters*, which returns the superior gaze of Europeans on the Orient, with Muslim characters questioning European cultural norms. These works are part of a distinct philo-semitic and heterodox cultural movement in the eighteenth century which rejected a Christian sacred history focused on the Israelites alone, admired Arabic literature and religion, and was attentive to the possibility of 'cultural, philosophical and religious exchanges between Europe and the Orient'.[74]

Moses Mendelssohn and Gotthold Ephraim Lessing were active promul-gators of the heterodox philosemitic Enlightenment of the eighteenth century. In one of his earliest published writings, the *Rettungen* (*Vindications*) of 1754, Lessing defended heretics and heterodox thinkers who had been historically ignored or dismissed, lending them a voice by which they could defend them-selves. One of Lessing's *Rettungen* of 1754, 'Rettung des Hier. Cardanus', was dedicated to the sixteenth-century Renaissance mathematician, philosopher, and physician Hieronymous Cardanus, who was reviled as an atheist and heretic for taking Islam seriously as a subject for theological discussion by comparing Islam and Judaism, albeit unfavourably, to Christianity.[75] Lessing defended Cardanus but also sharply criticized him for being unfair to the tenets of Judaism and Islam. Lessing reworks Cardanus's dialogue by having a Jewish and Islamic protagonist defend their religions. The Jewish character refutes the charge that the Jews' dispersal and exile is a sign of God's punish-ment and the Muslim defends his faith against the charge of being irrational and barbaric by stressing that Islamic monotheism, which believes in the unity of God and that God rewards and punishes as a measure of our actions in this world, is in accord with the purest conceptions of reason ('allerstrengesten Vernunft'). Lessing goes further, having his Muslim protagonist proclaim that the Christian religion is a hotch-potch of doctrines that no healthy reason could ever recognize ('Wirrwarr von Sätzen, die eine gesunde Vernunft nie für die ihrigen erkennen wird'), a critical perspective shared by Mendelssohn: 'in [Mendelssohn's] view Christianity was permeated with intolerance and the spirit of persecution'.[76]

Lessing, who did not believe in a final truth that could be possessed once and for all, leaves the question of the one true faith open, but his Muslim protagonist's powerful critique of Christian doctrines such as the Trinity is a 'return of the gaze' that also invokes the long literary history of imagining a 'world upside down' that parodies and criticizes official norms and established truths about the world.[77] I would suggest that Lessing is not simply criticizing Christianity in order to overturn a hierarchy of values, but that his critique aimed to provoke Christians into dialogue with those faiths which it disdains and oppresses. In a telling moment in the play, Lessing has Recha rebuke Daja, who has benefitted from the kindness and hospitality of the Jewish Nathan but nevertheless believes he will be damned to hell, as 'one of those fanatics who imagine that they know the only true and universal way to God' (3587–3589). As Leah Hochman contends, Mendelssohn's discussion of the divine without reference to specific theologies provided an alternative means of describing God and examples of Godliness in terms of God's perfection as realized in the natural world and in the self-cultivating practice of virtue. Mendelssohn's heterodox ethical monotheism could not be assimilated into established religious systems and empowered the spontaneous critical and receptive faculties, the *Bildung* of the individual, as against the authorized epistemologies of church and state.[78]

Mendelssohn/Nathan's Jerusalem

After Lessing's death Mendelssohn paid heartfelt tribute to his friend's tendency to side with the weak and the oppressed, and to socialize with outsiders and outcasts such as actors and soldiers. Mendelssohn's appreciation of Lessing's acute sense of justice is not surprising when we consider that in texts such as *Jerusalem* Mendelssohn himself articulated consistent philosemitic and subaltern sympathies: 'Reader! To whatever visible church, synagogue, or mosque you may belong! See if you do not find more true religion among the host of the excommunicated than among the far greater host of those who excommunicated them.'[79]

Rather than encouraging Jews to conform to German and Christian cultural norms, as he is often accused of doing, Mendelssohn's subversive strategy in *Jerusalem* was to remind Christians of Jewish and Muslim cultural and philosophical achievements, and of an impressive Judeo-Arabic heritage typified by the powerful Jewish contribution to culture and politics in Muslim lands. As Willi Goetschel suggests, Mendelssohn leaves us in no doubt that Christian Europe has a 'reprehensible past', and that the Jews' fortunes are better in Ottoman lands than in Europe where they are disenfranchised from most of the professions and from political participation.[80] Mendelssohn makes the following point in his 'Vorrede':

It may be true in our times that Jews in Christian states are in better circumstances than in Muslim states; but never have they been so cruelly persecuted, murdered, tortured, burnt, robbed and chased away naked than by Christian governments and theologians of the Middle Ages. Still nowadays Jews in Turkish lands pay only a moderate head tax and suffer little more than other subjects . . . The number of Jews in Muslim states is probably higher than in Christian states. Thanks to their excellent skills as physicians and also as state officials they often rise in Muslim states to a position of honor . . . Even now the prime minister of the Emperor of Morocco is a Jew called Sumbul.[81]

In this respect, the Jerusalem of Mendelssohn's famous work is also the Jerusalem of Lessing's *Nathan the Wise*, published only a few years earlier, a polyglot space protected by the mature and benign sovereignty of the Muslim leader Saladin, in which Jews, Christians, and Muslims are brought into a relationship of mutual respect. It is also a Jerusalem where Jews and Arabs must forge political alliances, as Nathan and Saladin do, to fend off ravaging Christian armies, a counter-narrative to Christian Europe's fear of invading Muslim hordes. Mendelssohn's Jerusalem is a site of negotiation and exchange between different cultures and faiths, a heterogeneous zone of contact that is capable of educating prejudiced Christians about civilized behaviour. It is the Jerusalem of the noble and principled Saladin, who spares the life of the Knight Templar and encourages intermarriage between Christians and Muslims. It is also the Jerusalem of Nathan, who instructs the initially anti-Semitic Knight Templar on the values of pluralism, like Jesus deploying the parable form in order to encourage the Knight Templar's acceptance of a shared humanity ('one gnarled branch must accept another'), reminding him that no single 'treetop' should assume that it alone did not spring from the ground, a reference to Christianity's violent attempts to suppress its Jewish origins (1283–1286).

Following Willi Goetschel, I think Mendelssohn should be interpreted as a vigorous 'cosmopolitan citizen' and anti-colonialist liberal, fiercely critical of ethnocentrism and refusing to concede to the State or the Church the right to sit in judgement on matters of religion and inner conscience.[82] As Goetschel writes, even Wilhelm von Humboldt, Mendelssohn's most prominent student, seems 'at moments to pale in comparison to Mendelssohn's unflagging accentuation of the individual's role, significance, and rights'.[83] Inheriting Spinoza's liberal republicanism and critique of the mischief caused by revealed religions, Mendelssohn conceives of Judaism as equally accessible in its ethical precepts, such as the notion of God's Providence, to every human being. *Jerusalem* harshly criticizes the universalist claims of revealed religions and the colonial institutions they require to promulgate their teachings. In what is probably an allusion to Diderot's fiercely anti-colonial and anti-imperialist contributions to the *Histoire philosophique des deux Indes* (1772–), edited by the Abbe

Guillaume-Thomas Raynal, Mendelssohn, following Spinoza, challenges the notion of a people chosen by Revelation:

> If therefore, mankind must be corrupt and miserable without revelation, why has the far greater part of mankind lived without true revelation from time immemorial? Why must the two Indies wait until it pleases the Europeans to send them a few comforters to bring them a message without which they can, according to this opinion, live neither virtuously nor happily . . . According to the concepts of true Judaism, all the inhabitants of the earth are destined to felicity; and the means of attaining it are as widespread as mankind itself . . . As often as it was useful, Providence caused wise men to arise in every nation on earth.[84]

The last statement finds its echo in Nathan's reassuring overture to the distrustful Knight Templar, who is suspicious of the pride and exclusivity of the Jews: 'Good people are produced in every land' (1273).

Saladin's sister Sittah also provides an acerbic commentary on the imperial violence of the Christian nations, which suggests that *Nathan the Wise* is keen to evoke 'the Crusades through Arab eyes':[85]

> Sittah: Their pride is: to be Christian, but not human.
> Even that mixture of humanity
> And superstition, which their founder gave to them,
> They love not for its human values,
> But because Christ teaches it, Christ did it.
> . . . Not his virtue; it's his name
> That must be spread throughout the world, that must
> Dishonour and devour the names of all
> Good people. For the name, the name alone,
> Is everything to them (868–879).

We are reminded of Lessing's comment in his famous treatise on aesthetic principles, the *Hamburg Dramaturgy*: 'These Crusades, which in their inception had been a political stratagem of the Popes, in practice led to the most inhuman persecutions of which Christian superstition has ever been guilty'.[86] As Hochman reminds us, as the scion of a Sephardic family that had escaped Inquisition-obsessed Portugal, Spinoza was horrified and traumatized by the terrors the Inquisition visited on friends and family still within its clutches.[87]

So far I hope to have indicated that *Nathan the Wise* is not an ahistorical or abstractly humanist drama but a powerful commentary on the nightmare of history, its cyclical violence, its hubris and folly, its redemptive possibilities. The character of Nathan has a choric function: he stands outside of history's madness. Late in the play, we find out that during the Crusades the Christians murdered all the Jews, including wives and children, in the Mediterranean town of Gath. In this massacre perished Nathan's wife and seven sons, all 'full of promise', burned to death in his brother's house (3040–3044). After he initially swore undying hatred for Christendom, Nathan's reason returns, and in another moment of all-too-human providence, a kindly Christian, the Lay Brother, presents him with the opportunity to bring up an orphaned Christian child, Recha. As the Lay Brother points out, when they are young, children need love more than they need Christianity, and anyway, was not all of 'Christianity founded on Judaism?' (3021–3220).

In a sense, then, Nathan is a redeemer figure and martyr, taking upon himself the burden of renewing and regenerating a world sundered by hatred, tyranny, and the desire for conquest. Yet he is not a messiah, nor the Christ; he represents no final revealed truth, no decisive historical event that compels recognition and obedience. Rather, Nathan redeems us from the very idea of a redeemer, of a sacred history that includes some groups and excludes others. The histories he evokes are multiple and the future he strives for open ended. He is the wandering Jew who mediates between different cultures. He is the unsettling stranger depicted by Georg Simmel, who comes today and stays tomorrow but is never reconciled to his adopted home, remaining sceptical, detached, wary, and observant of human nature.[88] Yet Nathan is also the garrulous and generously sociable sage Socrates, constantly drawing people into conversation, questioning the way they rationalize their own lust for power, disarming them with narratives, parables, and metaphors, humbly confessing his ignorance. As we shall see, the character of Nathan the Wise helped German Jewish thinkers to articulate a relational conception of Judaism as performing important critical social functions in relatively closed societies, a figure of the Jew as mediator and agent of cultural conversation that greatly appealed to liberal Jewish thought.

Moses Mendelssohn: The Pathos of History

It is a commonplace, contested but by no means eclipsed in recent criticism, that Mendelssohn, unlike contemporaries such as Herder, was mostly indifferent to the study of history, unable to integrate the chaos of human history into his tranquil rationalism and steadfast emphasis on natural law. However, we should remember that even in his oft quoted 1765 letter to his friend Thomas Abbt, in which Mendelssohn confesses that 'when I have to read something historical I feel like yawning', Mendelssohn then adds that this is not the case if the history is written in a stimulating manner. Later in the letter Mendelssohn politicizes his critique of historical writing by suggesting that as a 'man without a country' he has up until now struggled to relate to national and civic histories; nevertheless (perhaps influenced by Montesquieu's *The Spirit of the Laws*, 1748), he has come to realize that the histories of political constitutions and the larger history of mankind are interrelated, and that it simply won't do to be uninformed about the former.[89]

Mendelssohn's semi-public complaint about being deracinated, in some senses outside of and critical of the parochialism and self-aggrandizing nature of much historical writing, suggests less an indifference to history than an incipient German Jewish interest in a cosmopolitan world-historical temporality focused on the exemplary significance of robustly refractory, dissident individuals. Mendelssohn reminds his readers of the importance of the individual, fearing that the then fashionable conjectural and universal histories were too concerned with the rise and fall of cultures. Showing due respect for the pathos of history, Mendelssohn remained acutely aware of the recurrence of humanity's vices and follies, rejecting Lessing's speculative hypothesis, articulated in his *Erziehung des Menschengeschlechts* (The Education of the Human Race) (1780), that humanity as a whole as opposed to the individual, is capable of being progressively educated by history.

As Feiner argues, Mendelssohn's attitude towards the notion of any positive and enduring historical change in history was 'moderate and sceptical'; he was not only keenly aware, like Lessing, that the true disclosure of Christianity's arrogance and intolerance was realized in the barbarism of the Middle Ages and the Inquisition, and could occur once more, but he was also unconvinced that artistic and technological progress was accompanied by moral progress.[90] Mendelssohn seemed to adhere to a Viconian philosophy of history as a perpetual cycle of spiritual advancement and regression. Mendelssohn argues that as much moral conduct can be expected from the 'crude mode of conceiving things' as from 'refined and purified concepts'; the quantity and weight of morality was on balance about the same during all these various epochs.[91]

There were tensions in the Mendelssohn/Lessing friendship on just this point. In *Jerusalem* Mendelssohn criticized Lessing's speculative discussion of humanity's sanguine prospects in *Erziehung des Menschengeschlechts*, in which the human race's ever more refined conception of God will gradually encourage its progress towards a 'Third Gospel' transcending the warring monotheisms. Mendelssohn argued against Lessing's Leibnizian concept of Providence as guiding humanity from childhood to manhood, instead contending that in reality the human race is, in almost every century, child, adult, and old man at the same time.[92] Progress is for the individual; everyone goes through life in his or her own way, and we should not presuppose that the purpose of Providence is, as is commonly assumed, to provide for humankind's perfection in the course of time.[93]

As Edward Breuer writes, Mendelssohn, dedicated to *Bildung* as an ethos of critical independence, was acutely aware of the implications of progressive historicisms even of an implicitly post-Christian kind such as Lessing's, wary that the 'compelling linearity of such historicism would always result in the submersion of the individual and particular in the face of the general and universal'.[94] In other words, progressive theories of history were homologous in Mendelssohn's mind to those processes of colonial imposition and civic exclusion of which Mendelssohn, the Jewish outsider, was extremely critical.

Mendelssohn's Bildung

We have already situated Mendelssohn, in collaboration with Lessing, as a proponent of the philosemitic Enlightenment, meaning that we should regard his philosophy of *Bildung* or individual formation mediated by diverse experience as imbricated in anti-Eurocentric patterns of thought that are sensitive to the contemporary political implications of universal history and stadial theory. As Matt Erlin writes, in contrast with Lessing's concept of global moral progress, Mendelssohn 'proposes a model in which each individual follows his own trajectory of self-cultivation', a stance pithily epitomized in his 1782 letter to August Hennings: 'The aim of nature is not the perfection of the human race. No! It is the perfection of the human being, of the individual.'[95] Moreover, for Mendelssohn the assumption of human progress may lead to complacency and stunt the creativity and initiative of subsequent generations: 'What are our children supposed to do? Continue to march forward indefinitely? . . . They cannot continue where we left off, because they do not begin where we have begun. They bring with them a tension that finds no resistance and thus cannot work effectively.'[96] Erlin argues that it is not just that individual initiative and felicity is threatened by the sweeping temporality of progressive time; rather for Mendelssohn, eighteenth-century theories of progress as applied to Judaism and so-called nomadic peoples suggested that entire cultures were vestigial once their historical function had been fulfilled.[97]

Mendelssohn's response, which would have ssignificant repercussions for liberal Jewish discourse, is to suggest a theory of *Bildung* as dynamic self-cultivation that is less ahistorical than counter-historical. Contrary to Arendt's early condemnation of Mendelssohn's *Bildung* as an escape from historical consciousness, Mendelssohnian *Bildung* refrains from eulogizing the emergence of the state, commercial society, and civic institutions in the manner of stadial theory, and instead draws attention to luminous individuals, outsider figures such as Socrates and Spinoza who, in as much as they have left a characterological legacy focused on their sociable virtues, embody a tantalizing equilibrium of worldly and spiritual energies.[98] As Erlin suggests, for Mendelssohn, the character of Socrates, equally a philosopher, urbane citizen, and fearless warrior, is an exemplary model for *Bildung*, requiring, as Erlin puts it, the cultivation of 'interior and exterior, the physical and the mental, sense and reason'.[99] Mendelssohn's ideal of *Bildung* rejected the fatalism or complacency implicit in the stadial philosophy of history, emphasizing instead the importance of sociability, the desire to foster perfection in oneself and others. Mendelssohn describes an 'innate drive for self-improvement' that motivates human beings to form a social contract, in turn intensifying their drive to perfect themselves, an unceasing dialectic of self and society that cannot refer to nostalgic origins or any goal to history that would encourage human uniformity, stasis, and delusory self-regard.[100] As Willi Goetschel suggests, Mendelssohn's ethos of *Bildung*, articulated in a sophisticated philosophy of aesthetic and ethical perfection (*Vollkommenheit*), desires a Spinozist increase in the powers of self-determination, the 'emancipation of human nature from the internal powers of repression'.[101]

Rather than stressing humanity's intellectual and technological progress towards commercial civilization, Mendelssohn's theory of *Bildung* prioritizes expansive sociability and the refinement of the media of communication as the very matrix of an enlightened society:

> Bildung, Cultur, und Aufklärung sind Modificationen des geselligen Lebens, Wirkungen des Fleißes und der Bemühungen der Menschen, ihren geselligen Zustand zu verbessern.[102] (Education, culture, and enlightenment are modifications of our social life, effects of industry and of the efforts of men to improve their social condition.)

> Ueberhaupt ist die Sprache eines Volkes die best Anziege seiner Bildung, der Cultur sowohl als der Aufklärung, der Ausdehnung sowhol als der Stärke nach.[103] (In general, the language of a people is the best indication of their education, of their level of culture and enlightenment, in terms of both its extent and depth.)

As Willi Goetschel has argued, Mendelssohn's notion of *Bildung* cannot be equated with the form of aesthetic self-cultivation associated with Schiller and post-classicism. Mendelssohn's notion has a 'clear political and religious dimension', in which *Bildung* is the 'constitutive ground on which the state and enlightenment depend as much as religion and culture'.[104] Mendelssohn's innovative idea, that *Bildung* is a standard by which to measure culture, religion, the state, and the progress of enlightenment, is a profound harbinger of the liberal Jewish ethos, which refuses, with Nathan the Wise, any religious or political ontology which transcends the dense texture of lived relationships. As we shall see, Mendelssohn's vigorous cosmopolitanism, counter-historical energies, sympathy for outsiders, and pluralistic conception of Judaism as congenial to individual and collective flourishing, helped to establish a repertoire of Reform and liberal Jewish arguments for the historical vitality of diasporic Judaism.

Notes

1 An earlier version of this essay appeared in N. Curthoys. 2010. 'A Diasporic Reading of *Nathan the Wise*', *Comparative Literature Studies* 47(1), 70–95.

2 E. Said. 2003. *Freud and the Non-European*, New York: Verso, 76.

3 R. Brann and A. Sutcliffe. 2004. 'Introduction', in R. Brann and A. Sutcliffe (eds), *Renewing the Past, Reconfiguring Jewish Culture: From Al-Andalus to the Haskalah*, Philadelphia: University of Pennsylvania Press, 1. On Mendelssohn's contribution to the Hebrew renaissance of the *Haskalah* see D. Sorkin. 1999. 'The Mendelssohn Myth and its Method', *New German Critique* 77, 13–14.

4 D. Sorkin. 2008. *The Religious Enlightenment: Protestants, Jews, and Catholics from London to Vienna*, Princeton and Oxford: Princeton University Press, 167.

5 S. Feiner. 2004. *Haskalah and History: The Emergence of a Modern Jewish Historical Consciousness*, trans. C. Naor and S. Silverston, Oxford: The Littman Library of Jewish Civilization, 1.

6 For a discussion of the intensive German Jewish memorialization of the Lessing/ Mendelssohn friendship, which by 1879 had become a 'key element in the discourse of German-Jewish struggle for emancipation', see W. Goetschel. 2000. 'Lessing, Mendelssohn, Nathan: German-Jewish Myth-Building as an Act of Emancipation', *Lessing Yearbook* XXXII, 354. For a discussion of the commemoration of the 200th anniversary of Mendelssohn's birth as a summation of this memorial tradition, see M. Gottlieb. 2008. 'Publishing the Moses Mendelssohn *Jubiläumsausgabe* in Weimar and Nazi Germany', *Leo Baeck Institute Yearbook* 53(1), 57–75.

7 D. Sorkin. 1994. 'The Case for Comparison: Moses Mendelssohn and the Religious Enlightenment', *Modern Judaism* 14(2), 123.

8 J.L. Sammons. 1999. 'Who Did Heine think He Was?', in J. Hermand and R.C. Holub (eds), *Heinrich Heine's Contested Identities: Politics, Religion and Nationalism in Nineteenth Century Germany*, New York: Peter Lang, 11.

9 For an excellent discussion of Voltaire's notorious rationalist antipathy to Judaism as signifying 'primitivism, legalism, and blind reverence for tradition', see A. Sutcliffe. 2004. 'The Ambiguities of Enlightenment: Voltaire and the Jews', in A. Sutcliffe, *Judaism and Enlightenment*, Cambridge, UK: Cambridge University Press, 232.

10 For a discussion of the 'Lessing-Mendelssohn-Nathan complex' as a 'symbol for the chances and limits of the German-Jewish experience', see Goetschel, 'Lessing, Mendelssohn, Nathan', 343.

11 M.A. Meyer. 1989. 'Modernity as a Crisis for the Jews', *Modern Judaism* 9(2), 151.

12 Meyer, 'Modernity as a Crisis for the Jews', 155.

13 For a good overview of the German Jewish Renaissance, see Mendes-Flohr. *German Jews*, and P. Mendes-Flohr. 1991. *Divided Passions: Jewish Intellectuals and the*

Experience of Modernity, Detroit: Wayne State University Press. For a discussion of the Jewish Renaissance, see Rabinbach. 'Between Enlightenment and Apocalypse', 78–124.

14 F. Rosenzweig. 2000. 'Notes on Lessing's Nathan, December 1919', in *Cultural Writings of Franz Rosenzweig*, trans. B.E. Gall, New York: Syracuse University Press, 106.

15 Rosenzweig, 'Notes on Lessing's Nathan', 107.

16 Rosenzweig, 'Notes on Lessing's Nathan', 109.

17 Rosenzweig, 'Notes on Lessing's Nathan', 109.

18 Rosenzweig, 'Notes on Lessing's Nathan', 109.

19 Rosenzweig, 'Notes on Lessing's Nathan, 111.

20 F. Rosenzweig, 'A Pronouncement for a Celebration of Mendelssohn (1929)', in *Cultural Writings of Franz Rosenzweig*, trans. B.E. Gall, New York: Syracuse University Press, 103–104.

21 H. Arendt. 1997. *Rahel Varnhagen: The Life of a Jewess*, L. Weissberg (ed.), and trans. R. and C. Winston, Baltimore and London: The Johns Hopkins University Press, 104.

22 See, for example, Mendelssohn's famous 'Vorrede' to the German translation of Manasseh Ben Israel's 'Rettung der Juden' in which, contra Dohm, he defends Jews as an already, rather than potentially, productive people, specifically defending their mediating role as merchants and financial middlemen. See M. Mendelssohn, *Gesammelte Schiften: Jubiläumsausgabe*, eds. Ismar Elbogen, Julius Guttmann, and Eugen Mittwoch, continued by Alexander Altmann (Berlin: Akademie Verlag, 1929–1932; Breslau: S Münzs, 1938; Stuttgart-Bad Cannstatt: F, Frommann, 1971–2011) (hereafter cited by mentioning the volume and page number of the passage in question). See Mendelssohn *JubA*, 8: 13–14.

23 W. Goetschel. 2007. 'Mendelssohn and the State', *MLN* 122: 482.

24 H. Arendt. 2007. 'The Enlightenment and the Jewish Question' (1932), in J. Kohn and R.H. Feldman (eds), *The Jewish Writings*, New York: Schocken Books, 8.

25 Arendt, 'The Enlightenment and the Jewish Question', 8.

26 Arendt, 'The Enlightenment and the Jewish Question', 15.

27 Arendt, 'The Enlightenment and the Jewish Question', 8–9. By way of contrast with Arendt's narrative of Mendelssohn's original betrayal of Judaism, we now know, as Sorkin puts it, that 'Mendelssohn wrote in Hebrew on Jewish subjects virtually continuously throughout his adult life'. See Sorkin, 'The Mendelssohn Myth and its Method', 22.

28 Arendt's animus towards the quietism of Mendelssohn is still in evidence in *The Origins of Totalitarianism*, where she inaccurately represents Mendelssohn as being indifferent to his political or civil rights, referring more than once to Mendelssohn's 'complete satisfaction with the conditions under which he lived'. See H. Arendt. 1973. *The Origins of Totalitarianism*, New York: Harcourt Brace Jovanovich, 59.

29 G. Scholem. 1976. 'Against the Myth of German-Jewish Dialogue', in G. Scholem, *On Jews and Judaism in Crisis, Selected Essays*, W.J. Dannhauser (ed.), New York: Schocken Books, 62–63.

30 G. Scholem. 1976. 'Jews and Germans', in G. Scholem, *On Jews and Judaism in Crisis, Selected Essays*, W.J. Dannhauser (ed.), New York: Schocken Books, 75.

31   Scholem, 'Jews and Germans', 77.

32   Scholem, 'Against the Myth of German-Jewish Dialogue', 11.

33   Scholem, 'Jews and Germans', 74–75.

34   Scholem, 'Jews and Germans', 81.

35   S.L. Gilman. 1986. *Jewish Self-Hatred, Anti-Semitism and the Hidden Language of the Jews*, Baltimore and London: The Johns Hopkins University Press, 87.

36   'Mendelssohn wished to restructure the very definition of the Jew so as to make his . . . splitting of the good Jew from the bad Jew the norm rather than the exception'. Gilman, *Jewish Self-Hatred*, 105.

37   Gilman, *Jewish Self-Hatred*, 104.

38   Gilman, *Jewish Self-Hatred*, 84–85. For a related critique of Mendelssohn's disparagement of Yiddish as seminal for German Jewish self-perception, see J.A. Grossman. 2000. *The Discourse on Yiddish in Germany: From the Enlightenment to the Second Empire*, Rochester, NY: Camden House.

39   Gilman, *Jewish Self-Hatred*, 104.

40   The most significant and influential challenge to Gershom Scholem's post-war criticism, in essays such as 'Against the Myth of German-Jewish Dialogue', of nineteenth-century German Jewish responses to emancipation – a critique which has cast a long shadow over the field – is S. Heschel. 1998. *Abraham Geiger and the Jewish Jesus*, Chicago: University of Chicago Press. I am indebted to Heschel's rejection of Scholem's argument that the rationalist proponents of *Wissenschaft des Judentums* sought to 'bury' Judaism under the weight of historical criticism.

41   As Michah Gottlieb argues, the German Jewish editors of the 1929 Mendelssohn *Jubiläumsausgabe*, which celebrated the 200th anniversary of his birth, saw in Mendelssohn the 'promulgation of the classical spirit of German humanism, Jewish entry into German society, and the cultural renewal of Judaism'. See Gottlieb, 'Publishing the Moses Mendelssohn *Jubiläumsausgabe* in Weimar and Nazi Germany', 62.

42   D. Westerkamp. 2008. 'The Philonic Distinction: German Enlightenment historiography of Jewish thought', *History and Theory* 47, 534 and 536.

43   Feiner, *Haskalah and History*, 17.

44   Feiner, *Haskalah and History*, 51.

45   Feiner, *Haskalah and History*, 36.

46   A. Altmann. 1973. *Moses Mendelssohn, a Biographical Study*, London: Routledge and Kegan Paul, 752.

47   Altmann, *Moses Mendelssohn, a Biographical Study*, 33.

48   Altmann, *Moses Mendelssohn, a Biographical Study*, 34.

49   A. Sutcliffe. 2004. 'Quarrelling over Spinoza: Moses Mendelssohn and the Fashioning of Jewish Philosophical Heroism', in R. Brann and A. Sutcliffe (eds), *Renewing the Past, Reconfiguring Jewish Culture: from al-Andalus to the Haskalah*, Philadelphia: University of Pennsylvania Press, 181.

50   Sutcliffe, *Judaism and Enlightenment*, 134–135.

51   Sutcliffe, *Judaism and Enlightenment*, 137–138.

52   M. Mendelssohn. 1988. 'To the Friends of Lessing' (1781), in *The Spinoza Conversations between Lessing and Jacobi: Texts with Excerpts from the Ensuing Controversy*, trans. G. Vallée et al., Boston: Lanham, 130.

53   Altmann, *Moses Mendelssohn, a Biographical Study*, 35.

54 Quoted from L. Hochman. 2004. 'The Other as Oneself: Mendelssohn, Diogenes, Bayle, and Spinoza', University of Florida, *Eighteenth-Century Life* 28(2), 51. The English translation is M. Mendelssohn. 2003. *Philosophical Writings*, D.O. Dahlstrom (ed. and trans.), Cambridge, UK: Cambridge University Press, 106. Mendelssohn, *JubA* 1: 14–15.

55 See Westerkamp, 'The Philonic Distinction', 538.

56 Mendelssohn, *JubA* 8: 11. For a nuanced discussion of Mendelssohn's critique of Dohm's statism, see W. Goetschel. 2010. 'Voices from the "Jewish colony": Sovereignty, power, secularization, and the outside within', in R. Shilliam (ed.), *Non-Western Thought and International Relations: Retrieving the Global Context of Investigations of Modernity*, London: Routledge, 64–84.

57 Sutcliffe, 'Quarrelling over Spinoza: Moses Mendelssohn and the fashioning of Jewish Philosophical Heroism', 172. For a suggestive reading of *Nathan the Wise* through a Spinozist prism, see W. Goetschel. 2004. 'Negotiating Truth: On Nathan's Business', in W. Goetschel, *Spinoza's Modernity: Mendelssohn, Lessing, and Heine*, Madison: University of Wisconsin Press, 230–250.

58 Steven Nadler accurately describes Spinoza's rigorously anti-anthropomorphic conception of God: 'His God is not a lawgiver and judge in any traditional sense. He is not a source of comfort or reward or punishment, nor is he a being to whom one would pray.' See S. Nadler. 1999. *Spinoza: A Life*, New York: Cambridge University Press, 187.

59 Nadler, *Spinoza: A Life*, 231.

60 See the preface to B. de Spinoza. 1951. *A Theologico-Political Treatise*, trans. R.H.M. Elwes, New York: Dover Publications, 9.

61 As Edward Breuer argues, 'the spiritual sensibility of eighteenth-century Europe, if one can speak in these terms, was decidedly exoteric and socially inclusive'. See E. Breuer. 1996. 'Rabbinic Law and Spirituality in Mendelssohn's "Jerusalem"', *The Jewish Quarterly Review* 86(3/4), 302.

62 G.E. Lessing. 1994. *Nathan the Wise*, trans. S. Clenell and R. Philip, Milton Keynes: Open University Press. Hereafter cited by line number.

63 For Spinoza's principles of scriptural interpretation and his anti-clerical emphasis on natural reason, see 'On the Interpretation of Scripture' in B. de Spinoza. 2007. *Theological-Political Treatise*, trans. J. Israel and M. Silverthorne, Cambridge, UK: Cambridge University Press, 9–10, 83.

64 See the chapter 'Was the Enlightenment the Origin of the Holocaust?' in J. Docker. 2008. *The Origins of Violence: Religion, History, and Genocide*, Sydney: UNSW Press, 199–200.

65 Docker, *The Origins of Violence*, 197.

66 Docker, *The Origins of Violence*, 196. See also Nadler, *Spinoza: A Life*, 238. For an illuminating discussion of the centrality of imagination and embodiment to Spinoza's metaphysics and ethics, see M. Gatens and G. Lloyd. 1999. *Collective Imaginings: Spinoza, Past and Present*, London: Routledge.

67 'Der Wunder höchstes ist, Dass uns die wahren, echten Wunder so Alltäglich werden können, werden sollen.' G.E. Lessing. 2000. *Nathan der Weise*, Stuttgart: Reclam, ll.217–219, p. 14.

68 Sutcliffe, 'Quarrelling over Spinoza', 173.

69 Altmann, *Moses Mendelssohn*, 180.

70 J.I. Israel. 2001. *Radical Enlightenment: Philosophy and the Making of Modernity, 1650–1750*, Oxford: Oxford University Press.

71 Docker, *The Origins of Violence*, 203.

72 Docker, *The Origins of Violence*, 205–206.

73 Docker, *The Origins of Violence*, 207.

74 Docker, *The Origins of Violence*, 207–208.

75 G.E. Lessing. 1970–1979. 'Rettung des Hier. Cardanus', in K. Eibl and H.G. Göpfert (eds), *Theologiekritische Schiften I und II* of Lessing's *Werke*, 8 vols, Munich, vol. 7, 9–32.

76 Altmann, *Moses Mendelssohn*, 231.

77 For a discussion of Lessing's defence of Cardanus, see W. Goetschel. 2005. 'Lessing and the Jews', in B. Fischer and T.C. Fox (eds), *A Companion to the Works of Gotthold Ephraim Lessing*, Rochester, NY: Camden House, 194; and Silvia Horsch, 2004. *Rationalität und Toleranz. Lessings Auseinandersetzung mit dem Islam* (Ex Oriente Lux 5), Ergon, Würzburg.

78 Hochman, 'The Other as Oneself', 44.

79 Mendelssohn, *Jerusalem*, 73. Mendelssohn, *JubA* 8: 140.

80 Goetschel, *Spinoza's Modernity*, 140.

81 Quoted from Goetschel, *Spinoza's Modernity*, 141. See Mendelssohn, *JubA* 8: 35n.

82 See Goetschel, 'Mendelssohn and the State', 47: 'the notion that the state by definition entails an absolute claim to sovereignty, including the authority over the individual's natural and human rights, is starkly absent in Mendelssohn.'

83 Goetschel, 'Mendelssohn and the State', 486.

84 Mendelssohn, *Jerusalem*, 94. Mendelssohn, *JubA* 8: 161.

85 See A. Maalouf. 1984. *The Crusades through Arab Eyes*, trans. J. Rothschild, London: Al Saqi Books.

86 G.E. Lessing. 1962. *Hamburg Dramaturgy*, trans. H. Zimmern, New York: Dover, 20–21.

87 Hochman, 'The Other as Oneself', 53.

88 G. Simmel. 1950. *The Sociology of Georg Simmel*, K.H. Wolff (ed. and trans.), Glencoe, Il.: The Free Press, 402–408.

89 M. Mendelssohn, letter of 16 February 1765 to T. Abbt. Mendelssohn. 1975. *Selections from his Writings*, E. Jospe (ed. and trans.), New York: Viking Press, New York, 62–63.

90 Feiner, *Haskalah and History*, 42.

91 Mendelssohn, *Jerusalem*, 95. Mendelssohn, *JubA* 8: 162.

92 Mendelssohn, *Jerusalem*, 95–96. Mendelssohn, *JubA* 8: 162.

93 Mendelssohn, *Jerusalem*, 96. Mendelssohn, *JubA* 8: 163.

94 E. Breuer. 1995. 'Of Miracles and Events Past: Mendelssohn on History', *Jewish History* 9(2), 45.

95 M. Erlin. 2002. 'Reluctant Modernism: Moses Mendelssohn's Philosophy of History', *Journal of the History of Ideas* 63(1), 83 and 87.

96 Cited in Erlin, 'Mendelssohn's Philosophy of History', 87.

97 Erlin, 'Mendelssohn's Philosophy of History', 84.

98 On Mendelssohn's enthusiasm for Socrates, see Erlin, 'Mendelssohn's Philosophy of History', 89.

99 Erlin, 'Mendelssohn's Philosophy of History', 89.

100 Erlin, 'Mendelssohn's Philosophy of History', 90.
101 Goetschel, *Spinoza's Modernity*, 97.
102 M. Mendelssohn. 1784. 'Ueber die frage: was Heisst Aufklären?' *JubA*, 6:1: 115.
103 Mendelssohn, 'Ueber die frage: was Heisst Aufklären?', *JubA*, 6:1: 116.
104 Goetschel, 'Mendelssohn and the State', 481.

CHAPTER 2

✳

Diasporic Visions
The Emergence of Liberal Judaism

The era of Moses Mendelssohn enabled the emergence of a historically aware conception of Judaism that was sympathetic to the spiritual, philosophical, and aesthetic achievements of post-exilic diasporic Jews. Diasporic Jewish acumen in fields as varied as philosophy, poetry, biblical exegesis, diplomacy, astronomy, and medicine were interpreted by liberal and reformist German Jews from the late eighteenth century as the fruits of active Jewish participation in tolerant and progressive non-Jewish societies. This chapter discusses the pronounced tendency of post-Enlightenment German Jewish intellectuals to extol a narrative of Jewish resourcefulness and creativity in diaspora that begins with the Babylonian exile in the sixth century BCE, and then continues, after the fall of the Second Temple in 70 CE, in Egyptian Alexandria, the Levant and Mediterranean world, Moorish Spain, and then southern and western Europe, with particular reference to the Sephardic communities of the Iberian peninsula and their post-expulsion legacy in seventeenth-century republican Amsterdam. I shall argue that the transformation and enlargement of Jewish historical consciousness that begins with the German Jewish Enlightenment or *Haskalah* from the 1780s generated a dynamic conception of the vocation of Jews as a supra-national people with double-edged attributes, both loyal to the nation in which they reside and yet offering skills, values, and perspectives that enrich their host society.

I suggest that liberal Judaism's post-*Haskalah* articulation of Judaism as a progressive force in world history was not simply an inventive but ultimately apologetic justification for Judaism's continuing existence, nor did it seek to effect the dissolution of Judaism and the national life and historical traditions of the Jewish people into a spiritual ideal. Rather the emerging liberal Jewish interpretation of post-exilic Judaism represented a highly strategic re-interpretation of the contemporary social function of Jews as merchants, brokers, middlemen, diplomatic mediators, and as advisers; that is, as perennial travellers and translators between cultures. This increasingly secular concern with promulgating an affirmative social theory of diaspora Judaism anticipates Georg Simmel's famous sociological analysis of 'the stranger' who combines the productive and emancipative critical functions of participatory engagement and dispassionate objectivity. The argument for Judaism's participatory vitality developed by liberal German Jewish intellectuals in the nineteenth century articulated a resilient worldview that persisted into the twentieth century, eventually challenging, as we shall see in later chapters, the emergence of political Zionism and its rejection of the past, present, and future of the diasporic Jewish condition.

Beginning with Moses Mendelssohn, progressive German Jews critiqued the Christian assumption, legitimized by German philosophers such as Kant and Hegel, and reaching its apogee in Ernst Renan's conception of a non-Semitic or 'Aryan' Jesus, that Christianity has historically superseded an arid, legalistic Judaism and become the one true faith of world-historical significance. Historical thinking, even in the service of Enlightenment, continually threatened to condemn the Jews as degraded, inferior, and foreign in relationship to the dynamic and fructifying history of the Christian West.[1] German Jewish thinkers responded to this dilemma in the vigorous manner of Mendelssohn: by abjuring supercessionist historicisms, stressing the inclusive and imaginative dimensions of historical representation, and articulating cross-cultural and world-historical narratives.

In confronting Christianity's hubris and its often visceral disdain, begot of genealogical anxiety, for Judaism and the Jewish people, German Jewish intellectuals developed an energetic mode of historiography which was felicitously dubbed 'counter-history' by contemporary scholars of German Jewish history beginning with David Biale, and subsequently heuristically deployed by Susannah Heschel and Christian Weise.[2] Counter-historical approaches involve the reinterpretation of foundational sources which tend to be read against the grain; they involve a critical rethinking of values and tradition that disturbs reified identities and dominant political and ecclesiastical institutions.[3] In his writings on diasporic consciousness, James Clifford celebrates the creative and dissonant potential of diasporic 'counterhistories, [those] off-the-beat cultural critiques' that disrupt normative interpretations of historical reality and leave open the relationship between past and present.[4] In articulating a diasporic critique of historical narratives which revile and exclude the Jewish presence in German life, German Jewish historical consciousness was often subversive, critical of Eurocentric ideologies of modernity and progress, particularly those that justified colonialism, imperialism and racism. German Jewish liberals and reformers did not seek to subsume Jewish history within the unfolding story of Christian civilization; rather, they undermined Christian claims to superiority by embracing a decentred world history that was notably sympathetic to the Islamic world in which medieval Jewry prospered.[5]

Renewing the Past: The Haskalah and the Maskilim

While German Jewish and Enlightenment historiography has consistently drawn attention to the profound admiration of the *Maskilim* for historical exemplars such as Maimonides, cultured and rationalist Jewish individuals who enjoyed an intellectually fertile relationship with the non-Jewish world, it has not focused as explicitly on the *Haskalah's* imaginative investment in the symbiotic relationship between polyglot and sophisticated cultural contexts such as Andalusia (Moorish Spain) and the flourishing of Jewish philosophy, religious hermeneutics, and aesthetic expression. *Haskalah* reformists were profoundly interested, we might argue, in evoking diasporic Jews as cultural agents, as catalysts for new ideas and as creative translators between cultures and traditions, just as they had been at the forefront of intellectually vibrant and relatively tolerant societies such as medieval Al-Andalus and seventeenth-century Amsterdam. The historical consciousness of liberal Judaism does not simply isolate the transmissible content of the teachings of individual Jews such as Maimonides or Mendelssohn as they contribute to biblical translation and commentary, ethics, or influential interpretations of Halakhah or Jewish Law. It wishes in addition to evoke the forms of life and acculturated personae of such individuals, illuminated by their interactions with sometimes curious and sympathetic, sometimes hostile, non-Jewish interlocutors.

The emergence of an inclusive German Jewish historical consciousness, alert to the diverse experiences and cultural hybridity of post-exilic Jews who absorbed the language and mores of their host societies, can be traced back to a group of German and central European Jewish reformers, the *Maskilim*. These Jewish intellectuals were profoundly affected, as the first generation to have experienced it, by the emancipation of Jews from the ghetto and subsequent contact with the increasingly secular, dynamic intellectual culture of the German Enlightenment, with its humanist ideals and withering critique of dogmatic orthodoxy and religious bigotry. They were eager to promote a consonant but autochthonous German Jewish Enlightenment which sought to curb Talmudic exclusivity and advocated that Jews be educated in secular subjects such as history, science, geography, mathematics, and in vernacular European languages, including German.[6] In addition to their secularizing and integrationist tendencies, the *Maskilim* wanted to renew Jewish education and religious principles by reviving Hebrew grammar, biblical exegesis, and Jewish philosophy, a movement analogous to the critical and philological impetus of the Protestant Reformation.[7] Moses Mendelssohn, with his extensive Hebrew commentary on the Pentateuch and his seminal German translation of the Hebrew bible, was, as Schorsch argues, the progenitor of the *Haskalah*'s countercultural critique of the Ashkenazi aversion to serious Bible study.[8]

The *Maskilim* were deeply sceptical of the power of rabbinical authority in ghettoized Jewish communities and wanted to curb an over-emphasis in Jewish education on the study of the Talmud, the textual codification of an oral rabbinical tradition debating Jewish law, custom, and morality. Part of the problem for the *Maskilim*, who wished to edify and enlighten the Jewish masses, was that the biblical period of Jewish history was limited in its relevancy, for it was a bygone age when Israel possessed its own land, and its own political and social institutions. As Michael Meyer argues, modern diasporic Jewish existence in emancipation era Germany required 'as exemplars individuals who had combined adherence to Judaism with full participation in the non-Jewish world around them'. Such individuals were rare in Ashkenazi Judaism, the traditional heritage of central and Eastern European Jews, but could be found among the Sephardim, Iberian Jews and their descendants in seventeenth-century Holland who had inherited the secular culture that flourished under more tolerant regimes in Islamic Spain. As Meyer details, the regular column in *Ma'assef*, the periodical of the German *Maskilim*, entitled 'History of the Great Men of Israel', was devoted, aside from Moses Mendelssohn himself, to Sephardic luminaries such as the Andalusian philosopher and legal thinker Moses Maimonides, the widely learned Joseph Delmedigo of seventeenth-century Crete, and the Dutch rabbi and interlocutor with Christians, Menasseh ben Israel.[9] As we have discussed, Mendelssohn himself famously revived Manasseh ben Israel's significance by organizing a new German edition of his *Vindiciae Judaeorum* (1656) which argued the case for the admission of the Jews to England, to which Mendelssohn dedicated a preface defending the beneficial effects of Jewish economic activity and critiquing ecclesiastical coercion.[10]

Drawing upon Sephardic models, writes Meyer, meant widening the past of German Jews, evoking Jewish historical figures very different from the prominent rabbinical authorities of recent tradition, promoting an elastic conception of historical Judaism populated by figures that combined religious, philosophical and worldly virtues, proud defenders of Judaism but also skilled community advocates who encouraged dialogue with the non-Jewish world.[11] As Schorsch writes, the 'Sephardic image' construed by enlightened Ashkenazi intellectuals facilitated a Jewish posture 'marked by cultural openness, philosophical thinking, and an appreciation for the aesthetic'.[12] Brann and Sutcliffe suggest that the 'Sephardi Mystique' was a crucial formative element of the early *Haskalah*, in which revered luminaries of the Andalusian golden age such as Maimonides, Abraham ibn Ezra, and Judah Halevi were elevated to intellectual models for the *Maskilim*. An enthusiastic focus on the 'rationalist heroes of Muslim Spain' enabled the recuperation of an ethical, progressive, and rationalist tradition within Jewish history, and had the allegorical value of demonstrating to Christian Germany that Jews were capable of dynamic participation in societies in which culture and talent was more influential than religious affiliation.[13] As Andrea Schatz argues, while the adoption of Sephardi models of learning was intimately linked to self-assertion vis-à-vis the Christian world, the great interest in the Bible in its original Hebrew language in the Portuguese Jewish community of Amsterdam was not only indicative of attempts to regain a lost religious tradition after a history of expulsion, conversion, and migration, but was also consistent with the cultural ideals of the surrounding Christian community, since the Bible was held in great esteem by both Calvinists and Sephardim. Indeed, Schatz writes, biblical knowledge constituted common ground that could be turned into an arena of interpretive contest. Thus the Sephardic model of biblical and linguistic studies was attractive for reformists in the Ashkenazi world precisely because of its dialectical aspects, facilitating the articulation of Jewish difference while acknowledging shared concepts and values.[14] We can interpret the Sephardic posture as a multifaceted counter-history to the Ashkenazi focus on Jewish Law, a desire for Jewish renaissance which sought both to rejuvenate Judaism from within, to offer an alternative model of intellectual and ethical comportment to Christianity, and to provide continuity with the flourishing cultures of Jewish antiquity.[15]

I would suggest that the classical German ideal of *Bildung*, with its neo-humanist anti-scholastic ideal of rounded and harmonious personality, breadth of interests, and hunger for diverse experiences, influenced the *Maskilim* in their choice of historical Jewish exemplars. In the *Maskilim* periodicals of the late eighteenth century Sephardic Jews were praised and held up as examples for their polymathic talents; they studied the Bible and the Hebrew language, as well as science, philosophy, and secular languages, and were presumed to be open to stimulation by the non-Jewish world. The scholarly and political achievements of Iberian Jews such as Samuel ha'Nagid (993–1055), the eleventh-century vizier at the Muslim court of Granada educated in Arabic and the Koran as well as the Torah and Halakhah, military commander, and founder and patron of a very successful Yishuv for Talmudic and biblical scholarship, provided an exhilarating contrast to the weary rabbinic presumption that the 'essential contours of the relations between Jews and gentiles have been delineated long ago in rabbinic aggadah', foreclosing any real interest in the history of gentile nations.[16] The *Maskilim* marvelled at Maimonides, who was born in Andalusian Cordoba but spent a great deal of his life in Morocco and Egypt, wrote his innovative works in Arabic, studied Muslim and Greek philosophy, attempted to harmonize Jewish theology and law with Aristotelian principles, and influenced the thought of great Christian theologians such as Thomas Aquinas.[17]

As discussed, another exemplary diaspora Jew was Manasseh ben Israel, the seventeenth-century Dutch Rabbi and publisher who enjoyed extensive correspondence with Christian scholars and displayed considerable political skill in successfully seeking the readmission of Jews to England under the rule of Cromwell. The sudden shift in educated Jewish historical consciousness towards an appreciation of non-rabbinical Jewish personalities brought about a decisive transformation in the worldview of reform-oriented German Jews. Heavily criticized by the Rabbinate and by Orthodox religious Jews who considered their own form of Judaism to be permanent and unalterable, the *Maskilim* were deeply sympathetic to personalities who were peripheral to Judaism, including the Marranos. In early nineteenth-century periodicals such as *Sulamith*, the *Maskilim* spoke highly of figures such as Isaac Orobio de Castro, a seventeenth-century Portuguese Christian intellectual and prominent physician, and later rector of the University of Toulouse, who had been tortured by the Inquisition on suspicion of being a Jew and then joined the Jewish community in Amsterdam.[18]

Perhaps the Marranos fascinated Jewish advocates of *Haskalah* because they represented a 'grey area at the boundary of Judaism', allowing reformist Jews to meditate on the ubiquity of intolerance throughout history, and on the vitality of outsider figures who, like the *Maskilim* themselves, could no longer completely identify with a single culture or religious tradition. Meyer describes the increasing historical interest taken by the *Maskilim* in personalities who were not Jewish in an orthodox religious sense but who affirmed a Jewish sensibility despite the vicissitudes of history. The *Haskalah* thereby entailed a secularization of Jewish history and a polycentric conception of Jewish identity sensitive to Marrano experience.[19]

We have discussed Spinoza as a focus of 'confused fascination' for Enlightenment era Jews who sought to find historical models for mediation between Jewish and non-Jewish worlds.[20] For Spinoza was not just a scholar who corresponded with gentile scholars in an international republic of letters: according to Sutcliffe and Brann the Sephardic descended Spinoza was an 'intellectual bridge' between the secular Enlightenment and medieval Al-Andalus, continuing the Andalusian tradition of practical rationalism.[21] What is important to note here is that Spinoza could still be considered resiliently 'Jewish', despite his expulsion from Amsterdam's Jewish community and voluntary relinquishment of Jewish Law. We can consider the interest taken by Jewish reformers and intellectuals in Spinoza's personality and philosophy as an indication that in the era of *Haskalah* Jewish identity was interpreted in terms of more recent historical dynamics, in the sense that it was understood to be mediated by specific traditions and genealogies, political and cultural circumstances which produced a particular kind of acculturated Jewish sensibility and ethical personality. A good example of this tendency is the German Jewish author Berthold Auerbach's first novel, a fictionalized life of Spinoza, written in 1837, in which Auerbach represents Jewish Amsterdam as a continuation of the Sephardic tradition and 're-appropriates Spinoza for Jewish history' by presenting him as a reincarnation of Maimonides.[22] As Yosef Yerushalmi argues, the emergence of a post-emancipation Jewish historical consciousness lent itself to a version of Judaism that was inseparable from its evolution through time, from its 'concrete manifestations at any point in history'. Such a focus on concrete historical dynamics in post-biblical Jewish history eroded a sense of Jewish identity as amenable to *a priori* definition, but also increased interest in forms of Jewish sensibility and intellect forged in liminal, transformative, and revolutionary episodes of Jewish and world history.[23]

Wissenschaft des Judentums

The *Maskilim* were didactic reformers who endeavoured to make a continued adherence to Judaism defensible for modern, philosophically inclined Jews, and in that respect they were the progenitors of the Reform movement in Judaism. Emerging early in the nineteenth century, the Reform movement sought to replace traditional rabbinical authority and its ahistorical focus on Jewish law and observance with an interpretive model of Judaism as historically dynamic. As Meyer argues, 'the grounding of Judaism in the flux of history provided a . . . direct support for the Reform enterprise'. Reformers wanted to use modern historical scholarship to prove to Christians that Judaism was not a permanently ossified array of beliefs and practices but capable of self-reinvention; *Wissenschaft* would also demonstrate to traditionalists and the Orthodox rabbinate that 'variety and change were characteristic of Jewish tradition', evoking a Judaism that was 'at home in the modern world'.[24] Schorsch argues that recovery of the past became the means of reconstituting the present.[25] The demonstration of Judaism's religious diversity throughout history warned contemporary critics of Judaism against regarding it as an immutable monolith.[26]

Reform Judaism was given a powerful impetus in the early nineteenth century by the founding of a new scholarly movement, *Wissenschaft des Judentums* (the Science of Judaism), in 1819, by a group of young Jewish intellectuals who had been exposed to the historical, legal, and philological disciplines of German universities, and were motivated to combat the pervasive German anti-Semitism manifested in the notorious 'Hep Hep' riots of that year. This new and vigorous push for Jewish scholarship was the brainchild of the 'Verein für Cultur und Wissenschaft der Juden' (Society for the Culture and Science of the Jews) which included the luminous scholar of Judaism and philologist Leopold Zunz, the Hegelian scholar Eduard Gans, and the (in)famous poet and essayist Heinrich Heine. As scholars such as Heschel and Yerushalmi remind us, *Wissenschaft des Judentums* was a boldly independent, counter-hegemonic venture in tension with the German academic system, given that post-biblical Jewish studies was excluded from German universities and that Jewish scholars knew from the start they could not aspire to academic careers.[27]

The *Verein* sought to sponsor the scholarly study of Judaism and the history of the Jewish people using secular critical methodologies including historical criticism, modern biblical studies, and philology, deploying the latter's focus on historical documents and linguistic evolution. *Wissenschaft des Judentums* evinced a historically expansive research ethos which respected Herder's famous dictum that historically considered all is 'both means and an end'. The discipline combined, in Schorsch's words, a 'profound respect for the integrity of the individual entity', whether it be text, event, or person, with a synthetic approach to interpretation that respected context and chronology, contesting the disjointed and disjunctive way of reading texts sanctified by rabbinic tradition.[28]

In so doing members of the *Verein* formulated a flexible conception of Jewish 'culture' as the 'essence of all the circumstances, characteristics, and achievements of the Jews in relation to religion, philosophy, history, law, literature in general, civil life and all the affairs of man'.[29] The *Verein* wanted all educated Europeans to recognize the rich and nuanced reality of Jewish cultural life and hoped that educated Europeans would belatedly recognize Judaism as an essential aspect of their cultural and religious heritage and not just as a historically remote and reviled background to a nascent Christianity. The founders of the *Verein* wanted to demonstrate through comparative scholarly analysis of a wide range of religious and philosophical sources that Jewish culture flourished beyond the period of its biblical glory and contributed in a multiform fashion to the shaping of Europe's most refined intellectual and spiritual sensibilities. At the same time the Jewish desire to participate in modern European culture and lay claim to its attendant political rights would be strengthened by the extension of equal rights to the academic study of Judaism.[30]

One of the founders of *Wissenschaft des Judentums*, Leopold Zunz (1794–1886), widely regarded as the most respected Jewish scholar of the nineteenth century, wrote a programmatic essay in the first scholarly Jewish periodical *Zeitschrift für die Wissenschaft des Judentums* (1822–23) which he edited, arguing that Jewish scholarship should elucidate the 'inner life and striving of the Jews', their inherited and acquired ideas, in order to be able to 'separate the divine from the mundane'. Zunz held that the Reform movement in Judaism was not bound to all the present forms of external observance, but believed principally in 'the divine spirit of piety and knowledge'. As Maren Niehoff argues, Zunz modelled his ethically inspired hermeneutic of Jewish sources on the Jewish Prophets, arguing in a sermon of 1821 for a transition from the Torah as a 'crude legal text to the prophets' spiritual-ethical interpretation of it'. Significantly Zunz defines the progress of humanity in terms of a movement towards spiritual exegesis, which illuminates explicit underlying moral principles rather than becoming legalistically absorbed with the details of behaviour.[31] Zunz attributed central importance to the later Prophets, who became for him the true educators of humanity, an ideal of human historical progress inspired by Lessing and Herder. Establishing a distinction that would legitimize the Reform movement and instil a liberal Jewish enthusiasm for interpreting the vitality of the Prophetic tradition, Zunz, as Niehoff puts it, 'identifies prophecy with free spirituality, while the priests symbolize the petrification of Judaism'. Such ideas, as Niehoff remarks, can be traced back to Herder, who defined prophecy as the distinguishing characteristic of Israel's national spirit. Herder, Niehoff points out, contrasted Moses and Aaron as two types of religiosity: where Moses stood for authentic religion and ethics, prefiguring the Prophetic tradition, Aaron represented false religiosity, enticing the people to external and petty forms of worship.[32] As Sorkin argues, an ongoing precept of emancipative Jewish reform from the age of Mendelssohn was the attempt to render 'Judaism an "ethical", aesthetic and edifying religion rather than a ritualistic one'.[33]

In 1832 Zunz published *The Sermons of the Jews*, described by Schorsch as a 'classic of modern Jewish scholarship that galvanized a generation and launched a movement'.[34] Here Zunz extolled the Reform movement as the most significant contemporary impulse of Judaism, whose task was to create religious forms and institutions in keeping with the new political status of the Jews and as the fruit of scholarly research. Zunz suggested that edifying sermons had a precedent in Jewish life and could be found, for example, in medieval Midrashic exegesis and in the writing not just of rabbis but of laymen. As Niehoff remarks, Zunz's book is based on the assumption of a distinct similarity between the homiletics of the synagogue and the 'school of the prophets', in which rabbinic *Haggadah* – the free discourse and sermons that developed both in the synagogue and on social occasions connected to synagogue life – express the Prophetic spirit in a similar type of free, spiritual and moral exegesis.[35] Zunz therefore urged, against the clamorous opposition of rabbinic reactionaries and the Prussian government, the reintroduction of the sermon, thereby legitimizing the synagogue as the dominant form of Jewish expression and communal consciousness in the post-emancipation era, a medium of popular self-expression.[36] Zunz emerged as a committed communal advocate. When the Prussians forbade by law the use of Christian proper names by Jews, the Berlin Jewish community assigned to Zunz the task of writing an historical study proving that there was a long tradition of 'non-Jewish' names among Jews, a commission he resolutely discharged with the resonant claim that 'names always belong at first to a people and a language, never to a church and a dogma, never to this or that political or religious opinion'.[37] Zunz's motto – that 'true scholarship produces deeds' – set a precedent for liberal Jewish scholars who wished to contribute directly to a reformist critique of existing forms of Judaism, while at the same time articulating a spirited counter-historical interpretation of Judaism as a spiritual and ethical force in world history.[38]

Heinrich Heine's Marrano Pose

In his analysis of the iconoclastic German Jewish writer Heinrich Heine, a short-lived member of the *Verein*, Jeffrey Sammons argues for the importance of Heine's 'Marrano pose', his 'strong and intensifying identification with the golden age of medieval Spanish Jewry'. Sammons suggests that Heine chose a 'dignified and highly cultured Sephardic persona' in order to contrast his worldliness with the philistinism and backwardness associated with Ashkenazi Jews.[39] It is just as important to note Heine's elective affinity with the Sephardic and Marrano heritage as an anti-Eurocentric disposition, a rambunctious and cosmopolitan ethos of humanist critique in the spirit of Mendelssohn. As Goetschel comments, in his 1835 work *Religion and Philosophy in Germany* Heine offers a 'counterhistory of German philosophy'.[40] Heine displaces the centrality of Kant and Hegel as canonical German philosophers in the idealist tradition in favour of the profound and enduring influence of Spinozism on Lessing and Goethe. Mischievously, Heine describes a democratic, sensuous pantheism as the 'religion of our greatest thinkers', a creed brought to German soil by an outsider, the Marrano of Sephardic origins, Spinoza.[41]

Goetschel suggests that by insisting that a Dutch Jew was pivotal to the development of German philosophy, Heine portrays the vitality of intellectual life in Germany as owing to cross-cultural fertilization during the age of radical Enlightenment, marked by the methodological eclecticism of figures such as Pierre Bayle, John Toland, and Gotthold Ephraim Lessing who invoked unofficial histories of intellectual influence and sympathized with outsider figures and heretics.[42] In so doing Heine articulates a liberal German Jewish *Geistesgeschichte*, in which the unfolding of German history is defined less by power-political machinations culminating in German unification, or a primordial conception of the destiny of the German *Volk*, than by its ongoing struggle to realize the enduring Enlightenment ideas and principles of human dignity, equality, and political enfranchisement.

In *The Romantic School* (1836), his often insouciant history of the Romantic movement in Germany, written with caustic detachment and satirical élan for the benefit of a French readership, Heine draws a grim contrast between a cold, narrow-minded, xenophobic, coarse, and uncultured German patriotism that wants to be 'provincial' rather than a 'citizen of the world', and the 'magnificent and venerable convictions that Germany has produced'; these perennial values include humanism, cosmopolitanism, and the conception of the universal brotherhood of man exemplified by 'our great minds, Lessing, Herder, Schiller, Goethe, Jean Paul, which all educated Germans have always believed in'.[43] The promise of the future, for Germany and Europe, has issued forth from the European Enlightenment and German *Aufklärung* and has been manifested in the epochal friendship of Lessing and Mendelssohn; Heine evokes the latter as a Jewish Luther, the advocate of a pure Mosaic faith, a form of deism. Heine credits Mendelssohn with overthrowing the Talmud, repudiating outworn tradition, and declaring the Bible to be the source of true religion by translating the most important parts of it into German.[44] Claiming that Germany has never produced a better man than Lessing, Heine reserves special enthusiasm for the Lessing/Mendelssohn friendship: 'these two are our pride and our delight. In the gloom of the present we look up to their comforting figures, and they nod in affirmation of a brilliant promise'.[45] Arguably Heine is not simply responding to Mendelssohn as a secular model of bicultural achievement but to his profoundly influential articulation of a messianic universal faith rooted in the vision of the Jewish Prophets, in which the differences between the religions and the separation of the Jews from other nations will not last forever, but will be supplanted by forms of religious observance that will 'bind the hearts of all human beings in reverence for their creator and in mutual love and beneficence'.[46] As Michael Meyer argues, the universalization of the messianic vision, which is especially associated with German Liberal Judaism of the nineteenth century, 'clearly finds expression already in the writings of Mendelssohn'.[47]

Goetschel has suggestively contended that when Judaism surfaces in Heine's work, it is as narrative interruption, a challenge to monocultural assumptions and monochrome tonalities, as something inappropriate, indecent, and scandalous.[48] Heine's liberal Jewish historical consciousness is inflected by Mendelssohn's emphasis on unofficial histories and the release of the repressed. In his *History of Religion and Philosophy in Germany* Heine highlights Mendelssohn's admiration for Spinoza as an exemplary philosopher by comparing Europe's most reviled atheist with Jesus Christ:

It is a fact that Spinoza's life was beyond reproach and pure and spotless as the life of his divine cousin, Jesus Christ. Like Him, he too suffered for his teachings; like Him he wore the crown of thorns. Wherever a great mind expresses its thought, *there* is Golgotha.[49]

Heine's witty literary persona 'provincializes Europe' by critiquing European colonialism, Christian hubris, and national chauvinism, cheekily suggesting the need for Europe to 'raise itself to the level of the Jews', since from the beginning, an egalitarian Judaism has borne within itself the 'modern principles' of enlightened freedom and democracy that is only slowly unfolding among the nations of Europe.[50] Indeed for Heine it is Judaism itself, by way of the Prophetic tradition and its more heterodox modern exemplars such as Spinoza, that adumbrates the true principle of human progress. In Spinoza's writings, Heine enthuses, 'the air of the future seems to flow over us. Perhaps the spirit of the Hebrew prophets still hovered over their late-born descendant'.[51] Heine relates the fate of the Jewish people to a global post-colonial politics focused on the emancipation of oppressed peoples; as Goetschel puts it, 'a discussion of Heine's Jewish concerns cannot ... be separated from his emancipatory project'.[52] Prophetic Judaism's revolutionary and utopian impulses encourage Heine to announce the great task of his time as being 'not only the emancipation of the Irish, the Greeks, the Frankfurt Jews, the West Indian Blacks and other repressed people but the emancipation of the entire world'.[53]

Heine's sympathies are with the brilliant, pluralist history of the golden age of Moorish Spain as a culture of tolerance, and with the Orient more generally as a space of sensuous vitality and aesthetic refinement. In his historical play *Almansor* (1821), set in Granada around the year 1500, Heine laments the arrival and brutal monocultural hegemony of the conquering Christians, crystallized in the obscene Catholic despoliation of the Alhambra, and the burning of the Koran. Heine's Moorish hero, Almansor, leaps to his death along with his beloved rather than be converted by the Christians.

In his elegiac 1851 poem 'The Moorish King' (*Der Mohrenkönig*), Heine redeems the memory of the last Moorish sovereign of Granada, Boabdil, dwelling on his final, lachrymose glances back at his lost kingdom:

But Allah! What a sight!
Instead of the loved crescent of Allah,
The crosses of Spain and its banners
Sparkle over the towers of Alhambra.

Alas! With this sight deep sighs
Broke from the king's breast,
And suddenly, like torrents, tears
Flooded his cheeks, fell on his chest.

Boabdil is comforted and his fears of oblivion assuaged by his much loved paramour, who predicts his eternal fame in the manner of the defeated yet noble Trojan king Hector:

'Boabdil el Chico,' she said,
'My dearly loved one, take comfort,
From the abyss of misery,
A beautiful laurel will blossom forth.

Not only the man who triumphed,
Not just the victory-crowned
Favourite of the blind goddess,
The son of misfortune who has been bloodied,

The heroic warrior too,
Who succumbed to a monstrous destiny,
In the memory of his fellow-men,
Will live for eternity.'

The poet concurs, immortalizing Boabdil and the lost world of Andalusia as a perennial source of redemptive meditation upon those defeated and maligned by historical triumphalism:

His fame will never die away,
Not before the last string
From the last Andalusian guitar
Will jarringly break and spring.[54]

Heine's Sephardic poetics of memory, his profound sympathy towards Judaism's succour in Arab lands and the experience of both Moors and Jews at the hands of the Catholic Inquisition, scandalously celebrates the hybridity of *Mestizo* cultures. A particularly apt example is Heine's scurrilous poem 'Donna Clara', set in a Spain recently reconquered by the armies of Christendom. Here the suitor's conventional Petrarchan courtship of the beautiful Catholic maiden Donna Clara is suddenly interrupted by her sclerotic racism, anxiously repudiating Spain's disturbingly polymorphous past:

There is nothing false in me, my love,
Nor is there in my breast a single drop
Of blood, of the Moorish blood,
Or of that filthy Jewish mob.

Upon parting from their tryst, the smitten Donna Clara wants to know the name of the 'stranger Knight', leading to an explosive, comical revelation:

> And the knight, smiling and serene,
> Kisses his Donna over each finger,
> He kisses her lips and her forehead,
> And finally says these words to her:

> 'I, Señora, your lover,
> Am the son of the much praised
> Great Scribe, who has the honor
> To be Rabbi Israel from Saragossa.'[55]

Heine's poetic sensibility simultaneously evokes the figure of the cultured *sprezzatura* of the Sephardic Renaissance man and the Jewish *schlemiel*, merry and insouciant, proudly embracing his pariah status and exclusion from social hierarchies in order to deflate cultural mythologies and heroic pretensions.[56] Heine's representation of Jewish diasporic existence as a disturbing provocation to bounded identities and pure lineages reprises Mendelssohn's visionary philosophical articulation of Judaism as an ethical rational religion which is reverential towards a loving God, and whose survival and continuation mounts a robust challenge to religious bigotry and colonial violence towards subjugated others. For German Jewish writers and intellectuals such as Heine who lived in a liminal, fraught period of Jewish history in Europe, Sephardic Jewish history and its post-expulsion legacy in the seventeenth-century Holland of Spinoza offered a complex and dynamic model for the renaissance of Jewish culture in diaspora. The 'Sephardic mystique' offered post-emancipation Jewish intellectuals a site of imaginative investment that was proudly Jewish but in constant dialogue with other cultural traditions and intellectual inheritances.[57]

Heinrich Graetz

As Yerushalmi argues, it is a measure of the success of the *Wissenschaft des Judentums* movement that the famous historian of Judaism Heinrich Graetz was able to offer his multi-volume history as a grand synthesis of Jewish history, an achievement inconceivable only fifty years earlier.[58] Schorsch comments that Graetz had a strongly inclusive conception of Jewish history, guided by a sort of non-teleological Hegelianism in which the 'essential attributes of each of the major periods of Jewish history were preserved', a flexible approach entwining cultural and political history, the history of the Jewish people and that of Judaism.[59] While Graetz is often discussed as a proto-nationalist,[60] his eleven-volume *History of the Jews* (1853–1870) offers a dynamic, often celebratory account of Jewish diasporic existence that is strongly focused on Jewish intellectual achievement in Muslim lands, including the 'happy peninsula' of Sefarad/Al-Andalus. Graetz considers Hispanic Jews to have 'contributed almost as much' to the development of Judaism as Judea and Babylonia. Great centres of Jewish communal life in Al-Andalus, such as Cordova, Granada, and Toledo, are now as 'familiar to the Jews as Jerusalem and Tiberias'.[61] He notes the similar cultural traits and cognate languages of Jews and Arabs, two cultures which were often only distinguished by their religious beliefs.[62] Graetz enthuses over a productive Muslim-Arabic/Jewish-Hebrew symbiosis, elaborating on the fruitful interaction between Judaism and Islam, and between Jewish and Arab intellectuals. In establishing a refined, Abrahamic monotheism, Mahomet appreciated Judaism's 'highest aims', and founded Islam on a 'lofty basis' informed by Jewish strictures against idolatry.[63] Islam's renewed monotheism, Graetz writes, has exercised a 'wonderful influence' on the course of Jewish history and the evolution of Judaism.[64]

Graetz credits the enthusiasm of Islamic Arabs for the Koran, expressed in their philological and grammatical rejuvenation of classical Arabic, for stimulating similar sentiments in the hearts of Andalusian Jews. It was in Al-Andalus where thriving Jewish communities, who did not wish to 'blush in controversy with the Mahometans', rediscovered their love for the poetic and liturgical beauty of biblical Hebrew.[65] Graetz's description of an agonistic respect between two flourishing cultures, the reciprocal rationalist and classicizing influences between Muslim and Jewish scholars in Andalusia, is supported by recent scholarship. Consuelo López-Morillas discusses the development of Hebrew poetry from the tenth century in Andalusia as being in synergy with a new, widespread interest in Hebrew grammar and lexicography, inspired by the intensive research into Koranic Arabic by Syrian and Andalusian Muslim scholars. It was a hybridizing era in which Andalusian Jewish commentaries on the Hebrew Bible drew 'on both Arabic cognates and Arab syntax to explain the biblical text'.[66]

The complex Andalusian Jewish encounter with the cultivated and venerated lingua franca of the Muslim empire, Arabic, encouraged the birth of neo-Hebraic poetry and a turning away from the speculative subtleties of Talmudic exegesis towards the ethical sublimity and aesthetic pleasures afforded by the Hebrew Bible.[67] As Ross Brann puts it, classical literary Hebrew was to serve as the principal sign of the Andalusian Jews' newfound literary identity, an aesthetic, urbane identity which makes sense only in the context established by Arabic culture and Muslim society.[68]

Graetz sees the classical period of Muslim culture in Andalusian Spain in the three centuries following the Muslim conquest in 711 as a golden age of

ecumenical acculturation, a 'period of prosperity and vigor' under the guidance of noble principles and free from (Christian) prejudice against votaries
from other religions, in which scientific men and poets could be appointed
to the highest offices.[69] Articulating, in the manner of Mendelssohn, a
diasporic vision of Levantine culture as a counter-history to Christian *amour
propre*, Graetz reprises Mendelssohn's argument that in the early Middle Ages
the 'European Christian countries were still less fit to become the center of
Judaism than the Mahometan Kingdoms of Egypt and Northern Africa'.[70]

Graetz portrays Andalusia as a model of cross-cultural acculturation that
strengthened Jewish culture by giving Jewish intellectuals supple, humorous,
and agonistic forms of critical prosody and lyricism. Jewish Andalusian poets
took as their model the poetic forms of the Arabs, such as the *Muwashshah*,
writing panegyrics, love poems, and satire, as well as liturgical poetry.[71]
Graetz enlarges on the tenth-century dispute between two Jewish philologists
and their followers, the ambitious, brash, iconoclastic challenger Dunash
ben Labrat, of North African origin and the earnest establishment figure
Menahem ben Saruq, compiler of one of the earliest Hebrew dictionaries.
According to Graetz, it was a fierce contention resulting in 'virulent satire'
that helped to make the Hebrew language of the time 'pliant and rich'.[72] As
Maria Rosa Menocal points out, it was Dunash who advocated the use of
Arabic prosodic forms in Hebrew, which helped to bring Hebrew 'out of the
confines of the synagogue' and made it as 'versatile' as the quotidian Arabic
spoken in the Andalusian Jewish community. Graetz is deeply sympathetic to
the Andalusian revolution in Hebrew which was based, according to Menocal,
on the Andalusian Jews' 'profound appreciation of the tolerance and openness
of the universe of Arabic poetry'.[73]

For Graetz, like other post Enlightenment German Jews invested in
the humanist ideal of *Bildung* in which the formation of one's character is
mediated by a polymorphous or worldly education, the rounded personality
and cultural sophistication of Sephardic Jews was exemplary in transcending
religious identity and communal insularity. Andalusian Jews were held to
have eagerly participated in the learning and conversation of a cultivated,
multi-religious society, and to have driven intellectual and aesthetic innovation. Graetz writes that for Spanish Jews, as well as for Andalusian Muslims,
'many-sided knowledge' was a person's 'most beautiful ornament'.[74] Indeed
Arab Andalusians in the golden age of Arabic and Hebrew poetry were as
proud of Hebrew and Arabic language Jewish poets such as Judah Halevi
as the Jews were themselves.[75] The knowledge of the period, writes Graetz,
relishing a historical transposition of the privileged discourse of *Bildung*,
was neither 'one-sided nor barren', but saturated with healthy forms of life,
and with idealism rather than meanness. Andalusian Jews, stimulated by the
vitality of their environment, were not 'narrow specialists', but were equally

active in Bible exegesis, grammar, Talmudic study, philosophy, and poetry.[76] Graetz is almost giddy with pleasure when he surveys the versatile talents and intellectual acuity of Andalusian Jewry. He enthusiastically remarks on the willingness of Andalusian Jews to engage in incisive philological and linguistic critiques of biblical Hebrew and the Bible. Willing to acknowledge the so-called 'grey zone' of Jewish critical rationalism as it strains at the boundaries of Jewish fideism, Graetz considers Andalusian Jews as possessing a complex sensibility with contradictory attributes, a conjuncture of Jewish piety and rationalist critique that carried intellectual investigation to the 'borders of unbelief but not beyond'.[77]

Graetz writes in the edifying spirit of the *Maskilim*, who sought an account of Jewish history that invoked great Jewish sages of the diaspora as cultivated ethical exemplars. Graetz inscribes a number of luminous historical figures, including Judah Halevi, Maimonides, Spinoza, and Mendelssohn, against a background of Sephardic and Levantine acculturation and diasporic mobility, notably concentrating on their character and diverse sympathies as much as on their ethical and philosophical contributions to Judaism. Graetz describes Maimonides, for example, as a 'perfect Jewish sage', versed in Talmudic exegesis, philosophy, and medicine, who wanted to convince others of the 'truth of Judaism' by codifying Jewish Law.[78] Yet Graetz's Maimonides is also a model diaspora Jew and world-thinker at the point at which various cultures meet, moving freely through a cosmopolitan geography. Graetz boasts that Maimonides' name, due to his famous writings in Arabic, the *lingua franca* of his day, 'rang from Spain to India, and from the sources of the Euphrates and the Tigris to southern Arabia'.[79]

For Graetz, Maimonides was also a translator, advisor, and intermediary between personalities and cultures, transmitting Galen's important medical teachings to the Islamic world and then to Europe. When Saladin allowed Jews to settle once again in the city of their fathers, Jerusalem, in 1187, Graetz speculates that Maimonides, a physician at his court, was not 'unconnected with this act of noble-minded tolerance'; he may be associating Maimonides here with Lessing's urbane, hospitable Jewish character Nathan the Wise, Saladin's creditor and advisor.[80] Graetz credits Maimonides with the rejuvenation of Judaism, precisely because as someone fluent in Arabic, his influence and exemplary fame reached well beyond the Jewish world.[81] Constructing a Sephardic genealogy, Graetz interprets Moses Mendelssohn as being imbued with the 'spirit of Maimonides', as Mendelssohn contributed to a Jewish renaissance in eighteenth-century Europe by attaining unparalleled renown as a Jewish and European thinker.

For Graetz, Mendelssohn is a double figure of restoration and renewal, a Jewish sage and pedagogue who revived Hebrew – the original source of Jewish learning and culture – but who also adapted Judaism to the complex needs of modern diaspora Jews in a European cultural context.[82] Graetz is proud of the independent Mendelssohn and perhaps revives the tradition of post-ecclesiastical ethical admiration for Spinoza in representing Mendelssohn as a Jewish thinker who was self-educated rather than beholden to rabbinical authority, who attained complete 'self-mastery' over an often fiery temper but who was renowned throughout Germany and Europe for his calmness and gentleness.[83] Like most German Jewish thinkers and activists before 1933, Graetz unconditionally extols the friendship of Lessing and Mendelssohn as an elective affinity of a rebellious German intellectual sympathetic to outsider figures with a 'second Spinoza' destined to do honour to the Jewish people.[84]

In Graetz's view, which echoes Heine's praise of Mendelssohn as a latter-day Luther who restored the Bible to his people, Mendelssohn, in recovering a 'sense of the beautiful' for his Jewish brethren by translating the Pentateuch and other parts of the Hebrew Bible into eloquent German for their cross-cultural edification, understood the ancient Revelation 'as if it was a new one'.[85] Such was his polymathic intellectual mastery in the Maimonidean and Spinozist tradition, that Mendelssohn, the Jewish Socrates as he was often called, convinced Christians of the immortality of the soul and even advised Benedictine friars on questions of moral and philosophical conduct![86] While refusing to surrender 'an iota of his Judaism' – indeed, he courageously criticized Christian dogmas that were 'abhorrent to his reason' – Mendelssohn's heartfelt tolerance and true benevolence was a profoundly humane challenge to the hypocritical bigotry of 'official Christianity'.[87] Without Mendelssohn's rational humanism and proud assertion of Jewish difference, writes Graetz, the 'splendid drama' of Lessing's *Nathan* could not have been written.[88] Graetz's character portraits of exemplary diasporic Jewish intellectuals and their productive relationships with the non-Jewish world encouraged an interpretation of post-biblical Jewish history as a heterogeneous and picaresque narrative in which the Jewish people preserve their national identity but also reveal their vitality, adaptability, ethical commitments, and hermeneutic creativity in diaspora.

Notes

1 See, for example, Adam Sutcliffe's analysis of Voltaire's 'sustainedly disparaging and often vehemently hostile attitude to Judaism' in A. Sutcliffe. 2004. *Judaism and Enlightenment*, Cambridge, UK: Cambridge University Press, 231.

2 See D. Biale. 1979. *Gershom Scholem, Kabbalah and Counter-History*, Cambridge, Mass.: Harvard University Press. Heschel, *Abraham Geiger and the Jewish Jesus*. A. Funkenstein. 1993. *Perceptions of Jewish History*, Berkeley, CA: University of California Press, 36 ff. C. Weise. 2005. *Challenging Colonial Discourse: Jewish Studies and Protestant Theology in Wilhelmine Germany*, Leiden: Brill Publishers.

3 Heschel argues that the nineteenth-century Jewish theologian Abraham Geiger's argument for Jesus as a reformist Jew and Pharisee represents a 'potentially devastating critique' of Christian claims to represent Jesus, undermining the 'identification of Western civilization with Christianity' and inverting accepted European self-understanding. Heschel, *Abraham Geiger and the Jewish Jesus*, 3, and 14.

4 J. Clifford. 1997. *Routes: Travel and Translation in the late Twentieth Century*, Boston Mass.: Harvard University Press, 264. See Heschel, *Abraham Geiger and the Jewish Jesus*, 3 and 14.

5 Heschel, *Abraham Geiger and the Jewish Jesus*, 2. See also Schorsch, *From Text to Context,* in particular the chapter 'The Myth of Sephardic Supremacy'.

6 See Schorsch, *From Text to Context*, 73. Louise Hecht describes the *maskil* as a 'man raised in the bosom of traditional Jewry [prominent examples discussed by Hecht include Salomon Maimon, Peter Beer, and Lazarus Bendavid] who subscribes to the values of *Haskalah*. Which is to say he is actively involved in the project of Judaism's intellectual renewal and/or the reformation of Jewish society'. L. Hecht. 2002. '"How the Power of Thought can Develop with a Human Mind". Salomon Maimon, Peter Beer, Lazarus Bendavid: Autobiographies of *Maskilim* Written in German', *LBIYB* 47 (1) 21–22. For an important revisionist interpretation of the early *Haskalah* as a reformist response to the challenges to Judaism posed by scientific criticism and the Deistic emphasis on natural religion, see D. Sorkin. 2000. *The Berlin Haskalah and German Religious Thought: Orphans of Knowledge*, London and Portland: Vallentine Mitchell.

7 For an analysis of the *Haskalah* as in conversation with other post-Reformation religious Enlightenments in eighteenth-century Europe, see Sorkin, *The Religious Enlightenment.*

8 See Schorsch, *From Text to Context*, 73.

9 M.A. Meyer. 1988. 'The Emergence of Jewish Historiography: Motives and Motifs', *History and Theory* 27(4), 162.

10 M. Mendelssohn, *Manasseh Ben Israel, Rettung der Juden. Aus dem Englischen übersetz. Nebst einer Vorrede von Moses Mendelssohn* (Friedrich Nicolai, Berlin/Stettin, 1782), reprinted in Mendelssohn, *JubA* 8, 1–25.

11 Meyer, 'The Emergence of Jewish Historiography', 162.

12 See Schorsch, *From Text to Context*, 71.

13 Brann and Sutcliffe, 'Introduction', 14. See also J. Yahalom. 2004. 'Aesthetic Models in Conflict, Classicist versus Ornamental in Jewish Poetics', in R. Brann and A. Sutcliffe (eds), *Renewing the Past, Reconfiguring Jewish Culture: From Al-Andalus to the Haskalah*, Philadelphia: University of Pennsylvania Press, 43.

14 A. Schatz. 2007. 'Returning to Sepharad: Maskilic Reflections on Hebrew in the Diaspora', in R. Fontaine, A. Schatz, and I. Zwiep (eds), *Sepharad in Ashkenaz: Medieval Knowledge and Eighteenth-Century Enlightened Jewish Discourse*, Amsterdam: Koninklijke Nederlandse Akademie van Wetenschappen, 267.

15 See Schorsch, *From Text to Context*, 71.

16 Y.H. Zhakor. 2005. *Jewish History and Jewish Memory*, Seattle, WA: University of Washington Press, 36.

17 Feiner. *Haskalah and History*, 51–52.

18 See Meyer, 'The Emergence of Jewish Historiography', 162.

19 Meyer, 'The Emergence of Jewish Historiography', 162.

20 A. Sutcliffe. 2004. 'Quarrelling over Spinoza: Moses Mendelssohn and the Fashioning of Jewish Philosophical Heroism', in R. Brann and A. Sutcliffe (eds), *Renewing the Past*, 181.

21 Sutcliffe, 'Quarrelling over Spinoza', 173.

22 Schorsch describes Spinoza as a 'cultural hero of German Jews' who 'seemed to sum up the loftiest ideas of the Sephardic tradition'. Schorsch, *From Text to Context*, 81.

23 Zhakor, *Jewish History and Jewish Memory*, 91–92.

24 M.A. Meyer. 1988. *Response to Modernity: A History of the Reform Movement in Judaism*, New York and Oxford: Oxford University Press, 75.

25 I. Schorsch. 1988. 'Scholarship in Service of Reform', *Leo Baeck Institute Yearbook* XXXV, 73.

26 Schorsch, 'Scholarship in Service of Reform', 74.

27 Zhakor, *Jewish History and Jewish Memory*, 87.

28 Schorsch, *From Text to Context*, 153, 167.

29 Cited in H.G. Reissner. 1965. *Eduard Gans: Ein Leben im Vormaerz*, Tübingen: C.B. Mohr, 64 ff.

30 Here I draw on Mendes-Flohr, *Divided Passions*, 415. See also Schorsch, *From Text to Context*, 164.

31 M.R. Niehoff. 1998. 'Zunz's Concept of Haggadah as an Expression of Jewish Spirituality', *Leo Baeck Institute Yearbook* 43(1), 12.

32 Niehoff, 'Zunz's Concept of Haggadah', 11, 15.

33 D. Sorkin. 1995. 'Religious Reforms and Secular Trends in German-Jewish Life: An Agenda for Research', *LBIYB* 40(1), 172.

34 Schorsch, 'Scholarship in Service of Reform', 79.

35 Niehoff, 'Zunz's Concept of Haggadah', 17, 18.

36 Meyer, *Response to Modernity*, 76. See also Schorsch, 'Scholarship in the Service of Reform', 79–81.

37 Cited in M. Brenner. 2010. *Prophets of the Past: Interpreters of Jewish History*, trans. S. Rendall, Princeton, N.J.: Princeton University Press, 31.

38 Brenner, *Prophets of the Past,* 31.

39 Sammons, 'Who Did Heine Think He Was?', 11.

40 Goetschel, *Spinoza's Modernity*, 19.

41 H. Heine. 1959. *Religion and Philosophy in Germany*, J. Snodgrass (trans.), Boston: Beacon Press, 69–103.

42 Goetschel, *Spinoza's Modernity*, 230.

43 H. Heine. 1985. 'The Romantic School', trans. H. Mustard, in H. Heine, *The Romantic School and other Essays*, J. Hermand and R.C. Holub (eds), New York: Continuum, 21.

44 Heine, 'History of Religion and Philosophy in Germany', 193.

45 Heine, 'History of Religion and Philosophy in Germany', 195.

46 M.A. Meyer. 2006. 'German Jewish Thinkers Reflect on the Future of the Jewish Religion', *Leo Baeck Institute Yearbook* 51(1), 4.

47 Meyer, 'German Jewish Thinkers Reflect on the Future of the Jewish Religion', 5.

48 W. Goetschel. 1999. 'Rhyming History: A Note on the "Hebrew Melodies"', *The Germanic Review* 74(4), 271.

49 H. Heine. 1985. 'Concerning the History of Religion and Philosophy in Germany', trans. H. Mustard, in H. Heine, *The Romantic School and other Essays,* J. Hermand and R.C. Holub (eds), New York: Continuum, 173.

50 Goetschel, 'Rhyming History: A Note on the "Hebrew Melodies"', 273.

51 Heine, 'Concerning the History of Religion and Philosophy in Germany', 173.

52 Goetschel, 'Rhyming History: A Note on the "Hebrew Melodies"', 274.

53 Goetschel, 'Rhyming History: A Note on the "Hebrew Melodies"', 272.

54 H. Heine. 1851. 'The Moorish King', in *Werke*, translated from *Romanzero* (1851) by Joseph Massaad, http://www.heinrich-heine.net/haupt.htm, accessed 29 May 2012.

55 H. Heine. 1827. 'Donna Clara', in *Werke*, translated from *Buch der Lieder* (1827) by Joseph Massaad, http://www.heinrich-heine.net/haupt.htm, accessed 29 May 2012.

56 For a superb discussion of Heine's schlemiel sensibility and democratic *joie de vivre*, see H. Arendt. 2007. 'The Jew as Pariah: A Hidden Tradition', in H. Arendt, *Hannah Arendt, the Jewish Writings*, J. Kohn and R.H. Feldman (eds), New York: Schocken Books, 275–297.

57 For a discussion of the Sephardic mystique as a crucial, formative element of Jewish Enlightenment thought, see Sutcliffe and Brann's introduction to Brann and Sutcliffe, *Renewing the Past*, 3.

58 Zhakor, *Jewish History and Jewish Memory*, 87.

59 Schorsch, *From Text to Context*, 192–193.

60 Michael Brenner, for example, describes Graetz in familiar, and somewhat hackneyed terms, as a 'self-confident Jew who emphasized the national dimension of Jewish history'. See Brenner, *Prophets of the Past*, 13. Shlomo Sand's much discussed *The Invention of the Jewish People* also reads Graetz rather reductively as a 'nation-fostering' historian who focused on the exceptional destiny of the Jewish people, thus underestimating his *Bildung* inspired interest in post-biblical Jewry's multifarious and participatory self-formation nourished by diasporic conditions. See S. Sand. 2010. *The Invention of the Jewish People*, trans. Y. Lotan, London: Verso, 80–84.

61 H. Graetz. 1894. *History of the Jews*, six volumes, Philadelphia: The Jewish Publication Society of America, vol. 3, 41–42.

62 Graetz, *History of the Jews*, vol. 3, 56.

63 Graetz, *History of the Jews*, vol. 3, 71.

64 Graetz, *History of the Jews*, vol. 3, 71.

65 Graetz, *History of the Jews*, vol. 3, 111.

66 C. López-Morillas. 2006. 'Language', in M.R. Menocal, R.P. Scheindlin, and M. Selis (eds), *The Literature of Al-Andalus*, Cambridge, UK: Cambridge University Press, 45.

67 Graetz, *History of the Jews*, vol. 3, 111–112.

68 R. Brann. 2006. 'The Arabized Jews', in M.R. Menocal, R.P. Scheindlin, and M. Selis (eds), *The Literature of Al-Andalus*, Cambridge, UK: Cambridge University Press, 445.

69 Graetz, *History of the Jews*, vol. 3, 214.

70 Graetz, *History of the Jews*, vol. 3, 212.

71 Graetz, *History of the Jews*, vol. 3, 224. See T. Rosen. 2006. 'The Muwashshah', in M.R. Menocal, R.P. Scheindlin, and M. Selis (eds), *The Literature of Al-Andalus*, Cambridge, UK: Cambridge University Press, 166: 'The muwashshah is both the product and a microcosm of the cultural conditions peculiar to Al-Andalus. Its linguistic complexity reflects the fluid and diverse linguistic situation of the peninsula's population . . . Despite its status as an Arabic literary genre, it serves as a junction within a cultural space that encompassed non-Arabs as well . . . Hebrew poets maintained its linguistic hybridness in their secular poetry . . . It admits non-Arabic and nonlearned cultures, recognizes the female voice, and expresses both secular sentiments and religious yearning.'

72 Graetz, *History of the Jews*, vol. 3, 227.
73 M.R. Menocal. 2002. *The Ornament of the World: How Muslims, Jews, and Christians Created a Culture of Tolerance in Medieval Spain*, New York: Little, Brown and Company, 108–109.
74 Graetz, *History of the Jews*, vol. 3, 234.
75 Graetz, *History of the Jews*, vol. 3, 235.
76 Graetz, *History of the Jews*, vol. 3, 235.
77 Graetz, *History of the Jews*, vol. 3, 230.
78 Graetz, *History of the Jews*, vol. 3, 451.
79 Graetz, *History of the Jews*, vol. 3, 471.
80 Graetz, *History of the Jews*, vol. 3, 474.
81 Graetz, *History of the Jews*, vol. 3, 486.
82 Graetz, *History of the Jews*, vol. 3, 495.
83 Graetz, *History of the Jews*, vol. 3, 495.
84 Graetz, *History of the Jews*, vol. 5, 297.
85 Graetz, *History of the Jews*, vol. 5, 301.
86 Graetz, *History of the Jews*, vol. 5, 307–308.
87 Graetz, *History of the Jews*, vol. 5, 314, 325.
88 Graetz, *History of the Jews*, vol. 5, 326–327.

CHAPTER 3

Abraham Geiger
Rabbi and Writer

The leading theorist and intellectual founder of the Reform movement in Judaism, and perhaps the most influential liberal Jewish thinker of the nineteenth century, was the theologian, rabbi, scholar of Islam, historian of Judaism, and intellectual iconoclast, Abraham Geiger (1810–1874).[1] Geiger was a frustrated independent intellectual, for as a Jew he could neither obtain an academic appointment at a German university nor publish in the major Protestant theological periodicals of his day despite his cognate scholarly interests; moreover, due to his liberal views and perceived anti-Talmudic agitations he was also temporarily excluded from the Jewish seminary in Breslau, his position as first rabbi there having been hotly contested by traditionalists.[2] Geiger was a second-generation member of the *Wissenschaft des Judentums* movement, a university educated practising rabbi, a popular educationalist, and the first German Jewish scholar, as Susannah Heschel argues, to 'subject Christian texts to detailed historical analysis from an explicitly Jewish perspective'. Geiger sought to debunk Christianity's self-serving claims as a universal faith superseding an obsolete legalistic Judaism.[3] As a politically and socially engaged reformist scholar and writer inspired by the brilliant example of Leopold Zunz, Geiger conceived of *Wissenschaft* not only as an end in itself but as the guide to a construction of a living present and dynamic future for the Jewish people as a post-national diaspora.[4] A cosmopolitan humanist with ecumenical interests, Geiger felt it was important to pursue free enquiry while also analysing Judaism in the full light of broad general knowledge, for only in this way could Judaism assume its rightful place in world culture. Geiger was a visionary educationalist who like his *Wissenschaft* predecessors wished to dignify Judaism as a subject worthy of university scholarship; his long held ambition was to establish a Jewish theological faculty in a German university.[5]

In his influential three-volume work *Das Judentum und Seine Geschichte* (*Judaism and its History*, 1865–1871), based on an engaging series of public lectures he delivered after moving to Frankfurt am Main in 1863, Geiger defended Judaism by using counter-historical stratagems against Protestant theologians who wished to downplay the Jewish milieu in which Jesus emerged.[6] Heschel has described the attempts of liberal Protestant theology 'to elevate Jesus as a unique religious figure who stood in sharp opposition to his Jewish surroundings'. With deflationary bathos, Geiger claimed instead that 'Jesus was a Jew whose teachings were the typical liberal Pharisaic teachings of his day', going so far as to suggest that Jesus made no great impression on his Jewish listeners, a claim that infuriated Christian scholars.[7] In his famous essay 'Sadducaer und Pharisaeer' (Sadducees and Pharisees, 1863), Geiger contended that 'Jesus stands upon Pharisaic ground, and fights with Pharisaic weapons against Pharisaic half-measures', thus inscribing Jesus within a history of Jewish reform inspired by the Pharisees as early leaders of a progressive movement to democratize Jewish worship.[8] In *Judaism and its History* Geiger claims that Jesus taught nothing original or unique but merely repeated the common rabbinic wisdom of the time, indeed that it took Paul's dilution of Jewish monotheism by the admixture of polytheistic teachings to create a religion which was palatable to heathens.[9]

Writing in the iconoclastic spirit of great eighteenth-century anti-colonial critics such as Diderot and Mendelssohn, Geiger considered Christianity by immanent standards to be an aggressive institutional power; he decries its obscene sectarian pride in 'introducing prejudice into the souls of unsuspecting human beings by way of a most disgusting missionary institution'.[10] Exemplifying Ismar Schorsch's revisionist suggestion that the political arguments of German Jewish emancipationists influenced by Jewish *Wissenschaft* were frequently 'confrontational', Geiger probingly questions European Christianity's self-understanding as an original spiritual movement in world history, instead maintaining that it was and continues to be Jewish monotheism that preserves the authentic Christian faith, the faith of Jesus.[11] Geiger renews Mendelssohn's claim that Judaism mediates the relationship between humanity and a transcendent God in a consistently ethical fashion which adapts itself to historical circumstances; in contrast to puritanical Christianity, Judaism 'does not designate this earth as a "vale of tears"' or comprehend universal history through the ideal lens of a single person, Jesus.[12] Geiger lamented that Christianity's pagan monolatry easily degenerates into hero worship, mythic fetishism and iconophilia, and anti-Semitic scapegoating due to the insistent focus on the Passion.

Extending his subversive counter-history to the present state of Europe, Geiger argues that Christianity has failed to provide an ethos for fostering human relationships and progressive cultural exchange. It is a decided error, writes Geiger, to represent Christianity as the mother of modern culture, since it has always worked against scientific advances: 'to speak plainly the modern is not Christian and the Christian is not modern'.[13] Christianity, he claims, does not want to work as a spiritual power within mankind but wants to stand above and dominate it, so that it denies the significance of humanity itself in all its other relationships; this criticism echoes Sittah's bitter complaint about Christian invaders in *Nathan the Wise*.[14] By contrast, as Koltun-Fromm has suggested, as a reformer who sought to de-nationalize the Jewish religion by challenging nostalgia for Zion as one of its dominant liturgical and political emotions, Geiger evoked Judaism as a progressive religious ideal inspired by 'thick relations' internally and externally; for Geiger, modern Judaism is energized by the collective memory of diversification and transformation that points it towards its diasporic future. Modern Judaism is nourished by a hermeneutic which is sensitive to a post-biblical history of heroic individuals, those rabbis, intellectuals, and political activists whose interpretive creativity and imaginative advocacy continue to contribute to the cultural and spiritual elevation of Judaism in the post-emancipation era.[15]

Perhaps influenced by the *Aufklärung* philosemitism exemplified by thinkers such as Lessing, Mendelssohn, and Herder, Geiger interpolates Christianity into a comparative dialogue with other world religions. Imbibing Lessing's passionate distaste for Christian *amour propre*, Geiger provoked the Christian world by taking Islam, denounced by Christian theology as a derivative heresy, seriously as a subject for theological scholarship. Geiger enhances Judaism's claim to be a vital, ongoing matrix for ethical monotheism by demonstrating, in *Was hat Mohammed aus dem Judenthume aufgenommen?* (*What has Mohammed taken from the Jews?*, 1833), that some of Islam's central teachings derive from rabbinic literature. Geiger alleges that passages in the Koran which altered Old Testament stories were neither sheer invention nor imitative of Christian heretical teachings, but rather derived from Midrashic retellings of those same stories.[16] Martin Kramer has described Geiger as a 'partisan of Islam', who deploys Mendelssohn's subversive counter-historical strategies to favourably contrast the experience of Jews under Islam and Christianity. Throughout his oeuvre Geiger referred to Islam as youthful, congenial to the cultivation of science and philosophy, in stark contrast to an established Christian Church that finds science and reason repugnant.[17]

Geiger's provincializing of Christianity conditioned his influential reappraisal of Judaism as a diasporic religion, an energetic vessel for an unfolding *Geistesgeschichte* or history of the human spirit, accessible to a sympathetic interpreter as a 'world-historical phenomenon' and 'immortal traveler through history'.[18] By contrast to Christianity, which, through colonial and missionary activity, attempts to make the world acknowledge the decisive historicity and eschatological significance of Christ, Geiger praises Judaism's intellectual openness and fertile influence on a variety of cultures.[19] Geiger interprets the story of the Jews in relational and world-historical terms 'as a people rooted in the larger story of civilization'.[20] Seeking, like Zunz, to rejuvenate Jewish pride through the medium of historical consciousness, Geiger draws on Wilhelm von Humboldt's humanist approach to *Geistesgeschichte*, articulated in influential essays such as 'The Task of the Historian' (1821), which enjoined the historian to be sensitive to the revolutionary power of ethical ideas and suspicious of power politics as a barometer of the movement of history. In evoking Judaism as a noble and animating 'energy' (*Kraft*) free of dogma, Geiger invokes Judaism in Mendelssohnian terms as a rational and practically focused religion whose most basic ethical precepts are not anchored to Revelation, Law, or binding doctrines. For example, Geiger notes that Judaism has not allowed the concept of original sin to be grafted on to it; rather than focusing on Christ, Judaism's midrashic and self-revising interpretive traditions have allowed 'free play' in criticism of even its great men.[21]

In response to the left-Hegelian Bruno Bauer's polemical accusation in essays such as 'The Capacity for Present-Day Jews and Christians to Become Free' (1843) that Jews are an obdurate and ahistorical people who always react against the movements and changes of history, rendering them permanent outsiders to a dynamic European *Geist*, Geiger, Koltun-Fromm argues, provided a 'counterhistory of his own'.[22] Geiger posits Judaism as the protagonist in a drama in which a decentralized post-exilic Judaism has had to overcome not only the sectarianism of the Christian Church which continually seeks an exclusively Christian state, but also the concentration of power in the hands of the few typical of feudalism and later the stultifying of civic society under absolutist and aristocratic rule. These atavistic dimensions of European religion and politics are absent in Judaism, where 'prophet conquers priest, and Judaism's spiritual life supplants worldly church ambitions'.[23]

In a telling assault on reified Orthodoxy Geiger stresses that the great textual traditions of Judaism, such as the Hebrew Bible and the Talmud, represent fresh stages of religious and ethical development, thereby providing evidence that Judaism is 'not a system of truths' but responds to changing historical circumstances and is beholden to no single founder or revelation. Geiger historicized the Torah as the 'gradually unfolding ideas of the Jewish people', meaning that the identity of the Jewish people and the validity of Judaism cannot be located in any one body of law, ceremonial observance, or canonized textual tradition. In his famous work of biblical criticism, the *Urschrift und Uebersetzungen der Bible* (*The Original Text and Translations of the Bible*) (Breslau, 1857), Geiger contends that there is no fixed and absolute biblical text, that interpretation is not of the biblical text but intrinsic to the text itself, which can now be explained as a palimpsest, a communal and historical work that is shot through with alterations, reworkings, expansions, clarifications, symbolic explanatory schemes and translations which point to older variants. Relishing, like Graetz, agonistic dissension as a source of Jewish creativity, Geiger posits the biblical text as documenting a history of herme-neutic innovation, political intrigue, competing social forces, and attempts at religious reform.[24]

Geiger invoked Lessing's argument against Christian orthodoxy which held that the ethical truths of Christianity do not depend on the letter of the Bible but precede it and are thus a catalyst for its ongoing interpretation according to changing human needs. Similarly Geiger argues of the *Urschrift* that its 'eternal word' does not belong to a particular time, indeed could not be wholly dependent upon the time of its writing down, and thus could just as little dispense with what would become new truths and knowledges. Every age and direction of thought, every form of individual interpretation, brought to the Bible its own point of view; as such, Geiger avers, every demand for a fixed and objective point of view, every attempted reification of Judaism as outside of or transcending history, will be unsuccessful.[25]

Geiger's conception of Judaism is dynamic, replete with the idealistic and process focused vocabulary of the *Aufklärung*-inspired *Bildung* tradition. For Geiger, Judaism is a future oriented post-biblical phenomenon, an 'aspiration of the spirit' in pursuit of the 'loftiest ideals', a religious force that is pregnant with a 'mission for the future'.[26] Geiger's emancipative claim that Judaism is a vital living faith impels him to argue against the lachrymose version of Jewish history that pervades Jewish collective memory. Jewish history, he cautions, is not a tearful tragedy, for it does not simply consist of catastrophes on the empirical plane but 'contains a grand idea' and preserves a 'spiritual freshness' and 'original vigour'. Jewish life and hope expands when room is granted to it. The impressive history of the Jewish diaspora proves that post-biblical Jewish history is not merely a fatal tragedy, but rather continues to illuminate a 'power of resistance in Judaism' that preserves and creates in the domain of the spirit. The 'drama' of Jewish history, writes Geiger, borrowing a historio-graphical topos from Herder, Wilhelm von Humboldt, and Graetz himself, 'is not yet concluded'.[27]

Abraham Geiger and Heinrich Graetz shared a fluid conception of Jewish history as irreducibly entwined with world history. Both of these towering Jewish scholars ardently affirmed the beneficial effect of diasporic conditions on Jewish thinkers who creatively absorbed the science and philosophy of other cultures.[28] Geiger's imbrication of Jewish and world history also unfolds a picaresque drama of bold personalities and unexpected cross-fertilizations, of adaptation, appropriation, tactical agility, and cultural hybridization, in which Judaism is enriched and transfigured by the practical energies and inter-pretive élan of the Jewish people in myriad circumstances. Geiger is attentive to Jewish arts of survival that have developed under post-exile conditions. Geiger enthuses that one of the strengths of Jewish history is that it extends from remote antiquity to the present, that it both traverses and impels world history, as 'one of the noblest animating forces among mankind'.[29] Judaism is not compelled by a single, sacred history; it has survived and even flourished in Phoenicia, while the Jews lived under Persian sovereignty in general without oppression, for Cyrus 'understood the Jews'.[30]

Geiger describes how Judaism maintained close ties with neighbouring countries and could not ward off their intellectual influences. Far from always possessing an innate monotheism, the Jews learnt much from Persia's 'pure' religion of light worshipped as the emanation of the Deity. Once more Geiger draws on the depiction of humanity's evolutionary historical *Bildung* in Lessing's *Die Erziehung des Menschengeschlechts* (*The Education of Humankind*) (1780) with its immanent and deterritorializing or non-Palestine centric interpretation of Judaism's religious and ethical development as it was exposed to the cultural influences and cosmologies of neighbouring civilizations. Judaism, Geiger enthuses, survived and took root in countries which long before had produced the first fruits of civilization: in Egypt, Phoenicia, Syria, Assyria, and Babylonia. Geiger avers that Judaism maintained close ties with Syria and Assyria, and absorbed their intellectual influences, including the doctrine of immortality, and a more sublime sense of God's unity. Judaism united with Hellenism to give birth to Alexandrianism. However, Judaism developed its 'fullest potential in closest union with the Arab civilization' and thus helped to communicate to medieval Christianity the heritage of antiquity which was rescued from oblivion during the Arab era.[31] It is Geiger's liberal emphasis on religious progress that sets him apart from the historical sobriety, if not pessimism, of his illustrious forebear, Moses Mendelssohn.[32]

Geiger's spirited, broadly philosemitic counter-narrative continues with the suggestion that Jews benefitted when Islam became an important historical power, as it projected a 'youthful' spiritual energy that carried the torch of science and learned culture at its head for a thousand years, preventing the 'spirit from going to sleep' as it had in medieval Europe.[33] Geiger embraces the efflorescence of Jewish communities in Islamic Spain as a genuine, if tragically interrupted, homecoming for the Jews, rather than as a distressing story of exile from a longed-for Zion. Iberian Jews, the self-styled 'Sephardim', 'regarded their Spain with noble pride', glorified it in poetry, and clung to it with all the fervour of their hearts. Here, those weary wanderers, the Jewish people, had found a new and beautiful abode, such that they no longer looked nostalgically backwards towards the past, but fell in love with the present.[34] Imbued with an ethico-religious sense of Judaism's mission in the world, the Iberian Jew felt that it was 'his task to establish lasting habitations in order to live with and among men and work for their elevation'.[35] Geiger felt that the vibrant Jewish participation in Muslim lands exemplifies a particular trait of the Jews: their willing participation in and loyalty to 'new cultures' which encourage untrammelled spiritual and mental development.[36] Jews were in the midst of Andalusian culture precisely because they fulfilled an exemplary social function as propagators of cultural innovation, as philosophers and translators, carrying Greek thought everywhere and 'scattering the seeds' of the new culture far and wide.[37] Transfiguring a mundane, degrading anti-Jewish trope into an ethical vocation, Geiger writes that while the Jews are mocked at as business brokers and middlemen, as old-clothes men peddling cast-off clothes from house to house, they have carried the 'cast-off garments' of ancient cultures into the nations of Europe; in the same way, the Aristotelian Maimonides was a 'teacher for all of Europe'.[38]

In 'honouring' the Spanish-Arabian development of Judaism, Geiger privileges Judeo-Arab intellectuals as 'lasting intermediaries' of sciences such as astronomy, medicine, and mathematics, while medieval Europe was still culturally and philosophically benighted. Geiger sees Iberian Jews as precursors to modern post-emancipation Jews who participate in contemporary European culture by alerting it to recent critical and aesthetic innovations.[39] Geiger suggests that Andalusian Jews adumbrated the contemporary challenge of Judaism – not to look back passively to Jerusalem, which Geiger pungently describes as a 'tomb', but to 'draw from the living present and labor in it'; for if 'we do not identify ourselves with mankind, we do not do our duty'. In contrast to an eschatological Christianity that reviles human history as a profane prelude to the day of judgment, Judaism does not consider the world's history as closed or determined but rather lauds human progress and brightens it with its 'mild rays'.[40] If Christianity is bound to the institutions of the state, Judaism is free to develop progressively, unhindered by political considerations, and to drive forward religious and moral development within society as a whole.[41]

A disciple of Mendelssohn and Zunz, Geiger extols a cosmopolitan and Prophetic vision of Judaism as a progressive faith, one which recognizes that 'man is not limited to certain spots of the world for his abode'. Indeed Judaism has a humane character that can 'acclimatize itself everywhere' and 'carry its seeds' into the popular life of many different cultures.[42] We Jews, he proposes, are not professors of the Mosaic religion exclusively, we do not cling to the letter of the law only, but are responsive to the Prophetic message of the 'great men' who appeared in Judah, the Isaiahs and the Jeremiahs, the poets of the Psalms, and Job – a great 'spiritual stream'.[43] Geiger's celebration of the Bible's textual variety and diachronic creativity is a reminder of the epochal effects of Mendelssohn's strategy to reclaim the Bible as a stimulating *paedeia* for Judaism, an ethical and aesthetic inspiration and a repository of spoken language that would revive colloquial Hebrew and restore biblical exegesis and the discipline of philosophy to the Jewish people.[44] In his various roles as practising rabbi, scholar of Judaism, and Jewish reformer, Geiger elaborated an ethical version of Judaism that Meyer calls 'Prophetic Judaism'. For Geiger, as for the Reform movement of which he was a leading proponent, Prophetic Judaism was the most important component of Judaism. Of particular importance, as Meyer argues, was the Prophets' 'concern for the poor and downtrodden, their contempt for ritual acts unaccompanied by social morality, and their vision of peace for all humanity'. These qualities made Amos, Isaiah, Micah, and other Jewish heroes both timeless and contemporary.[45]

Acknowledging the rationalist critique of religious supernaturalism which began with Spinoza, Geiger praises the Prophets because they did not stand out by virtue of miraculous acts but had a powerful effect upon the spirit of the people through their high ideals of religion and ethics.[46] Intrinsic to Geiger's Prophetic religion is the desire to anthropomorphize the sources of Jewish morality, to see the Jewish Prophets as exemplary models for *Bildung* or self-formation. Geiger argued that the Prophets vividly demonstrated that 'a new idea can only originate in a strong personality'.[47] Drawing on Graetz's Plutarchan relish for rounded biography, Geiger accentuates the Prophets' varied characteristics and passionate contradictions, tactically prefiguring the ambivalence of reformist Jews such as himself who were compelled to relate to their people as both insiders and outsiders, both communal advocates and spirited critics:

> [In the Prophets] we behold personalities of serene grandeur and simple dignity; these were men of fiery passion coupled with calm prudence; their boldness was coupled with profound humility and resignation . . . Each Prophet is a complete, well-rounded personality in his own right, with a distinct individuality of his own.[48]

The Prophetic tradition that Geiger appeals to is a Spinozist inspired version of religious humanism which is intended to demonstrate that the essence of Judaism is love of man and mutual regard – for 'the rest is commentary'.[49] For Geiger, the Prophetic tradition of acute social critique and reformist agitation inaugurates a tradition of acculturated ethical Jewish sages who adapted to the practical demands of diasporic existence. One such was Geiger's hero, the Babylonian Jewish sage Hillel, a 'genuine reformer' and a 'man of living, continuous development' who 'exerted a decisive effect on Judaism'. Hillel wanted 'actual practical life' to decide upon questions of measure and form. He once commented on a contractual dispute in Jewish Law as follows: if we 'stick to the letter' all morality will be lost.[50] Geiger's Hillel is strongly redolent of Mendelssohn, who insisted in *Jerusalem* that Jewish ceremony must awaken a sense of ethical duty and is best nourished and sustained orally, through dialogical human relationships.

In the passionate manner of Graetz, Geiger argues for the interdependence of Jewish cultural development and propitious diasporic conditions.

Babylonian Jews such as Hillel 'felt themselves at home in a vigorous country in which endeavour could develop untrammeled', in which 'life was not outside of the present', a milieu lending itself to a 'healthier realism' than was the case in Jewish Palestine where the Jewish community refused to accommodate itself to other temporal powers or to religious and legal innovation.[51] Koltun-Fromm suggests that Hillel was a model for reformers like Geiger since Hillel rejoins that Prophetic stream which is concerned with the moral and political life of religious communities; Geiger felt that Hillel, as a man immersed in public life, 'invigorated and elevated the life of Judaism in every way'.[52] A model of meekness, simplicity, refinement, and kindness, Hillel possesses all the traits with which Geiger described those biblical women he took a special interest in, such as Ruth and Rebecca.[53]

Commensurate with his enthusiasm for the practical morality and present-centred interests of post-exilic Judaism, Geiger experienced a profound affinity with Lessing's Levantine Jew, Nathan the Wise. In Nathan Geiger saw not an anaemic Jew abstracted from his religion but a 'representative of Judaism' as a man of the world and also a sage. Geiger's Nathan is a well-rounded subject of *Bildung* who draws experience from life, knows it, thoroughly comprehends its weaknesses, but who still looks upon others with tolerance and kindness. Nathan sees in every human being a noble foundation and nourishes the joyful hope of being able to forward his own development through them.[54]

Drawing on the Prophetic tradition and the cosmopolitan values of the German *Aufklärung*, as a reformer and post-Enlightenment liberal Geiger felt strongly that nationalistic longing and a distinct sense of ethnic exclusiveness are not essential to Judaism but reflect the hostile conditions under which it has endured. In order to thematize the historically unstable relationship between Jews and other peoples, Geiger, as Heinrich Graetz once observed, read 'against the text' of the Bible using the philological techniques of historical criticism. Geiger noted that various passages which discussed Israel's eternal hatred towards and struggle against Ammon and Moab are contradicted by earlier moments when the Ammonites, Moabites, and Israelites were once close and friendly neighbours, as well as biblical passages such as Deuteronomy, 2:18–19 which are mild in their depiction of other peoples. Geiger historicizes and relativizes these conflicting accounts, arguing that national jealousies often accounted for discrepancies in these portrayals, and that far from being paradigmatic, the condemnation of non-Israelites as eternal foreigners to God's community in Deuteronomy 23:3–4 reveals a time when Israelites desired national independence soon after their restoration from Babylonian exile.[55]

Far from being obsolete, Judaism for Geiger is characterized by its ethical vocation in world history. Judaism's 'mission' is not to convert or annihilate, but rather to propound an idea, that of ethical monotheism, an idea which goes beyond Jewish national existence.[56] Geiger affirms that 'Israel's mission was not accomplished by the achievement of its nationality', since Judaism itself represents the aspiration of the spirit towards the ideal.[57] Energetic endeavour in the world and the recognition of a unified humanity is the basis of Judaism.[58] It is a 'remarkable trait' of Judaism that wherever a country offers mental and spiritual liberty, Jews will regard it as their home.[59] Judaism is not primarily a nationality but a 'religious force' and a 'mission for the future'.[60] Like the redemptive character of Nathan who suffers for the sake of maintaining dialogue with other people, Judaism is nourished by amicable cross-cultural relationships; using metaphors of agricultural fertility Geiger suggests that Jewish history is the soil from which the noblest fruits of human life have ripened and are still being harvested, providing fresh spiritual sustenance for the present and future. Jews cannot perform this fertilizing task unless they shun atavistic nationalism and live, as Nathan did, in the midst of humanity.[61]

Symbols of Reform

Geiger's liberal principles led him to spiritualize Judaism. He wanted modern Jews to speak, as Koltun-Fromm terms it, a 'new language' of symbolic prayer and edifying historical memory that repudiates biblical literalism, ethnic sectarianism, and an ardent nostalgia for Zion which hinders Jewish participation in the world's affairs. Geiger edited the prayer books of his congregation so that Reform principles 'concerning the spiritual unity of God, ethical monotheism, Jerusalem as "symbol", and messianic ideas are everywhere in force'.[62] He warned against false romantic enthusiasm for the Holy Land and 'gave careful and sympathetic study to the fate of Jews the world over'.[63]

Geiger was at the forefront of a movement to restructure the rabbinate, ensuring that rabbis would be community leaders and scholars educated at German universities. Geiger agitated for a modern rabbinate that, in the words of Koltun-Fromm, was 'fully immersed in local politics, one that prepared and motivated communities to engage larger social and cultural issues'.[64] Geiger felt that Judaism must renounce for all time the cult of nationalism; it must realize that the whole world is its sphere of action, and it must not wilfully isolate itself from other cultures.[65] In a famous letter to Zunz in March 1845, Geiger queries Zunz's keeping of the Kosher dietary laws which he feels are 'thoroughly lacking in spirit' (*Geistloses*). Geiger protests that the reform movement in Judaism should stimulate, in Jewish liturgy and practice, the 'higher, vigorous meaning that refers to the idea. Reform practice is to always signify the higher idea that underlies it'.[66] The ideas that sustain Jewish religious observance in turn emerge from the flourishing of

Jewish life in its manifold relationships with the broader culture. Critiquing theocratic centralism and rabbinic authoritarianism, Geiger contributed to the crucial rabbinic conferences of the 1840s by arguing that rabbis should avoid binding resolutions and norms in order to respect the freedom and diversity of individuals and autonomous communities.[67] One of Geiger's most resolute precepts was that Jewish principles of faith could never be established once and for all: witness the dialectical fierceness of Talmudic discourse and the fantastic depths of Jewish mysticism that retain the 'freshness' of the Jewish spirit. Invoking the liminal 'greyzone' of Jewish identity which has, paradoxically, contributed so much to Jewish scholarship, theology, and political critique, Geiger was adamant that grounding norms of faith would only create 'illegitimate borders of identity' and work to disenfranchise Jews who remain outside the established margins.[68]

In justifying his own career as a practitioner of *Wissenschaft* and a practicing rabbi, an outsider shunned by both mainstream Protestant theological scholarship and reviled by the Orthodox and Conservative movements in Judaism that emerged to contest his liturgical reforms and de-nationalizing arguments, Geiger reprises a *Haskalah* fascination with the possible social and ethical roles that can be played by Jews in the modern world. Significant in this respect is his 1838 essay 'Die zwei verschiedenen Betrachtungweisen: Der Schriftsteller and der Rabbiner' ('Two Different Approaches: The Writer and the Rabbi'). Geiger describes the Jewish theological writer or intellectual as someone who bridges Jewish and European communal space and Jewish and historical studies. The 'Jewish-theological writer' encourages Judaism to abandon its 'one-sidedness' and, without shedding its distinctiveness, become a 'member of the human organism'. Assuming the figure of the hortatory orator, the writer motivates Jewish communities, in 'vivid expressive' language, to engage with broader humanistic trends, leading the community from 'insular self-certainty into more expansive realms of human activity'. The Jewish writer has the difficult, frequently painful and often misunderstood task (*verkannte Aufgabe*) of grasping the present and its prevailing ideas in their complete unity, and the position of Judaism within it. Recognizing that Judaism's eternal kernel, its higher religious ideas, have been damaged and that Judaism, in its over-reliance on external forms, has become one-sided (*einseitig ausgebildet habe*) because of the unfavourable historical conditions under which it has developed, the writer, if he is to be true to his Prophetic-critical vocation of rejuvenating Judaism in its relationships with the general culture and purifying its eternal religious ideas, must communicate in a lively and penetrating manner and without compromise.[69] The Jewish writer is thus a tormented figure who serves a larger purpose, looking beyond the insular 'house' of Judaism towards the 'relations of the world' and the 'needs of the time'. Not accepted at home, the writer reaches out for a broader community of 'progressive minds', perhaps an allusion to the participation of liminal Jewish figures from Spinoza to Heine and Börne in a European republic of letters.[70]

Geiger ruminates on another role he has held within the Jewish community: the reforming rabbi. While the writer, as a visionary, always has in view the totality of Judaism and its different elements in their relationship to the present age, the rabbi is directed towards his own circle of activity: his community, its level of education and the social relationships that pertain within it.[71] Geiger explains that the modern rabbi is a scholar who can no longer remain within the 'small circle' of communal Jewish life, and must broaden its borders to include opposing tendencies and political conflict, challenging those customs considered to be confining and insular ritual practices. If history is messy and disruptive, then the rabbi must engage with those conflicts rather than withdraw from them, thereby pro-actively educating his congregation rather than allowing its innocence to be disrupted and vitiated by potentially hostile transformations in the wider society.[72]

This youthful essay of Geiger, which accepts a degree of Prophetic martyrdom for a necessary ethical and educative task, is also indicative of his mature approach to the reform of Jewish worship, which combines critical idealism with a pragmatic spirit of compromise. Geiger was dismayed by the strong national and religious feeling brought forth by the liturgical invocation of the 'people of Israel' ('*das Volk Israel*'), an ethno-national concept which he felt 'no longer lives in the heart and wishes of the present'; it would be better, Geiger felt, to highlight the fortunes of Israel as a 'holy teaching' than to stress the character of a chosen people.[73] Emphasizing 'spiritual (*geistige*) significance' as against sensual representation and preferring, like Kant in *Religion within the Boundaries of Mere Reason*, the 'power of interiority' (*Kraft der Innerlichkeit*) in public prayer to external observance, Geiger wanted Jews to retain a strong connection to their past but for that attachment to be coloured by modern ethical commitments and diverse relationships with the surrounding society.[74] Jews can still invoke the people of Israel, but not as the chosen people, rather as the 'bearers of divine teaching'. Paradigmatic figures of enmity towards the Jews, such as Amalek and Haman, will still draw Jews back to a horrifying past but only in order to teach moral and spiritual lessons for the future.[75] Geiger artfully deployed translation in his two prayer books of 1854 and 1870, leaving the Hebrew untouched but, in the edifying spirit of Mendelssohn's epochal translation of the Pentateuch into German, using the German translation on the same page to offer a reworking of the Hebrew prayers based on liberal principles and philosophical rationalism. For example, in the second benediction to the Amidah prayer, Geiger's German text requests 'ever clearer' knowledge of God and does not mention a return to the past; God does not literally revive the dead, rather the dead achieve salvation in a new eternal life.[76]

In the spirit of the edifying sermon called for by Zunz, Geiger countered communal insularity and Zionistic longing by instructing his readers and congregation in the characterological diversity of Jewish history and Jewish literature. During the 1850s, in his scholarly contributions Geiger analysed and discussed many vibrant, heterodox personalities in relatively recent Jewish history; in that decade he published studies on the great medieval Jewish poets Judah Halevi, Abraham and Moses Ibn Ezra, Judah ben Shelomo Alharizi, and Kalonymos ben Kalonymos. Geiger was attracted to the critical spirit and cultivation of Sephardic Jewry. He wrote a brief biography of Judah Halevi, and produced several essays in which he tried to imitate the style of the older Sephardic poets.[77] In connection with his second series of lectures on Judaism and its History (1869–1871) Geiger prepared a biography of the Andalusian Hebrew poet and philosopher Solomon Ibn Gabirol (1021(?)–1058). He was fascinated by the Jewish controversialist, the Venetian Rabbi Leon da Modena (1571–1648). Impressed by the latter's independent critical attitude, Geiger wistfully imagines a German Jewish friendship; if only Lessing, that classical polemicist and argumentative free spirit, could have known da Modena as a kindred spirit![78] Geiger was also interested in Isaac Troki, another Jewish religious critic who had refuted the assertion of the Church that the Holy Scriptures of the Hebrews contained allusions to Christ.[79]

As an edifying sermonist and humanist orator in the manner of Zunz,[80] Geiger wished to provide a propaedeutic or repository of pedagogical resources for contemporary Judaism. Geiger did not confine himself to Jewish sources or Jewish publications but readily quoted Christian theologians. In his 'Lectures on Jewish history' Geiger sought to educate his congregation in Jewish contributions to recent European history and the latest intellectual developments, discussing controversial German Jewish personalities such as Ludwig Börne and Heinrich Heine (both converts to Christianity), the writer Berthold Auerbach, and the emancipation advocate Gabriel Reisser.[81] Graetz was adamant that Börne and Heinrich Heine belonged to Jewish history, and an entire chapter of his *History of the Jews* was devoted to them.[82] Many of Geiger's sermons touched on the 1848 revolutions.[83] Geiger's sermons were impressively eclectic, exampling notes from the memoirs of Henriette Herz, characteristic utterances from the brilliant legal and political career of Adolphe Crémieux, interspersed with passages from the letters of Wilhelm von Humboldt advocating Jewish emancipation.[84] As a reporter on contemporary history and as a would-be political educator of the Jews, Geiger sustained a productive tension between his Jewish commitments and varied intellectual interests, between his internal critique of aspects of Jewish religious identity and his fierce defence of Judaism against the demoralizing affronts of Christian anti-Judaism.

It was the great neo-Kantian philosopher Hermann Cohen, a disciple of Abraham Geiger's, who inherited the complex social, political, and pedagogical role of the liberal reformist Jew: someone who lives both inside and outside the Jewish community, as an advocate of ecumenical dialogue and a fierce combatant of Christian hubris.

Notes

1 See K. Koltun-Fromm. 2006. *Abraham Geiger's Liberal Judaism: Personal Meaning and Religious Authority*, Bloomington and Indianapolis: Indiana University Press, 1. For a discussion of Reform Judaism's theological, ceremonial, and communal innovations extending up to the 1970s, see Meyer, *Response to Modernity*.

2 For a detailed description of the ferocious campaign to prevent Geiger's assumption of a rabbinical post in Breslau, an important centre of Jewish activity, see 1906. 'Abraham Geiger', *The Jewish Encyclopedia*. Retrieved on 6 June 2012 from http://www.jewishencyclopedia.com/articles/6560–geiger-abraham.

3 Heschel, *Abraham Geiger and the Jewish Jesus*, 2.

4 A. Geiger. 1962. *Abraham Geiger and Liberal Judaism: The Challenge of the Nineteenth Century*, trans. E.J. Schlochauer, Philadelphia: The Jewish Publication Society of America, 14.

5 Koltun-Fromm, *Abraham Geiger's Liberal Judaism*, 117.

6 For an excellent study of the Protestant theological background to the Nazi redefinition of Jesus as an 'Aryan', see S. Heschel. 2010. *The Aryan Jesus: Christian Theologians and the Bible in Nazi Germany*, Princeton: Princeton University Press, especially chapter one, 'Draining Jesus of Jewishness'.

7 S. Heschel. 1999. 'Revolt of the Colonized: Abraham Geiger's Wissenschaft des Judentums as a Challenge to Christian Hegemony in the Academy', *New German Critique* 77, 73, 78.

8 Koltun-Fromm, *Abraham Geiger's Liberal Judaism*, 55.

9 Heschel, 'Revolt of the Colonized', 73.

10 Heschel, 'Revolt of the Colonized', 76.

11 Heschel, *Abraham Geiger and the Jewish Jesus*, 7. See Schorsch's own 'counterhistorical' argument that in its search for great power support for a Jewish homeland, the Zionist movement turned its back on the 'confrontation politics of the emancipationists'. Schorsch, *From Text to Context*, 127.

12 A. Geiger. 1985. *Judaism and its History in Two Parts*, trans. C. Newburgh, Lanham MD: University Press of America, 110.

13 Geiger, *Judaism and its History in Two Parts*, 392.

14 Geiger, *Judaism and its History in Two Parts*, 157–158.

15 Koltun-Fromm, *Abraham Geiger's Liberal Judaism*, 140.

16 Heschel, 'Revolt of the Colonized', 70–71.

17 M. Kramer. 1999. 'Introduction', in M. Kramer (ed.), *The Jewish Discovery of Islam, Studies in Honor of Bernard Lewis*, Tel Aviv: The Moshe Dayan Center for Middle Eastern and African Studies, Tel Aviv University, 11.

18 Geiger, *Judaism and its History in Two Parts*, 13.

19 Geiger, *Judaism and its History in Two Parts*, 21.

20 J. Lassner. 1999. 'Abraham Geiger: A Nineteenth-Century Jewish Reformer on the Origins of Islam', in M. Kramer (ed.), *The Jewish Discovery of Islam*, 105.

21 Geiger, *Judaism and its History in Two Parts*, 160.

22 Koltun-Fromm, *Abraham Geiger's Liberal Judaism*, 19. For Bauer's controversial writings on Jewish emancipation, see B. Bauer. 1843. *Die Judenfrage*, Braunschweig; and Bauer. 1843. 'Die Fähigkeit der heutigen Juden und Christen, frei zu werden', in G. Herwegh (ed.), *Einundzwanzig Bogen aus der Schweiz*, Zurich and Winterthur, 56–71.

23 Koltun-Fromm, *Abraham Geiger's Liberal Judaism*, 19.

24 Koltun-Fromm, *Abraham Geiger's Liberal Judaism*, 41, 45.

25 Koltun-Fromm, *Abraham Geiger's Liberal Judaism*, 47.

26 Geiger, *Judaism and its History in Two Parts*, 10, 21.

27 Geiger, *Judaism and its History in Two Parts*, 162.

28 See, for example, Heinrich Graetz's argument in 'The Diaspora, Suffering and Spirit' that for post-exilic Jews, 'migrations brought the Jewish people new experiences; homeless, they exercised and sharpened their gaze . . . even the plenitude of their suffering contributed to broadening the horizon of Jewish thinkers' who, to an extent, have 'participated in all the overwhelming events of world history'. H. Graetz. 1977. 'The Diaspora, Suffering and Spirit', in N.N. Glatzer (ed.), *Modern Jewish Thought, A Source Reader*, New York: Schocken Books, 21.

29 Geiger, *Judaism and its History in Two Parts*, 23.

30 Geiger, *Judaism and its History in Two Parts*, 83.

31 A. Geiger. 1962. 'A General Introduction to the Science of Judaism', in A. Geiger. *Abraham Geiger and Liberal Judaism: The Challenge of the Nineteenth Century*, trans. E.J. Schlochauer, Philadelphia: The Jewish Publication Society of America, 153.

32 On this point see Meyer, 'German Jewish Thinkers Reflect on the Future of the Jewish Religion', *Leo Baeck Institute Yearbook* 51(1), 5.

33 Geiger, *Judaism and its History in Two Parts*, 249.

34 Geiger, *Judaism and its History in Two Parts*, 168.

35 Geiger, *Judaism and its History in Two Parts*, 168.

36 Geiger, *Judaism and its History in Two Parts*, 92.

37 Geiger, *Judaism and its History in Two Parts*, 170.

38 Geiger, *Judaism and its History in Two Parts*, 171.

39 Geiger, *Judaism and its History in Two Parts*, 352.

40 Geiger, *Judaism and its History in Two Parts*, 175–176.

41 M. Meyer. 2006. 'German Jewish Thinkers Reflect', 9.

42 Geiger, *Judaism and its History in Two Parts*, 92.

43 Geiger, *Judaism and its History in Two Parts*, 81.

44 E. Breuer and D. Sorkin. 2003. 'Moses Mendelssohn's First Hebrew Publication: An Annotated Translation of the Kohelet Musar', *Leo Baeck Institute Yearbook* 48(1), 4–6.

45 Meyer, *Response to Modernity*, 95–96.

46 Geiger, *Abraham Geiger and Liberal Judaism*, 158.

47 Geiger, *Abraham Geiger and Liberal Judaism*, 158.

48 Geiger, *Abraham Geiger and Liberal Judaism*, 150.

49 Geiger, *Judaism and its History in Two Parts*, 117.

50 Geiger, *Judaism and its History in Two Parts*, 114, 117, 118.

51 Geiger, *Judaism and its History in Two Parts*, 240–241.

52 Koltun-Fromm, *Abraham Geiger's Liberal Judaism*, 82.

53 Koltun-Fromm, *Abraham Geiger's Liberal Judaism*, 81.
54 Geiger, *Judaism and its History in Two Parts*, 228.
55 Koltun-Fromm, *Abraham Geiger's Liberal Judaism*, 46 and 47.
56 Geiger, *Judaism and its History in Two Parts*, 55, 56, and 70.
57 Geiger, *Judaism and its History in Two Parts*, 80.
58 Geiger, *Judaism and its History in Two Parts*, 228.
59 Geiger, *Judaism and its History in Two Parts*, 92.
60 Geiger, *Judaism and its History in Two Parts*, 10.
61 Meyer, 'German Jewish Thinkers Reflect', 9.
62 K. Koltun-Fromm. 2000. 'Historical Memory in Abraham Geiger's Account of Modern Jewish Identity', *Jewish Social Studies* 7(1), 121.
63 Geiger, *Abraham Geiger and Liberal Judaism*, 59.
64 Koltun-Fromm, *Abraham Geiger's Liberal Judaism*, 88.
65 Geiger, introduction to *Abraham Geiger and Liberal Judaism*, 60.
66 Koltun-Fromm, *Abraham Geiger's Liberal Judaism*, 77.
67 Koltun-Fromm, *Abraham Geiger's Liberal Judaism*, 93.
68 Koltun-Fromm, *Abraham Geiger's Liberal Judaism*, 122.
69 A. Geiger. 1942. 'Die zwei verschiedenen Betrachtungsweisen: Der Schriftsteller und der Rabbiner', in Ludwig Geiger (ed.), *Abraham Geiger's Nachgelassene Schriften*, vol. 1 (first publ. 1885), Andover-Harvard Theological Library 1942, (492–504), 495–496.
70 Koltun-Fromm, *Abraham Geiger's Liberal Judaism*, 108.
71 Geiger, 'Die zwei verschiedenen Betrachtungsweisen', 498.
72 Koltun-Fromm, *Abraham Geiger's Liberal Judaism*, 106–107.
73 Koltun-Fromm, 'Historical Memory in Abraham Geiger's Account of Modern Jewish Identity', 118.
74 'Religion within the Boundaries of Mere Reason', in I. Kant. 2006. *Religion and Rational Theology*, Cambridge, UK: Cambridge University Press, 210, n: 'In that wish, which is the spirit of prayer, the human being only seeks to work upon himself (to give life to his disposition by means of the *idea of God*)'.
75 Koltun-Fromm, 'Historical Memory in Abraham Geiger's Account of Modern Jewish Identity', 119.
76 Koltun-Fromm, *Abraham Geiger's Liberal Judaism*, 35.
77 Geiger, introduction to *Abraham Geiger and Liberal Judaism*, 46.
78 Geiger, introduction to *Abraham Geiger and Liberal Judaism*, 46.
79 Geiger, introduction to *Abraham Geiger and Liberal Judaism*, 46.
80 For an evocative description of Zunz as an 'enthusiastic preacher' intent on rediscovering Jewish literature, history, and culture, see Niehoff, 'Zunz's Concepts of Haggadah'.
81 Geiger, *Abraham Geiger and Liberal Judaism*, 35.
82 See M.A. Meyer. 1986. 'Heinrich Graetz and Heinrich von Treitschke: A Comparison of their Historical Images of the Modern Jew', *Modern Judaism* 6(1), 5.
83 Koltun-Fromm, *Abraham Geiger's Liberal Judaism*, 106.
84 Geiger, *Abraham Geiger and Liberal Judaism*, 35.

CHAPTER 4

❋

Hermann Cohen's Prophetic Judaism

'Modern Judaism is history-oriented; it derives its sense of self from its historical development'.

Hermann Cohen, 'An Argument against Zionism'

The German Jewish philosopher Hermann Cohen (1842–1918) was perhaps the most influential theorist of Prophetic Judaism and, as I shall argue, one of the greatest exponents of the emancipative historical consciousness and confrontational politics of *Wissenschaft des Judentums*. Cohen is perhaps best known today (or vaguely remembered) as having founded the influential Marburg school of neo-Kantian philosophy. However, during his lifetime he was one of the most prominent defenders of the German Jewish community, an influential advocate for Jewish adult education, and a leading proponent of a philosophically and historically informed curriculum for Jewish studies in the *Wissenschaft des Judentums* tradition.[1]

After his retirement from his position in Marburg, Cohen moved to Berlin in 1912 and taught general and Jewish philosophy at the Academy for the Scientific Study of Judaism (*Lehranstalt für die Wissenschaft des Judentums*). It was during this period in particular that Cohen established a reputation as a 'highly significant modern Jewish theologian' over and above his contributions to the history of philosophy.[2] Cohen's Jewish writings are prolific. He published some seventy essays on matters relating to Jewish religious studies and Jewish life in diaspora, discussing topics as diverse as 'Jewish philosophy, Jewish history, Jewish biblical literature, the Talmud, Jewish education, and Jewish contemporary political affairs'. Most of these essays were published during his lifetime in various Jewish journals and newspapers.[3]

As the German Jewish political theorist Leo Strauss recalls, 'I grew up in an environment in which Cohen was the center of attraction for philosophically minded Jews who were devoted to Judaism; he was the master whom they revered'.[4] Hans Liebeschütz, in a now classic essay that helped to revive interest in Cohen as a Jewish thinker, describes Cohen as an 'outstanding representative of German Jewry', an 'effective publicist' who dealt with 'events of contemporary Jewish history in concrete terms'. Those who heard his lectures and read his articles felt that his 'witness gave authority and meaning to their own desire for the continuation of a Jewish existence in the midst of modern civilization'.[5]

As Avi Bernstein-Nahar details, between 1904 and 1917, in the scholarly and semi-popular Jewish press, Cohen wrote 'numerous articles promoting a particular self-understanding for the modern Jew', in which he suggested that Judaism, as a form of ethical monotheism, is 'well suited to contribute to the *Kultur* of the modern state, and to inform the ethical commitments (*Sittlichkeit*) of its citizens'.[6] Cohen appeared for the first time in public as a speaker before a Jewish audience as early as 1869; his lecture, on the importance of the idea of Sabbath in the history of civilization, belonged to a series established for the financial support of the *Zunzstiftung*.[7] In 1880, Cohen cemented his reputation for Jewish advocacy in his response, initially published as a separate pamphlet, to the eminent Prussian historian Heinrich von Trietschke's infamous attack on German Jews as unassimilable. Cohen suggested on the contrary that there was hardly 'any difference between Israelite monotheism and Protestant Christianity'.[8]

While still a philosophy professor at Marburg, in 1888 Cohen gave expert testimony to a Marburg court, refuting the slanderous anti-Semitic accusation that Jewish Talmudic law allowed Jews to rob and cheat gentiles. Cohen's testimony, which later appeared as a pamphlet called 'Die Nachstenliebe im Talmud', presented a theory of Noahide law in 'order to show that Judaism indeed has a doctrine of universal law, one concerned with the rights of gentiles as well as Jews'.[9] Cohen inherited not only the rebellious hermeneutic spirit of Jewish *Wissenschaft* but also a post-*Haskalah* desire for the renewal of Judaism through the creative interpretation of its literary and historical sources. As Eva Jospe observes, Cohen's formative years 'coincided with a richly creative period in the intellectual life of German Jewry'. The young Cohen was influenced by reformist Jewish scholars such as Leopold Zunz, Abraham Geiger and Samson Raphael Hirsch.[10] In his essay 'Heinrich Heine and Judaism', published anonymously in 1867, Cohen augmented the liberal Jewish tradition of sympathy for the Jewish Marrano and outsider by reclaiming the notorious Christian convert and Spinozist for Judaism. Cohen stressed, as Liebeschütz argues, Heine's 'strong feeling of responsibility for the Jewish community'. Heine, under the 'influence of Zunz's circle', which included the *Verein für die Wissenschaft des Judentums*, had, according to Cohen, accepted the idea and duty of Jewish learning as a medium through which the individual 'could fight for his own honour by defending his ancestors and their tradition'.[11] Developing Geiger's cultural-historical interpretation of post-biblical Judaism, Cohen argued that Heine, like Spinoza with whom he had such a profound intellectual affinity, was formed and educated by Judaism as a productive cultural-historical energy (*Grundgedanken hervorwirkenden Kultur-kräfte*) that gave rise to fundamental conceptions of the relationship between God and world, humanity and its destiny. Amongst a number of cultural elements which united to shape Heine's intellect and character (*zur Bildung seines Geistes und seines Charakters vereinigt haben*), Jewish thought – with its providential concept of humanity and purified conception of God – made a deep and enduring impression, ensuring a lasting affinity between Heine's emancipative vision of the future and the spirit of the Hebrew Prophets. In Cohen's reading Heine embodies the Prophetic spirit of protestation on behalf of the downtrodden that had inspired a 2000–year struggle against social oppression and religious violence.[12] From an early stage in his career, therefore, Cohen had evoked the personality of the 'modern Jew' as defined by a creative, even heterodox commitment to the ongoing theological, ethical, and political interpretation of diverse biblical and post-biblical Jewish sources, sources that could be recuperated as a matrix of ethical idealism and political struggle. As Almut Sh. Bruckstein suggests, 'Cohen's reading of Western philosophical sources throughout reflects the promise of an ethics that draws its life from Jewish sources'.[13]

Hermann Cohen's Protestant Judaism

Even though there has been a recent renaissance of interest in the 'Jewish' Cohen, partially stimulated by influential introductions to his religious philosophy by the illustrious Jewish philosophers Franz Rosenzweig and Leo Strauss, there lingers the influential verdict of Gershom Scholem that Cohen was one of those philosophically inclined Jewish thinkers – these include Leo Baeck for example – who, 'under a dominant Protestant influence', tended to regard Judaism in essentialist terms as a 'purely spiritual phenomenon', instead of interpreting it as a spiritual phenomenon bound to an historical phenomenon, 'namely, to the Jewish people and the Jewish nation'.[14] Jacques Derrida, in his influential 1991 essay 'Interpretations at War', shares Scholem's dismay at Cohen's attempts to synthesize his German and Jewish identities. It is with Cohen as the figure of the German Jew, Derrida argues:

> that Rosenzweig, like Scholem and Buber in a different way, will eventually break, despite the respect that Cohen still inspired, this great figure of rationalist German Judaism, liberal and non-Zionist if not assimilationist, this Jewish *and* German thinker.[15]

Derrida devotes most of the essay to an analysis of Cohen's notoriously Germanocentric 1915 essay *Deutschum und Judentum*. While Cohen's fervently patriotic wartime essay might well have been condemned by Rosenzweig, Scholem, Buber, and many Zionists, Derrida argues, it nevertheless represents 'something then typical of a certain Jewish-German intelligentsia', the very same class who were either exiled or ended up in the camps some twenty-five years later, that is, a 'certain type of militant patriotism in the Jewish-German community'.[16] Derrida is wary of Cohen's aggressive privileging in *Deutschum und Judentum* of a 'Judeo-German psyche' which excludes other hybrid Jewish identities, such as the 'Judeo-Moslem or Judeo-Catholic'. Cohen's ideal cultural symbiosis, Derrida writes, is 'strictly Judeo-Protestant – that is to say, thanks to Luther, Judeo-German'.[17] Derrida argues that Cohen, like Heidegger in the 1930s, gives a 'double privilege' to the German spirit in its process of becoming, in the concatenation of its spiritual events, both philosophical and religious. According to Derrida, this is because Cohen's historico-philosophical interpretation of the German spirit privileges the tradition of German idealism on the one hand, and on the other the Lutheran Reformation as a religious form of rationality opposed to the dogma of ecclesiastical institutions: 'The Reformation, something irreducibly German in Cohen's eyes, places the German spirit "at the center of world history"'.[18]

When Cohen speaks of the 'historical spirit of Protestantism', this spirit is not, Derrida argues, to be confused with an empirical history of factual events, but is a force or telos, one so strong, internal, and undeniable that 'even the non-Protestants, the Catholics and the Jews, must recognize it'. It is as if, Derrida suggests, Cohen were asking these communities to recognize the superior essence of Protestantism as a form of free conscience, a manoeuvre that Derrida describes as a logic of 'conversion to Protestantism, of conversion in general'.[19] Cohen's monocultural genealogical idealism, in overlooking or glossing over actual German anti-Semitism including that of Luther himself, 'presents at each moment a bouquet to all the dormant – or rather ever wakeful – [Jean-Marie] Le Pens, who do not concern themselves overmuch with detail'.[20] Recent scholarship on Cohen has proved more generous in its willingness to consider his contributions to Jewish ethics and philosophy over a more than fifty-year period. Nevertheless, the supposition that Cohen's conception of a Jewish-German symbiosis verges on a delusional and dangerously evangelical assimilationism is evident, for example, in David Myers' somewhat naïve judgement that Cohen's genealogy of philosophical idealism, stretching from Plato to Maimonides, Luther, Kant, and Cohen himself, suggests that he viewed 'Jewish and Protestant-German identities as harmonious, if not identical'.[21]

Taking a broader view of Cohen's Jewish activism and counter-historical energies, I would suggest that despite what seems to be an apologetic evocation of Judaism's congeniality with the spirit of Lutheran Protestantism, Cohen often deployed the confrontational tactics of Jewish *Wissenschaft*, and demanded that Judaism be recognized as a formative and independent contributor to modern culture. In so doing Cohen developed a liberal Jewish hermeneutic of symbolic interpretation that undermined the coupling of Christianity with spiritual interiority and ethical progress. Cohen, like Geiger, Graetz, and Heine before him, sought to undermine Christianity's proud claim to spiritual uniqueness as the first truly moral and post-conventional monotheistic religion. In this chapter, I argue, *pace* Scholem's critique of Geiger and Cohen as abrogating Jewish identity and solidarity in their apparent concessions to the rationalist demands of a dominant German Protestant culture, that we should interpret Cohen's engagement with Protestantism as a stratagem and rhetorical ploy. I would describe Cohen's frequent paeans to the spirit of Lutheran Protestantism as a *concessio*, in which an interlocutor seemingly concedes to the opponent's point of view while undermining the entire edifice on which their argument and self-perception rests.

As Alan Mittleman argues in his introduction to a later Cohen essay written during the First World War, 'The Jew in Christian Culture' (1917), Cohen's approach to German Protestantism was positionally flexible and dialectically conceived. Cohen wanted to recognize the formative influence of Protestantism on German culture because its critique of ecclesiastical dogma and emphasis on hermeneutic freedom signalled the historical emergence of a rational and secular vision of German culture and statehood that would encompass different nationalities and embrace religious heterogeneity. On the other hand, Cohen's appeal to Protestantism in its theological and ethical guises hid an audacious counter-historical stratagem – apparently a concession to Christianity as the motor of modern historical progress, in effect a wholesale transvaluation of its originality and causality – which was to 'root the constitutive ideas of the Reformation, of German Protestantism generally, in Hebrew, biblical monotheism'.[22] Cohen also sought to historically educate and boost the morale of his German Jewish compatriots pressured by both anti-Semitic calumnies and the increasingly influential Zionist critique of a viable Jewish life in Germany. Cohen argues that 'Christian culture' only seems to be foreign and threatening to Jews, for it is not a 'thorough and independent creation of Christian ideas'. Rather, and here Cohen reprises Geiger's trenchant disdain for Christianity's supercessionist claims, Judaism shares 'in the origins and further development of Christian culture . . . in its deepest intellectual essence'.[23]

In the first place, Cohen suggests, Judaism participates in the idealizing and spiritualizing tendencies of post-Reformation religious development in contributing to the leading religious ideas of the Protestant age. Cohen congratulates modern Protestant Christianity for liberating its conception of Christ's suffering from the dogmatic meaning of salvation for a sinning humanity. For the modern Christian, this suffering has 'rather a symbolic meaning, which gives to suffering the role of chief value or content for the whole of human life'. Without pause, however, Cohen goes on to argue a point that must be unacceptable to any Christian, when he suggests that in light of the 'metaphysical symbolization process' inaugurated by Protestantism, the 'question of the historicity of Jesus, as well as of his passion, recedes into irrelevance. Dogma and history retreat behind symbolism'. Moreover Cohen reminds us, as Mittleman explains, 'that Jesus as sufferer is based, historically, on Isaiah's suffering servant', an interpretation that runs directly contrary to the supercessionist Christian interpretation of the beleaguered servant of the Hebrew Bible as prefiguring the advent of Christ the humble redeemer. A radical religious humanist, with considerable interpretive élan and not a little chutzpah, Cohen, the comparative biblical critic and combative Zunzian philologist, dares the 'enlightened' scholarly Protestant theologian to repudiate his emphasis on the spiritual affinity of Judaism and Christianity considered as higher ethical religions.[24]

In an earlier address, 'The Significance of Judaism for the Religious Progress of Humanity', given to the International Congress of Free Christians and Other Religious Liberals in Berlin in 1910, Cohen reminded his ecumenical audience that historical research into religion necessitates sympathy with religions other than one's own; 'idealization' is thus a methodological precondition of historically minded theological scholarship, which should aspire to the enlightened, pluralist recognition that 'genuine idealization represents general religious progress in every religion'.[25] The criterion and goal of religious progress is morality. Thus the task of Cohen's address, which he inherits from Abraham Geiger, is to refute the conventional wisdom of Judaism's Pharisaic legalism and demonstrate Judaism's religious progress towards a higher morality.[26]

Cohen reinforces his point that religion is a vessel for ethical idealism and moral reason when, adapting Kant's attempted philosophical purification of religion as necessarily in accordance with a disposition towards the moral law as the kingdom of ends, he symbolically reinterprets the Holy Spirit as the 'spirit of holiness', a spirit that already appears in Psalm 51 as a moral striving that binds, but does not unite, humanity and God.[27] In the tradition of Mendelssohn and Lessing, Cohen's methodology of symbolic idealization replaces an exclusivist Christian tenet – the dogma of the Trinity – with a post-ecclesiastical ethics of virtue focused on ethical dispositions that enhance the dialogical correlation, but not anthropomorphic identification, of the human and divine.[28] Appropriating a cherished representative of German national awakening only to subvert his ardent Christology, Cohen allegorizes Luther's Christ as an 'ideal figure of faith', grounded 'neither in an historical nor in a literary fact, but in an ideal form, in an image of religious imagination'. Cohen remarks that the Lutheran Christ, although drawn from the materials of the gospels and 'taken freely from the prophets and psalms', is 'actually a creation of reason'.[29]

Cohen's palimpsestial Judaic Christ figure, which recalls Geiger's revisionist interpretation of Jesus as a reformist Pharisee, is a provocative reminder of Nietzsche's ironic recognition that Protestant theological scholarship's interest in the historical Christ eventually undermined the veridical claims of Christianity entirely. Cohen's adversion to the incomplete idealism of the Lutheran reformation also subtly suggests, as Mittleman puts it, that Judaism is a superior monotheism that has made further progress down the road of demythicization.[30] In this 1910 address, Mittleman argues, Cohen does not pander to his largely Christian audience. While shaping his presentation of Judaism to comply with the modernist proclivities of liberal Christianity, he 'does not shrink from attacking their conceits or subverting their stereotypes'.[31] Referring to the egalitarian communal institution of the Sabbath, Cohen emphasizes the worldly orientation of Judaism as compared to Christian asceticism, the free constitution of the Jewish community as opposed to the dominance of the Christian church, and Christianity's tardiness with regard to 'educated humanity's' faith in moral progress, since even in its liberal forms 'Christianity must still struggle with a mystical-sacramental view of Christ as a personal saviour', an understanding of salvation 'at odds with progressive, Jewish messianism'.[32] Where Judaism remains an ethical religion focused on the concept of God, even within Protestantism there are interpretive 'difficulties associated with the person of Christ, however idealized he is', a subtle reference to Christianity's residual Paganism.[33]

Nevertheless Cohen's philological and comparative focus on shared figures of suffering and redemption is intended in a spirit of ecumenical dialogue. Cohen's concept of religion as ethically effective through symbolic archetype and exemplary personality promises a shared ethical orientation and inward piety common to both Judaism and Christianity. Reminding his inter-faith audience of the transcendent power of friendship, Cohen narrates his initial encounter with the German philosopher and Social Democrat Friedrich Albert Lange, under whom he wanted to write his *Habilitation*. Lange, Cohen says, came out of 'an arid, Protestant orthodoxy'. When Lange warily acknowledged their different conceptions of Christianity upon Cohen's first visit, anxious about a perceived Jewish antipathy to Christianity, Cohen helped to bring about a 'candid understanding' between the two by responding, 'What you call Christianity, I call prophetism'. With a single stroke their souls were 'bound together', Lange enthusiastically affirming this conciliatory gesture by showing Cohen the Prophetic passages of his Bible that he had underlined.[34] Cohen's conciliatory anecdote demonstrates a shared textual heritage awaiting hermeneutic revivification and prioritizes friendship and dialogue over religious sectarianism. Cohen's anecdote appeals to the communicative and self-transforming ethics of *Bildung*. As Reinhart Koselleck suggests, the eighteenth-century historical critique of religion, and specifically of Protestant theology, contributed to transforming 'religion into religiosity', a form of piety in which dogmatic beliefs could be transformed back into myths. This new religiosity could forgo both church and ecclesiastical dogmatism without having to give up a religious self-interpretation or social reforming praxis.[35] Cohen appeals to *Bildung*'s emphasis on a process of self-discovery that relies upon interpersonal relationships, in which self-formation through experimental sociability has an emancipative function because it is 'directed against all authorities', and is constituted outside the state and 'differences of social estate and ecclesiastical precepts'. Cohen's attempt to soften Lange's apprehensions recalls the conversational sphere initiated by *Bildung*, the salon culture in which Jews and women 'shared in equal rights' and could take the initiative.[36] Cohen's illustration of an inter-religious friendship is intended to have an exemplary power, since, as Peter Schmid observes, for Cohen friendship, which ensures the lasting connection of people, is the 'social cement which effectively enables and preserves society and state'.[37]

Returning to 'The Jew in Christian Culture', Cohen speaks to both Jewish and Christian audiences in desiring to 'refute the prejudice that the Jew must flee the general culture in order to be able to remain an independent, self-sufficient Jew'. Positing *Bildung*'s most cherished ideal of courageous self-disclosure through communicative participation, Cohen affirms that the Jew 'retains a good, perhaps the best, part of his own world, in its deepest intellectual essence, so far as he offers himself, spirit and soul, to the general culture'. The Jew should not be alienated by Christian culture since there is an 'essential [Jewish] contribution [to that culture] in the beginning as well as in the Middle Ages', which was renewed at the beginning of modern times, and remains to the present day. The Jewish contribution will remain as long as the 'Christian world' retains its religious and moral framework, its ideal personality.[38]

Cohen makes it clear, however, that the Jewish contribution to European modernity does not lack complexity or contradiction. It is a combination of ethical monotheism and innovative modernism, piety and reform, loyalty to the host society but retaining the potential for critical detachment. Cohen's protean historical consciousness and his liberal Jewish receptiveness to Judaism's complex personality – with its liminal greyzones and creative adaptation to diasporic conditions – were necessary to combat the anti-Semite who disavows Judaism's intellectual fertility and reifies the Semitic mentality as arid, imitative, and inherently sterile. Wary of the ingrained Christian image of a theocratic and heteronomous Judaism, Cohen reminds his audience that while Christian education in Germany only knows the Judaism of the Old Testament, in order to form a judgement about the religious progress of Judaism one must 'also know the postbiblical period, its literature and contemporary way of life'. No less important is the knowledge of the living Judaism of today; for despite all 'development and differentiation, inner struggles and external influences, Judaism has maintained itself as a living, historical unity'.[39]

Cohen was a rigorous monotheist in terms of his ethics, but his liberal investment in the richness of post-biblical Judaism gave him a necessary resource in the struggle against increasingly popular anti-Semitic arguments. In 'The Jew in Christian Culture' Cohen upbraids the 'much-read nationalist Odysseus' and anti-Semitic pseudo-intellectual Houston Stewart Chamberlain for vigorously denying that Goethe's pantheism has its source in the Jewish Spinoza. Chamberlain instead maintained that Goethe had the anti-Jewish Giordano Bruno to thank for his identification of God with nature. Yet, as Cohen points out, even if this were true, Bruno took his pantheism from the Iberian Jew 'Salomon ibn Gabirol', 'a poet of the synagogue with a deep sensitivity towards the lyricism of the Psalms'. Gabirol was better known to Bruno, who cited him with great approbation, by his philosophical name 'Avicebron', and therefore considered him to be an Arab Muslim. Bruno, Cohen enthuses, had unwittingly 'drawn his nourishment from Jewish sources', so that if 'Goethe had read Bruno more than Spinoza, his pantheism would nevertheless not have been any less Jewish'.[40] Yet this 'demonic game of intrigues, which does not want to thank the Semitic spirit for the dubious good of pantheism', has been ironically resolved. Appealing to a proud intellectual tradition of German Jewish pan-Semitism, Cohen remarks that it was the nineteenth-century German Jewish Orientalist Salomo Munk, a friend of Zunz and a devotee of Maimonides and Judeo-Arab literature, 'who had to leave Germany [Prussian universities did not employ Jewish academics] in order to find an honourable influence in Paris', who 'rediscovered the Jew in the Arab'.[41]

In 'The Jew in Christian Culture' Cohen goes on to affirm that German philosophy itself owes much to the Jewish Middle Ages 'when our philosophers of religion, with our revered Maimonides at their head, flourished'. The first German philosopher, the cardinal legate Nicholas of Kusa, 'appealed to Maimonides for the theory of attributes and with this the fundamental problem of the knowledge of God'. Abruptly returning to the historical imaginary of Islamic Andalusia as a homeland of the Jewish spirit, Cohen declares to his Jewish audience that 'we do not require Protestantism for the grounding for our faith', since for Luther himself that faith developed out of the Psalms. This was because, as Joseph Ballan argues, the psalmists and the Prophets, designated by Cohen as 'poet-thinkers', conceive of God as an idea or archetype rather than an image or semblance.[42] As Jews, Cohen proclaims with pride, we still 'live in *our* Middle Ages', an age of cultured rationalism and refined philosophical theism, very 'different from the Christian Middle Ages'.[43]

Cohen further inverts the Christian temporal schema when he suggests that it is the Jewish faith which fulfils the (failed) promise of Lutheran Protestantism as a rational religion without dogma or salvific works. Following Mendelssohn and Geiger, Cohen avers that it is Judaism which realizes a free or uncoerced piety towards God without institutional mediation; Judaism has nourished the development of an autonomous ethical personality, sustaining the 'character-task' of *Bildung* which is to attain the 'harmony of self-consciousness'.[44] In the Jewish faith 'we recognize the inexhaustible ground of revelation in our own hearts . . . we shape for ourselves continuously our believing, responsible personality'.[45] Reviving the Mendelssohnian trope of Judaism as an egalitarian faith of oral instruction and transmission that educates character through living example, in 'The Significance of Judaism' Cohen had criticized the Reformation for failing to seriously address social equality: 'The Reformation made only a little progress in principle here vis-à-vis Judaism'. For it was not the Bible alone but the study of the so-called oral teaching, the Talmud and its commentaries, that has informed the content of the spiritual life of the poor as well as of the rich Jew.[46] Critical of the Pietistic focus on confessional interiority and by extension Kant's instrumentalization of public prayer as a prop for the resolved ethical will, Cohen, as Ballan argues, admired the 'socializing power' of Jewish prayer, its creation of a 'common language' that can be shared by rich and poor, young and old.[47]

Prophetic Judaism

Before analysing Cohen's famous conception of Prophetic Judaism in more detail, it is important to recognize that his Prophetic ethics gave him significant tactical flexibility both as a Jewish intellectual in conversation with German Christians and as a Jewish reformer who sought a greater focus in Jewish life on philosophical training and ethics. As a liberal German Jew and a socialist Cohen faced withering criticism from Orthodox Jewish communities and from anti-Semitic elements in German society, while his socialist-inspired idealism attracted opprobrium from the ranks of German philosophers. If Judaism sustains the ethical personality, it is Prophetic Judaism which models that personality as robust, critical, progressively minded, and closely engaged with social and political questions. More than any other contemporary Jewish thinker, Cohen propounds modern Judaism in his Jewish writings as an ethical religion beholden to the teachings of the biblical Prophets. For the

Prophets, Cohen reminds us, Judaism's special distinctiveness is not 'in its concerns with mankind's past but in its hope for the future'.[48]

In his essay 'The Style of the Prophets' (1901), Cohen remarks that the Prophets are not theologians; to them God's teaching is an exclusively moral teaching. It is the relation of God to man and hence also to nature which is the concern of Prophetic teaching.[49] Yet the Prophets do not start out with the (Protestant) relationship between the individual and God; rather, for them, 'man means nation or other nations. They do not even regard their own people as representative of the concept man but instead those nations or states with which their country establishes a more or less close contact'. This is because 'politics is the native soil of prophetic religion, their moral teachings have topical overtones; voiced within wide practical contexts, they open important perspectives and give rise to basic questions of morality'.[50]

In evoking a passionate monotheism which articulates God's love for a suffering humanity, the Prophets rebuke polytheism's focus on collective guilt and inexorable fate and introduce an ethics of social love and compassion for the poor man and the stranger as archetypal beneficiaries of God's love. 'God loves the stranger' and thus man has to love the stranger; the Israelites are sternly reminded in the Bible that they too 'were strangers in the land of Egypt' (Leviticus 19:34).[51] God loves the stranger and the poor man such that his love does not stop at love for Israel, which is only an historical point of departure for his love of men as a totality. As Samuel Brody argues, for Cohen Israel's election has a purpose or vocation, which is to generate within the national body of a people the 'unheard-of idea of a unified mankind, the prophetic ethic, the idea of Messianism'.[52] Prophetic religion reminds the Israelites that in Israel God loves nothing other than the human race, that God loves Israel 'only as a model, a symbol of mankind'.[53] Cohen continues Geiger's cautiously denationalizing hermeneutics, in which Judaism's inherited vocabulary of election is displaced and extended rather than extinguished. As Brody argues, Cohen maintains in 'The Style of the Prophets' that Israel's chosenness is not a mark of arrogance; rather chosenness means 'Israel's vocation to proclaim the one God as the redeemer of mankind', conceptually subordinating Israel's election to the unity of humanity.[54]

Cohen details the ways in which the Prophets were concerned with politically educating the Jewish people and expanding their knowledge and historical consciousness of the gentile nations. By referring repeatedly to 'Israel's Canaanite origins', the Prophets introduce a perspective that combines both national and supranational views.[55] Amos, for instance, reproaches Phoenicia and Egypt for forgetting their '"brotherly covenant" with Judah'. Israel remains God's inheritance; but now Egypt too is called '"My people and Assyria the work of My hands" (Isaiah 19:25)'.[56] In this way, Cohen avers in the critical spirit of Geiger, a 'naïve pan-semitism' helps to demolish national conceit and arrogance, and prepares the way for the 'universalism of mankind': for mankind is the 'archetypal, the fundamental Gestalt envisaged by moral man'. The Prophets are dismayed at how far removed the nations are from this ideal of mankind, and they recognize that any war waged by a nation against its neighbours will soon rage within its own borders: as with *The Iliad*, 'the prophets' awesome imagination depicts all of war's horrors'.[57] In his *magnum opus Religion of Reason out of the Sources of Judaism* (1919), Cohen associates the Prophetic ethos with the *Aufklärung* for the Prophets arose 'as if they had come from a new world', exhorting 'men to a kind of politics as if they were akin to eighteenth century cosmopolitans'. The messianic conception of mankind prefigures Kant's cosmopolitan concept of mankind as well as Herder's 'universal humanitarianism'.[58]

The concept of a unification of all nations into one mankind under Israel's religious guidance indubitably represents the highest triumph as well as the most profound substance of prophetic patriotism. And yet, Cohen muses, this concept is inherently painful for the Prophets, such that it results in frequent changes of mood. A new concept emerges: the Prophet must lose his country, for mankind will become his country; for Jerusalem to be a moral concept of the new world historical interpretation of Judaism's vocation, it must cease to be a political concept.[59] Israel's election now means 'Israel's vocation to proclaim the One God as the redeemer of mankind'. The realization that Israel must sacrifice its peoplehood for its God, its national status for its transformation into a community (*Gemeinde*), is both exhilarating and melancholic, evoking both patriotic and more universal emotions.[60]

The 'inner necessity of our wanderings', Cohen feels, is 'a note of human suffering sounded even in moments of sublime human joy'.[61] Israel's loneliness necessitates the loss of the state and its social misery begets its existence as the social analogue of the poor man. Israel has an exemplary power; it is not an anachronistic remnant but the 'prototype of suffering', a 'symbol of human suffering', of the human creature in general. Thus God's love for a wandering Israel expresses God's love for the human race.[62] The proper course of Israel's history begins when it broke with all the national treasures of this world and started a new existence, its 'world mission'. Yet Israel's suffering has no tragic connotations, for it does not have national particularism as its motivation; rather its exemplary vicarious suffering as a people without land or national sovereignty expresses the reconciliation of man with God.[63] Suffering, Cohen argues, is the characteristic feature of religion, and it is the 'task of monotheism that is symbolically expressed through the suffering of those who professed Jewish monotheism'.[64] As Brody points out, Cohen's articulation of Israel's vicarious suffering for humanity displaces Jesus as the singular, historically decisive Messiah figure who died for the sins of the world with a dispersed people's ongoing task to serve as an exemplary witness of the humanism and ethical idealism of the God-idea, and as a catalyst for an eventual messianic transformation of a present mired in injustice.[65]

Cohen's discussion of the ambivalence of the Jewish Prophet as insider and outsider to their community opens a discursive space for the internal, far-sighted critic of the Jewish community, someone for whom the relationship between Jew and Gentile is of crucial importance. The Prophetic critics acknowledge but do not submit to weariness and pessimism; in the face of scepticism from their own community, and the hostility of external forces, they proclaim a new heaven, and a new earth, acutely aware of the people's 'disinclination for this new and great idea'.[66] The new heaven is the new morality; and the new earth, a new mankind.[67] In his essay 'On Messianism' Cohen suggests that the Jewish God-concept reaches its ultimate perfection in the Messianic idea, an idea which grew out of an historical development as all ideas do.[68] The Prophets, in the midst of political decline, proclaimed the reestablishment of their state long before its fall; but the Prophets did not make the renascence of their own state the primary subject of their public pronouncements. On the contrary, they 'announced the eventual restoration also of those states and nations that had fought against their own people. Faced with events of the past, they conceived the notion of a future'; this is the true significance and real discovery of their Messianic thinking.[69]

Nevertheless, initially the Messianic concept had a strong empirical element; the Messiah is conceived of as a scion of the house of David, one who is anointed, 'who is like a king'. But soon the prophetic image of the redeemer changes, as the anointed one, no longer a king, is 'transfigured into a symbol of human suffering'. True hope emanates from this 'symbolic figure alone', and in this humble figure mankind can see a true warrant for its restoration.[70] Through this process of symbolization which, like the Judge of Lessing's ring parable, translates the scriptural and territorial locus of religious adherence into a temporality of recessive origins demanding ethical praxis, the Messiah comes to be thought of in universalistic terms as a 'symbol of universal peace' when all Mankind will gather around as one flock to worship the One God. No longer passively awaiting the advent of an individual national saviour, and overcoming its own patriotic grief at the loss of Zion, Israel's enduring task, transfiguring its exile and immiseration, is to be a 'light of the nations', making wars disappear and preparing the way for a future in which life can be lived in harmony and justice.[71] No triumphalism, no thirst for the restoration of national glory should colour the Messianic vision, for this Messianic ideal is pregnant with a dream of the future that banishes inequality, yet does not seek the re-establishment of normative social relations.

As the Prophetic vision of the future is refined, the Messiah is represented as a 'poor man who is depicted with the warmth or the fire of empathy'; he is destitute and without beauty, and rides not a splendid horse but a donkey, yet God's spirit emanates from him.[72] He will 'end all social misery' as the Prophets are very clear that the poor must be given their rights.[73] Cohen remarks that compassion and pity for the poor of the earth are poured into this Prophetic portrayal of the servant of the Lord. The Prophetic 'poetry of social compassion' points, with all the magic of hope, towards the future, in which poverty will be ended. However, the present, 'with all its unfulfilled needs, unnatural oppression, glaring injustices, vain conceits, and bragging untruths', deserves no pity.[74] For the actualization of the Messianic era 'constitutes a specific task' of social criticism and utopian imagination, a transcendence of the perpetual struggle for existence and a recognition that the fact that things are today as they were yesterday does not necessarily mean that they have to be that way tomorrow.[75]

The future, according to Cohen, is a postulate of religious faith and indeed its most wondrous flower, but such a future can only be realized through healthy realism and transformative action in the present.[76] With a *Bildung* inflected emphasis on communicative self-formation and the importance of balanced personal virtues in the tradition of Aristotelian ethics, Cohen clearly distinguishes the Prophets from augurs and mystic visionaries. The prophet is primarily interested in humanity rather than a shadowy image of the 'beyond'; he is a politician interested in social legislation whose thoughts constantly turn to history, indeed he is the 'originator of the concept of world history'. Historically sensitive to the progress of human universal history, the messianic age in the Prophets' poetic depictions is an age of 'culture' governed by knowledge rather than Rousseau's projection of a golden age of natural innocence. It is the outcome of moral *Bildung* rather than utopian projection.[77] Turning to a contrast with the Greek historians, Cohen alleges that they never thought of a 'history that has the future' as its content. Their mytho-poetic history is directed to their origins, it is a history that 'narrates the past of its nation'.[78]

Cohen's Prophetic Judaism recalls the mature Geiger and his emphasis on the ongoing world-historical task of the Jews, which in modernity takes place within history rather than outside of it. Cohen's emphasis on the radical social criticism and interpretive freedom of the Jewish Prophets is a reminder of Geiger's counter-historical claim that 'unlike Christianity, which is tied to the institutions of the state, Judaism is free to develop progressively . . . to push forward religious and moral development within society as a whole'.[79]

Debate with Martin Buber

Cohen's prophetic convictions inform his famous 1916 debate with Martin Buber (1878–1965). Cohen's response to Buber's attack on his liberal Jewish antipathy to Zionism in *Der Jude* (July 1916) was published in *K.C.-Blaetter*

(July–August 1916) as 'An Argument against Zionism: A Reply to Dr. Martin Buber's Letter to Hermann Cohen'. Buber was a Jewish religious philosopher and cultural Zionist, well known for educating bourgeois German Jews about East European Jewry by translating Hasidic folk tales into German, and for his translation, in collaboration with Franz Rosenzweig, of the Hebrew Bible into German.[80] Cohen was outraged that Buber presented himself as the custodian of authentic Judaism and felt that he dismissed Jews who were neither Zionist nor Orthodox as preserving a 'fictitious Judaism' that prevented the true renaissance of Jewish life in a Jewish homeland. Buber had rejected Cohen's conception of Jews as a nationality, but not a nation, that can find a home in a modern nation-state which could unite disparate peoples within its rational and distributive legal framework and pluralist national identity.[81] He argued instead that the messianic idea of Judaism cannot be realized if Jewish nationhood is not actualized, and that the Jewish people must struggle for a homeland in order to realize their freedom and creativity, rather than remaining in diaspora as a 'brittle fact of nature appended to an ever more diluted confessional religion'.[82] In his reply Cohen disputes the Zionist claim that Jews are only living a sort of 'half-life' in diaspora and that the diaspora Jew's imagined synthesis of German and Jewish history and religious spirit is an expression of false consciousness.

A critical focus of the debate between these two Jewish philosophers is the significance of post-biblical Jewish history. Cohen incredulously asks of Buber:

> Are all the other roads and directions our history has taken really nothing but devious paths that necessarily lead to degeneration? And what is the criterion by which to decide whether the road to Palestine alone will determine the shape of our future?[83]

Zionism, Cohen feels, is attempting to tailor Jewish existence to fits its own preconceived notions, circumscribing Jewish reality ever more narrowly. Only in Palestine, and only in a Jewish state, can a 'silted-over, a "fictitious" Judaism be extricated from the undesirable accretions of diaspora-existence'. Yet, laments Cohen, drawing on the affirmative historical consciousness of *Wissenschaft des Judentums*, the entire history of Judaism is hereby ideologically distorted, all cultural endeavours of Jewish history condemned as illusory, as belaboured abstractions having nothing to do with authentic Judaism. The 'problems and predicaments' of modern life simply do not exist for this narrow nationalism. Here the 'Jew is a Jew only insofar as he is conscious of his Jewish nationality'.[84] Cohen's version of liberal Judaism is, as we have seen, syncretic, nourished by Enlightenment cosmopolitanism and the German ideal of *Bildung* as the formation of the principled ethical personality regulated by humanist ideals and in constant dialogue with other individuals and cultures.

Cohen's vigorous response to Buber evokes the Prophetic theodicy of Israel's suffering in exile as exemplary for humanity, and advocates the modern Jew's integration into the enlightened nation-state. Cohen reminds Buber of the liberal Jewish embrace of the diasporic condition: 'we are aware of the fact that we continue to live as divine dew among the nations; we wish to remain among them and be a creative force for them'. Cohen affirms that 'all our prophets have us living among the nations, and all view "Israel's remnant" from the perspective of its world mission'.[85] Cohen then reminds Buber of the idealistic symbolic language of Prophetic religion, which looks simultaneously towards the past and future of Judaism. He argues that 'Palestine is not merely the land of our fathers; it is the land of our prophets, who established and perfected the ideal of our religion'.[86] It is a Holy Land in the sense that our timeless, sacred heritage originated there. Just as the Prophets reminded the Israelites of their peripatetic history as strangers and sojourners in other lands, today Jews cannot afford to shut themselves off from the vagaries of gentile and world history, for 'we regard the moral world as it unfolds throughout history as our real Promised Land'.[87] As David Novak argues, Cohen rejected Zionism because it was an attempt to 'fixate the national identity of the Jewish people at the level of a nation-state like any other', whereas he conceived the task of the Jewish people as a religious community affirming and deriving cultural advantages from the modern secular state while simultaneously anticipating the unification of the nations in the Messianic age.[88]

Unsurprisingly Cohen's liberal hermeneutics humanizes and spiritualizes the more nationalistic aspects of the Hebrew Bible. He affirms Judaism's post-exilic history and the progressive politics of the modern German Jewish community as being sustained by both Jewish ethical sources and *Aufklärung* inspired German humanism. Cohen suggests that liberal German Jews 'draw our spiritual sustenance largely from the treasure-troves of the German mind (and surely not from the Bible or Talmud alone)'.[89] The German spirit is the spirit of classical humanism and true cosmopolitanism. After enumerating a list of German poets and thinkers including Leibniz, Kant, Lessing, and Herder who animate German Judaism's *Geistesgeschichte*, Cohen fuses Prophetic universalism and German humanism by declaring that 'all these German thinkers are prophets of one humanity' (*Die Deutschen Geister sind allesamt Propheten der Humanität*).[90]

Cohen revisits Geiger's anxiety that Palestine-centric thinking by contemporary Jews inhibits realistic political engagement with the modern state and surrounding society. Like Mendelssohn, he wants to maintain Jewish ethnic group distinctiveness as bound to the observance of Jewish Law but also urges political integration into and ethical obligation towards the modern nation state, which he understands as a prerequisite and guarantee of Jewish religious survival.[91] Cohen warns against a return to an indifference towards gentile geo-politics when he argues that the 'state represents more than merely one of many cultural phenomena to be subsumed under our religion'. Invoking a long standing trope of worldly Jewish engagement with surrounding cultures, Cohen remarks that even our ancestors in Arab Spain, in which cultural milieu they flourished, 'were hardly that limited in their thinking'.[92] Cohen alludes to Andalusian Jews in order to remind Buber of a supposedly untenable combination of Jewish creativity, spiritual sincerity, and loyalty to one's host society.

Moreover, the modern state, Cohen continues, lets us participate in the ever-changing manifestations of its national spirit, enlarging our horizons and granting the formative guidance of ethics and scientific philosophy to our religion. Our ancient sages, Philo and Maimonides, were already approaching this methodological procedure of examining our religion in the light of rational awareness and cross-cultural fertilization.[93] What is thus required by the German Jew is a 'vital and constructive concern for the country of which he is a citizen and a full affirmation of his own past history, so that his German and his Jewish consciousness are fused into one'.[94]

The relationship of Jews to their history is pivotal in this disagreement between Zionism and liberal Judaism as to the future of Jews in the diaspora. For the essential difference between liberal Judaism and Zionism, Cohen feels, is akin to the difference between Jewish classicism and romanticism, where the classical concept points towards the future of mankind, rather than the hallowed past of an ethnic community.[95] Reaffirming the Prophetic ideal of Judaism as a world-historical vocation, in his essay 'Religion and Zionism' Cohen once again cautions against a sectarian concept of the Jewish God, counselling that 'Judaism and its basic teachings are not reserved alone for the Jewish people', that the Zionist recourse to Jewish exceptionalism denies the One God of Messianic mankind preached by the Prophets.[96] Since the Jew dwells within history and, like Herder, articulates a vision of humanity immanent to its unfolding, the liberal Jew interprets the 'entire historical world as the future abode of our religion', and it is this future alone which 'we acknowledge as our true home'.[97] As Brody argues, for Cohen 'Israel only *becomes* itself in exile. It is defined only by its Teaching and its task', just as Job suffers 'for the sake of *others*'.[98]

As Michael Meyer points out, this universalization of the messianic vision, which is especially associated with German liberal Judaism of the mid to late nineteenth century, had already found a forceful articulation in the writings of Mendelssohn. In his *Jerusalem*, Mendelssohn formulated a mission for Jews in the modern world: he defined them as a people chosen by Providence to call unadulterated ideas of God continually to the attention of humankind.[99]

We shall find a similar defence of the liberal Jewish ethical task in Cassirer's writings on Judaism in the next chapter. In considering Cassirer's philosophy of symbolic forms, we shall be alert to its continuity with the idealizing hermeneutics of Cohen's liberal Judaism. The philosophy of history which buttresses Cassirer's philosophy of symbolic forms, moreover, suggests the formative influence on Cassirer's philosophy of *Wissenschaft des Judentums'* counter-historical energies.

Notes

1 Cohen's place in intellectual history is, however, being reappraised. As Gregory Moynahan comments, 'as new research on Cohen has progressed . . . the tremendous importance of his work, and the severe limitation of his designation simply as a "neo-Kantian" has become clear'. See G.B. Moynahan. 2003. 'Hermann Cohen's *Das Prinzip der Infinitesimalmethode*, Ernst Cassirer, and the Politics of Science in Wilhelmine Germany', *Perspectives on Science* 11(1), 41.

2 D. Novak. 1981. 'Universal Moral Law in the Theology of Hermann Cohen', *Modern Judaism* 1, 101.

3 See A.S. Bruckstein. 2004. 'Introduction', in H. Cohen, *Ethics of Maimonides*, trans. A.S. Bruckstein, Madison, Wisc.: The University of Wisconsin Press, xxii.

4 L. Strauss. 1995. 'Introduction', in H. Cohen, *Religion of Reason out of the Sources of Judaism*, Atlanta: Scholars Press, xxiii. David Myers suggests that Cohen was 'alternately mentor, polemical target, and intellectual foil to the extraordinary cadre of German-Jewish intellectuals – e.g. from Martin Buber and Franz Rosenzweig to Gershom Scholem and Walter Benjamin – that has attracted so much attention in recent decades'. Myers invokes Scholem's account – in *Walter Benjamin: The Story of a Friendship* – of how he and Benjamin attended Cohen's classes at the Lehranstalt für die Wissenschaft des Judentums in Berlin, admired him, and read his Kantian writings carefully. See D.N. Myers. 2001. 'Hermann Cohen and the Quest for Protestant Judaism', *Leo Baeck Institute Yearbook* 46, 195.

5 H. Liebeschütz. 1968. 'Hermann Cohen and his Historical Background', *Leo Baeck Institute Yearbook* 13, 3.

6 A. Bernstein-Nahar. 1998. 'Hermann Cohen's Teaching Concerning Modern Jewish Identity', *Leo Baeck Institute Yearbook* 43(1), 27.

7 Liebeschütz, 'Hermann Cohen and his Historical Background', 4.

8 Cited in Myers, 'Hermann Cohen and the Quest for Protestant Judaism'. See H. Cohen. [first published 1880], 'Ein Bekenntnis in der Judenfrage', in Bruno Strauß (ed.), 1924. *Hermann Cohens Jüdische Schriften*, vol. 2, New York: Arno Press, 73.

9 Novak, 'Universal Moral Law in the Theology of Hermann Cohen', 104. For a discussion of 'Die Nachstenliebe im Talmud' as an early illustration of Cohen's idealizing methodology, and as a reappraisal of the concept of Jewish election that seeks to demonstrate how Jewish national feeling can and does lead Jews to a universal commitment to a common humanity, see S.H. Brody. 2010. 'Reason, Revelation, and Election: Hermann Cohen and Michael Wyschogrod', *Toronto Journal for Jewish Thought* 1, 4.

10 Eva Jospe, 'Introduction', in H. Cohen. 1971. *Reason and Hope: Selections from the Jewish Writings of Hermann Cohen*, trans. E. Jospe, New York: W.W. Norton and Company, 15.

11 Liebeschütz, 'Hermann Cohen and his Historical Background', 6.

12 H. Cohen. 1980. 'Heinrich Heine und das Judentum', (1867) in *Jüdische Schriften II*, 2–3, 5.

13 Bruckstein, 'Introduction', xxiii.

14 See G. Scholem. 1997. 'What is Judaism' (1974), in G. Scholem, *On the Possibility of Jewish Mysticism in our Time and Other Essays*, trans. J. Chipman, Philadelphia: The Jewish Publication Society, 115.

15 J. Derrida and M. Ron. 1991. 'Interpretations at War: Kant, the Jew, the German', *New Literary History* 22(1), 43.

16 Derrida and Ron, 'Interpretations at War', 48.

17 Derrida and Ron, 'Interpretations at War', 54.

18 Derrida and Ron, 'Interpretations at War', 55.

19 Derrida and Ron, 'Interpretations at War', 59.

20 Derrida and Ron, 'Interpretations at War', 69.

21 D.N. Myers. 2003. *Resisting History: Historicism and its Discontents in German-Jewish Thought*, Princeton, NJ: Princeton University Press, 42.

22 A. Mittleman. 2003. 'Introduction', in '"The Jew in Christian Culture" by Hermann Cohen: An Introduction and Translation', *Modern Judaism* 23, 54.

23 Mittleman, 'Introduction', in '"The Jew in Christian Culture" by Hermann Cohen', 55.

24 Mittleman, 'Introduction', in '"The Jew in Christian Culture" by Hermann Cohen', 55.

25 H. Cohen. 2004. 'The Significance of Judaism for the Religious Progress of Humanity', trans. A. Mittleman, *Modern Judaism* 24(1), 44.

26 Cohen, 'The Significance of Judaism for the Religious Progress of Humanity', 44.

27 Cohen, 'The Jew in Christian Culture', 66.

28 For an illuminating discussion of Hermann Cohen's neglected theory of the virtues as indispensable to a principled ethical life, see P.A. Schmid. 2005. 'Hermann Cohen's Theory of Virtue', in R. Munk (ed.), *Hermann Cohen's Critical Idealism*, Amsterdam: Springer, 231–258.

29 Mittleman, 'Introduction', in '"The Jew in Christian Culture" by Hermann Cohen', 56.

30 Mittleman, 'Introduction to "The Significance of Judaism for the Religious Progress of Humanity"', 36.

31 Mittleman, 'Introduction to "The Significance of Judaism for the Religious Progress of Humanity"', 37.

32 Cohen, 'The Significance of Judaism for the Religious Progress of Humanity', 42.

33 Cohen, 'The Significance of Judaism for the Religious Progress of Humanity', 55.

34 Cohen, 'The Jew in Christian Culture', 63.

35 R. Koselleck. 2002. 'The Anthropological and Semantic Structure of "Bildung"', in *The Practice of Conceptual History, Timing History, Spacing Concepts*, trans. S. Presner with others, Stanford: Stanford University Press, 184–185.

36 Koselleck, 'The Anthropological and Semantic Structure of "Bildung"', 181–182.

37 Schmid, 'Hermann Cohen's Theory of Virtue', 243.

38 Cohen, 'The Jew in Christian Culture', 62.
39 Cohen, 'The Significance of Judaism for the Religious Progress of Humanity', 44.
40 Cohen, 'The Jew in Christian Culture', 67.
41 Cohen, 'The Jew in Christian Culture', 67.
42 J. Ballan. 2010. 'Dialogic Monologue: Hermann Cohen's Philosophy of Prayer', *Toronto Journal of Jewish Thought* 1, 4.
43 Cohen, 'The Jew in Christian Culture', 71.
44 Schmid, 'Hermann Cohen's Theory of Virtue', 246.
45 Cohen, 'The Jew in Christian Culture', 71.
46 Cohen, 'The Significance of Judaism for the Religious Progress of Humanity', 48.
47 Ballan, 'Dialogic Monologue', 5.
48 Jospe, 'Introduction', in Cohen, *Reason and Hope*, 27.
49 H. Cohen, 'The Style of the Prophets', in Cohen, *Reason and Hope*, 107–108.
50 Cohen, 'The Style of the Prophets', 109.
51 Cohen, *Religion of Reason out of the Sources of Judaism*, 145–147.
52 Ballan, 'Dialogic Monologue', 4.
53 Cohen, *Religion of Reason out of the Sources of Judaism*, 148–149.
54 Cohen, 'The Style of the Prophets', 116. Brody, 'Reason, Revelation, and Election', 4.
55 Cohen, 'The Style of the Prophets', 109–110.
56 Cohen, 'The Style of the Prophets', 115.
57 Cohen, 'The Style of the Prophets', 110.
58 Cohen, *Religion of Reason out of the Sources of Judaism*, 241–242.
59 Cohen, 'The Style of the Prophets', 115.
60 Cohen, 'The Style of the Prophets', 116.
61 Cohen, 'The Style of the Prophets', 116.
62 Cohen, *Religion of Reason out of the Sources of Judaism*, 149.
63 Cohen, *Religion of Reason out of the Sources of Judaism*, 234.
64 Cohen, *Religion of Reason out of the Sources of Judaism*, 234.
65 Brody, 'Reason, Revelation, and Election: Hermann Cohen and Michael Wyschogrod', 7.
66 Cohen, *Religion of Reason out of the Sources of Judaism*, 243.
67 Cohen, 'The Style of the Prophets', 114.
68 Cohen, 'On Messianism', in Cohen, *Reason and Hope*, 119.
69 Cohen, 'On Messianism', 120.
70 Cohen, 'On Messianism', 120.
71 Cohen, 'On Messianism', 120–121.
72 Cohen, 'The Style of the Prophets', 118.
73 Cohen, 'The Style of the Prophets', 118–119.
74 Cohen, 'The Style of the Prophets', 119.
75 Cohen, 'The Messianic Idea', in Cohen, *Reason and Hope*, 126.
76 Cohen, 'The Messianic Idea', 127.
77 Cohen, *Religion of Reason out of the Sources of Judaism*, 249–250.
78 Cohen, *Religion of Reason out of the Sources of Judaism*, 249–250.
79 Meyer. 'German Jewish Thinkers Reflect on the Future of the Jewish Religion', 8–9.
80 For a redacted version of the Cohen/Buber debate in English with helpful biographical notes, see P.R. Mendes-Flohr and J. Reinharz (eds). 1980. *The Jew in the Modern World, a Documentary History*, Oxford: Oxford University Press, 448–453.

81 Mendes-Flohr and Reinharz (eds), *The Jew in the Modern World*, n.1, 452, and see also D. Novak. 2005. 'Hermann Cohen on State and Nation: A Contemporary Review', in R. Munk (ed.), *Hermann Cohen's Critical Idealism,* Amsterdam: Springer, 259–282.

82 Mendes-Flohr and Reinharz (eds), *The Jew in the Modern World*, 448–449.

83 H. Cohen, 'An Argument against Zionism: A Reply to Dr. Martin Buber's Letter to Hermann Cohen', in Cohen, *Reason and Hope*, 167.

84 Cohen, 'An Argument against Zionism', 166.

85 Cohen, 'An Argument against Zionism', 168.

86 Cohen, 'An Argument against Zionism', 169.

87 Cohen, 'An Argument against Zionism', 170.

88 Novak, 'Hermann Cohen on State and Nation', 268–270.

89 Cohen, 'An Argument against Zionism', 168.

90 Cohen, 'An Argument against Zionism', 169.

91 Cohen, 'An Argument against Zionism', 166, 169.

92 Cohen, 'An Argument against Zionism', 167.

93 Cohen, 'An Argument against Zionism', 167.

94 Cohen, 'An Argument against Zionism', 167.

95 Cohen, 'An Argument against Zionism', 170.

96 Cohen, 'Religion and Zionism', in *Reason and Hope*, 171.

97 Cohen, 'An Argument against Zionism', 170.

98 Brody, 'Reason, Revelation, and Election', 6.

99 Meyer, 'German Jewish Thinkers Reflect', 5.

CHAPTER 5

✳

Ernst Cassirer and the Ethical Legacy of Hermann Cohen

'History as well as poetry is an organ of our self-knowledge, an indispensable instrument for building up our human universe.'

Ernst Cassirer, *An Essay on Man*

'There are structures of Bildung, once conceptualized, which remain effective and stretch across epochs.'

Reinhart Koselleck, 'The Anthropological and Semantic Structure of "Bildung"'

The German Jewish philosopher Ernst Cassirer (1874–1945) was perhaps the greatest representative of the liberal Jewish tradition in philosophy, ethics, and political thought in the twentieth century. Carrying on Hermann Cohen's public-intellectual efforts on behalf of the German Jewish community, Cassirer was Cohen's greatest disciple and supporter, consistently defending his philosophical legacy and unique contribution to German philosophy and Jewish thought. Cassirer was arguably Germany's pre-eminent philosopher of the early twentieth century until the ascendancy of Heidegger. A polymath with wide-ranging interests, he contributed to fields as diverse as the philosophy of science, the history of ideas, linguistics, aesthetics, legal theory, the study of myth, literary history, and Renaissance studies. As John Michael Krois observes, Cassirer had a significant influence on the work of the art historian Erwin Panofsky, the theologian and existentialist philosopher Paul Tillich, the aesthetician Susanne Langer, the Renaissance scholar Paul Oskar Kristeller, and, although unacknowledged by him, the famous literary critic Mikhail Bakhtin.[1] Yet Cassirer's breadth of interests has complicated his philosophical reception. Still known primarily as a neo-Kantian epistemologist and philosopher of culture, Cassirer has been consistently criticized for lacking metaphysical profundity and a normative ethical position. The suspicion lingers that Cassirer is more the philosophical proponent of a liberal, acculturated German Jewish 'worldview' than an original thinker.

Edward Skidelsky's recent intellectual biography of Cassirer, *Ernst Cassirer: The Last Philosopher of Culture* (2008), is exemplary in this regard. Skidelsky criticizes Cassirer's philosophy for being relativistic and indeterminate, and for lacking a fixed conception of human nature, a philosophical stance he deems irreconcilable with Cassirer's normative defence of inalienable human rights.[2] He indicts Cassirer's signature philosophy of symbolic forms as placid, conciliatory, and divorced from social reality. Indeed, according to Skidelsky, it is only thanks to Cassirer's friendship with the German Jewish art historian Aby Warburg, who analysed myth as a perennially dangerous force in contemporary mass culture, that Cassirer's philosophy became something more than a 'piece of elegant escapism'.[3] Skidelsky goes on to suggest that Cassirer's philosophy can be read as a 'characteristically Jewish attempt' to preserve the liberal ideal of culture under increasingly hostile conditions, a 'rearguard action' on behalf of a 'vanishing civilization'.[4] Echoing George Mosse's lament for the 'noble illusion' of German Jewish *Bildung* in *German Jews Beyond Judaism*, Skidelsky caricatures Cassirer as a naïvely optimistic and politically ineffective liberal German Jew: this 'German who wasn't really a German, this Jew who wasn't really a Jew, this man of the eighteenth century adrift in the twentieth' who even as late as 1944 could only see man 'in the light of his cultural products' rather than the 'darkness of his earthly struggle'.[5] According to Skidelsky, it was culture, not politics, that remained for Cassirer the supreme forum of self-expression and self-liberation, indicative of an 'apoliticism' that reflects the indifference of Germans, and particularly German Jews, to a public sphere that was by and large closed to them.[6] Reprising an all too common allegorical reading of German Jewish history, Skidelsky indicts Cassirer's 'failure' to comprehend the menace of the age as not just that of an individual, 'but of an entire cultural tradition'.[7] While Cassirer's universal philosophy spanning the breadth of human civilization was a 'humane and happy dream' that casts a reproachful shadow on our present age, we can only lament his symptomatic failure to ground his admirably liberal political convictions in his philosophy of culture.[8]

Skidelsky's searching critique of Cassirer's philosophy of symbolic forms as a philosophical expression of his aestheticism demonstrates the resilience of a dismissive social-historical critique of German Jewish attempts at cultural assimilation, of which Cassirer's mien and thought is held to be representative.[9] Skidelsky invokes much earlier criticisms made by Leo Strauss in his review of Cassirer's posthumously published final work *The Myth of the State* (1946). While noting Cassirer's attachment to the Enlightenment doctrine of the Rights of Man, Strauss argues that a more adequate challenge to those philosophies that favour the political myths of our time, such as Heidegger's and Spengler's, would not have been 'an inconclusive discussion of the myth of the state, but a radical transformation of the philosophy of symbolic forms into a teaching whose center is moral philosophy, that is, something like a return to Cassirer's teacher Hermann Cohen, if not to Kant himself'. For how, Strauss asked, can 'Cassirer challenge the aestheticism of the romantic revolt against the enlightenment if aestheticism is the soul of his own doctrine?'[10] In a 1956 memorial lecture for Kurt Riezler, delivered before the graduate faculty of the New School for Social Research, Strauss intensified his criticism of Cassirer: Cassirer at the Davos debate with Martin Heidegger had represented the 'established academic position'; he was a distinguished professor of philosophy but 'no philosopher', erudite and lucid but lacking in sensitivity to genuine philosophical and ethical problems. As Peter Eli Gordon remarks, when contemplating Heidegger's charismatic power Strauss felt that Cassirer embodied 'the retreat of modern liberalism into political quietism and its abandonment of philosophy's highest ethical mission'. Cassirer, Strauss lamented, had transformed Cohen's philosophical system, the centre of which was ethics, into a 'philosophy of symbolic forms in which ethics had silently disappeared'.[11]

Cassirer's philosophy has been interpreted not only as lacking anthropological norms but also as offering an impoverished ethics centred on the transcendental subject. In his fine recent introduction to Emmanuel Levinas's writings on humanism, Richard Cohen remarks that Levinas's post-war engagement with Cassirer's thought is tempered by his dissatisfaction with Cassirer's focus on cultural forms as indispensable media of ethical formation. Cohen argues that for Levinas *pace* Cassirer, 'moral obligation effects a deformalization more pressing, more immediate, than the immediacy of self-awareness'. Levinas felt that Cassirer's philosophy of culture 'inevitably falls into the very cultural relativism of which it accused Heidegger. It loses its capacity of moral judgment'.[12]

Peter Eli Gordon's monumental study *Continental Divide: Heidegger, Cassirer, Davos* (2010) offers a much more sympathetic and balanced appraisal of the ethical dimensions of Cassirer's philosophy, noting Cassirer's idealistic investment in the 'expressive spontaneity of the human mind', and his ethos, influenced by the Warburg Institute, of 'cultural pluralism and renaissance humanism'.[13] He notes *pace* Strauss that Cassirer did in fact recognize the crucial place of religion within his own philosophy, and that Cassirer's claims for Judaism as a demythologizing, ethical religion, was a 'direct homage to Hermann Cohen', qualifying Strauss's 'brittle contrast' between Cohen's 'theological ethico-political fortitude and Cassirer's ostensibly superficial retreat into aestheticism'.[14] Yet despite his comprehensive analysis of Cassirer's political, ethical, and religious commitments, Gordon insists that the famous 1929 Davos encounter between Cassirer and Heidegger 'remained confined to matters of philosophy alone'. Gordon avers that the Davos debate was not essentially adversarial, and that the interpreter should first acknowledge the 'philosophical world' that Heidegger and Cassirer shared before reading the encounter as a political 'allegory'.[15]

In order to consolidate his more irenic view of the philosophical substance of the Davos encounter, Gordon reconstructs Cassirer as a 'philosophical as well as cultural political moderate' whose 'progressivist doctrine' required that 'modernity be understood as both a *triumph over* and a *displacement* of myth'.[16] Evident in all of Cassirer's writings was a tone of 'rational moderation, even in the midst of political conflict'.[17] Gordon goes on to suggest that it was only later, as an exile, that Cassirer 'ramified' his philosophy of human spontaneity into a politicized critique of Heidegger's philosophical fatalism and privative metaphysical concerns.[18] Gordon rounds off his characterization by describing Cassirer as a 'private man who was typically reticent about his felt attachment to religion' but whose later writings defending Judaism were motivated out of a 'fortified solidarity with the émigré community' and can thus be considered a 'belated paean' to Judaism as a religion of 'ethical idealism'.[19] Cassirer's mature defence of Judaism, a 'direct homage to Hermann Cohen', should be read according to Gordon as a '*spiritual return* to Marburg neo-Kantianism, endorsing its religion, if not its philosophy'.[20] I think Gordon's secularist reading of Cassirer underestimates the latter's thoroughgoing embrace of Cohen's passionate liberal Jewish idealism from a relatively early stage in his philosophical career. Swayed by a residual image of Cassirer as an ineffective liberal, Gordon could have been more attentive to Cassirer's energetic ethos of *Bildung*, with its solicitude for the worldly formation of character and its concern for the principled virtues of friendship. Reading Cassirer's testaments to Cohen as a homage, Gordon is insufficiently sensitive to the exemplary ethical and political power of Cassirer's many expressions of abiding loyalty to the memory of Cohen, in which the desire to affirm the dignity, virtue, and creative contribution of a besieged German Jewish intellectual takes precedence over the impersonal asseveration of philosophical doctrine, a theme we will encounter in Arendt's critical comportment.[21] As I shall argue, Cassirer's willingness to communicate the philosophical idealism he shared with Cohen to a variety of potentially hostile publics exemplifies the ideal, as Koselleck describes it, of '*Persönlichkeitsbildung* ("building of character"): the demand to . . . conduct one's life in society in a responsible way', a demand that at one time 'initiated the concept of *Bildung*'.[22]

In this chapter and the next I argue that critics have generally overlooked the extent to which Cassirer's philosophy is a faithful continuation of Hermann Cohen's liberal conception of Judaism, reprising Cohen's vigorous counter-historical articulation of Judaism as a superior ethical monotheism with an important world-historical mission to propound ethical ideals such as the unity and universality of God. I analyse the not infrequent passages in Cassirer's oeuvre where he explicitly espouses Cohen's religious humanism, that is, Cohen's projection of a cosmopolitan humanity to come as adumbrated by the Jewish Prophets. As we shall see, Judaism plays a privileged role in Cassirer's philosophy of symbolic forms because it offers a regulative ideal for the formation of the individual moral subject, the ethically responsible personality. I argue that Cassirer by no means shied away from articulating a politicized, historically aware Jewish ethics that implicitly repudiated Christian supercessionist arguments for the obsolescence of Judaism but also remained focused on the clear and present dangers of authoritarianism, nationalism, and racism. Cassirer held dear the notion that Judaism, in its ideal-historical passage from sectarian tribalism to universal monotheism, from the externalities of ritual and dogma to the inward cultivation of ethical principles and transcendent ideals, has a special role to play in cultivating our personal freedom and moral imagination. In his philosophy of symbolic forms, together with his substantial body of political, occasional, and ethical writings, Cassirer can be situated, I would contend, as a loyal heir to the confrontational political animus and counter-historical vigour of the *Wissenschaft des Judentums* movement.

In focusing on the prominence of Jewish ethics in Cassirer's oeuvre, I seek to redress a significant gap in Cassirer scholarship. Scholars of his work have generally failed to acknowledge his sincere readiness to continue the bold public-intellectual activity and liberal Jewish philosophy of Cohen, his close friend and mentor. Such an omission is all the more puzzling given Cassirer's evident devotion to Cohen. The two had a close friendship that coincided with the mature Cohen's energetic ecumenical activism and theological writings on behalf of Judaism. The friendship also matured during a particularly fertile period in Cohen's religious thought after his resignation from the University of Marburg in 1912, a period that culminated in Cohen's magnum opus, *The Religion of Reason from the Sources of Judaism*, published posthumously in 1919.

I stress that Cassirer's public appearances and political interventions of the late Weimar era were closely aligned with his struggle to stoutly defend not only Cohen's philosophical reputation but also the often excoriated role of German Jewish intellectuals in German public life. I am indebted to Toni Cassirer's memoir *My Life with Ernst Cassirer* (completed 1948, published 1981), which poignantly evokes Ernst's repeated attempts, most notably in his famous 1929 debate with Heidegger in Davos, Switzerland, to prevent Cohen's neo-Kantian epistemological and ethical idealism from being historically erased by a resurgent tide of exclusionary German nationalism and its complicit philosophical counterpart, Heidegger's *Lebensphilosophie*. In Chapter 6 I contend that Cassirer's counter-historical interventions into German *Geistesgeschichte* of the late 1920s and early 1930s, including his resolute defence of the pan-European Enlightenment and the German *Aufklärung*, constituted an attempt to challenge a parochial and exclusivist interpretation of German intellectual history and to warn Germany of the potential danger that illiberal ideology posed to its cosmopolitan heritage.

Ernst Cassirer's Defence of Hermann Cohen

One of the most prominent themes of Ernst Cassirer's wife Toni Cassirer's fascinating memoir *Mein Leben mit Ernst Cassirer* is Ernst Cassirer's close and devoted friendship with Hermann Cohen, for whom, according to Toni, he had 'extraordinary love and admiration'.[23] In a section of the memoir devoted to their relationship, Toni Cassirer (*née* Bondie, a distant cousin of Ernst's) remarks that in only one instance, in the case of Cohen, did she have the impression that the independently minded and intellectually robust Ernst Cassirer stood under someone's 'influence'.[24] In a 1902 letter to Toni, a young Ernst Cassirer wrote that he felt better understood and more justly judged by the sixty-year-old Cohen than by many others.[25]

It was Cohen, Toni Cassirer argues, who helped to make Cassirer aware of the extent of anti-Semitism in late Wilhelmine Germany, a realization strengthened by Cassirer's failed attempts, which had been enthusiastically supported by Cohen, to become a university lecturer in the decade before the First World War. Cohen's vulnerable and anomalous situation, as the only openly Jewish Ordinarius for Philosophy in Germany, was emblematic to Cassirer of the besieged status of German Jewish intellectuals in Germany and the fragility of the achievements of the Marburg School of neo-Kantian philosophy founded by Cohen.

According to Toni Cassirer, the pursuit of a Habilitation was not important in itself to Ernst Cassirer but because it would help him to propagate Cohen's ideas, which everywhere faced tremendous opposition.[26] For Ernst Cassirer, she writes, Cohen represented the very embodiment of philosophy ('Verkörperung der Philosophie'), impressing Cassirer not just as a scholar but as an imposing yet humane and forgiving personality who would allow no formalities to stand in the way of an open and unreserved friendship with the younger Ernst Cassirer. In Cohen, Ernst Cassirer truly experienced the unity of a man with his work ('Erlebnis-Einheit des Menschen mit seinem Werk'), a unification of theory and practice, intellectual and ethical comportment, which suggests that Ernst Cassirer held Cohen up as a luminous model of *Bildung*. Cohen, Cassirer writes to Toni, was untiring in his rigorous critical demands concerning the matter at hand, but also full of the warmest understanding and tender sympathy for the idiosyncrasies and flaws of each individual.[27]

To the younger Cassirers, the fiery and argumentative Cohen presented himself as much in the aspect of an 'Old Testament Prophet' as a modern philosopher.[28] In his notes, according to Toni, Ernst described Cohen reverentially as the 'teacher of the Ideal' ('Lehrer im Ideal'), since it is the 'Idea', the very 'task of philosophy itself', which Cohen evoked in such an exemplary manner.[29] Toni remarks how both she and Ernst were deeply affected by Cohen's dedication to Judaism, the way in which he was entirely bound to Jewish tradition and wholeheartedly identified with the suffering of the Jewish people wherever it occurred. The son of a Jewish teacher and cantor at the local synagogue in Coswig, central Germany, Cohen remained closely attached to his Jewish origins and was deeply and empathetically pained by the persecution of Jews in Poland and Russia. On his deathbed in 1918, Ernst and Toni celebrated Passover with Cohen, and were greatly moved by Cohen's sudden, angry, yet ultimately prescient denunciation of the anti-Semitic lie of ritual murder, which he lambasted as an attempt to 'destroy' the Jews; on his deathbed Cohen solemnly exhorted the Cassirers to keep steadfastly to their religion.[30]

Ernst Cassirer's 1918 eulogy at the gravesite of Hermann Cohen lends credence to Toni's account of the special bond between the young Ernst and the elder Cohen, and to the possibility that Cohen's fierce dedication to Judaism, manifested in his prolific religious writings and his ongoing ecumenical dialogue with Christian scholars, had a transformative impact upon Ernst Cassirer. We should note that the context of Ernst's heartfelt eulogy was a funeral service at which former non-Jewish colleagues of Cohen in the philosophy faculty of the University of Berlin were notoriously absent, lending a particular urgency, pathos, and broader political significance to his testament.

Cassirer insisted to the gathered audience that he was speaking not only as a commentator but as Cohen's 'student and friend'. Cassirer defied the gloom by insisting that history itself would unequivocally acknowledge the significance of Cohen's work in the course of time.[31] Well before meeting him, Cassirer had been enthralled by Cohen's seminal books on Kant; for what was illuminated there, what shone forth through the pages of those conceptually difficult books, was the image of a great personality (*großen Persönlichkeit*) with an unconditional sense for the truth and a bold and unique approach to philosophical interpretation.[32] When first acquainted, Cassirer was almost too shy to approach the man that represented so much to him, whom he had viewed for so long as the very embodiment of the true substance of philosophy.[33] However, the warmth that Cohen exuded had quickly broken through all the barriers of convention that separate a young and mature man, a teacher and student, resulting in a deep and intimate friendship of more than twenty years standing.[34]

That friendship, remarks Cassirer, has truly disclosed the essence of Hermann Cohen, for the secret of this remarkable man is the incomparable unity of his will and intellect, of his human and spiritual existence ('menschlichen und . . . geistigen Seins').[35] Cohen's thinking was permeated by a powerful and unshakable exertion of will, and his temperament and personal preferences were immediately discernible even in his asseverations of pure thought.[36] While still penetrating the depths of Cohen's difficult prose, Cassirer relates that the 'form of the thinker' (*Gestalt des Denkers*) was already clear from the beginning in an unconditional sense for the truth, a boldness and idiosyncrasy of interpretation, and the courage (*Mut*) to pursue that interpretation to its last, systematic consequences.[37] Cassirer's affective hermeneutics is appropriate because in Cohen's thought the ethical and the critical, the philosophical and the religious, cannot ultimately be divorced from one another. Cohen sought the highest, ultimate abstractions that thought is capable of precisely so that he could understand and ground his fundamental ethical-religious impulses (*sittlich-religiösen Grundtrieb*).[38] Cohen knew of no theory divorced from life, he united the enthusiasm and passion of the ethicist (*Ethiker*) with the most refined critical reflection; his doctrines evolved from life and immediately re-entered the stream of life, while on the other hand the fundamental laws of truth determined his interpretation and construction of ethics. The idealism of the concept was for Cohen identical to the idealism of the act; even where he spoke as a logician and dialectician, he knew of no theory that could be divorced from lived existence; all that was achieved by the pure activity of his thought exceeded intellectual limitations and sought to be tested in relation to the great national and social problems of the time. For Cohen there could be no rigorous distinction between theory and praxis, since theory sought not merely to describe and represent, but possessed the very power of shaping and transforming reality itself (*Gestaltung und Umgestaltung der Wirklichkeit*).[39]

It is from this holistic vantage point, Cassirer suggests, that one must understand the deep inner affinity between Cohen's religious and philosophical development, between his concept of God (*Gottesbegriff*) and his concept of truth. Nowhere is this inner affinity of the ethical and epistemological, the religious and the philosophical, more pellucid for Cassirer than in Cohen's posthumously published religious-philosophical work *Religion of Reason out of the Sources of Judaism* (1919), of whose existence, Cassirer poignantly admits, he had only just become acquainted some weeks earlier. Goethe once remarked, Cassirer reflects, that wherever faith in the one God manifests itself in history, it is spiritually uplifting, because it refers Man back to the unity of his being. This is how Cohen understood monotheism. For Cohen the idea of God was the means by which the pure concept of humanity and the idea of the ethical personality (*sittlichen Persönlichkeit*) could be developed and brought to completion.[40]

Cassirer suggests that in the correlation of the concept of God and the ethical personality, Cohen recalled a passage in the Second Book of Moses, a passage that no one other than Cohen has ever read and explicated in such depth.[41] In response to Moses' anxious query as to how God should be named if the suspicious populace inquires of him, God magnificently replies 'I am that I am. Say to them, the "I am" has sent me to you'.[42] Cassirer remarks that it is this final and supreme abstraction of the 'I', this comprehension of the person free of all empirical contingency, this overcoming of everything sensuous and figuratively represented through the pure intellectual principle of personality, that is at the root of the 'unique power of monotheism and its world-historical mission' ('*die eigentliche Kraft des Monotheismus und seine weltgeschichtliche Mission*').[43] While pantheism may express the unity of the world as the unity of God's attributes, only monotheism penetrates into the very kernel of the 'I', into the principle and genesis of human self-consciousness, so that through a relational consciousness of self the meaning and content of the divine can be discovered. In turn, the Jewish Prophets discovered a new God and a new concept of the World (*Weltbegriff*), a new heaven and a new earth; through them, a new concept of humanity (*Begriff der Menschheit*), in all its social, ethical, and religious significance, was developed.[44]

Cassirer reminds his audience of Cohen's love for Germany's *Geistesgeschichte*, its great representatives of cosmopolitan humanism and ethical idealism. As Paul Mendes-Flohr tells us, Cohen, in a defiant speech before the Kant Gesellschaft of Berlin immediately after the outbreak of war, castigated those who would allow the euphoria of war to elevate German warriors and statesmen above German poets and thinkers. Germany, Cohen had proclaimed, 'remains in continuity with the eighteenth century and its cosmopolitan humanity', a statement surely more hortatory than descriptive.[45] Cassirer adverts to the syncretic tendencies of Cohen's humanist philosophy by reminding us that in the *Critique of Judgment* Kant had once remarked that there is no more sublime passage in the Old Testament than the forbidding of image worship. Indeed, Kant's own doctrine relied entirely on non-sensuous and non-visual grounds. Cohen read Kant's philosophy as resting on pure thought, on that which is comprehensible only in thought and in the inner self-activity of the will ('*der inneren Selbsttätigkeit des Willens*').[46] Drawing on Schiller's *Bildung* inflected interpretation of Kant's philosophy as the great teaching of the person's self-formation and the mind's self-activity, of the logical, ethical, and artistic spontaneity of consciousness, Cassirer submits that Cohen's philosophy surpasses even Kant in its emphasis on the priority of activity over passivity, of the independent mind over the sensuous world of things. Cohen insisted on the pure origin and principle of thinking and willing, of artistic and religious consciousness, an origin entirely independent of what is merely inertly 'given' by nature or circumstance.[47]

Cassirer then discusses the religious insight supporting Cohen's critical idealism, his homologous method of genetic analysis or logical reflection upon origins. Just as Cohen's critical idealism posits and demands the concept of the 'Origin' so that through it we can secure what we call Being (*was wir Dasein nennen*) and ground the flux of phenomena in the permanent structures of thought (*in dauernden Gedanken zu befestigen*), so Cohen's metaphysical and religious thought deploys the concept of Creation (*Schöpfung*), so that, as Cohen maintains in *The Religion of Reason from the Sources of Judaism*, all physical and natural phenomena can be traced back to a spiritual origin (*geistigen Urgrund*).[48] In commenting on the cross-cutting significance of Cohen's theory of the dynamic spontaneity of origins, Cassirer evokes the ethos of *Bildung* as described by Koselleck: it is 'open and connectable in many directions', opening 'countless points of connection' between fields of knowledge and ethical discourse, such that 'religion ... history, language ... art, and science' refer to and mutually justify one another in the medium of *Bildung*.[49]

Anticipating his own extensive commentary on the philosophy of history in his later work, Cassirer ruminates on Cohen's exemplary articulation of the ethos of philosophy as a critical *Geistesgeschichte*, the dialogical relationship of philosophy with its history. Cassirer enthuses that while Cohen's greatness as a teacher rested on his fundamental conviction that an educator is independent and encourages that active quality in others, nonetheless he never succumbed to the obstinate ambition to be an 'original' philosopher and inveighed strongly against any form of philosophizing that sought to stand outside the general overview afforded by the great and ongoing historical-systematic work of philosophizing (*geschichtlichen Gesamtarbeit*) within a hermeneutic horizon. Yet on the other hand what fresh and vital immediacy he, Cohen, was able to contribute to this history! Cohen felt, with a modest pride, that he was a part of a great chain of philosophical idealism, a golden chain stretching from Plato, through Descartes, to Leibniz, and Kant. By virtue of this systematic philosophical-historical context, the historical past was completely accessible to Cohen in the plenitude of an immediate present. Cohen never related the 'History' of Philosophy (*Geschichte der Philosophie*), he reported nothing as definitively past and completed; rather he stood in the midst of the very stream of these intellectual phenomena, probing and weighing, evaluating and taking positions. One could disagree with the positions that Cohen took while appreciating that he had opened up a perspective from which the history of philosophy could be mastered afresh and inspired by new energies.[50]

Cassirer's testament to Cohen's historical vigour and its ethical immediacy is consonant with what Mendes-Flohr has described as Cohen's 'fiercely anti-Hegelian historical spirit'. Cohen deemed it as 'both philosophically inane and politically reactionary to view, as Hegel had, the real, empirical world as rational'. Cohen maintained that there was a 'world of difference' between Kant and Hegel, for as Cohen paraphrased Kant, 'what is rational is not actual but ought to become'.[51] As early as 1918 Cassirer was sensitive to the ethical implications of Cohen's counter-history of German and European idealism, as, in the words of Mendes-Flohr, an 'ideal construct meant to disclose the shortcomings of the present reality'.[52] In the posthumously published *The Myth of the State* (1946) Cassirer would pursue a critique of Hegelian historicism in very similar terms, contrasting Kant's self-legislating idealism of the ethical will with Hegel's attempt to reconcile reason and reality by interpreting human history and the given order of things as the true ethical substance.[53]

Cassirer reminds his audience that Cohen not only taught the history of philosophy but was also a vital part of that history, representing its unfolding essence as a concrete, living embodiment.[54] Cohen's version of the history of philosophy was not mere dates and facts, let alone general rubrics and ideological slogans; rather his audience felt the breath of the very spirit (*Geist*) from which the great philosophical systems have emerged and matured.[55] It was by virtue of Cohen's liveliness, personal warmth, and his critique of convention and intellectual constraint, that his principal legacy will not be that of a philosophical doctrine or asserted truth but the creation of an active research community (*Forschungsgemeinschaft*) held together not by its results but by the universal and ideal orientation of its investigations and questioning.[56] Cohen leaves behind no mere doctrine or dogma but rather has shown, through his own illustrious example, how a great human being can discover for himself and for others a new form of being (*Gestalt des Seins*) and life's deeper and richer significance.[57]

Cassirer's Ethico-Political Task

One senses in his 1918 eulogy that Cassirer is willing to accept a quasi-paternal injunction: the ethico-political task of a liberal Jewish philosopher as exemplified by the vigorous personality of Cohen. Cassirer signals that he stands ready to defend the neo-Kantian legacy and reiterate the ethico-political task of the research community established by Cohen; he will defend the ideality of the 'idea' itself as the task of a philosophy of critical idealism, uniting philosophy's logical, ethical, political, and religious enquiries and thus refusing to accede to the fragmentation of philosophy into scientist and metaphysical schools. Cassirer's focus on Cohen's personal qualities and ethical animus, the indissoluble unity of the passionate historical individual and his critical methodology, indicates that Cassirer is ready to continue Cohen's public-political activities, in conversation with German and Jewish audiences, in defence of a liberal conception of Judaism. Cassirer subtly situates himself as the willing heir of a long post-*Wissenschaft des Judentums* struggle to defend the vital role of Judaism in world history and contemporary culture. In conversation with Toni Cassirer's extraordinary testament to the character and ethos of Ernst Cassirer, I will dwell on the ethical qualities and intellectual attributes that made him eminently suitable for the task of continuing Cohen's legacy.

As Toni Cassirer relates in her wonderful memoir *Mein Leben mit Ernst Cassirer*, Ernst Cassirer's intellectual disposition was holistic and affectively inspired; he was not a pure researcher (*rein Wissenschaftler*). His capacious knowledge was not in itself essential to him but was rather the medium (*Rüstzeug*) that Ernst Cassirer needed to ground his ideas.[58] Cassirer, Toni argues, had a powerful elective affinity with Goethe and particularly his humanist *Bildungsideal*, the drive to expand his field of vision, to extend his knowledge into almost all areas so as to secure his judgement and to protect himself from one-sidedness (*vor Einseitigkeit zu schützern*). Cassirer sought to elevate himself above the vicissitudes of personal experience and to distance himself from the transient pull of contemporary events. His harmonious personality and sensitivity to form had the hallmark of Goethe, while his enduring belief in the value of the human personality and his aversion to any violent disturbance in himself or his environment evinced a repugnance for ideological, political, or religious slogans.[59] Nonetheless, while noting, in Nietzsche's sense of the term, Cassirer's 'untimely' formation by virtue of his devotion to Goethe's harmonious worldview, Toni strongly rejects any notion that Cassirer was an elitist or insular (*Weltabgewandter*) intellectual. Such an accusation, she stresses, is completely false: the world in which Cassirer lived and moved was not opposed to ours but richer and deeper.[60]

Toni adduces, as evidence of Cassirer's diverse interests, his intellectual freedom and adventurousness; despite a regular, tranquil work routine, Cassirer travelled regularly, exposing himself to new experiences and excluding nothing as unimportant if it helped him to research and understand something as yet unknown.[61] During one such journey, a trip they took to Paris in 1910, Cassirer enthusiastically related that city's historical and political background to Toni as they passed through streets such as Place de la Bastille and encountered monuments to Robespierre, Danton, and Marat. At that juncture Toni felt how strongly Cassirer's philosophical thought was affected by the immediate present. Reminding us of Cassirer's attention to Cohen's energetic, present centred historical consciousness, Toni suggests that for Cassirer previous epochs were not merely dry products of thought (*Gedankengut*), but rather lived in him and were intimately bound up with the world in which he was situated.[62] It was during this trip, Toni notes, that Cassirer conceived his famous 1932 book *The Philosophy of the Enlightenment*.[63] In the preface to *The Philosophy of the Enlightenment*, Ernst Cassirer stressed that 'no account of the history of philosophy can be oriented to history alone', but should be accompanied by 'philosophical re-orientation and self-criticism'.[64] Gordon aptly describes Cassirer's powerful study of the pan-European Enlightenment as a 'synthetic tribute to the Enlightenment as a living resource for the modern world', as not merely a construction but 'a *retrieval* of Enlightenment philosophy'.[65]

In a remarkable chapter on 'History' in *An Essay on Man* which anticipates that discipline's linguistic turn, Cassirer argues that historical understanding demands not just empirical but symbolic reconstruction, in which the sympathetic historian, engaging with the findings of the linguist and philologian, learns to 'read and interpret' the 'living messages' of the past.[66] Affirming a famous aphorism of Friedrich Schlegel, Cassirer stresses that historical consciousness is also a form of 'prophecy', such that a 'new understanding of the past gives us at the same time a new construction of the future'. Historical inquiry is a 'stimulus to intellectual and social life'. Historical knowledge answers definite questions, which must be given by the past, but these questions are dictated by our intellectual interests, 'our present moral and social needs'.[67] Invoking the *Bildung* tradition's cosmopolitan interest in ethical exemplars and arts of living, Cassirer suggests that historical interpretation should draw our attention to what is 'highly characteristic'. As a discipline attentive to its rhetorical form, history is attuned to the 'historical portrait' of 'personality and character', and to 'intellectual and moral physiognomy'. In the spirit of Mendelssohn Cassirer draws attention to legendary characters that provoke recursive meditation, such as the enigmatic, variously interpreted character of Socrates, one of those world historical figures who ensure the 'process of historical interpretation never comes to a complete standstill'.[68]

Toni Cassirer stresses that far from being a marker of Olympian isolation in a tumultuous present, Ernst Cassirer's *Bildungsideal* expressed his 'unshakeable conviction' that philosophy should never isolate itself as a peremptory meta-discourse, that it should articulate its interests through the sympathetic study of other disciplines, disclosing a relational and pluralist character sensitive to the vulnerability of knowledge formation in a politically polarized world. Significantly, Cassirer cautioned his son Heinz against the isolated pursuit of philosophy and suggested that the specialized disciplines were necessary stages on the way to philosophy; Heinz subsequently agreed to study ancient languages.[69] Cassirer was so convinced of the value of 'humanisticher Bildung' as a process of rounded and gradated education that he only reluctantly agreed to his younger son Georg giving up on ancient languages during his secondary schooling.[70] In late 1934, now living in Sweden, Cassirer gave an interview to a Göteborg newspaper in connection with his forthcoming appointment as a professor of theoretical philosophy at the University of Göteborg. In that interview he candidly regretted that mathematicians, physicians, and astronomers were not regularly invited to philosophy conferences and stressed that knowledge was furthered through interdisciplinary co-operation rather than by the formation of schools of thought. Cassirer lamented the tendency of philosophers to deprecate everything that did not fit into their ready-made systems and expressed regret that they did not show a greater interest in what was going on outside their country's borders.[71] We learn from Toni Cassirer's memoir, moreover, that Cassirer particularly enjoyed his first few months at Yale University in 1941, because there he participated in a general seminar with colleagues from different faculties. This was entirely according to Cassirer's wishes, Toni suggests, since it had always been his desire to unite philosophy with the specialized disciplines.[72]

Cassirer's desideratum for philosophy to play an active role in contemporary culture and knowledge formation was paralleled by a dynamic philosophy of historical interpretation that challenged received histories and was oriented, in the spirit of Cohen, towards redemptive possibilities. As Toni remarks, Cassirer was inspired by Goethe's historical ethos, in which events from different historical epochs, as well as materials from art and one's own life, flow together and unify to form a living background against which the thought of the future starts to emerge (*Gedanke an die Zukunft zu einstehen beginnt*). Only the unproductive human being, Cassirer claimed, complains about the past: the productive historical consciousness looks forward, moulding together what lies behind it, whether it be ten, a hundred, or a thousand years in the past, so as to begin to form itself towards the truly new, thus adumbrating a vision of the future (*Schau der Zukunft*).[73]

While Ernst Cassirer's holistic ethos closely resembles Cohen's idealistic and engaged emphasis on the dialectical interpenetration of scholarship with pressing ethical concerns, Toni Cassirer's memoir makes it clear that Ernst Cassirer's sense of political exigency, his willingness to expose himself and actively defend Jewish intellectuals and Judaism in the German public sphere, was powerfully influenced by their difficult experiences of the First World War and of the intensifying German anti-Semitism of the Weimar era. Anti-Semitic prejudice in the Germany university system meant that, despite being a well-known scholar, Cassirer did not receive an appointment at an independent university in Germany before the First World War. He remained a *Privatdozent* for thirteen years in Berlin until his appointment to the University of Hamburg in 1919.[74] Toni remarks that during this time she cannot remember any member of a Berlin philosophical faculty visiting Ernst's Berlin lectures, with the single exception of the philosopher and aesthetician Max Dessoir. Cassirer was rarely openly challenged in these years; rather, he was simply ignored, or bypassed. Later, when it became difficult to ignore Cassirer's growing international reputation his name would appear on job shortlists, though always ranked second.[75]

However, despite these degrading experiences, Cassirer sought to make a contribution to Germany during the dark days of the First World War. Unable to join the German army, he taught German and literary history at a boys' *Gymnasium* in Berlin and at secondary schools, displaying an enthusiasm for public education in the spirit of Abraham Geiger, Hermann Cohen and Franz Rosenzweig. Everywhere confronted by a 'blind nationalism', particularly pervasive amongst German Jews and regrettably including Cohen himself, and working in a military propaganda section where he had to selectively quote from the French press, Cassirer nevertheless realized that Germany would lose the war two years before it ended. It was under these oppressive conditions that Cassirer composed his book *Freiheit und Form* (1918), salvaging for himself a counter-historical image of the indestructible and immortal Germany, rationalist and republican in its orientation, which was increasingly becoming unrecognizable.[76]

While the advent of the Weimar Republic opened up new opportunities for German Jewish academics, upon their arrival at the University of Hamburg the Cassirers were ominously confronted by the activities of a right-wing student group distributing leaflets which called for the boycott of Jewish professors.[77] In the initial post-war years, with anti-Semitism becoming increasingly open and widespread in Weimar Germany, Toni and her children were subject to an appalling anti-Semitic verbal assault by their neighbours ('*Sie gehören ja alle nach Palästina*'), silently witnessed by complicit spectators, which drew an immediate and sharp epistolary response from Ernst.[78]

Toni's memoir suggests that Ernst Cassirer, following Cohen, responded vigorously to intensifying German Judeophobia and sought to participate actively in the ethical, political, and even legal debates of the Weimar republic.[79] As early as 1916 Cassirer had written a rebuttal of the philosopher Bruno Bauch's claim that neo-Kantianism smacked of 'Jewish formalism', that as a Jew Cohen was unable to appreciate Kant's philosophy, and that the editorial board of the leading journal *Kantstudien* was 'Jew-ridden' (*verjudet*); Cassirer decried 'Bauch's faulty conception of national identity', as Gordon puts it.[80] At the height of Cassirer's philosophical reputation in Germany, the mayor and the senate of Hamburg approached him to give the *Festrede* on 11 August 1928, in order to celebrate the Weimar Republic's 'constitution day'. Toni was energetically opposed to Cassirer speaking as she did not want him to be involved in the politics of the university or to be too closely associated with the widely loathed Weimar Republic, given the general perception that German Jews were already overly involved in the fate of the nation. Cassirer, however, did not share her attitude and felt that as a citizen of a German university, a teacher of German students, and a representative of philosophical idealism, he might be able to have an effect where he was most needed, displaying not a little of that *Mut* that he had ascribed to the late Hermann Cohen.[81] Indeed

Cassirer confided to Toni, in a confrontational mood, that he intended to 'annoy' his opponents. He would demonstrate in his speech, 'The Idea of the Republican Constitution', which I will discuss in more detail in the next chapter, that those ideas which form the basis of the French Revolution did not arise in the hated France, but in Germany itself.[82] Later, in 1929, despite Toni's misgivings, Cassirer became the first openly Jewish Rector of a German University, performing his various public duties with alacrity.[83]

In the winter of 1929, Cassirer participated in a philosophical debate in Davos with a prominent opponent of his Kant-interpretation, a young Martin Heidegger. Heidegger's disdain for social convention, his enmity towards the neo-Kantians, and particularly Cohen, and his inclination to anti-Semitism, were no stranger to the Cassirers, according to Toni Cassirer. At the opening night dinner Toni Cassirer had to sit next to Heidegger, who, Toni Cassirer relates, had resolved to grind Cohen's legacy into the dust and, if possible, to destroy Ernst Cassirer.[84] Much of Toni Cassirer's crafty strategy to defuse the malignant intent of Heidegger centred on pretending she knew nothing of his personal antipathy to Hermann Cohen. Toni Cassirer decided to innocently relate to Heidegger the shameful treatment that Cohen, an exceptional scholar, had received as a Jew, such as the fact that no Berlin philosophy faculty member was present at his burial. Toni Cassirer triumphantly narrates how in this conversation her subsequent descriptions of Ernst Cassirer's academic struggles saw Heidegger soften 'like a biscuit dipped in milk', resulting in a surprisingly cordial debate with Cassirer.[85]

Perhaps Toni could also have added as an example of the exclusionary tactics of Germany's mandarin class that when the Berlin Academy, under the guidance of Wilhelm Dilthey, designed and executed the plan of a comprehensive edition of Kant's works in order to commemorate the two hundredth anniversary of his birth in 1924, Cohen and his School of neo-Kantians were not invited to co-operate. It was Ernst Cassirer who succeeded, in collaboration with his cousin, the publisher Bruno Cassirer, in 'bringing about an edition of equal standing under the aegis of the [Marburg] School', an edition which has kept its place besides the 'volumes of the Academy on the shelves of the great libraries of the world' and was for some time the standard reference work for Kant scholarship in Europe.[86] The title page of what was known simply as the 'Cassirer-edition', since it was published under Cassirer's editorial leadership, paid homage to the late Hermann Cohen, who authored one of its volumes. Cassirer's counter-hegemonic efforts to defend the honour of Hermann Cohen suggests that his 1918 eulogy was a promissory gesture that fortified his lifelong Mendelssohnian dedication to the values of friendship, loyalty and justice to the departed, marginalized and forgotten.

Toni Cassirer's interpretation of the *mise en scène* of the 1929 Davos disputation as an antagonistic and politicized struggle over Cohen's legacy and the value of neo-Kantianism is, to my mind, validated by the contours of the debate itself. Cassirer's opening sally in the debate queried Heidegger's interpretation of neo-Kantianism, which, he feelingly complains using terminology that hints at a broader anti-Jewish context, has become the 'scapegoat [*Sündenbock*] of the newer [existential] philosophy'. Cassirer then smilingly attempts, as he will fruitlessly throughout the debate, to establish some common ground for the discussion with Heidegger, by suggesting that neo-Kantianism should be understood 'functionally rather than substantially', not as a doctrinal system but as a direction for question-posing; in that sense, Cassirer genially suggests, Heidegger too might be an unwitting neo-Kantian.[87]

Heidegger unsmilingly responds to Cassirer's urbane refusal of a friend-enemy distinction, a gesture that was perhaps inspired by the symposium's symbolic purport to promote 'understanding and cooperation between nations'. Disregarding Cassirer, he narrows his definition of the neo-Kantianism promulgated by Cohen to a 'mathematico-physical theory of knowledge', a theory of science that he interprets as unfaithful to Kant's own metaphysical and ontological problematic.[88] Cassirer draws on his 1918 eulogy by replying more firmly that one only understands Cohen correctly if one understands him 'historically, not merely as an epistemologist'.[89] Nor, Cassirer loyally affirms, does he conceive of his own philosophical development as in any way a defection from Cohen.[90] Cassirer quickly transposes the discussion onto an ethical plane, arguing that for Kant the transition from the receptive to the productive powers of the imagination is crucial in breaking through to the *mundus intelligibilis*, in which morality (*das Sittliche*) leads beyond the world of appearances, such that the laws established are now valid for all rational creatures.[91] In the ethical (*Ethische*), Cassirer avers, a 'point is reached which is no longer relative to the finitude of the knowing creature'.[92] Does Heidegger want to renounce 'this entire Objectivity, this form of absoluteness, which Kant advocated in the ethical and theoretical, as well as in the *Critique of Judgment?* Does he want to withdraw completely to the finite creature or, if not, where for him is the breakthrough to this sphere?'[93] As Deniz Coskun has argued in an illuminating discussion of the Davos dispute, for Cassirer Kant's great contribution was to have linked freedom explicitly to our ability to create moral archetypes for evaluating particular and local actions, in which 'Man acts as an intelligent and free personality when he gives meaning to his own life and places himself under the law of (pure) reason, i.e., the categorical imperative'. Cassirer's ethics, aptly described by John Michael Krois as 'personalistic', are derived from the Kantian conception of rational beings as 'persons' whose form of willing indicates that they are ends in themselves, thus worthy of respect.[94] As Krois remarks, personality for Cassirer is 'consistency of action'. Cassirer emphasizes personality because, as he puts it, 'by virtue of this persistence of personality we can count on such a person; we rely on his remaining true to himself and on his arriving at a decision not by mood and arbitrariness but by an autonomous law, by that which he recognizes and acknowledges as right'.[95]

In Cassirer's subsequent 1931 lead essay in *Kant-studien*, which criticizes Heidegger's interpretation of Kant, and which should be read as an extension of the Davos disputation, Cassirer is more sharply critical of Heidegger's aggressively polemical style, which, he remarks, threatens the degeneration of their debate into two interlocutors talking past each other.[96] Cassirer maintains that he simply will not be drawn into a purely polemical discussion, even though Heidegger has been manifestly unjust to neo-Kantianism's historical service to philosophy, and also to the seminal and foundational interpretations that Cohen has given in his books on Kant. Cassirer will avoid the temptation to dispute on this issue since the present argument is not about 'historical justice' (*historische Gerechtigkeit*) but a question of factual and systematic correctness.[97] Cassirer then draws Heidegger's attention to Kant's Platonist confidence in the ideas of reason, which 'burst free from the circle . . . of merely-temporal existence'. As Gordon argues, Cassirer firmly rejects Heidegger's attempts to read Kant's philosophy without reference to the unconditional character of its ethical concepts, since this expunges what Kant himself called a 'wonder in the phenomenal world', the spontaneity of the will. In Kantian ethics, Cassirer reminds Heidegger, one's being is no longer conditioned ultimately by one's sensual being; rather the '"I" is at bottom only what it makes of itself'.[98] Nor was it accidental, as Gordon points out, that at the beginning of this essay Cassirer draws attention to a famous letter of Kant to his friend the German Jewish physician Marcus Herz, his most intimate philosophical companion, thereby deliberately recalling a moment of 'German Enlightenment sociability' reminiscent of Cohen's testament to his friendship with Lange.[99]

It is puzzling, then, that Gordon reads Cassirer's 1931 essay as a movement away from the 'philosophical disagreement' of Davos towards a 'broader and more ramified cultural-historical meaning'.[100] For surely Cassirer interrogated the potentially disastrous ethical implications of Heideggerean finitude in 1929? Was Cassirer's distaste in 1931 for Heidegger's polemical violence and historical 'injustice' not a vigorous extension of his response to Heidegger's mischaracterization of Cohen and neo-Kantianism (a mischaracterization echoing a vituperative disdain for Jewish 'formalism') and refusal of a common discursive ground in 1929, a refusal of conversation Cassirer held to be all too redolent of the rhetorical and institutional exclusion of German Jews from German intellectual life? Moreover, Cassirer's attempt to performatively exemplify his 'ramified' conception of philosophy as dialogical and urbane in spirit seemed evident in 1929 as well as in 1931. I am not convinced that the much discussed 1929 debate should be distinguished from the many occasions on which Cassirer offered a politicized defence of the rich contribution of German Jewish intellectuals to German culture.

Cassirer's public loyalty to Jewish intellectuals such as Hermann Cohen and Aby Warburg, and his resilience in the face of anti-Semitism, continued unabated throughout the Weimar era.[101] While Cassirer was not invited, with one exception, to any of the commemorations of the centenary of Goethe's death in Germany, he did receive and gave a lecture on Goethe at the University of Paris in February 1932.[102] Like Cohen, Cassirer was also politically prescient and vigilant towards anti-Semitism. As soon as Hitler became Chancellor, Cassirer was convinced that the situation was hopeless for people of their background and convictions, that Nazism was not an ephemeral phenomenon, and that its evil effects would live on long into the future.[103] Cassirer was not really prophetic in this instance, Toni remarks; rather, his ongoing research into history and myth, the fruit of his collaboration with the Hamburg based Warburg Institute throughout the 1920s, had taught him the power that such mass movements could have over the minds of men. These insights would culminate in his posthumously published book *The Myth of the State* (1946). Toni had to restrain Cassirer from leaving Germany as soon as possible.[104] After departing for Sweden in 1935 Ernst Cassirer, in conversation with Toni Cassirer, suggested that what had begun in Germany was not simply the persecution of the Jews but an attempt at their complete destruction, for it was in the nature of the National Socialist regime that every opposition to it can and will be broken.[105] After the annexation of Austria in 1938, Cassirer anticipated that Hitler would attack country after country until war with England became inevitable; the Nazi system, he repeatedly commented, cannot suffer stability, it must demonstrate success after success, otherwise it cannot continue.[106]

Yet Cassirer did not meet the Nazi threat with resignation or vacillation. He stood resolute and assured of his principles in the turbulence of the times. He was formed, Toni reminds us, by the 'Goethesche Weltbild'; thus fear played no decisive role in his life.[107] Such was Cassirer's anger at Hitler's notorious pronouncement, 'Recht is, was dem Führer dient' (The Law is whatever serves the Führer), that he wanted every legal scholar in Germany to oppose vigorously this tyrannical edict, for otherwise, as he saw it, 'Germany is lost'. Not a single voice was raised in protest from the legal community.[108] In 1933, Cassirer wanted to write a powerful critique of the National Socialist movement but Toni dissuaded him, as it would endanger their immediate family in Germany as well as other German Jews.[109] While Cassirer refrained from public pronouncements against the Nazis, in a letter of 27 April 1933 he clarified his reasons to the University of Hamburg for leaving his position. The university wished to save itself embarrassment, and so publicized his grounds for leaving as private and health related. In that letter, Cassirer stressed his 'purely principled' solidarity with German Jews, having relinquished his position upon learning of the boycott movement against them. He could only have continued to work at a German university under conditions of collegial equality. He goes on to express his profound sadness over the fate of German Jews.[110] Cassirer also considered advertising his principled resignation to the newspapers only to learn that he had already been relieved of his position. Upon his arrival in Switzerland, as Hansson and Nordin note, Cassirer became one of the first German refugee scholars to form the *Notgemeinschaft deutscher Wissenschaftler im Ausland*, with its objective of placing about '300 unabsorbed intellectuals in the universities of the world'.[111]

Cassirer's unconditional empathy for Jewish persecution was one of his most abiding and resolute principles, perhaps complicating Gordon's suggestion that Cassirer was a 'private man and typically reticent about his felt attachments to religion'.[112] Where Toni was disturbed by the appearance of Jewish refugees in European countries and wondered aloud whether the difficulty Jews had conforming to the behavioural protocols of other countries contributed to anti-Semitism, Cassirer replied bitingly that it was not the 'bad Jews' who had given succour to anti-Semitism, but envy and malice towards the 'good Jews'; like the rest of the world's impoverished masses (*Pöbel*), the bad Jews could have been simply ignored.[113] Where Toni Cassirer suggested that Jews who lost contact with their tradition and converted to Christianity should not be resented, Cassirer, like Cohen before him, was sharply opposed to this form of 'apostasy'. In contrast to his usually tolerant, genial nature, he saw such a drastic step at this historical moment as a fundamental denial of character (*Versagen des Charakters*) which he could in no way excuse. Indeed, even those Jews that Cassirer recognized as inwardly inclined towards Christian doctrine should be well disposed to their fellow Jews for whom Judaism does have a deep significance, and who are persecuted for their beliefs.[114]

There was another form of apostasy that outraged Cassirer, and that was the betrayal of Cohen's friendship and neo-Kantian legacy by recent German converts to the Nazis. Toni relates the episode of Cassirer receiving a letter from Albert Görland, a one-time leftist disciple of Hermann Cohen who had now turned completely and sold his soul to the Nazis in exchange for an academic position, abruptly discovering, as Cassirer put it sardonically in a withering letter of 26 November 1938 to Görland, the 'ideas of 1933'. In that caustic letter, Ernst Cassirer angrily denounced Görland for his traitorous actions in a moment of great danger, for forgetting and denying his relationship to his teacher, his friends, and his earlier convictions. Görland's betrayal was particularly galling to Ernst Cassirer because he, Görland, was not blind like other anti-Semites but could see the situation of the Jews clearly. With acid irony, Cassirer reminded Görland that he once knew what Jews and

Judaism really were; he once recognized what the so-called 'pernicious influence (*verderblichen Einfluß*) of Judaism on German philosophy' had meant for him, a beneficiary of Cohen's tutelage. He, Görland, understood the intellectual achievement of Hermann Cohen, without which he could not have written a single line of his own work. Quoting Cohen to the effect that ethics is truly demonstrated through friendship, Cassirer mordantly asked Görland which version of ethics pertained to his friendship with Cohen?[115]

Even after the outbreak of the Second World War, as Toni Cassirer relates, Cassirer remained steadfast, never vacillating or sceptical. The Jewish problem (*Das Jüdische Problem*), however, was never far from his thoughts, and Cassirer acknowledged that a war would be necessary to overcome Nazi violence.[116]

Cassirer's Prophetic Judaism

After arriving in America in 1941, Cassirer was not simply a grateful refugee, his *Bildungsideal* guaranteeing critical scrutiny of his adopted homeland. He was critical of the overly scholastic method of university study in the United States, which was too prescriptive in terms of what students should read. The American university encouraged students to learn enormous amounts and in depth, but Ernst Cassirer, ever attentive to the need for critical independence and the autonomous cultivation of character, asserted that American students were not learning the important things, such as independent thought ('*selbständige Denken*').[117]

Toni Cassirer relates how Ernst Cassirer became much more sceptical towards the United States over time, wearying of the American pursuit of private happiness, which amounted to a false understanding of the republican spirit of their constitution.[118] Listening attentively to the radio, Cassirer studied propaganda techniques in advertising, remarking that whether it be 'soap' or the idea of a 'master race', 'scouring powder', or 'Jew hatred', all can be conquered by marketing techniques.[119] In 1943, the Cassirers' daughter Anne became a member of the American Jewish committee, reading German newspapers and closely following statistics of Jewish persecution.[120] In preparing his perhaps long suppressed response to Nazism, posthumously published as *The Myth of the State* (1946), Cassirer wanted to give various talks at US universities about its analysis of the political potency of myth before it appeared; he advertised the book by publishing an article-length version of its argument in the popular 'Fortune' magazine.[121]

Despite turning his back on Germany after his departure, by declining Paul Tillich's request to join an effort to reconstruct Germany and encourage democratic movements there, Cassirer refused to blame Germany's moral collapse on perennial national characteristics. Cassirer responded in his usual steadfast manner to the trite idea that one could talk of a specifically German national spirit that had led to Nazism; as Cassirer calmly opined, 'es gibt nur Geist oder Ungeist'.[122]

In a remarkable tribute, 'A Reminiscence of Ernst Cassirer', the rabbi, scholar, and Jewish communal leader Arthur Hertzberg's account of his friendship with Cassirer in the short period before his death in 1945, Hertzberg confirms many elements of Toni Cassirer's portrait of Cassirer as a loyal and politically active Jewish intellectual. Cassirer had come to Columbia in the winter of 1944–1945 as a visiting Professor in the Philosophy Department. Hertzberg, then a young rabbi, was surprised to learn that what he knew of Cassirer's personal history was only a 'half-truth', that is that Cassirer had always been 'very assimilated'.[123] Cassirer surprised Hertzberg in conversation by willingly discussing 'Jewish matters', expressing his regret for not having learnt Hebrew, and mentioning his participation in the scholarly celebration of the 200th anniversary of the birth of Moses Mendelssohn in 1929 as well as his time on the Board of the *Hochschule für die Wissenchaft des Judentums* in the 1920s.[124] Hertzberg came away convinced that Cassirer's regret at not having been more involved in Jewish learning and not having made his Jewish self more central to his entire being came from his 'very depths'.[125]

After learning of Cassirer's sudden death from a heart attack while walking near Columbia campus on 13 April 1945, Hertzberg was asked to deputize as a presiding rabbi, as the presence of a rabbi was consonant with the known wishes of Cassirer. At Cassirer's funeral service, Hertzberg read the traditional psalms and the *El Moleh Rahamim* in Hebrew. A few days later Hertzberg visited his widow, Toni Cassirer, who was kind enough to tell him that it had meant something to Cassirer to have a young rabbi in his last seminar.[126]

Cassirer's loyalty and dedication to Hermann Cohen and his philosophical legacy continued unabated until his death in April 1945. In a testament to Cohen written for the New School's journal *Social Research* in 1943, Cassirer lamented that no German philosophical review or contemporary German philosopher had as much as noted the date of the centennial of Cohen's birth. Sadly, in today's Germany, remarks Cassirer, the 'greatest efforts have been made to forget the name of Hermann Cohen, and to efface or suppress his philosophical work'. Cassirer consoles his readers that these efforts will, however, prove useless: future historians of German philosophy in the second half of the nineteenth century will regard Cohen as one of the greatest representatives of that period.[127] Praising Cohen as an independent and original thinker, Cassirer devotes ample space to his Jewish origins and ethically focused philosophy of religion. Cassirer's remarks are significant as they address Jewish critics of Cohen such as Martin Buber, who claimed that Cohen's conception of God was simply a rationalist philosophical 'idea' rather than the living God of the Jewish faith. By contrast, Cassirer describes how Cohen, who was 'animated by a deep religious faith', finally granted religion autonomy within his philosophical system after an 'inward struggle'.[128]

Cassirer discusses Cohen's recognition that religion is mythical, rather than intellectual or ethical in origin, and that even in its highest stage religion 'can never deny or forget this mythical background'.[129] The roots of the historical existence and real meaning of religion are to be sought in our emotional and imaginative life: religion is neither a system of thought, nor a code of moral demands, but is consistent with our freedom and spontaneity. Religion, for Cohen, in its true and genuine sense, is to be 'proved by the strength of man, not by his weakness or infirmity'.[130] Cohen did not contest or minimize the intimate and indispensable connection between myth and religion, but he saw it as a preliminary step toward a monotheistic conception of God purified of anthropomorphism.[131] Cohen described the evolution of religion from mythical thought and feeling to Prophetic thought and feeling. In the books of the Prophets, in Isaiah and Jeremiah, Cohen found the consummation, the culminating point of religion, in which mythical elements, while not eradicated, are 'overshadowed by a new ideal'.[132] Cassirer situates Cohen's conception of Judaism within a liberal Jewish interpretive framework, in which historical Judaism is not scorned or negated but regenerated by rational interpretation and enlightened ethical ideals.

According to Cassirer, Cohen did not fear the objection that his interpretation of the fundamental ideas of Judaism and of religion in general was not an historical description but an 'idealization of the religious facts'. This is because Cohen was one of the most 'resolute Platonists that has ever appeared in the history of philosophy', firmly rejecting the notion that an idea should be subordinated to phenomena, to the empirical. The 'idea' was for Cohen the *Urbild* rather than the *Abbild*, the archetype and not the mere copy of things. Without such an ideal archetype, we could never understand the true life, the deepest tendency, of religion. Such an idealization is by no means a mutilation or falsification of the historical facts but their purification, and it is 'only in this continual process of purification that the true sense of religious facts can be discovered'. The process of purification requires a sympathetic presupposition that in all 'mature religions true humanity, or, what means the same, true divinity is striving for its development'.[133] Notably, Cassirer quotes Cohen's ecumenically spirited public lecture discussed in the previous chapter, 'The Significance of Judaism for the Religious Progress of Humanity', and its injunction that 'idealization is the first condition – for everyone who confesses a religion and just as much and no less for everyone who wishes to judge its value'.[134]

In his philosophy of symbolic forms Cassirer emulated Cohen's liberal Jewish method of idealizing religion in its monotheistic form, while paying more attention to a phenomenology of the civilizing process. This ethically normative liberal Jewish trajectory from a mythical to a monotheistic conception of time, subjectivity, and ethics correlates closely with the ideal history charted by Cassirer's philosophy of symbolic forms, which traces the development of the moral subject from sensuous entanglement and collective fatalism to the free and spontaneous awareness of the self that engages with, but does not reject, a world of affectively laden images and signs. Take as an example Cassirer's 1921 lecture to the *Kulturwissenshaftliche Bibliothek Warburg*, 'The Concept of Symbolic Form in the Development of the Humanities', the first lecture in which Cassirer elaborated his philosophy of symbolic forms.[135] Cassirer praises Warburg's collection for applying the insights of art history, the study of religion, and myth-history, as well as linguistic and cultural history, to a common and ideally conceived focal point.[136]

Cassirer's problematic is allied to, but different from, Warburg's in that he is not interested in a philological or historicist inquiry as to what particular symbols signify and perform in domains such as art, myth, and language, but in a question motivated by critical idealism: to what extent language as a totality, myth as a totality, and art as a totality bear within themselves the universal character of symbolic formation (*symbolischer Gestaltung*).[137] Cassirer proceeds to give his famous definition of a symbolic form as that energy of the spirit (*Energie des Geistes*) through which an intellectual significance or meaningful content is attached to a concrete, sensuous sign and becomes internally dedicated to it (*innerlich zugeeignet wird*).[138] It is in this sense that we encounter language, the mythical-religious world, and art as symbolic forms, since in all of them our consciousness is not satisfied with the mere reception of phenomena, but permeates and fuses every impression with the free activity (*freien Tätigkeit*) of expression. Thus a human world of self-created signs and images opposes itself to what we are used to calling the objective reality of things, and maintains itself against them with its independent plenitude and originating power.[139]

Cassirer's broad cultural interests, so attuned to the Warburg ethos, are soon engaged with Warburg's question as to how symbolic forms enable the individual to be gradually freed from the enthrallment of daemonic religion and astrological powers. Cassirer argues that language only attains to its specific meaning, its proper achievement as a symbolic form, when it surpasses the mimetic and analogical stages of expression typical of 'primitive' cultures, no longer striving to be a copy of the objective world. Language obtains, through this detachment, a new intellectual content, and a reflexive enhancement of the self and its interior life.[140] In a parallel process and ideal-historical narrative, art progresses from the mimetic stage, which ultimately only produces a restrictive view of the object, to the emergence of mannerism, which colours the object with a characteristic viewpoint. It then progresses to the highest stage, that of 'stylistic' vision, which expresses the true objectivity and free play of the artist.[141] Analogously, the progress of knowledge and the sciences (and Cassirer here has the theoretical achievements of Albert Einstein and the emergence of quantum mechanics in mind, once more a coded defence of Jewish modernism) has been enhanced by the gradual realization that the language of signs it deploys is not mimetic but symbolic, grounded in the 'free spontaneity' of the human spirit.[142]

In a narrative we shall encounter many times in Cassirer's subsequent writings, such that we might call it his signature narrative, Cassirer moves on to describe a process of human emancipation by which the 'religious' worldview frees itself from mythic enthrallment to the power of words and images. While the mythic imagination continues to nourish all genuine world-historical religions, the characteristic form of religion as such is only attained when it consciously breaks away from its mythic substrate and opposes its conscious power of intellectual critique to mythic images. Cassirer's chosen example for this indispensable emancipative process is a familiar one, an invocation of the Prophetic ethics of Hermann Cohen. Cassirer contends that the Jewish Prophets obtained the form and content of the idea of the monotheistic God (*Gottesidee*) by virtue of an energetic and spirited critique of the mythic worship of images. The banning of image-worship constitutes a firm dividing line between the mythic and Prophetic consciousness. All meaning and relevance is to be found in another, purely spiritual sphere. Before the heroic power of abstraction that typifies Prophetic thought, and which determines Prophetic religious feeling, the images of myth are 'simply nothing'.[143]

Or consider the second volume of Cassirer's *Philosophy of Symbolic Forms*, *Das Mythische Denken* (Mythical Thought) which was published in 1925. Here Cassirer argues for a 'critical phenomenology of the mythical consciousness', which starts neither from the godhead as an original metaphysical fact, nor from mankind as an original empirical fact. A critical phenomenology of the mythical consciousness, Cassirer enjoins, should apprehend the subject of the cultural process, the human spirit, 'in its pure actuality and diverse configurations, whose immanent norms it will strive to ascertain'. It is only in these spiritual activities as a whole that 'mankind constitutes itself in accordance with its ideal concept and concrete historical existence'. For Cassirer myth is not the pre-history of civilized humanity but the medium of its 'spiritual consciousness'. It is through myth that human beings attain the progressive differentiation of subject and object, of I and world, a movement by which 'consciousness issues from its stupor', its captivity in 'sensory impression and affectivity'.[144]

Cassirer's ideal concept of mankind as historically constituted through immanent norms of ethical and spiritual development describes myth dialectically as an historical stage containing the seeds of its own negation and sublation by religious consciousness. Myth is not simply naïve; it does raise a certain barrier against the world of passive sense impression. Like art and cognition, myth arises in a process of separation from immediate reality, but in the figures and images with which it replaces this world of the immediately given it merely 'substitutes for things another form of materiality and of bondage to things'.[145] As a spiritual force, however, myth already contains within itself the immanent precondition for its own future dissolution, the potentiality of a 'spiritual process of liberation' that is effected in the progress from 'the *magical-mythical* world view to the truly *religious* view'. The condition for this development, which Cassirer traces in detail throughout the volume and which serves as a leitmotif for his liberal Jewish argument for the difference between myth and religion as modes of subjectivity, is that while the religious spirit still lives in and makes use of the world of images and signs, it discovers a new relation to them, attaining a 'greater understanding of them, and thus rising above them'.[146]

Significantly – and this is very much in the tradition of Abraham Geiger's diachronic conception of Judaism's religious evolution – in the second volume of his philosophy of symbolic forms Cassirer does not quarantine Judaism and the Hebrew Bible from an ideal-historical narrative of progress from mythic enthrallment to sign and image to an iconoclastic religious disposition that criticizes but also reflexively deploys the symbols it inherits. In a section entitled 'The Formation of Time in the Mythical and Religious Consciousness', Cassirer argues that in the religious consciousness of the Prophets there is a sharp turn away from nature and from the temporality of natural processes. This development is discernible in the Hebrew Bible. The Psalms still praise God as the creator of nature, as Him to whom day and night belong, who assigns a fixed course to the sun and the planets. However, there is a markedly different perspective introduced by the books of the Prophets, for although these great images still appear in the Prophetic writings, for them the divine will has created no symbol of itself in nature; indeed 'nature becomes a matter of indifference for the purely ethical-religious pathos of the Prophets'.[147] Moreover, belief in God is interpreted by the Prophets as superstition if, whether out of fear or hope, it 'clings to nature'.[148]

For the Prophetic consciousness, cosmic and astronomical time disappears along with nature; in its place, there arises a 'new intuition of time' that has 'reference solely to the history of mankind'. The Prophetic history of mankind, Cassirer suggests, is not simply 'seen as past history but as a religious history of the future'. It is for this reason that the legend of the Patriarchs was removed from the centre of religious interest by the 'new Prophetic self-consciousness and consciousness of God' in which all 'true consciousness of time becomes a consciousness of the future'. In reference to the Prophetic renewal of the monotheistic ethical disposition, Cassirer refers us to Isaiah's dictum, 'Remember ye not the former things, neither consider the things of old' (Isaiah 43:18).[149]

In support of an idealized elucidation of Prophetic consciousness, Cassirer approvingly refers to Cohen's *The Religion of Reason*, for it is Cohen 'who of all modern thinkers has felt this fundamental idea of the Prophetic religion most deeply and renewed it in the greatest purity'. Cassirer quotes a passage from *The Religion of Reason* which evokes Cohen's redemptive messianic idealism:

> Time becomes future and only future. Past and present are submerged in this time of the future. This return to time is the purest idealization. Before this idea, all existence vanishes. The existence of man is transcended in this future being . . . What Greek intellectualism could not create, Prophetic monotheism succeeded in creating . . . The Prophets are the idealists of history. Their seerdom created the concept of history as the being of the future.[150]

By invoking the messianic ethics of Cohen, Cassirer substantiates his argument that for the Prophetic consciousness, the whole present, that of man as well as things, must be reborn out of the idea of the future: the theogony and cosmogony of myth and of the 'mere natural religions' are surpassed by a spiritual principle of an entirely different form and origin. The idea of the Creation disappears almost entirely, at least in the pre-exilic Prophets.[151] Cassirer is following Cohen's critique of a mythical ontology of origins, which, as Almut Sh. Bruckstein has argued, is expressed in the decisive contrast between myth's interest in the ontological origin of things (motion, matter) and monotheism's focus 'upon the origins of this world's *purpose* – arriving at God's word as the grounds of goodness, of justice, and of love of one another'.[152] In a summation of the ideal trajectory from mythic to religious consciousness, Cassirer deploys a liberal Jewish hermeneutic, arguing that the 'religious significance of an event depends no longer on its content but solely on its form', that is, the 'spiritual aspect in which it is seen'.[153]

In a poignant late essay, 'Judaism and the Modern Political Myths', published in the journal *Contemporary Jewish Record* in 1944, an essay which I think should also be read as implicitly critical of Zionism, by then the dominant form of Jewish politics, Cassirer explains to his readers that the Nazis, purveyors of the potent 'myth of the twentieth century', detested Judaism because it was 'Judaism which first made the decisive step that led from a *mythical* to an *ethical* religion'.[154] Cassirer laments, in a manner remarkably similar to that of Walter Benjamin's critique in his 'Theses on the Philosophy of History' of the faith of Marxists and Social Democrats in the 'homogenous time' of historical progress, the inability of the intellectual and political leaders of Weimar Germany, most of them determined Marxists, to recognize the 'explosive force of the political myths', since for them myth was a form of 'primitive' thought which had long ago lost its force and meaning.[155] That was a great error, in that it failed to explain why the 'new political mythology' had assaulted Judaism. This is because 'from its very beginnings' Judaism had attacked and rejected all those mythical elements which had hitherto pervaded and governed religious thought. In its proscription of the graven image as simulacrum, simile, likeness, Judaism attacked imagery, the 'very core of mythical thought', for to 'deprive myth of imagery is to insure its decay'.[156]

The slogan 'blood and soil', Cassirer remarks, is only a 'caricature' of a 'primeval mythic conception' of blood fellowship that connects man with God through sacrifice, though in the Nazi slogan the secularized connection is between man and his race. Cassirer reminds us that the religious and ethical ideals of the Prophets constituted a 'fierce protest' against primitive mythical motives requiring a sacrificial scapegoat: 'To what purpose is the multitude of your sacrifices unto me? saith the Lord . . . Bring no more vain oblations; incense is an abomination unto me' (Isaiah 1, 11, 13).[157] The merely mythical creeds and purely ritual ceremonies are done away with by the Prophets who stress 'religious and ethical duties' to their fellow human beings.[158] While nothing is so characteristic of the German political system as the 'denial and complete destruction of the ideal of individual responsibility', in which the only conceivable '"moral" subject' is the community, nation, or race, the 'new spirit' of Prophetic consciousness no longer allows, as in 'early Judaism', the punishment of a transgression or crime that has not been committed by an individual, meaning that the individual is the only 'moral subject'.[159] Referencing Jeremiah's new covenant with the house of Israel ('I will put my law in their inward parts, and write it in their hearts', Jeremiah 31: 29ff.), Cassirer praises 'this pure interior religion' for removing the binding force of previous social bonds, such that it is no 'longer blood-relationship or nationality that determines the moral will'.[160]

While the Jewish God has been unfairly represented 'time and time again' as a fiercely national God, in fact from its first and elementary stages Judaism conceived an ideal of monotheism incompatible with a narrow nationalism, even if its conception of individual and moral responsibility was not 'reached all at once'.[161] In his 1943 testament to Hermann Cohen with which we began this chapter, Cassirer quoted Cohen's statement in 'The Significance of Judaism for the Religious Progress of Humanity' that man is not at liberty to seek his salvation 'simply in his nationality' or in 'his pretended race', rather 'he must open his heart to more universal historical motives'.[162]

Cassirer emphasizes once again that a mature Judaism's stress on the individual moral will and its higher ideals, as opposed to the family, tribe, or community, is entirely compatible with ethical universalism. For if the 'bond that unites man and God' is no longer a physical bond of consanguinity, if religious duty no longer consists in the performance of specific rites, then it becomes clear that 'the new approach, the approach by man's ethical life, is open to everyone'. Religion is no longer the privilege of a caste of priests, nor is it the privilege of a single nation. It breaks with all restrictions. In the new Prophetic religion, Judaism must still fulfil a special task, but its call is a universal one, no longer confined within the limits of the life of a single nation ('a light of the Gentiles', Isaiah 42, 6). When the remnant of Israel that has been saved returns to Jerusalem and rebuilds the temple, Cassirer affirms in the post-national spirit of liberal Judaism, the worship in the temple will no longer be a national worship: 'At that time they shall call Jerusalem the throne of the Lord; and all the nations shall be gathered unto it, to the name of the Lord' (Jeremiah 3:17).[163] From this universalism the ideal of a 'perpetual peace' arises, a conception in its origin that is 'purely religious' rather than philosophical, an ideal never dreamt of by the ancient Greek thinkers such as Heraclitus who considered war the 'father and king of all'.[164]

Perhaps anticipating the objection of political Zionists, Cassirer agrees that the Prophetic ideal of transforming swords into ploughshares, and spears into pruning hooks, is 'utopian'. But it is an ethically energetic utopianism in accord with Goethe's dictum that to 'live in the idea means to treat the impossible as if it were possible', thereby helping to realize a 'great ethical and religious promise', that of a 'new heaven and a new earth'.[165] In *An Essay on Man* Cassirer affirms the humble virtues and visionary imaginations of the Prophets, for without these 'great individual religious reformers . . . religion would not have found its way'.[166] It is the Prophets' noble conception of 'man's ethical, social and religious life' that is so strikingly different from 'our modern myths' such as Nazism, which seeks to perpetuate and intensify war. Where the Prophets dissolve the 'blood-relationship' between human beings, the modern myths acknowledge no other duty than that which arises from a community of blood. Where the German leaders promised the German conquest of the whole world, the Prophets promised not the 'glory of the Jewish nation but its decline and fall, its deepest misery'. Where the political myths deify a super-race, the Prophets predict an age in which all nations shall be united under the worship of the one God. Cassirer maintains that there can be no reconciliation between these conceptions.[167]

No Jew, Cassirer writes feelingly in 'Judaism and the Modern Political Myths', 'can and will ever overcome the terrible ordeal of these last years'. Yet there is one relief amongst the inflicted wounds, the horrors and the miseries. We may be firmly convinced that these sacrifices were not made in vain, since what the 'modern Jew' had to defend in this combat was not only his physical existence and the preservation of the Jewish race. Much more was at stake. 'We had to represent all those ethical ideals that had been brought into being by Judaism and found their way into the general human culture', into the 'life of all civilized nations'. These ideals cannot be and have not been destroyed. If Judaism has contributed to breaking the power of the modern political myths, it has done its duty, 'having once more fulfilled its historical and religious mission'.[168] Even in Judaism's darkest hour, Cassirer once more returns faithfully to Cohen's argument, memorably advanced in his quarrel with Martin Buber, that the Jewish people must fulfil their role as a 'divine dew in the midst of the peoples', helping to realize the 'world mission' of the remnant of Israel. There can be no doubt that even at this terrible juncture Cassirer sought to reinstate Cohen's challenge to Martin Buber in 1916, in which he argued that for the Jewish people the 'moral world, as it evolves in history' is 'our true promised land'.[169]

I have argued, then, that we should recognize Cassirer as an heir to the confrontational politics and messianic impulse of *Wissenschaft des Judentums* historiography. He was engaged, as Christian Weise puts it, in a 'counter-history to the Christian portrayal of Judaism as an outdated, dead religion'. Weise makes this comment in relation to the work of another student of Hermann Cohen, Leo Baeck's 1905 *Das Wesen des Judentums* (The Essence of Judaism), which was a response to Adolf von Harnack's book *Das Wesen des Christentums*, and its denigration of ancient Judaism. Baeck's book, says Weise, postulated Judaism's 'religious and ethical superiority' in which Jewish religion and culture were not 'merely a living part of Western culture but indeed the "religion of the future"'. Judaism is represented in *Das Wesen des Judentums*, Weise writes, as a '"classical" religion that views human beings as subjects of their own moral actions, endowing them with responsibility for worldly justice'.[170] Weise could well have been speaking of Cassirer's arguments for Jewish monotheism and Prophetic religion as guarantors of ethical individuality in an age of mythic enthrallment to dogma and emotive symbolism. In the next chapter, we shall discuss how Cassirer responded to a powerful romantic and irrationalist assault on the significance of the Enlightenment with a counter-historical portrayal of that intellectual and cultural movement's imbrication in the history and future of Germany. As we shall see, Cassirer's argument for the Enlightenment era's religious humanism, cosmopolitanism, and dynamic interpretation of reason will resonate powerfully in the post-war thought of Hannah Arendt.

Notes

1 J.M. Krois. 1987. *Cassirer: Symbolic Forms and History*, New Haven and London: Yale University Press, ix. For Bakhtin's unacknowledged debt to Cassirer, see B. Poole. 1998. 'Bakhtin and Cassirer: The Philosophical Origins of Bakhtin's Carnival Messianism', *South Atlantic Quarterly* 97, 537–578.

2 Skidelsky, *Ernst Cassirer*, 232–233, 236.

3 Skidelsky, *Ernst Cassirer*, 94.

4 Skidelsky, *Ernst Cassirer*, 3.

5 Skidelsky, *Ernst Cassirer*, 213.

6 Skidelsky, *Ernst Cassirer*, 230.

7 Skidelsky, *Ernst Cassirer*, 6.

8 Skidelsky, *Ernst Cassirer*, 236.

9 Skidelsky shares Peter Eli Gordon's dismissive caricature of Cassirer in a recent review of Thomas Meyer's biography: 'politically progressive, but disinclined to controversy, Cassirer was the very paradigm of the Jewish *Bildungsbürgertum*'. P.E. Gordon. 2008. 'Review of Thomas Meyer, *Ernst Cassirer*', *AJS Review* 32(2), 435–437. Interestingly, Gordon avoids descriptions of this kind in his much more nuanced *Continental Divide: Heidegger, Cassirer, Davos* (2010), perhaps because the mounting evidence of Cassirer's frequent public intellectual engagements and robust defence of the Weimar Republic made such a stereotype untenable. P.E. Gordon. 2010. *Continental Divide: Heidegger, Cassirer, Davos,* Cambridge, Mass.: Harvard University Press.

10 L. Strauss. 1947. 'Review of Ernst Cassirer's *The Myth of the State*', *Social Research* 14(1/4), 127–128.

11 Gordon, *Continental Divide*, 344–345.

12 R.A. Cohen. 2006. 'Introduction', in E. Levinas, *Humanism of the Other*, trans. N. Poller, Urbana and Chicago: University of Illinois Press, xxxi.

13 Gordon, *Continental Divide*, 16, 22.

14 Gordon, *Continental Divide*, 318–319.

15 Gordon, *Continental Divide*, 37–38.

16 Gordon, *Continental Divide*, 11, 22.

17 Gordon, *Continental Divide*, 24.

18 Gordon, *Continental Divide*, 41 and 268–291.

19 Gordon, *Continental Divide*, 317–318.

20 Gordon, *Continental Divide*, 319, 321.

21 Almut Sh. Bruckstein points out that Cassirer gave no less than eight published talks on Cohen in his lifetime, from 1912 up until 1943. Bruckstein could have added Cassirer's 1944 essay 'Judaism and the Modern Political Myths', which is profoundly indebted to Cohen's Prophetic Judaism. For the full list, see A.S. Bruckstein. 2008. 'Practicing Intertextuality: Ernst Cassirer and Hermann Cohen on Myth and Monotheism', in J.A. Barash (ed.), *The Symbolic Construction of Reality: The Legacy of Ernst Cassirer*, Chicago: The University of Chicago Press, 187, n. 16.

22 Koselleck, *The Practice of Conceptual History*, 207.

23 'Ernst schilderte mir Hermann Cohen, den er außerordentlich bewunderte und liebte'. T. Cassirer. 2003. *Mein Leben mit Ernst Cassirer*, Hamburg: Felix Meiner Verlag, 40. All translations are my own.

24 'Ich . . . habe eigentlich nur in einem einzigen Falle-im Falle Cohens-den Eindruck gehabt, daß Ernst unter einem "Einfluß" stand'. T. Cassirer, *Mein Leben mit Ernst Cassirer*, 90.

25 T. Cassirer, *Mein Leben mit Ernst Cassirer*, 43.

26 T. Cassirer, *Mein Leben mit Ernst Cassirer*, 40.

27 T. Cassirer, *Mein Leben mit Ernst Cassirer*, 91.

28 T. Cassirer, *Mein Leben mit Ernst Cassirer*, 93.

29 'Es ist *die Idee, die Aufgabe der Philosophie selbst,* die er uns vorbildlich gedeutet hat'. T. Cassirer, *Mein Leben mit Ernst Cassirer,* 94.

30 T. Cassirer, *Mein Leben mit Ernst Cassirer,* 95.

31 E. Cassirer. 2004. 'Hermann Cohen. Worte gesprochen an seinem Grabe am 7. April 1918 von Ernst Cassirer', in B. Recki and T. Berber (eds), *Ernst Cassirer, Aufsätze und kleine Schriften (1927–1933),* Hamburg: Felix Meiner Verlag, 284.

32 Cassirer, 'Hermann Cohen. Worte gesprochen', 284, 285.

33 'Ich so lange Zeit [Cohen] die eigentliche Verkörperung der Sache der Philosophie and ihrer Sachlichkeit gesehen hatte'. Cassirer, 'Hermann Cohen. Worte gesprochen', 285.

34 Cassirer, 'Hermann Cohen. Worte gesprochen', 285.

35 Cassirer, 'Hermann Cohen. Worte gesprochen', 285.

36 Cassirer, 'Hermann Cohen. Worte gesprochen', 285.

37 Cassirer, 'Hermann Cohen. Worte gesprochen', 285.

38 Cassirer, 'Hermann Cohen. Worte gesprochen', 286.

39 Cassirer, 'Hermann Cohen. Worte gesprochen', 286.

40 Cassirer, 'Hermann Cohen. Worte gesprochen', 286.

41 Cassirer, 'Hermann Cohen. Worte gesprochen', 286.

42 Cassirer, 'Hermann Cohen. Worte gesprochen', 287.

43 Cassirer, 'Hermann Cohen. Worte gesprochen', 287.

44 Cassirer, 'Hermann Cohen. Worte gesprochen', 287.

45 Mendes-Flohr, *German Jews: a Dual Identity,* 20.

46 Cassirer, 'Hermann Cohen. Worte gesprochen', 287.

47 Cassirer, 'Hermann Cohen. Worte gesprochen', 287, 288. For an illuminating discussion of how 'Cohen's great student Ernst Cassirer summarized his teacher's intention at Cohen's grave' as the 'logic of the origin', see J. Habermas. 2002. 'The German Idealism of the Jewish Philosophers', in E. Mendieta (ed.), *Religion and Rationality: Essays on Reason, God, and Modernity,* Cambridge, Mass.: The MIT Press, 42.

48 Cassirer, 'Hermann Cohen. Worte gesprochen', 288.

49 Koselleck, *The Practice of Conceptual History,* 183, 187, 199.

50 Cassirer, 'Hermann Cohen. Worte gesprochen', 288.

51 Mendes-Flohr, *German Jews: A Dual Identity,* 60.

52 Mendes-Flohr, *German Jews: A Dual Identity,* 60–61.

53 See E. Cassirer. 1946. *The Myth of the State,* New Haven: Yale University Press, 257.

54 Cassirer, 'Hermann Cohen. Worte gesprochen', 288, 289.

55 Cassirer, 'Hermann Cohen. Worte gesprochen', 289.

56 Cassirer, 'Hermann Cohen. Worte gesprochen', 290.

57 Cassirer, 'Hermann Cohen. Worte gesprochen', 290.

58 T. Cassirer, *Mein Leben mit Ernst Cassirer,* 45.

59 T. Cassirer, *Mein Leben mit Ernst Cassirer,* 88.

60 T. Cassirer, *Mein Leben mit Ernst Cassirer,* 81.

61 T. Cassirer, *Mein Leben mit Ernst Cassirer,* 107.

62 T. Cassirer, *Mein Leben mit Ernst Cassirer,* 107.

63 T. Cassirer, *Mein Leben mit Ernst Cassirer,* 107–108.

64 E. Cassirer. 2009. *The Philosophy of the Enlightenment,* trans. F.C.A. Koelln, J.P. Pettegrove, Princeton: Princeton University Press, xvii.

65 Gordon, *Continental Divide,* 292.

66 Cassirer, *An Essay on Man*, 177.
67 Cassirer, *An Essay on Man*, 178.
68 Cassirer, *An Essay on Man*, 180, 182, 196.
69 T. Cassirer, *Mein Leben mit Ernst Cassirer*, 135.
70 T. Cassirer, *Mein Leben mit Ernst Cassirer*, 140.
71 J. Hannson and S. Nordin (eds). 2006. *Ernst Cassirer: The Swedish Years*, Bern: Peter Lang, 47–48.
72 T. Cassirer, *Mein Leben mit Ernst Cassirer*, 303.
73 T. Cassirer, *Mein Leben mit Ernst Cassirer*, 89. Toni is referring to Ernst Cassirer's discussion of Goethe's dynamic philosophy of history in E. Cassirer. 1995. *Goethe und die geschichtliche Welt* (1932), Hamburg: Felix Meiner Verlag.
74 T. Cassirer, *Mein Leben mit Ernst Cassirer*, 108.
75 T. Cassirer, *Mein Leben mit Ernst Cassirer*, 109. For a discussion of Cassirer's nomination for the prestigious philosophy chair in Berlin in 1930, which was subsequently vetoed, see Gordon, *Continental Divide*, 40–41.
76 T. Cassirer, *Mein Leben mit Ernst Cassirer,* 117–120.
77 T. Cassirer, *Mein Leben mit Ernst Cassirer,* 124.
78 T. Cassirer, *Mein Leben mit Ernst Cassirer*, 131–132.
79 See, for example, Cassirer's essay 'Vom Wesen und Werden des Naturrechts', based on a public address he gave to the legal society of Hamburg in February 1932, in which he defends the idealistic and universalist principles of natural law as animating a form of concrete ethical praxis. Significantly, Cassirer refers to the Dreyfusards in their challenge to the flawed procedures of the military court in Rennes. A genuine public conscience, Cassirer writes, can never be satisfied with written laws alone but must be mindful of other standards of judgement, those 'unwritten laws' which animate the very concept of justice itself. E. Cassirer. 1932. 'Vom Wesen und Werden des Naturrechts', *Zeitschrift für Rechtsphilosophie in Lehre und Praxis* 6, 26–27.
80 Gordon, *Continental Divide*, 56.
81 T. Cassirer, *Mein Leben mit Ernst Cassirer,* 179.
82 T. Cassirer, *Mein Leben mit Ernst Cassirer,* 181.
83 T. Cassirer, *Mein Leben mit Ernst Cassirer,* 182.
84 T. Cassirer, *Mein Leben mit Ernst Cassirer,* 188.
85 T. Cassirer, *Mein Leben mit Ernst Cassirer,* 188.
86 Liebeschütz, 'Hermann Cohen and his Historical Background', 19 and 20.
87 M. Heidegger. 1997. *Kant and the Problem of Metaphysics*, fifth edition, trans. Richard Taft, Bloomington: Indiana University Press, 193.
88 Heidegger, *Kant and the Problem of Metaphysics,* 193–194.
89 Heidegger, *Kant and the Problem of Metaphysics,* 194.
90 Heidegger, *Kant and the Problem of Metaphysics,* 194.
91 Heidegger, *Kant and the Problem of Metaphysics,* 194.
92 Heidegger, *Kant and the Problem of Metaphysics,* 195.
93 Heidegger, *Kant and the Problem of Metaphysics,* 195–196.
94 D. Coskun. 2006. 'Cassirer in Davos. An Intermezzo on Magic Mountain (1929)', *Law and Critique* 17, 22. In *The Myth of the State* Cassirer celebrates the Enlightenment's rejection of Hobbes' subjection of the rights and freedoms of the individual to sovereign power. Cassirer reiterates a theory of natural rights, arguing

that if a 'man could give up his personality he would cease being a moral being' who could promise and contract; this 'fundamental right, the right to personality, includes in a sense all the others'. Cassirer, *The Myth of the State*, 175.

95 Krois, *Cassirer: Symbolic Forms and History*, 104.

96 E. Cassirer. 2004. 'Kant und das Problem der Metaphysik. Bemerkungen zu Martin Heidegger's Kant-Interpretation' (1931), in B. Recki and T. Berber (eds), *Ernst Cassirer, Aufsätze und kleine Schriften (1927–1933)*, Hamburg: Felix Meiner Verlag, 225.

97 Cassirer, *Aufsätze und kleine Schriften*, 225.

98 Gordon, *Continental Divide*, 276.

99 Gordon, *Continental Divide*, 270.

100 Gordon, *Continental Divide*, 281.

101 See, for example, Cassirer's poignant eulogy, given while chancellor of the University of Hamburg, to his friend and close intellectual associate of the last decade, Aby Warburg. E. Cassirer. 2004. 'Nachruf auf Aby Warburg' (1929), in B. Recki (ed.), *Gesammelte Werke: Hamburger Ausgabe*, Bd. 17: *Aufsätze und Kleine Schriften, 1927–1931*, Hamburg: Felix Meiner, 368–374.

102 T. Cassirer, *Mein Leben mit Ernst Cassirer*, 191.

103 T. Cassirer, *Mein Leben mit Ernst Cassirer*, 194–195.

104 T. Cassirer, *Mein Leben mit Ernst Cassirer*, 194–195.

105 T. Cassirer, *Mein Leben mit Ernst Cassirer*, 237.

106 T. Cassirer, *Mein Leben mit Ernst Cassirer*, 263.

107 T. Cassirer, *Mein Leben mit Ernst Cassirer*, 269.

108 T. Cassirer, *Mein Leben mit Ernst Cassirer*, 195.

109 T. Cassirer, *Mein Leben mit Ernst Cassirer*, 202.

110 T. Cassirer, *Mein Leben mit Ernst Cassirer*, 203.

111 See Hansson and Nordin, *Ernst Cassirer: The Swedish Years*, 33.

112 Gordon, *Continental Divide*, 317.

113 T. Cassirer, *Mein Leben mit Ernst Cassirer*, 238.

114 T. Cassirer, *Mein Leben mit Ernst Cassirer*, 238–239.

115 T. Cassirer, *Mein Leben mit Ernst Cassirer*, 264–266.

116 T. Cassirer, *Mein Leben mit Ernst Cassirer*, 268–269.

117 T. Cassirer, *Mein Leben mit Ernst Cassirer*, 303.

118 T. Cassirer, *Mein Leben mit Ernst Cassirer*, 313.

119 T. Cassirer, *Mein Leben mit Ernst Cassirer*, 314.

120 T. Cassirer, *Mein Leben mit Ernst Cassirer*, 314.

121 T. Cassirer, *Mein Leben mit Ernst Cassirer*, 318–321, 328.

122 T. Cassirer, *Mein Leben mit Ernst Cassirer*, 326, 330.

123 A. Hertzberg. 1970. 'A Reminiscence of Ernst Cassirer', *Leo Baeck Institute Yearbook* 15, 245. Cassirer was also a founding member of the Akademie fur die Wissenschaft des Judentums in 1920.

124 Hertzberg, 'A Reminiscence of Ernst Cassirer', 245–246.

125 Hertzberg, 'A Reminiscence of Ernst Cassirer', 246.

126 Hertzberg, 'A Reminiscence of Ernst Cassirer', 246.

127 E. Cassirer. 1943. 'Hermann Cohen, 1842–1918', *Social Research* 10(1), 219.

128 Cassirer, 'Hermann Cohen, 1842–1918', 227–228.

129 Cassirer, 'Hermann Cohen, 1842–1918', 229.

130 Cassirer, 'Hermann Cohen, 1842–1918', 229.

131 Cassirer, 'Hermann Cohen, 1842–1918', 228.

132 Cassirer, 'Hermann Cohen, 1842–1918', 229.

133 Cassirer, 'Hermann Cohen, 1842–1918', 231.

134 Cassirer, 'Hermann Cohen, 1842–1918', 231.

135 E. Cassirer. 1923. 'Der Begriff der Symbolischen Form im Aufbau der Geisteswissenschaften', in *Vorträge der Bibliothek Warburg 1921/1922*, Leipzig: B.G. Teubner, 12.

136 Cassirer, 'Der Begriff der Symbolischen Form', 11–13.

137 Cassirer, 'Der Begriff der Symbolischen Form', 14.

138 Cassirer, 'Der Begriff der Symbolischen Form', 15.

139 Cassirer, 'Der Begriff der Symbolischen Form', 15.

140 Cassirer, 'Der Begriff der Symbolischen Form', 21.

141 Cassirer, 'Der Begriff der Symbolischen Form', 22.

142 Cassirer, 'Der Begriff der Symbolischen Form', 24.

143 Cassirer, 'Der Begriff der Symbolischen Form', 28.

144 E. Cassirer. 1955. *The Philosophy of Symbolic Forms, Volume Two: Mythical Thought*, trans. R. Manheim, New Haven: Yale University Press, 13.

145 Cassirer, *Mythical Thought*, 24.

146 Cassirer, *Mythical Thought*, 24–25.

147 Cassirer, *Mythical Thought*, 119.

148 Cassirer, *Mythical Thought*, 119–120.

149 Cassirer, *Mythical Thought*, 120.

150 Cassirer, *Mythical Thought*, 120. Cassirer quotes from H. Cohen. 1919. *Die Religion der Vernunft aus den Quellen des Judentums*, Grundriss der Gesamtwissenschaft des Judentums, Leipzig: Fock, 293 ff., 308.

151 Cassirer, *Mythical Thought*, 120.

152 H. Cohen. 2004. *Ethics of Maimonides*, trans. A.S. Bruckstein, Madison, Wisc.: The University of Wisconsin Press, 114.

153 Cassirer, *Mythical Thought*, 260.

154 E. Cassirer. 1944. 'Judaism and the Modern Political Myths', *Contemporary Jewish Record* 7, 115.

155 Cassirer, 'Judaism and the Modern Political Myths', 116.

156 Cassirer, 'Judaism and the Modern Political Myths', 117.

157 Cassirer, 'Judaism and the Modern Political Myths', 120.

158 Cassirer, 'Judaism and the Modern Political Myths', 120–121.

159 Cassirer, 'Judaism and the Modern Political Myths', 121–122.

160 Cassirer, 'Judaism and the Modern Political Myths', 122–123.

161 Cassirer, 'Judaism and the Modern Political Myths', 121–122.

162 Cassirer, 'Hermann Cohen, 1842–1918', 231.

163 Cassirer, 'Judaism and the Modern Political Myths', 123.

164 Cassirer, 'Judaism and the Modern Political Myths', 123–124.

165 Cassirer, 'Judaism and the Modern Political Myths', 124. Interpreting the Prophets as ideal subjects of *Bildung*, Cassirer stresses that the Prophets, despite their determination to articulate their divine inspiration, were not misanthropic mystics, but were tied to their social environment by a 'thousand bonds'. See Cassirer, *An Essay on Man*, 102.

166 Cassirer, *An Essay on Man*, 102.

167 Cassirer, 'Judaism and the Modern Political Myths', 124.

168 Cassirer, 'Judaism and the Modern Political Myths', 126.

169 See Martin Buber and Hermann Cohen. 1980. 'A Debate on Zionism and Messianism', in P.R. Mendes-Flohr and J. Reinharz (eds), *The Jew in the Modern World, a Documentary History*, Oxford: Oxford University Press, 451.

170 C. Weise. 2009. '"Let his Memory be Holy to Us!": Jewish Interpretations of Martin Luther from the Enlightenment to the Holocaust', *Leo Baeck Institute Year Book* 54(1), 112, 114.

CHAPTER 6

❄

Ernst Cassirer

The Enlightenment as Counter-History

'In Kant's actual existence, as Goethe – doubtlessly correctly – says, thought, in its objective content and its objective "truth", not only rules life but receives in return the characteristic stamp of the life to which it imparts its form.'

Ernst Cassirer, *Kant's Life and Thought*

In this chapter I explore Peter Eli Gordon's heuristic suggestion that Cassirer's important study *The Philosophy of the Enlightenment* (1932) is not simply a reconstruction but a *retrieval* of Enlightenment philosophy as a philosophical resource for the modern world which carries a 'specific contemporary resonance'. This was at a time, as Gordon points out, when Heidegger was 'turning away from philosophical modernity as an era condemned to ontological oblivion'.[1] Interestingly, in his 1927 account of the History of the Philosophy Chair at Marburg, Heidegger himself had recognized Hermann Cohen's contribution to the revitalization of Kantian philosophy as speaking with renewed immediacy to ethical and aesthetic concerns:

The boundary between theoretical knowledge on the one hand, and the moral-practical and artistic-formative conduct of the subject on the other, presses for a correspondingly far-reaching interpretation of Kant, which Cohen presented in his works *Kants Begründung der Ethik* (1877) and *Kants Begründung der Asthetik* (1889).[2]

Cassirer continued Cohen's expansive interpretation in retrieving the ethical, aesthetic, anthropological and political Kant. Indeed, Kant was a medium through which Cassirer refined his unified, personalistic approach to the history of thought, evoked in his graveside eulogy to Hermann Cohen and subsequent testaments to his friend and mentor.

In his influential 1918 biography *Kant's Life and Thought*, Cassirer reprised not only the significance of Kant for the history of philosophy, but renewed our conception of him 'as an individual intellectual personality', one whose person and way of life can be recast into a 'truly unified spiritual whole'.[3] Cassirer traces a process of 'inner self-development' which can be disclosed only by conceiving Kant's life history and the systematic evolution of his philosophy as one.[4] The task of the intellectual biographer of Kant is to rule out the narration of mere external vicissitudes and events and illuminate the '*Lebensform*, the form of life, corresponding to his form of thinking'.[5] As we have seen in his various paeans to the character of Cohen, for Cassirer the disclosure of the intellectual personality does not involve reductive psychological explanation or the enumeration of a conglomeration of characteristics but is thoroughly relational and historical. This means being attentive to the significant anecdote and epistolary correspondence which reveals the importance of sympathetic dialogue in the thinker's development as well as the ongoing struggle to master one's inclinations and shape one's life in the various critical phases of the thinker's philosophical self-formation.[6] In his biography and in a number of his writings and public presentations on Kant that stretch into the 1930s, Cassirer portrays the sage of Königsberg as being ardently engaged in the events of his time, principally the different phases of the French Revolution. According to Cassirer, Kant was ethically indebted to thinkers such as Rousseau, whose discovery of a noble conception of human 'nature' with profound normative import helped Kant to formulate the 'autonomous moral law in its pure, unchangeable validity and obligation'.[7] In a later study in comparative intellectual biography, *Rousseau, Kant, Goethe, Two Essays* (1945), Cassirer reflects that despite their very different temperaments, Kant regarded Rousseau as the thinker who 'possessed a new conception of the nature and function of philosophy, of its vocation and dignity'. Rousseau taught Kant to forsake the hubris of the philosopher who despises the ignorance of the common man and instead learn to 'respect human nature' and thus 'establish the rights of man'.[8]

Thus the neo-Kantian Cassirer, while affirming the importance of Kant's transcendental philosophy, deflects the image of him as a dry and aloof theoretician and evokes a practical moral thinker sensitive to various Enlightenment efforts to represent humanity as a subject of rights. Cassirer situates Kant in a pan-European Enlightenment republic of letters in which his philosophical ethos is informed by a horizon of passionate humanist concerns. In the remainder of the chapter I will consider how Cassirer's characterological approach to the intellectual history of the Enlightenment reprised that era in order to articulate a normative interpretation of the philosophical vocation as conversationally inclined, unflinchingly idealistic, and willing to continually disclose its function as an arbiter of civilized values through ethical activity.

Reconfiguring the origins of German philosophy, Cassirer draws attention to the stylistic élan and philosophical breadth of Moses Mendelssohn as exemplifying enlightenment philosophy as a diverse social practice.

In Chapter 5 we briefly discussed Toni Cassirer's remarks on the importance of Cassirer's August 1928 lecture, 'Die Idee der republikanischen Verfassung' (*The Idea of a Republican Constitution*), a robust defence of the Weimar constitutional republic. It was an address, Toni Cassirer writes, that was intended to provoke the republic's many enemies. I would suggest that 'The Idea of a Republican Constitution' was delivered in the spirit of Wilhelm von Humboldt's historiographical manifesto, 'The Task of the Historian' (1821), a text that inspired German Jewish intellectuals who admired its reappraisal of historical consciousness as imaginatively creative, ethically vigorous, and attentive to those powerful world-historical ideas that are not immediately visible to the historian concerned with power politics and the rise and fall of states.[9] Recalling Wilhelm von Humboldt's essay, in his address Cassirer invokes the ongoing reciprocal interaction between the world of action and the world of thought, the evolution of world-historical ideas and the constitution of political and social reality.[10] In respect of this historical interplay of intellectual and social agency Cassirer cites as an example the intimate relationship between theory and praxis in the venerable tradition of German philosophical Idealism, a tradition which reached its pinnacle in the work of Kant, in *The Critique of Pure Reason* (1781) and *The Critique of Practical Reason* (1788). The French constituent assembly's Declaration of the Rights of Man and the Citizen in August 1789 immediately followed the publication of the latter, an event which marked the beginning of the French Revolution.[11]

A spectator (*Zuschauer*) to the great world historical drama of the French Revolution, Kant was passionately interested in the events as they unfolded, impatiently seeking all available newspaper coverage. Cassirer gives us an image of Kant that contradicts the conventional view of the great philosopher as a sedate and abstract thinker, aloof from pressing social concerns. Cassirer instead endorses Heinrich Heine's witty aperçu in *On the History of Religion and Philosophy in Germany*, that with the French Declaration of the Rights of Man the world became the 'signature' of the words of great eighteenth-century thinkers such as Rousseau. Cassirer nonetheless disputes Heine's privileging of Rousseau in any discussion of the intellectual origins of the French Constituent Assembly's Declaration of the Rights of Man and of the Citizen of 26 August 1789. This is because Rousseau, regrettably, sacrificed the individual to the will of the community, dismantling the inalienable rights of the individual.[12]

Cassirer instead offers another genealogy of the revolutionary discourse of human rights, one informed by German idealist thought from Leibniz to Wolff and then Kant, a mode of thinking where one feels oneself in the 'immediate pulsation' of the historical life of the era and its pressing political and social problems.[13] Leibniz, Cassirer argues, was the first great European thinker to stress the fundamental and inalienable right of the individual as a rational soul, a stance that led him to impose severe restrictions on the exploitation of slaves.[14] In turn Leibniz's philosophical systematizer Christian Wolff proclaimed the fundamental thesis of the absolute equality of subjects before the law, as well as rights to personal security and freedom from the arbitrary impositions of the state. This philosophical doctrine of natural right influenced various declarations of the American free states, such as that of Virginia in 1776, with its important proclamation of the original and innate rights bequeathed to human beings by nature. The epochal American Bill of Rights, the model for the 1789 French Declaration, soon followed these declarations.[15]

If the pure 'world-moving' idea of humanity as a supranational legal subject entitled to inalienable rights was diminished by the terrible events that followed the deposing of Louis XIV in France, it was Kant's critically detached but profoundly engaged analysis of the historical and philosophical significance of the French Revolution that restored the equilibrium between actions and ideas as vectors of world history.[16] While repudiating the deposition of a monarch and the revolutionary violence that followed as unjustifiable, Kant nevertheless advanced the 'rational belief' that, from the ideal perspective of the spectator of the Revolution, it did not matter whether the French Revolution empirically succeeded or failed. For the spectator attuned to its world-historical significance, it nevertheless portended an age of republican constitutions and the 'cosmopolitan condition' of perpetual peace among states, which was to be achieved providentially, by a 'ruse of nature'. Kant argued that the 'ideas of reason' are never reliant on mere empirical facts or the winners and losers of power politics; rather, such ideas project us from the realm of being into the realm of the 'should', replacing acquiescence to history and tradition with an ethical imperative to understand events 'symbolically', as pregnant with future significance.[17] Cassirer's discussion of the role of symbolic perception, which is not bound to an interpretation of a narrow concatenation of events, is a reminder of Wilhelm von Humboldt's exhortation that 'History's true and immeasurable usefulness lies . . . in its power to enliven and refine our sense of acting on reality, and this occurs more through the form attached to events than through the events themselves'.[18]

Cassirer's peroration to 'The Idea of a Republican Constitution' should also be read, I would suggest, as a subtle allegory of the indigenous role played by Jews, as agents of critical idealism, in German and European intellectual history and cultural life. Cassirer reminds his audience in coded terms that the idea of a republican constitution is in no way a stranger or 'external intruder' [*äußerer Eindringling*] to Germany, but has grown up on the same soil [*Boden*] and has been nourished by its very own powers, the energies [*Kräfte*] of idealistic philosophy. Cassirer remarks that even this important historical insight would be fruitless if it did not instil in all those present the faith and confidence that the intellectual energies from which the republican tradition originated can also illuminate our path towards the future [*Weg in die Zukunft*] as well as helping us to actively bring forth that future.[19]

The year after his address in defence of the Weimar constitutional republic, Cassirer contributed an article, 'Die Philosophie Moses Mendelssohns', to a special edition of the *Encyclopaedia Judaica* commemorating the 200th anniversary of Mendelssohn's birth. The publication concluded the extensive commemorative events organized by the German Jewish community in honour of Mendelssohn and the Mendelssohn-Lessing friendship.[20] Recalling his imbrication of Cohen's ethical and intellectual interests, Cassirer describes Mendelssohn's work in the fields of metaphysics, logic, psychology, epistemology (*Erkenntnislehre*), aesthetics, and the philosophy of religion, as animated by a unified critical spirit (*einheitlichen Geiste beseelt*) and predicated on systematic fundamental principles.[21] Once more Cassirer's approach is revisionist, historically embedding Mendelssohn in the holistic *Bildungsideal* that he helped to initiate, thus critiquing his reception as a rationalist disciple of Wolff and Leibniz, while also stressing Mendelssohn's profound contributions to Jewish philosophy and Jewish political advocacy.

Mendelssohn was one of the first thinkers in Germany, notes Cassirer, to express himself in a 'free literary form' that was profoundly congenial to his personality and which made him one of the most 'effective pioneers of the spirit of the *Aufklärung*'. Mendelssohn helped to establish and propagate the Enlightenment in Germany. He substantially enriched the *Aufklärung*, not just within the limits of the Wolffian system of logic and metaphysics of which he was a leading representative, but by helping to make broad areas of intellectual life such as empirical psychology, literary criticism, and aesthetics newly accessible to critical discourse.[22] Mendelssohn particularly enriched the new discipline of aesthetics in Germany, a field of enquiry that enabled the full disclosure of his personality and interests.[23] In rigorously distinguishing the enjoyment of the beautiful from any kind of possessive desire, Mendelssohn was a notable forerunner of Kant's conceptual determination of the beautiful as 'disinterested pleasure' which in turn inspired Schiller's conception of aesthetic humanism.[24]

In a powerful and detailed section on Mendelssohn's philosophy of religion and the state, Cassirer argues that despite Mendelssohn's profound contribution to the development and promulgation of the fundamental ideas of German Enlightenment philosophy, his greatest and most historically decisive achievement did not belong in that field alone. Mendelssohn's philosophical achievement was not purely theoretical but of a more practical kind.[25] Mendelssohn had always regarded the touchstone of any theoretical truth to be its practical consequences, that is, whether it plays a fruitful and beneficial role in the ethical and political formation (*Gestaltung*) of a human life. Cassirer would seem to be referring to Mendelssohn's commitment to a practical ethic of *Bildung* encouraging the reflexive cultivation of virtue as a habit and proficiency disclosed in worldly interaction.[26] Mendelssohn always related his principal insights and doctrines to 'practical ethical goals' which he intended his theoretical work to serve.[27] Cassirer displaces a still prevalent conception of Mendelssohn as an outmoded pre-critical metaphysician, and instead recontextualizes him as an important Jewish philosopher, an illustrious progenitor of liberal Judaism's humanist emphasis on practical ethics as more important to the religious disposition than doctrines of personal salvation.[28]

Cassirer maintains that Mendelssohn's relationship to Judaism is another pertinent example of the overall unity of his thought. Just as his 'ethical universalism' arose upon and was continually nourished by the religious powers of Judaism ('*religiösen Kräften*', a vocabulary reminiscent of Abraham Geiger's conception of Judaism as a creative power of world-historical significance), so Mendelssohn's ethical commitments ensured that he continually returned to questions pertaining to the Jewish religion and to the problem of the legal and political status of the Jews. In this respect, *Jerusalem* (1783) represents the summation and crowning effort of his philosophical life's work. Here Mendelssohn draws the ultimate consequences from his fundamental metaphysical and ethical convictions and applies them to the form of the Jewish religion and to the determination of the tasks (*Aufgaben*) which religion, and Judaism in particular, can fulfil in the entire life of the state and the construction of the social order.[29]

Cassirer then explicates Mendelssohn's theory of the distinct prerogatives of the state and of religion in the education and formation of humanity (*Bildung des Menschen*), in which the former governs and the latter educates human beings to social virtues, thus giving up all legal powers, such as that of clerical or rabbinical excommunication. Cassirer enthusiastically endorses Mendelssohn's famous address to members of the three monotheistic faiths, Christianity, Judaism, and Islam, in which he asks his ecumenical readership to consider whether there is not more true religion in the ranks of the excommunicated than in the numerically superior ranks of those who have condemned them.[30] For Mendelssohn, the separation of church and state is not to be understood in the disenchanted sense of an atomizing process of secularization, but as a principled and ethically necessary division of social and educative tasks between the compulsory legality of the state and a religion that instructs and persuades. A genuine religion, Mendelssohn argued, wants no action without an accompanying disposition, no work without spirit (*Geist*), and no deed without an ethical significance or higher meaning. Cassirer quotes Mendelssohn's precept, so important for Reform and Liberal Judaism, that religious actions without religious thoughts are mere empty puppetry (*Puppenspiel*), and of no genuine service to God.[31]

Cassirer suggests that Mendelssohn derives his relationship to Judaism from his ethically and pedagogically motivated interpretation of the task and vocation of religion as inspiring by example rather than coercing by punitive threats. Mendelssohn insists on a rigorous distinction between the spiritual content (*geistegen Gehalt*) of the Jewish religion and Judaism as it incarnates particular commandments and statutory laws. The latter can only receive their validity on historical grounds.[32] The whole content of Jewish ritual and ceremonial law belongs to this domain. They are supported by tradition as their particular and unique legal basis (*Rechtsgrund*). The validity of this historical grounding of Jewish religious practice is neither doubted nor disturbed by Mendelssohn, since he holds that no human community is conceivable without the binding force of a tradition fortified by collective historical memories.[33]

As regards the historical forms of the Jewish religion, according to Mendelssohn here we remain within the sphere of 'Revelation' as it affects the individual who receives teaching that has been passed down through the generations. However, this merely passive relationship to tradition loses its meaning and justification when we deal with the issue of religious conviction, because fundamental doctrines about God and the relationship of humanity to God must be open to the scrutiny of reason; there can be no eternal truths which rely on Revelation alone, that is, on trust and faith.[34] Cassirer concludes his essay by praising Mendelssohn's profoundly influential re-orientation of Judaism. He evokes Mendelssohn's conviction that it is only the Jewish religion that contains such articles of faith as can be comprehended as necessary by human reason, as eternal truths that our active critical powers *(menschliche Kräfte)* can not only apprehend but also demonstrate and enact; here Cassirer situates Mendelssohn as a precursor to Cohen's precept that religion affirms the strength of humanity's ethical and intellectual powers, not its weakness.[35]

Cassirer then subtly adverts to Judaism's contemporary quarrel with Christianity. Mendelssohn interpreted Judaism's lack of doctrinal compulsion as a fundamental difference between Judaism and Christianity. As Mendelssohn famously argued, Jewish legislation, prayers, injunctions, rules of living, and ethical teachings pertain to temporal and eternal felicity, but are not saving truths and fundamental propositions of reason *qua* Christianity. Judaism's fundamental rational propositions, such as the providential nature and immortality of God, are, for Mendelssohn, only legible through nature and worldly relationships (*Sache*), and not through words and signs that can be dogmatically codified. In this respect, Cassirer points out, Mendelssohn's interpretation of religion agrees with his philosophical convictions: Judaism is the most perfect and complete expression of the fundamental truths of reason and of the generous ethical universalism that animated Mendelssohn's theoretical and practical philosophy.[36]

Lessing's Dynamic Reason

In April 1929 Cassirer delivered an address, 'Die Idee der Religion bei Lessing und Mendelssohn' ('The Idea of Religion in Lessing and Mendelssohn'), celebrating the tenth anniversary of the *Akademie der Wissenschaft des Judentums*, an institution that Hermann Cohen had helped to found. The lecture was part of the Lessing-Mendelssohn commemorations of the German Jewish community and was delivered to the three Jewish lodges in Hamburg. At the time Cassirer was a well-known professor at the University of Hamburg, one of the few who were openly Jewish. It is clear that Cassirer was willing to put his (fragile and contested) prestige in the service of the Jewish community, emulating Moses Mendelssohn's mature willingness to trade on his illustrious philosophical reputation for the sake of Jewish advocacy.

In this address Cassirer argues vigorously that the Mendelssohn and Lessing friendship was not merely of secular significance as a creative collaboration, an epistolary correspondence which produced influential aesthetic theories of the nature of genres such as drama, epic, tragedy and the affective states pertaining to their reception.[37] Much more interesting and remarkable is the fact that the Jewish Mendelssohn and the Protestant Lessing shared an assured understanding as to the form of religious belief they both represented; here we see a wondrous coincidence of worldviews between the son of a Protestant pastor and a child of the Talmud on the problem of religion, a coincidence that only the century of the *Aufklärung* could have enabled.[38]

Indeed, it was precisely in their struggles with the problem of religion that Mendelssohn and Lessing reached a deep understanding from an early stage in their relationship.[39] These two young men found each other in a similar disposition (*gleichen Gesinnung*) and in a common striving for reform (*reformatorischen Streben*).[40] Their shared interpretation of the meaning of religion was predicated on the assumption that religion denies itself and its real spiritual content when it attempts to detach itself from reason and to give itself over completely to faith understood as the simply 'irrational'.[41] Lessing spoke for his age when he wrote that all of our experiences (*Empfindungen*) of God cannot suffice alone to ground religion if they cannot at the same time withstand the test of rational thought.[42]

Lessing was, however, sensitive to the fact that the rational is only one particular root of religious belief, which has been an effective power in human affairs only to the extent that it has arisen in historical form. The form of religion can never simply be metaphysical or bound to a conceptual system; it is dependent on the unique and individual realm (*Reich*) of Revelation. Godliness is not so much conceptualized as immediately apprehended, and it depends not so much on a doctrine as on the existence and reality of a teacher, of a founder and a propagator of religion. Their being, their life, and their words must be historically attested to.[43] Religious belief, according to Lessing and Mendelssohn, is secured in the present by the millennial memory of the tidings brought forth by its founders. Thus Lessing and Mendelssohn understood religion not simply as a rational sphere of necessary and eternal truths, but rather assumed it to be a dialectical conundrum, a concrescence of the phenomenal and the eternal that has been artificially separated in logical and philosophical thought. For religion to educate human beings, the eternal necessarily appears through the temporal, the infinite through the finite, and the unconditioned and absolute through the conditioned.[44]

Cassirer suggests that three solutions have been offered to Lessing and Mendelssohn's conundrum. Orthodox (Catholic and Protestant) theological systems construct a bridge between the temporal and eternal, whereby the eternal significance and necessary truths arising from an historical event are secured through the mediation of either the Church or the irrefragable truth of the Bible, considered as those media which secure the truth of God in the human world.[45] However, it was not only Lessing and Mendelssohn, but the entire philosophy of the Enlightenment that objected to the logical circularity of this system in which the truth of Revelation relies on the Church or the Bible, while the holiness of the Bible or Church can on the other hand only be secured through an appeal to Revelation.[46]

The second solution, offered by Mendelssohn, was to transcend the contingent and merely historical and thereby secure access to the unconditioned, the necessary truths of God, through the immutable laws of our own reason. For Mendelssohn these truths served as an Archimedean point around which the world of the spirit could revolve, necessitating a supplanting of supernatural revelation (*lumen supranaturale*) with the self-revelation of reason (*lumen naturale*). In the self-revelation of reason there is the knowledge of God, the determination of the ethical vocation of humanity, and the knowledge of the immortality of the soul.[47] In the innate ideas of God and the innate truths of reason, Mendelssohn finds the very source of the Godhead, which is not restricted to particular times, lands, and nations, but is continually renewed by each and every one of us, since it is legible only through the created world itself and its inner relationships.[48] Cassirer explains Mendelssohn's defence of the historical content of religion *qua* Revelation in *Jerusalem* as inaugurating a process of education and instruction by which Judaism fulfils the evolving ethical task of addressing human beings in their particular historical circumstances through oral law, and through commands and prescriptions that are sensitive to circumstance. Inaugurating liberal Judaism's combination of Jewish loyalty and ethical universalism, Mendelssohn interprets Judaism as an exemplary rational religion preserved by the Jewish people and their Law. For Mendelssohn, while Judaism needs to be understood as an historically conditioned community of fate that must never be dissolved, its rational precepts do not exclude the possibility of a truly universal human community.[49]

The third response to the paradoxes with which religion confronted Enlightenment thought was provided by Lessing, a response which respected but could not share Mendelssohn's aversion to the erroneous course of history. This aversion, as we have discussed, was manifested in Mendelssohn's rejection of Lessing's notion of humanity's historical progress, which Cassirer somewhat harshly describes as Mendelssohn's history denying 'flight' from the unpredictable and contingent into the immutable laws of reason. Cassirer then argues that Lessing, in principle, no longer recognized Mendelssohn's version of a universal and necessary reason.[50] Lessing was indeed a great rationalist, but his version of reason did not exclude becoming and development: it was not static, but 'dynamic'. For Lessing reason does not jettison but rather wants to learn the immanent laws of historical movement. It is a form of reason that eagerly immerses itself in the stream of becoming.[51]

Cassirer contends that where orthodox systems of belief establish religious certainty in light of the past, Mendelssohn sees it in the light of the present, as that clear natural light of reason which, according to Spinoza, illuminates error and entails a truth that is immediately present to intellectual vision. Lessing, however, interprets religion dynamically, that is, exclusively in light of the future.[52] The difference between Mendelssohn and Lessing, Cassirer explains, is owing to differences in their original educational milieu (*Bildungselemente*). If Mendelssohn was self-educated by immersing himself in logic, philosophy, and metaphysics, Lessing's thinking emerges from a deep acquaintance with history and philology; Cassirer is perhaps suggesting that Lessing was one of the true precursors of the philological and historical methods of *Wissenschaft des Judentums*.[53]

Lessing's conception of religious truth, Cassirer remarks, is genuinely Heraclitean in its emphasis on renewal and becoming; it is not a classical rationalist conception of truth as being immediately present to intellectual vision through the logical categories of ratiocination.[54] For Lessing, whoever believes they are in possession of the truth has already lost it, since truth is only visible as long as it is continually brought forth anew by the efforts of human beings.[55] The version of truth that Lessing endorses, a version that could only appear as sacrilege to dogmatic theological and philosophical systems, and which was even foreign to his great friend Mendelssohn, sees truth as arising provisionally, from the productive forces of doubt, confusion, and error.[56] It is Lessing who lends the noble Enlightenment concept of tolerance (*Toleranz*) its specific affective character, that of reverence (*Ehrfurcht*) and modesty, for unlike the *Aufklärung* as a whole, Lessing's tolerance is not a compassionate condescension towards historical error, but the recognition, implying faith and confidence in the human intellect, that error is not simply antithetical to truth but an indispensable and unavoidable moment in the quest for it.[57]

Cassirer argues that while Lessing did not simply reject religion, his conception of religion no longer relied on obeisance to an otherworldly and transcendent God, but was rather invested in humanity as the subject of history (*Menschen als Subject der Geschichte*).[58] When Lessing, in *Erziehung des Menschengeschlechts*, refers to humanity's 'education' (*Erziehung*) and formation by religion, he does not mean a supernatural Revelation but a gradual historical process, a slow and steady maturing of the idea of the divine which is not given all at once to us by a majestic dispensation from above but is won through the tireless pursuit of circuitous pathways and in the struggle with doubt and error. It is a sublime idea of divinity which humanity must bring forth by the light of its own rational and ethical powers.[59] One senses distinct affinities between Lessing's humanist evocation of religion as temporally constituted, as the slow awakening of an ethical subject, and Cassirer's historical phenomenology of the emergence of a higher, idealistically inclined religious subjectivity in the second volume of *The Philosophy of Symbolic Forms* (1925). There Cassirer traces the slow yet ideal-historical transition from the magical-mythical worldview 'to the truly *religious* view'. Cassirer notes for example that as human civilization progresses, there is a movement from nature myths to culture myths, in which myths such as the story of Prometheus seek to explain not so much the world or its objects but rather human cultural achievements.[60] The outcome of this dialectical development is that while the religious spirit still lives in and makes use of the world of images and signs, it discovers a new relation to them, attaining a 'greater understanding of them, and thus rising above them'.[61] Cassirer also transposes this phenomenology of the slow maturation of the reflexive ethical subject onto his philosophy of human culture. In *An Essay on Man* he appeals in Kantian fashion to the idea of 'humanity' as a projective 'idea' of reason that subtends his interpretation of human acculturation. Cassirer argues that if the term humanity means anything at all, it signifies that in spite of all the differences and oppositions existing among its various forms, these are, nevertheless, 'all working toward a common end'.[62] In all of the particular symbolic forms there is a certain directionality in their order, a certain manner by which they develop from elementary to more complex forms, and it is the task of a philosophy of symbolic forms to 'ascertain the ideal "orientation" of each symbolic form' by providing a universal, synthetic view.[63]

Returning to the 1929 address, Cassirer maintains that Lessing had an open sense of the future; he was not a 'rationalist' in the classic sense derived from the seventeenth-century emphasis on clear and distinct ideas, because for him the shortest line was not necessarily the straightest.[64] Lessing's humility (*Demut*) and reverence before human history contained an element of Promethean pride that refused to be subjected to the will of an alien and transcendent divine power. Cassirer suggests that Lessing represented his Promethean animus towards an alien and supra-mundane divine power in the modest judge of the rings parable of *Nathan the Wise*. The judge of the rings dispute knows that the moment of divine judgement is perhaps infinitely deferred, that human beings are created for activity and not simply for rational demonstration; it is a question not just of the rational or dogmatic grounding of faith but of the capacity of religion to exemplify its moral attributes over time. The judge knows, therefore, that a definitive judgement on humanity's religious progress cannot yet be passed, and thus that there is no 'true' eschatological religion that stands outside of human history.[65]

In remarks that echo Cohen's articulation of an idealized Protestantism that reprises the rigorous ethical spirit of Jewish monotheism, Cassirer praises Lessing as the founder and creator of a new form of Protestantism. Lessing, Cassirer comments admiringly, was a Lutheran 'of the spirit' who would not prevent any person from discovering their own discretionary road to truth.[66] While religious intuition, for Lessing, remains under the guidance of critical interpretation, of a luminous and vigilant form of thinking, it does not arise from mere rational understanding (*bloßen Verstande*), but is nourished by other independent creative energies (*selbständigen Kräften*).[67]

Cassirer embarks on a hortatory peroration, asking his audience portentously whether Lessing and Mendelssohn's ideas of religion belong only to the past, or, whether they are still significant for our present and our religious future. This is not difficult to answer in the case of Judaism, for Mendelssohn himself, a great theoretician of Jewish religious philosophy as a 'religion of reason', was not simply a Wolffian and philosophical rationalist as Germans perceive him; Mendelssohn was decisively influenced by Maimonides's *More Newuchim* (*Guide for the Perplexed*), which he reverenced.[68] Today, Cassirer feels, the most original and fruitful perspectives of the modern Jewish philosophy of religion pursue the same path as Mendelssohn. Hermann Cohen, for example, in paying homage to Maimonides as a classic rationalist, entitled his religious-philosophical magnum opus *Die Religion der Vernunft aus den Quellen des Judentums* (*The Religion of Reason out of the Sources of Judaism*). Yet this great work of Cohen's was also influenced by Lessing's religious insights, since Cohen locates the unique essence of Judaism in the religion of the Prophets, as evinced in the idea of messianism. In the creation of messianism, the religion of reason is fulfilled as the religion of the future, in which the past must disappear in the light of the messianic ideal, in which all that has existed heretofore disappears before the standpoint of the idea of humanity. For Cohen humanity (*Menschheit*), Cassirer explains, has not lived in the past and does not live in the present: only the future illuminates its luminous form.

Cohen's Prophetic idea of humanity, Cassirer clarifies, is to be realized through ethical imagination and social activity; it is not simply a shadow of the beyond. Cohen effects a synthesis of the religious content of Judaism, as he understood it, and the intellectual content of philosophical idealism, to which his earlier work on Kant had contributed new profundities. In Cassirer's view, it takes little effort to demonstrate how close this synthesis of the idealistic thought of a rational religion as a religion of the future (*Zukunftsreligion*) is to the spirit of Lessing's *Erziehung des Menschengeschlechts*. The two providential streams of Mendelssohn's Maimonidean rational Judaism and Lessing's historically immanent conception of religion ensure that neither should be merely recognized as legendary historical figures but also understood and honoured as heralds of a spiritual future.[69]

Amongst a variety of observations we could make about Cassirer's subtle analysis, we should remark his liberal Jewish pride in Mendelssohn's twinning of a secular reputation as a great philosopher with a profound contribution to the Maimonidean tradition of Jewish philosophical rationalism. Cassirer's erudite reading of Mendelssohn's contribution to Jewish philosophy and religious thought goes well beyond an apologetic celebration of Mendelssohn as a benign figure of German Jewish acculturation. Cassirer's characterological interpretation of the Enlightenment, in the robust spirit of Heine, draws attention to an era of social experimentation that produced unique personalities and heterodox friendships. Of a piece is Cassirer's German Jewish assumption that the Enlightenment is a living and productive legacy of emancipatory thinking rather than an antithetical background to the rise of Romantic historicism and national consciousness. Finally, in the inclusive and syncretic spirit of liberal Judaism which prizes and reclaims the German idealistic tradition as contributing to post-biblical Jewish thought, Cassirer suggests that because of his historically immanent conception of reason, Lessing, a non Jew, is in many respects a more significant contributor to the ethos of modern Judaism, incarnated by Hermann Cohen, than the Jewish Mendelssohn.

The Philosophy of the Enlightenment

There are several aspects of Cassirer's defence of Enlightenment thought in his 1932 *The Philosophy of the Enlightenment* that follow on from his endeavours of the late 1920s to highlight not just the epistemological but also the ethical, legal, political, and religious significance of Enlightenment thought as mediated by exemplary personalities who were immersed in the hopes and desires of their times. In the oft discussed preface to *The Philosophy of the Enlightenment* Cassirer rejects a prevalent German critique of the ('French') Enlightenment's thin rationalism, atomistic materialism, and ahistorical universalism. Cassirer defends the Enlightenment's robust and vibrant legacy and the prism it affords for social critique. He will revise the 'verdict of the Romantic movement on the Enlightenment' that is still 'accepted by many without criticism', and in so doing repudiate the canard of the 'shallow Enlightenment' that is still in vogue.[70]

The ethos which Kant called the motto of the Enlightenment itself, *Sapere aude*, 'dare to know', should forestall, Cassirer feels, such a derogatory attitude, particularly as reflections on the history of philosophy 'must always be accompanied by philosophical re-orientation and self-criticism'. Indeed, Cassirer admonishes, 'more than ever before ... the time is again ripe for applying such self-criticism to the present age, for holding up to it that bright clear mirror fashioned by the Enlightenment. Much that seems to us today the result of "progress" will be sure to lose its luster when seen in this mirror'. Most importantly the recovery of the Enlightenment's intellectual curiosity is more urgent that ever before: 'the age which venerated reason and science as man's highest faculty cannot and must not be lost even for us'.[71]

In the preface to *The Philosophy of the Enlightenment*, Cassirer articulates an innovative methodological approach. He is less interested in the philosophical content of the Enlightenment, its particular axioms, theories, and positions, than in its dynamic *form* and ceaseless *activity*, for the 'true nature of the Enlightenment' can only be understood in the 'process' of doubting and seeking, and in 'action', the constantly evolving process of thought.[72] In the Enlightenment Cassirer detects the pulsation of an inner intellectual life that 'breaks through the rigid barriers of system' because it attributes to thought not merely an imitative function but the 'power and task of shaping life itself', of bringing about that order of things which it conceives as necessary.[73]

Perhaps with his recent characterization of Mendelssohn in mind, Cassirer evokes the *esprit* of the Enlightenment, which opposes the 'spirit of systems' and wants 'philosophy to move freely' as an 'immanent activity'.[74] The philosophy of the Enlightenment is no longer situated above the principles of natural science, law, and politics, but is the 'comprehensive medium' in which such principles are formulated, developed, and founded. Philosophy is now very much of this world, no longer representing the 'isolated substance of the intellect' but rather the 'totality of the intellect in its true function'.[75] The eighteenth century, Cassirer suggests in the first chapter of *The Philosophy of the Enlightenment*, the 'Mind of the Enlightenment', understands reason in a more modest sense than the seventeenth century; reason is not the sum of 'innate ideas' given prior to all experience, it is not a heritage but an acquisition, an 'original intellectual force' which guides the 'discovery and determination of truth'. The 'whole eighteenth century' understands reason in this more dynamic and practical sense: not as a sound body of knowledge, principles, and truths, but as a 'kind of energy' which is fully comprehensible only in its 'agency and effects'. What reason is, and what it can do, can never be known by results, but 'only by its function', one aspect of which is to dissolve everything that is merely factual, all simple data of experience, and 'everything believed on the evidence of revelation, tradition, and authority'.[76] Cassirer's conception of Enlightenment thought as dynamically self-disclosing, dispensing with the apodictic rationalism of the seventeenth century, reminds us of Koselleck's illuminating suggestion that *Bildung* is a 'processual state that constantly and actively changes through reflexivity', a conceptual medium that can only 'substantiate itself – actively and reflexively at the same time – in the medium of diachronic change'.[77]

Cassirer affirms that Lessing's famous saying – that the power of reason is to be found not in the possession but the acquisition of truth – has its 'parallels everywhere in the intellectual history of the eighteenth century', including Montesquieu and Diderot's *Encyclopedia* which sought to bring about a 'change in the mode of thinking'.[78] In the fourth chapter on 'Religion', which recapitulates to a large extent 'The Idea of Religion in Lessing and Mendelssohn', Cassirer claims once more that Lessing represents the pinnacle of the eighteenth century's conception of dynamic reason, in which reason 'does not exclude motion [but rather seeks] to understand the immanent law of motion'. It is an approach, Cassirer maintains, that influenced Herder's thought, a thinking that evolves from the Enlightenment and 'matures on its soil', opening up the 'whole horizon of the historical world'.[79]

While Cassirer's thought has often been described, usually unflatteringly, as irenic or conciliatory, his brilliant interpretation, that began in the late 1920s, of the Enlightenment's vital, socially engaged, and historically sensitive conception of reason was intended to challenge the reified version of reason critiqued by its romantic, historicist, and existentialist antagonists.[80] His purpose was also to warn an educated German public against fatally closing their minds to fructifying external influences. *The Philosophy of the Enlightenment* not only represented his futile attempts to remind Germany of its cosmopolitan and idealistic inheritance, but was also a superb embodiment of his counter-historical philosophy of history. In *An Essay on Man*, Cassirer will encapsulate his tireless effort, inspired by Cohen, to keep open the question of historical 'origins', describing historical thought as an active symbolic form, in which a 'new understanding of the past gives us at the same time a new prospect of the future, which in turn becomes an impulse to intellectual and social life'. Historical inquiry, Cassirer reminds us through his proud recovery of the Enlightenment's critical élan and breadth of purpose, is not an accumulation of empirical data but rather the answer to 'definite questions' which are dictated by the present, by our 'present intellectual interests and our present moral and social needs'.[81]

The Enlightenment in Exile

In order to grasp Cassirer's conception of the Enlightenment as a model of philosophy's possible relationship with the world, we should recall that after his emigration from Germany in 1933 and his lengthy periods in Sweden (1934–1941) and the United States (1941–1945), he expressed harsh criticisms of modern philosophy's failure, since the rise of positivism and materialism in the nineteenth century, to defend civilized values and encourage independent thought. In October 1935 Cassirer gave an inaugural lecture, 'Bedeutung und Aufgabe der Philosophie' ('The Meaning and Task of Philosophy', later translated into English by Donald Verene as 'The Concept of Philosophy as a Philosophical Problem'), at the University of Göteborg in Sweden, upon his appointment there as professor of theoretical philosophy.[82]

Cassirer was acutely mindful in this address of the ominous shadow that National Socialism cast over Europe. He invoked Kant's humanist philosophical ethos as exemplary and profoundly germane to the present crisis. It was Kant, Cassirer suggested, who learnt from Rousseau no longer to despise the mob but to 'respect human beings' and establish the 'rights of humanity'. For Kant all philosophy became henceforth inextricably allied with 'that basic question which stirred the eighteenth century so deeply', the 'eternal, immutable, and inalienable rights of man'.[83] From the time of his acquaintance with the thought of Rousseau, Kant was no longer interested in a scholastic conception of philosophy as the perfection of knowledge, but rather articulated a 'cosmic' (*conceptus cosmicus*) conception of philosophy as 'personified . . . in the ideal *philosopher*' and thus ethically inspiring: philosophy is the science of the relation of all knowledge to the ends of human reason, and the philosopher is the lawgiver of human reason.[84] In postulating the basic value of the moral law as consonant with the rights of man and human dignity, Kant ensured that a logical and epistemological conception of philosophy passed over into a 'conception of philosophy as related to the world'.[85]

Cassirer is adamant that the question that Kant and the eighteenth century posed – the relation of all forms of knowledge to the essential aims of reason itself – was not simply a youthful dream of human reason that we have now left behind. Rather, it 'arises more urgently and imperatively than ever before', not only for the philosopher, but for all of us who 'partake in the life of knowledge and the life of spiritual culture'.[86] Today the 'urgency of the time' means that there is once again a question for philosophy that involves its ultimate and highest decisions: is there an ideal of morality, of humanity? Are there general and binding supra-individual, supra-state, supra-national ethical claims? The inner 'ideational power' of a philosophy that once again asks such questions can never be diminished or weakened by derision and scepticism; indeed the preservation of these ideas is the only means by which philosophy can once again 'have an effect on outside existence and events'.[87]

Today, Cassirer warns, we must give ourselves over less than ever before to Hegel's famous, optimistic remark, that what is rational is real, and what is real rational. The true nature of reason cannot be grasped in 'bare existence', in the 'finished and extant'. We must instead seek reason in the 'continual self-renewing work of spirit': this is 'not a *given* but a *task*'. Reason is not, as Hegel hoped, a substantial, metaphysical world spirit which peacefully completes its immanent work and transcends all individual desires and plans. No, Cassirer intones in a surprisingly Heideggerean vein, rather 'it is the question of a problem which is placed before us and for which we must struggle'.[88] After outlining an active conception of reason immanent to historical time in the spirit of Lessing, the recently exiled Cassirer promised his Swedish audience that he would make every attempt to restore philosophy's relationship to the world and to other areas of knowledge. Cassirer commits to a new research community modelled, perhaps, on Cohen's vitality and warmth. He promises not to work in isolation but to put his philosophical endeavours into the 'closest connection with the particular disciplines, in lively community, in close personal touch with their representatives'.[89]

It is more than likely that Cassirer not only conducted highly desirable interdisciplinary conversations but also upheld his Jewish commitments during his Swedish period; Cassirer had given a lecture on Cohen's philosophy of religion to the Oxford Jewish Society in June 1935.[90] According to Hansson and Nordin, Cassirer lectured on more than one occasion in the Jewish community and likely made the acquaintance of the Chief Rabbi of Sweden, Marcus Ehrenpreis, who had studied at the *Hochscule für die Wissenschaft des Judentums* in Berlin, where he had come into contact with Hermann Cohen. By November 1935, Cassirer had agreed in principle to give a lecture for the Jewish Literary Society in Stockholm, offering lectures on Lessing and Mendelssohn, Spinoza's place in the history of ideas, and Hermann Cohen's philosophy and its relationship to Judaism.[91]

I would suggest that Cassirer's response to the fatalistic turn of German philosophy was to revive the 'anthropological culture of the *Aufklärung*' as described by John Zammito, a philosophical movement that attempted to bring the scholar back into the world. This anti-scholastic humanist philosophical ideal, initially articulated in the late seventeenth century by Christian Thomasius, desired an accessible philosophical discourse conducted with eloquence and *esprit*. Through the efforts of Mendelssohn and Lessing in the fields of philosophy and aesthetics, from the middle of the eighteenth century the ideal of a *Popularphilosophie* became associated with enlightened progress through periodicals and convivial associations (such as the famous *Mittwochgesellschaft* of which both Kant and Mendelssohn were members), the public use of one's reason, and informed public opinion.[92] Cassirer's turn towards philosophical anthropology in a moment of historical crisis was an attempt to reinscribe philosophy's public-political orientation as a bulwark against the fragmentation and specialization of knowledge, the impersonality of scientific discourse, technological automatism, and the ethical danger to civilized values posed by atavistic nationalism and the revival of political 'mythologies' on a grand scale.[93] Cassirer's inspired 1935 address to his anxious Swedish audience was not a belated reaction to the shock of his own sudden exile from Germany, but, as we have seen, once more conveys the urgent tenor of his critical discourse, often in the form of a public address, that began in 1928 and culminated in *The Philosophy of the Enlightenment*.

After his retirement from teaching at Göteborg, Cassirer was offered a guest lectureship at Yale; the Cassirers departed for the United States in May 1941. In a lecture entitled 'Philosophy and Politics', given at Connecticut College in the United States in April 1944, Cassirer resumed his discussion of the ethos and task of philosophy, defining philosophy as the 'great effort of thought to embrace and unify all the different activities of man – to bring them into a common focus'.[94] As a living exemplar of this philosophical ideal, Cassirer admiringly discusses the German thinker and humanitarian Albert Schweitzer, a hero of his mature philosophy, of whom Cassirer had commented in 'The Concept of Philosophy' that he is 'respected as much as a man as he is a thinker'.[95] Cassirer sympathetically quotes Schweitzer's lament that philosophy's universalism and capacity to care for human civilization as a whole has waned, leaving society susceptible to organized political ideologies. Where once, in the eighteenth century, 'philosophy led and guided thought in general', concerning itself with society and humanity, producing a 'living popular philosophy' that maintained the enthusiasm for civilization, 'all this was lost during the nineteenth century'. According to Schweitzer, during the nineteenth century philosophy became a 'stranger to the world' such that the 'problems of life which occupied man and the whole thought of the age had no part in its activities'.[96]

The decline of the social relevance of philosophy, Cassirer argues, does not mean we should discount the baleful influence of German thinkers such as Spengler and Heidegger on the intellectual atmosphere in Germany between the wars. It was the fatalism and passive attitude of their new philosophical doctrines that helped to enfeeble and slowly undermine the forces that could have resisted the modern political myths. A philosophy of history that consists in sombre predictions of the decline and inevitable destruction of our civilization and a theory that sees in the *Geworfenheit* ['thrownness'] of man one of his principal characters have given up all hope of an active share in the construction and reconstruction of man's cultural life. Such philosophy renounces its own fundamental theoretical and ethical ideals. It can be used, then, as a pliable instrument in the hands of the political leaders.[97]

This strain of philosophical fatalism 'can no longer do its duty' of instilling rational autonomy; it can no longer, Cassirer implies, fulfil the character-task of *Bildung*, which must 'teach man how to develop his active faculties in order to form his individual and social life'.[98]

One of the last and greatest works of Cassirer, *An Essay on Man* (1944), the first version of which he wrote in Sweden, articulated just such an attempt to encourage individual *Bildung*. In the second chapter, 'A Clue to the Nature of Man: The Symbol', Cassirer advocates a philosophical anthropology that acknowledges the ethical importance of defining humanity as a rational being while acknowledging that definition's limitation as a description of religion, culture, and ethics. Reason, Cassirer avers, is a 'very inadequate term' with which to comprehend the 'forms of man's cultural life' in their richness and variety. Recognizing all these forms as active and creative means redefining the human being not as an *animal rationale* but as an *animal symbolicum*, and thus acknowledging the specific difference of human being as an orientation towards culture and civilization: a 'human being in the construction of his human world is not dependent upon the quality of his sense material'.[99] As exemplified in the utopian and reformist proclivities of many great thinkers, it is in 'the very nature and character of ethical thought that it can never condescend to accept "the given"'.[100] While Cassirer's idealistic desideratum might seem in tension with Hannah Arendt's emphasis on realism in politics, as we shall see, Arendt's growing sympathy with the critical independence of the Enlightenment and her 'Prophetic' Jewish universalism helped her to contend with Zionist ethnocentrism and articulate a diasporic conception of recent Jewish history.

Notes

1 Gordon, *Continental Divide*, 292.
2 Heidegger, *Kant and the Problem of Metaphysics*, 214.
3 E. Cassirer. 1981. *Kant's Life and Thought*, trans. James Haden, New Haven: Yale University Press, 6 and 10.
4 Cassirer, *Kant's Life and Thought*, 11.

5 Cassirer, *Kant's Life and Thought*, 6.

6 'When [Herder] again and again stresses freedom and joyousness of soul as the foundation of Kant's nature, he does not seem fully aware that this harmonious balance
   was not for Kant a direct gift of nature and fate, but that it was won instead by hard
   intellectual struggles'. Of Kant's friendship and correspondence with the German
   Jewish physician Marcus Herz, Cassirer writes: 'The exchanges of letters [between
   Kant and Herz from the decade 1770–1780] . . . are quite spasmodic and seem to
   have ceased entirely for a while, but Kant, who was rendering in them an account
   to himself of how his thinking was progressing, seems always to have felt the need to
   begin them anew'. Cassirer, *Kant's Life and Thought*, 84 and 122.

7 Cassirer, *Kant's Life and Thought*, 89.

8 E. Cassirer. 1947. *Rousseau, Kant, Goethe, Two Essays*, Princeton: Princeton University Press, 1–2. For a more sustained study of Rousseau's ethical idealism, philosophy of
   education, and political theory, which seeks to imbricate the content and meaning
   of his work in the 'foundation of personal life', see E. Cassirer. 1989. *The Question of
   Jean-Jacques Rousseau*, trans. P. Gay, New Haven: Yale University Press, 40.

9 'Die Warheit alles Geschehen beruht auf dem Hinzukommen jenes . . . unsichtbaren
   Theils jeder Thatsache, und diesen muss daher der Geschichtschreiber hinzufügen.
   Von dieser Seite berachtet, ist er selbstthätig, und sogar schöpferisch, zwar nicht
   indem er hervorbringt, was nicht vorhanden ist, aber indem er aus eigner Kraft bildet,
   was er, wie es wirklich ist, nicht mit blosser Empfänglichkeit warnehmen konnte'.
   W.V. Humboldt. 2002. 'Ueber die Aufgabe des Geschichtschreibers', in *Über die
   Sprache, Reden vor der Akademie*, Tübingen: A. Francke Verlag, 34. (The truth of any
   event is predicated on the addition of that invisible part of every fact which the historian has to add. Regarded in this manner, the historian is active, even creative – not
   by bringing forth what does not exist, but in giving shape from his own powers to
   that which by mere intuition he could not have perceived as it was in actuality.) For
   an English translation see W.V. Humboldt. 1967. 'On the Historian's Task', *History
   and Theory* 6(1), 57–71.

10 E. Cassirer. 1927–1931. 'Die Idee der republikanischen Verfassung. Rede zur
    Verfassungsfeier am 11. August 1928' (1929), in *Aufsätze und kleine Schriften* (1941–
    1946), edited Birgit Recki. 2007. *Cassirer Gesammelte Werke* (24 vols), Hamburger
    Ausgabe (ECW), Meiner Verlag. Vol. 7, 291.

11 Cassirer, 'Die Idee der republikanischen Verfassung', 291.

12 Cassirer, 'Die Idee der republikanischen Verfassung', 294.

13 Cassirer, 'Die Idee der republikanischen Verfassung', 295.

14 Cassirer, 'Die Idee der republikanischen Verfassung', 295, 296.

15 Cassirer, 'Die Idee der republikanischen Verfassung', 298–299.

16 Cassirer, 'Die Idee der republikanischen Verfassung', 300, 302.

17 Cassirer, 'Die Idee der republikanischen Verfassung', 303.

18 Humboldt, 'Ueber die Aufgabe des Geschichtsreibers', 37 / Humboldt, 'On the
    Historian's Task', 61.

19 Cassirer, 'Die Idee der republikanischen Verfassung', 307.

20 For a discussion of Cassirer's role on the honorary board overseeing the Jubilee editon
    (*Jubiläumsausgabe*), see M. Gottlieb. 2008. 'Publishing the Moses Mendelssohn
    Jubiläumsausgabe in Weimar and Nazi Germany', *Leo Baeck Institute Yearbook* 53(1),
    58–59.

21 E. Cassirer. 2004. 'Die Philosophie Moses Mendelssohns' (1929), in *Aufsätze und kleine Schriften* (1927–1931), Birgit Recki (ed.), Hamburg: Felix Meiner Verlag, 117.

22 Cassirer, 'Die Philosophie Moses Mendelssohns', 117.

23 Cassirer, 'Die Philosophie Moses Mendelssohns', 126.

24 Cassirer, 'Die Philosophie Moses Mendelssohns', 128.

25 Cassirer, 'Die Philosophie Moses Mendelssohns', 132.

26 For a discussion of Mendelssohn's analysis of Judaism as congenial to the *Bildungsideal*, see my article 'Redescribing the Enlightenment: The German-Jewish Adoption of Bildung as a Counter-normative Ideal', *Intellectual History Review* 23 (3), 2013, forthcoming.

27 'True perfection is a living flame, constantly fanning out and becoming stronger and stronger the more it is able to fan out. The inclination to communicate itself and to reproduce the good that one enjoys is implanted in the soul as much as the instinct to preserve oneself. We become more perfect, if everything that surrounds us is perfect; we become happier if we are able to make everything around us happy'. M. Mendelssohn. 2003. 'Rhapsody or Additions to the Letters on Sentiment', in *Philosophical Writings*, trans. D.O. Dahlstrom, Cambridge, UK: Cambridge University Press, 152.

28 Cassirer, 'Die Philosophie Moses Mendelssohns', 132. In an unpublished 1928 manuscript Cassirer criticizes Heidegger's ontological philosophy in *Sein und Zeit* as a 'religious-individualistic comprehension of history' whose repudiation of discourse as 'mere talk' leaves no access to transpersonal meaning. To Heidegger's Lutheran conception of death as profoundly isolating, Cassirer opposes the '*idealistic* meaning of religion and the idealistic meaning of history' which promises 'liberation and deliverance' from the 'anxiety' which is the signature of finite Dasein. E. Cassirer. 1996. *The Philosophy of Symbolic Forms, Volume 4, the Metaphysics of Symbolic Forms*, trans. J.M. Krois, New Haven: Yale University Press, 202–203. For an illuminating discussion of Cassirer and Heidegger's differences over the philosophical significance of death as very similar to the dispute between Erasmus and Luther over human free will, see J.M. Krois. 1983. 'Ernst Cassirer's Unpublished Critique of Heidegger', *Philosophy and Rhetoric* 16(3), 147–159.

29 Cassirer, 'Die Philosophie Moses Mendelssohns, 132.

30 Cassirer, 'Die Philosophie Moses Mendelssohns', 133.

31 Cassirer, 'Die Philosophie Moses Mendelssohns', 134.

32 Cassirer, 'Die Philosophie Moses Mendelssohns', 135.

33 Cassirer, 'Die Philosophie Moses Mendelssohns', 135.

34 Cassirer, 'Die Philosophie Moses Mendelssohns', 135, 137.

35 Cassirer, 'Die Philosophie Moses Mendelssohns', 137.

36 Cassirer, 'Die Philosophie Moses Mendelssohns', 137.

37 'Ernst Cassirer. 1929. 'Die Idee der Religion bei Lessing and Mendelssohn', *Festgabe zum zehnjahrigen Bestehen der Akademie fur die Wissenchaften des Judentums, 1919–1929*, Berlin: Akademie Verlag, 23.

38 Cassirer, 'Die Idee der Religion bei Lessing and Mendelssohn', 23–24.

39 Cassirer, 'Die Idee der Religion bei Lessing and Mendelssohn', 24.

40 Cassirer, 'Die Idee der Religion bei Lessing and Mendelssohn', 24.

41 Cassirer, 'Die Idee der Religion bei Lessing and Mendelssohn', 25.

42 Cassirer, 'Die Idee der Religion bei Lessing and Mendelssohn', 25.

43 Cassirer, 'Die Idee der Religion bei Lessing and Mendelssohn', 26.

44 Cassirer, 'Die Idee der Religion bei Lessing and Mendelssohn', 26.

45 Cassirer, 'Die Idee der Religion bei Lessing and Mendelssohn', 28.

46 Cassirer, 'Die Idee der Religion bei Lessing and Mendelssohn', 28.

47 Cassirer, 'Die Idee der Religion bei Lessing and Mendelssohn', 29.

48 Cassirer, 'Die Idee der Religion bei Lessing and Mendelssohn', 29–30.

49 Cassirer, 'Die Idee der Religion bei Lessing and Mendelssohn', 31.

50 Cassirer, 'Die Idee der Religion bei Lessing and Mendelssohn', 32.

51 Cassirer, 'Die Idee der Religion bei Lessing and Mendelssohn', 33.

52 Cassirer, 'Die Idee der Religion bei Lessing and Mendelssohn', 33.

53 Cassirer, 'Die Idee der Religion bei Lessing and Mendelssohn', 32.

54 Cassirer, 'Die Idee der Religion bei Lessing and Mendelssohn', 33.

55 Cassirer, 'Die Idee der Religion bei Lessing and Mendelssohn', 33–34.

56 Cassirer, 'Die Idee der Religion bei Lessing and Mendelssohn', 34.

57 Cassirer, 'Die Idee der Religion bei Lessing and Mendelssohn', 34.

58 Cassirer, 'Die Idee der Religion bei Lessing and Mendelssohn', 36.

59 Cassirer, 'Die Idee der Religion bei Lessing and Mendelssohn', 37.

60 Cassirer, *Mythical Thought*, 203.

61 Cassirer, *Mythical Thought*, 24–25.

62 Cassirer, *An Essay on Man*, 70.

63 E. Cassirer. 1978. 'The Problem of the Symbol and its Place in the System of Philosophy', trans. J.M. Krois, *Man and World* 11(3–4), 417.

64 Cassirer, 'Die Idee der Religion bei Lessing and Mendelssohn', 37.

65 Cassirer, 'Die Idee der Religion bei Lessing and Mendelssohn', 37–38.

66 Cassirer, 'Die Idee der Religion bei Lessing and Mendelssohn', 39.

67 Cassirer, 'Die Idee der Religion bei Lessing and Mendelssohn', 40.

68 Cassirer, 'Die Idee der Religion bei Lessing and Mendelssohn', 40–41.

69 Cassirer, 'Die Idee der Religion bei Lessing and Mendelssohn', 41.

70 Cassirer, *The Philosophy of the Enlightenment*, xvii.

71 Cassirer, *The Philosophy of the Enlightenment*, xvii.

72 Cassirer, *The Philosophy of the Enlightenment*, xv.

73 Cassirer, *The Philosophy of the Enlightenment*, xiv, xv.

74 Cassirer, *The Philosophy of the Enlightenment*, xiii.

75 Cassirer, *The Philosophy of the Enlightenment*, xiii.

76 Cassirer, *The Philosophy of the Enlightenment*, 13.

77 Koselleck, *The Practice of Conceptual History*, 176.

78 Cassirer, *The Philosophy of the Enlightenment*, 14.

79 Cassirer, *The Philosophy of the Enlightenment*, 195–196.

80 As Gordon points out, Friedrich Meinecke's *Die Entsehung of Historismus* (1936) is perhaps the most famous indictment of the Enlightenment's supposed failure to understand historicity and historical difference. Gordon, *Continental Divide*, 293.

81 Cassirer, *An Essay on Man*, 178.

82 For a fine discussion of Cassirer's 'especially prolific' period in Sweden, see J.M. Krois. 2006. 'Introduction', in J. Hannson and S. Nordin (eds), *Ernst Cassirer: The Swedish Years*, Bern: Peter Lang, 7–30.

83 Cassirer, 1979 [1935]. 'The Concept of Philosophy as a Philosophical Problem', in D.P. Verene (ed.), *Symbol, Myth, and Culture: Essays and Lectures of Ernst Cassirer, 1935–1945*, New Haven and London: Yale University Press, 58.

84 Cassirer, 'The Concept of Philosophy', 58–59.

85 Cassirer, 'The Concept of Philosophy', 58.

86 Cassirer, 'The Concept of Philosophy', 59.

87 Cassirer, 'The Concept of Philosophy', 60–61.

88 Cassirer, 'The Concept of Philosophy', 62. In his lecture 'Hegel's Theory of the State' (1942), given as part of a course on the Philosophy of History which Cassirer taught at Yale in 1941–1942 (typically involving a close collaboration with a representative of another discipline, the historian Hajo Holborn), Cassirer sharply criticizes Hegel's critique of Kant's idealistic distinction between *Sein* and *Sollen*, between what is and what should be. Hegel's political realism, his disdain for the natural rights of the individual as articulated by the Enlightenment, and his worship of the state, means that his 'philosophy is to a large degree responsible for our modern theories of the omnipotent state'. See E. Cassirer. 1979 [1942]. 'Hegel's Theory of the State', in Verene, *Symbol, Myth, and Culture*, 112–115.

89 Cassirer, 'The Concept of Philosophy', 63.

90 In that 1935 address Cassirer was keen to disabuse his Anglophone audience of the image of Cohen as an abstruse and scientist neo-Kantian philosopher, while implicitly bolstering his own claim to be a committed Jewish philosopher. There was never a day after the commencement of his friendship with Cohen, relates Cassirer, when he 'did not start a conversation with me about a special problem of Judaism, about a problem of Jewish tradition, of Jewish religious, moral or political life'. E. Cassirer. 1996. 'Cohen's Philosophy of Religion', transcribed D. Kaegi, *Internationale Zeitschrift für Philosophie* 1, 91.

91 See J. Hannson and S. Nordin. 2006. *Ernst Cassirer: The Swedish Years*, Bern: Peter Lang, 65.

92 J. Zammito. 2002. *Kant, Herder, and the Birth of Anthropology*, Chicago: University of Chicago Press, 6, 10, and 37.

93 Zammito, *Kant, Herder, and the Birth of Anthropology*, 18.

94 Cassirer. 1979 [1944]. 'Philosophy and Politics', in Verene, *Symbol, Myth, and Culture*, 219.

95 Cassirer, 'The Concept of Philosophy', 59.

96 Cassirer, 'Philosophy and Politics', 232.

97 Cassirer, *The Myth of the State*, 293.

98 Cassirer, 'Philosophy and Politics', 230.

99 E. Cassirer. 1944. *An Essay on Man*, New Haven: Yale University Press, 26 and 35.

100 Cassirer, *An Essay on Man*, 61.

CHAPTER 7

※

Hannah Arendt
The Task of the Historian

'If the historian succeeded in effacing his personal life he would not thereby achieve a higher objectivity. He would on the contrary deprive himself of the very instrument of all historical thought.'

Ernst Cassirer, 'History', *An Essay on Man*

Cassirer's powerful reappraisal of the pan-European Enlightenment and the German *Aufklärung* in the 1920s and 1930s, which culminated in *The Philosophy of the Enlightenment*, was conceived as an urgent ethical resource, a counter-history to historical narratives that legitimized German exceptionalism and Romantic nationalism. As an expression of his philosophy of history Cassirer's inspired reconstruction of Enlightenment thought was a testament to the fragility of human creations, a reminder that in order to endure the 'works of man must be constantly renewed and restored'.[1] In order to 'possess the world of culture', Cassirer argued in a chapter discussing history as a symbolic form in *An Essay on Man*, we must 'incessantly reconquer it' by historical recollection. Such recollection is not merely 'reproduction' but a 'new intellectual synthesis' or 'constructive act'. In this reconstruction the human mind moves in the opposite direction from the original process of works of culture which originate in acts of solidification and stabilization. Behind the petrified works of human culture, history detects the 'original dynamic impulses'; it is the gift of the great historians to 'reduce all mere facts to their *fieri*, all products to processes, all static things or institutions to their creative energies'.[2]

Cassirer's engaged historical ethos was evident in his passionate defence from the late 1920s of Germany's Enlightenment heritage and its republican and natural law traditions.[3] Cassirer's lucid reflections on the task of the historian are also testament to the enduring impact of Hermann Cohen's theory of historical origins as being open to imaginative reinscription and idealistic reconstruction, an approach to the history of philosophy and of Judaism that was informed by the vigorous, emancipative historicity of *Wissenschaft des Judentums*, a stream of German Jewish historical scholarship that remained in fruitful dialogue with the ethos of *Geistesgeschichte* inaugurated by Wilhelm von Humboldt. As the epigraph suggests, Cassirer's refractory philosophy of history eschewed the methodological norms of impersonality and objectivity that were intrinsic to history as a professional discipline. He strongly disagreed with Ranke's stated desideratum of extinguishing one's own self in order to be the pure mirror of things and see events as they actually occurred. Cassirer writes that if I, as an historian, were to 'put out the light of my own personal experience I cannot see and I cannot judge the experience of others'.[4] As a performative demonstration of his own historical tact, which reads against the grain and illustrates the significance of the historian's personal qualities, Cassirer does not condemn Ranke but instead illuminates the 'ethical conception of his [historical] task, of the dignity and responsibility of the historian'.[5] Cassirer enthuses that in his historical works on religious and political ideas, in which he was neither a 'zealot' nor an 'apologist', Ranke displayed the 'sympathy of the true historian', a sympathy that does not imply intimate friendship or partisanship for a cause, but 'embraces friends and opponents'.[6] Ranke's 'universal sympathy could embrace all ages and all nations'.[7]

The radical methodological implications of Cassirer's conception of the ethical and imaginative task of the historian are often underestimated. Influenced by a tradition of liberal Jewish scholarship which was sensitive to the ethical and political implications of dominant historical representations, Cassirer intimates that humanistic disciplines such as history, which pretend to social scientific status, must be energetically redescribed in stylistic, characterological, and dispositional terms as world constitutive modes of human activity. It is not therefore surprising that in his lectures of the 1930s discussed above, Cassirer was adamant that contemporary philosophy must eschew a fatalistic rejection of political agency by couching its ontological claims in sweeping historical narratives. The task of the philosopher is the active formation of individual and social life in response to the impingements of the cultural moment. This self-formation in multifarious circumstances finds its ancillary in a revisionist conception of history in which we 'never look upon deeds or action alone' but seek the 'expression of character', of intellectual and moral physiognomy.[8] For Cassirer history is anthropomorphic, it is a form of self-knowledge in which 'man constantly returns to himself'. This is no mere egotism however, for in making us cognizant of the 'polymorphism of human existence', history frees us from the 'freaks and prejudices of a special and single moment', entailing an enrichment and enlargement, rather than effacement of the self.[9] In a recommendation strongly reminiscent of Wilhelm von Humboldt's seminal essay, Cassirer stresses that the task of the historian is two-fold. It requires a keen sense for the empirical reality of things combined with the 'free gift of imagination' upon which any genuine historical synthesis depends.[10]

While there is some evidence that after her emigration to the United States Arendt did engage with Cassirer's reconstruction of Enlightenment philosophy as a critical resource, and may have been aware of his discussion in *An Essay on Man* of the transformative task of the historian, her reappraisal of the Enlightenment's intellectual freedom and humanist concerns after the Second World War, combined with her critique of the nostrum of historical objectivity in favour of an ethos of cosmopolitan historical 'impartiality', suggests a sustained affinity with Cassirer's philosophy of historical representation.[11] In her famous reply to Eric Voegelin's criticism of *The Origins of Totalitarianism*, Arendt admits that she has 'parted quite consciously' with the tradition of *sine ira et studio* since her particular subject matter, the unprecedented nature of totalitarianism, demands a reconsideration of problems of style and disposition, allowing affects such as indignation and the power of metaphor to inform her immanent approach to historical description.[12] Her historical approach to totalitarianism has been influenced by that form of 'personal experience which is necessarily involved in an historical investigation that employs imagination consciously as an important tool of cognition'. Arendt then invokes the historiographical relevance of Kant's faculty of imagination (*Einbildungskraft*), as an ancillary to historical understanding.[13]

In her essay 'The Concept of History' Arendt demurs at Ranke's desideratum of the historian's self-extinguishment, and raises anew the issue of 'impartiality' and narrative form. The impartiality of true historiography, Arendt claims, begins when Homer decided to sing the deeds of the Trojans and not just those of the Achaeans, rejecting the overriding interest in one's own side typical of nationalist historiography as well as the alternative of victory or defeat which modern historians have felt expresses the 'judgment of history itself'. In the histories of Herodotus and Thucydides the exploration of 'diverse points of view' was not an expression of detachment but rather of their immersion in polis life and its combative rhetoric, in which the world we have in common is explored from an 'infinite number of different standpoints', and where the citizen is encouraged to 'understand' the world from another's standpoint.[14] As Dean Hammer argues, in *The Human Condition* Arendt also invokes the Roman historiographical tradition, where the political energies, the beliefs, ideas, habits, and principles that move humans to act are not only portrayed but also experienced.[15] In Roman histories, Arendt identifies a 'form of writing in which the animating forces of politics are given form through the impressions, reactions, and conclusions of political actors', encouraging readers of history to become 'spectators participating in a living past'.[16] Along with Hammer I would agree with Margaret Canovan's felicitous suggestion that Arendt sees in historiography a 'repository of human experience' by which we can find 'permanent human possibilities that are wider than those known and expected within our own culture', a protection against *Einseitigkeit* that was intrinsic to Cassirer's historical approach.[17] Finally, as we shall see, Arendt also follows Cassirer in fulminating against meta-narratives of history which reconcile the philosophical judgement of history with historical reality, typified in Hegel's supercessionist narrative of the Absolute Spirit as it manifests itself in pivotal epochs of world history.

Arendt's ongoing effort to elaborate an ethically charged historiography steeped in political experience raises some interesting questions about her approach to the history of Judaism and the Jewish people. What did Arendt contribute to Jewish historiography, to the unfolding and politically invested continuum of historical representations by which Jewish scholars attempted to wrest the representation of their history, religion, and culture, from the dominant supercessionist narrative inspired by Christianity? How did she translate her precept that historical writing must recapture authentic political experiences into narrating Jewish history? How did her ongoing dialogue with Enlightenment philosophies of history intersect with her ambition to revitalize our historical conception of Jewish political agency? I would like to suggest that Arendt's sympathetic rediscovery of the *Aufklärung* from the late 1930s correlated with a rethinking of what the *Aufklärung* meant for Jews and Judaism, suggesting historiographical principles for how a 'hidden tradition' of Jewish agency and diasporic sensibility might be written. In extraordinary essays such as 'The Jew as Pariah: a Hidden Tradition', which I explore in depth in Chapter 8, Arendt advances a version of Jewish history that illuminates Jewish characteristics forged in hybrid diasporic milieux, thus reprising a liberal Jewish interest in the pluralist social worlds that post-biblical Jewry has helped to create. Where Arendt once interpreted the Enlightenment as inimical to the feeling for historical continuity that would sustain and renew Jews as a distinct people, she came to appreciate the significance of the Enlightenment's cosmopolitanism and 'Prophetic' idealism as being in many respects highly compatible with her image of Judaism and Jewish history as profoundly imbricated in the unfolding drama of world-history. In the concluding section I query whether a liberal Jewish articulation of the Enlightenment as intrinsic rather than alien to Jewish interests informs Arendt's famous 1963 epistolary exchange with Gershom Scholem. There Arendt invokes the principle of *Selbstdenken* and the inviolability of friendship, while gesturing towards the threatened universalism of Prophetic Judaism, in order to rebuff Scholem's aggressive interrogation of her loyalty to Judaism. Perhaps now interpreting herself as an active contributor to the creative tradition of German Jewish *Geistesgeschichte*, Arendt reprises the Enlightenment as embodying the promise, dear to her, of creative Jewish participation in world history.

From Herder to Kant

It should come as no surprise, given our discussion of Arendt's forceful criticism of Mendelssohn in Chapter 1, that Arendt's initial attraction to Zionism as a political movement coincided with her powerful critique of the *Aufklärung* as an abortive emancipation of the Jewish people. In her illuminating biography *For Love of the World*, Elisabeth Young-Bruehl argues that around the period 1931–1932, when ominous storm clouds were appearing on the historical horizon and the recrudescence of anti-Semitism was laying bare the unfulfilled promise of Jewish assimilation into German culture, Johann Gottfried von Herder emerged as Arendt's intellectual 'hero' due to the respect he paid to historically developed differences among peoples.[18]

> Against the Enlightenment elevation of 'truths of reason' over 'truths of history' – present in Lessing's work, adopted by Moses Mendelssohn, and then used by Jews of Rahel [Varnhagen's] generation like David Friedlander to deny the 'historical' religion of Judaism – Herder emphasized the importance of history for individuals and peoples. Just as he challenged the Jews to give up the notion that their historical existence had come to an end with the destruction of the temple in Jerusalem and the notion that Judaism was a 'religion of reason' awaiting amalgamation with the universal reason of mankind, so too he challenged the Germans to admit the Jews, as a people, into the German state.[19]

It was also during the period of 1931–1932, Young-Bruehl argues, that Arendt was influenced by Zionism's defiant emphasis on the historical primacy of Jewish identity and its call for the political redemption of the Jewish 'nation'. Arendt shared Zionism's scorn for the perceived futility and treachery of Jewish assimilation into Gentile societies. As Dagmar Barnouw argues, the 'single most important influence on Arendt during the early thirties was that of the German Zionist Kurt Blumenfeld', chairman of the Zionistische Vereinigung für Deutschland (1924–1933), whom she had met in 1926 when he lectured to the Heidelberg Zionist Students' Club.[20] Arendt had drafted much of *Rahel Varnhagen, the Life of a Jewess* between 1929 and 1938, working under the 'influence of the Zionist critique of social assimilation' in which she had educated herself under the tutelage of Kurt Blumenfeld, 'who had been as naively assimilated as she had been in the late 20s'. In the historical study *Rahel Varnhagen*, Barnouw notes, Arendt was influenced by a Zionist pedagogical imperative; she sought to demonstrate that Jews could not really live like human beings under the diasporic condition of legal emancipation and social assimilation. Arendt, beholden to her withering critique of the disloyal Jewish parvenu whose treachery was emboldened by Enlightenment rationalism, felt that for a good part of her life Rahel had imitated the shallowness and opportunism of Mendelssohn and his wealthy follower, David Friedländer, in denying or seeking to evade uncomfortable historical facts for the sake of social acceptance.[21]

As already noted, in her 1932 essay, 'The Enlightenment and the Jewish Question', Arendt rejected the Enlightenment's elevation of the truths of reason over the reality of history as represented by the abstract rationalism of Lessing and Mendelssohn. Arendt complains in that essay that Lessing's vision of total equality demanded of Jews 'merely that they be human beings', a transformation, Arendt acerbically notes, that Mendelssohn felt Jews could readily achieve once they had undergone an education guided by *Bildung*, but which in reality 'destroyed all of the contents of history which formerly sustained them'.[22] As Barnouw suggests, Arendt's distaste for Mendelssohn, the progenitor of the German Jewish comi-tragedy of assimilation up until 1933, prevented her from recognizing the ways in which he differed from Christian-Wilhelm Dohm. Arendt failed to acknowledge Mendelssohn's radical proposal for a truly secular state that would abolish the political and judicial rights of the churches, a stance which would 'distinctly modify the concept of assimilation to a Christian environment'.[23] In 'The Enlightenment and the Jewish Question', Arendt laments that when Jews such as Mendelssohn and his reformist successor David Friedländer adopted the era's 'unhistorical argumentation' in order to claim their rights as pure human beings, the end result was a 'people without a history within history'. This is because, Arendt avers, the Enlightenment conception of *Bildung* as the education of the self through culture depended entirely on adapting to a secularized European world, a 'non-Jewish world'.[24] As Richard Bernstein points out – and this is revealing in regards to her severe distaste for Mendelssohn in *Rahel Varnhagen* – Arendt interpreted assimilation as '*aggressively* active', requiring the sacrifice of every 'natural impulse' and the suppression of passion, thus involving lying to oneself and forced self-deception. Moreover, the logic of assimilation required the internalizing of society's anti-Semitism, so denying one's own origin and cutting oneself off from those who have not yet done so, an action that 'becomes a scoundrel', or, as Cassirer would have put it, a fundamental denial of character.[25]

As a thinker who had recently embarked upon an intensive historical consideration of the 'Jewish question' and was thus primarily interested in the baleful effects of the *Aufklärung* on Jewish identity, Arendt sympathizes in 'The Enlightenment and the Jewish Question' with Herder's 'critique of his own age, the age of Enlightenment'.[26] Herder repudiated Lessing's rationalist suggestion that 'man receives nothing in his education that does not already lie within him', with its idealistic Enlightenment faith in a kind of 'virtual human sameness' based on the 'pure possibility' of each human existence.

He instead emphasized the historically differentiated 'reality' of each human existence and extolled the 'endlessness of history', refusing to recognize pure reason or the possibility of one single truth. Rather than being a 'mind of pure reason', Herder preferred to simply be 'a man', to 'move as a wave upon the sea of history' as he put it.[27] Herder's historically conditioned model of *Bildung* suggested that reason is not the judge of historical reality but is itself the result of the 'human race's total experience'; ergo 'reason is subject to history' since there are no abstract laws governing the historical process.[28]

Herder's discovery of the irrevocability of all that has happened made him 'one of the first great interpreters of history'; in particular, Herder rendered Jewish history 'visible' as primarily defined by Jewish possession of the Old Testament.[29] Herder approached the history of the Jews in terms of their own self-understanding as 'God's chosen people' and was arrested by the 'unique sense of life' of the Jewish people, which 'holds to the past and tries to hold what is past within the present'.[30] Herder understood that the Jewish religion is neither a source of prejudice, as anti-emancipationist Christians argued, nor 'Mendelssohn's religion of reason', but rather an inalienable heritage of the Jewish people, which stands or falls with their obedience to Mosaic Law. Historical Judaism, moreover, is ineluctably a 'religion of Palestine'.[31]

Importantly, where Lessing and Christian Dohm's discussion of the Jewish question arose primarily out of the problem of a foreign religion and its toleration, Herder interpreted Jewish assimilation into Germany as a political issue, that of emancipating and incorporating another nation within Germany, of admitting the Jews as a people into the German state.[32] Herder wished for the Jews to emerge from their 'parasitical' status and be a truly humanized and productive population within German culture. But this would not entail an Enlightenment process of *Bildung*, of thinking for oneself as a pure human being capable of reason, since such an ideal does not arise out of any experience and lacks a sense of reality. Such a notion of rational self-formation cannot 'form man, since it forgets the reality out of which he comes and in which he stands'. For Herder, the true formation of the Jews in present-day European culture, understood as an ongoing process, will be 'governed by the past', the eternal power of precedent, a past the Enlightenment had failed to preserve.[33] Arendt notes, however, that in Herder's secularized version of history such a past is understood as unique and transient rather than obligatory and binding, so that the formative function of the past in the present inheres in 'the understanding per se'.[34] In encouraging an energetic historical hermeneutic of the Jews as a people, Herder renders history a 'special and legitimate concern of the Jews'.[35]

Herder's enthusiasm for the unique histories that shape the destiny of peoples complemented Arendt's desire, articulated in *Rahel Varnhagen*, to reconfigure the authentic Jew as a self-identified 'pariah', defiantly performing and politicizing their historically conditioned difference rather than succumbing to the misleading assimilationist seductions of Enlightenment humanism.[36] Particularly in the early 1930s, since her position during and after the Second World War was much more ambivalent, Arendt regarded Zionism as a realistic response to the Nazi menace, a necessary though by no means sufficient political mobilization in the face of organized anti-Semitism. Zionism's withering critique of assimilationist apologetics had in her view decisively revealed the pariah status of Jews in contemporary European culture.[37] While she never identified as a Zionist in ideological terms, she was influenced by the 'criticism, the self-criticism that the Zionists spread amongst the Jewish people'.[38] As well as an appreciation of Zionism's pedagogical critique of Jewish assimilation, it seems that Arendt's continuing friendship with the great Jewish historian of Jewish mysticism, Gershom Scholem, which began in the early 1930s through a shared friendship with Walter Benjamin, also gave her an appreciation of cultural Zionism's rejuvenation of Jewish historical consciousness and its emancipative effects. As Young-Bruehl writes, in Scholem's momentous work, *Major Trends of Jewish Mysticism* (1941), which Arendt, Heinrich Blücher, and Benjamin spent many hours discussing during the winter of 1939/40, Arendt could see an 'historical precedent for a future reconciliation of Jewish history with the history of Europe'.[39] Reviewing Scholem's work in 1948, Arendt effusively praised his 'new presentation and appreciation of Jewish mysticism', which 'changes the whole picture of Jewish history', clarifying, for the first time, the 'role played by the Jews in the formation of modern man'.[40] Scholem's discovery of the historical and political significance of Kabbalism, Arendt enthuses, is more likely to reconcile Jewish history with the history of Europe than those apologetic Jewish histories which try to prove the impossible, the identity between Jews and other nations.[41] This is because Jewish mystical thought 'prepared its followers for action', breaking with the 'mere interpretation of the Law and with the mere hope for the coming of the Messiah'. Where the diaspora had been regarded as either a punishment for Israel's sins or a test of Israel's faith, it can now also be regarded as a mission of redeeming the fallen sparks of God's creation. For the first time, Arendt quotes Scholem, 'the role of the "protagonist in the drama of the world" was defined in terms which applied to every Jew'.[42]

As early as in her 1935 essay 'A Guide for Youth: Martin Buber', Arendt limns the possibility of a collective *Bildung* for the Jewish people informed by a renewed relationship to its history. She extols the cultural Zionist and spiritual leader of the Jewish Renaissance, Martin Buber, as 'German Judaism's incontestable guide', praising him for mediating between a narrowly focused political Zionism and a 'fossilized Orthodoxy' that is in danger of 'hardening into traditional rites'. A passionate Zionist, Buber understands that the 'renaissance of the Jewish people can only come about through a radical return to its great past and its living religious values', thereby helping to reconcile Jewish youth to a spiritual Judaism from which they had become estranged.[43] Buber's 'positive Judaism' renders Jewish *Wissenschaft* relevant to the present day, unlike the *Wissenschaft des Judentums* movement which sought for generations to 'bury a living people under the monument of exact philology and dead history'.[44] Buber's importance, Arendt enthuses, lies in the fact that he didn't bury himself or Judaism under a great past, but 'knew how to rediscover the living roots of this past to build an even greater future'.[45] Arendt supported Buber's cultural Zionism on the grounds that it embraced political Zionism's critique of Jewish assimilation but remained sceptical of its narrow territorial concerns with Jewish emigration to Palestine. In a 1934 address in Frankfurt, Buber had warned against Zionism as a movement of 'national egotism' preoccupied with political and military success, which in the end must lead to 'catastrophe'. More important than a narrow concern with national liberation was the 'supernational task', the 'panhuman, moral, social, eternal work of the nation', which was consequent upon a return to the land.[46] What we call 'Israel', Buber reminds his audience, is not merely the result of biological and historical development but the product of a decision made long ago, in favour of a 'God of justice' rather than egotism, a God who leads his people into the land in order to prepare it for its 'messianic work in the world'.

Arendt's concern that Jews embrace a vibrant past in order to construct a dignified future in the non-Jewish world is, of course, ironically reminiscent of the *Wissenschafts des Judentums* ethos she seemingly rejects. Arendt's blunt critique can be read as a relatively conventional Zionist condemnation of a scholarly movement perceived as rationalist and driven by apologetic embarrassment at Judaism's anomalous position within a progressive Western modernity. As Gershom Scholem argued in an influential post-war critique of *Wissenschaft des Judentums*, 'the attempt to disregard the most vital aspects of the Jewish people as a collective entity dominated in the work of the most significant representatives of the Science of Judaism' since 'apologetics played an enormous role' in their scholarship.[47]

Turning Points

As Young-Bruehl explains, Arendt became acutely aware after her emigration from Germany in 1933 of the dangers of Romantic historicism. She no longer sympathized with Herder's focus on an individual people's 'organic' development, his patriotic commitment to a German cultural and national awakening, and his embrace of the nation and the chain of historical tradition. Arendt, writes Young-Bruehl, came to construe Herder's autochthonous notion of individual peoples (*Volk*) as a denial of ethical autonomy, an elevation of historical process and communal fate (*Schicksalgemeinschaft*) over individual freedom and judgement. Revising her earlier jaundiced disdain for Enlightenment precepts such as humanity, progress, and reason, and now fully aware, according to Young-Bruehl, of the 'enormous political role' of nineteenth-century historical thinking in her own time, Arendt came to look on the Enlightenment 'with new eyes'.[48] Particularly from the 1950s onwards, Arendt worked through the problem of historical orientation in 'dark times' with the help of *Aufklärung* thinkers such as Lessing, whose critical ethos maintained constant reference to the world, and Kant, whose politically salient conception of reason and judgement postulates an 'enlarged mentality' that draws on the perspectives of others.

What historical events and experiences influenced Arendt's movement away from a Zionistic emphasis on the continuity of Jewish history sustained by the memory of Palestine? Her important friendship with Walter Benjamin, who challenged homogenizing historical narratives, may have played a significant role. While they had initially met in Berlin they became good friends in the émigré circles of Paris after Arendt moved there to escape the Nazis in the autumn of 1933. In 1934 Benjamin delivered his lecture 'The Author as Producer' to an audience that included Hannah Arendt.[49] Young-Bruehl relates how the last time they met in Marseilles Walter Benjamin entrusted his 'Theses on the Philosophy of History', in manuscript form, to Arendt and her husband Heinrich Blücher. In Lisbon, in 1940, while they waited for the ship that would take them to a new life in the United States, Arendt and Blücher read Benjamin's stirring philosophy of history aloud to each other and to the refugees gathered around them.[50] This oral performance to interested spectators may have been another instance of Arendt's steadfast conviction, shared by Cassirer, that historical interpretation can never be detached in a scientistic manner but must be nourished by the responsive presence of others.

Arendt, Young-Bruehl informs us, was inspired by Benjamin's historical 'Theses', themselves probably influenced by Scholem's book on Jewish mysticism, to oppose not only the reified images of the past that historicism had created to guide people according to the values of victorious peoples, but also the false hopes offered by historical materialisms such as Marxism. Along with Benjamin, Arendt hoped that a time filled by the presence of the Now (*Jetztzeit*) would yield a 'realistic, action-oriented sense of the past and future'.[51] It was Benjamin, Arendt writes retrospectively in 1968, who knew that the 'break in tradition and the loss of authority which occurred in his lifetime, were irreparable', and who therefore concluded that he 'had to discover new ways of dealing with the past'.[52] Arendt affirms Benjamin's recognition that the 'transmissibility of the past had been replaced by its citability' and that, in place of the authority of tradition, the past has now settled down in the present in piecemeal fashion so as to 'deprive it of "peace of mind", the mindless peace of complacency'.[53] Importantly, and very much consonant with Cassirer's hermeneutic emphasis on the critical and imaginative agency of the historical subject, Arendt drew attention to the Benjaminian persona of the 'pearl diver' who delves into the depths of the past: not in order to resuscitate the past 'the way it was' and contribute to the 'renewal of extinct ages', but to recover those 'thought fragments' that are 'rich and strange' for the world of the living.[54]

In her portrait of Benjamin in *Men in Dark Times*, Arendt is adamant that Benjamin's choice in the 1920s to study the German Baroque Age was an 'exact counterpart' to Scholem's strange decision to approach Judaism via the Kabbala, an aspect of Hebrew literature that is 'untransmitted and untransmissable' in terms of tradition and has a 'disreputable' odour. Benjamin and Scholem's choice of study, Arendt suggests, shows that there was no such thing as a '"return" either to the German or the European or the Jewish tradition', since obligative truths had been replaced by what was in some sense significant or interesting.[55] Arendt's familiarity with what David Biale has described as Scholem's 'anarchistic' philosophy of Jewish history and Benjamin's conception of a divinely inspired 'pure' language of names that captures the essence of its object should problematize the all too common conception, articulated by Richard Bernstein for example, that Arendt had 'little interest in, or feeling for, the religious aspects of Judaism' except insofar as they affected political questions, issuing in a 'thin' understanding of Judaism and Jewishness.[56]

In her interview with Günter Gaus in 1964, Arendt refused to identify herself as a philosopher, preferring to talk of herself more modestly as a political theorist. We can consider this refusal of Olympian contemplation that attaches to the moniker of philosopher as a gesture of solidarity with stateless peoples – 'we refugees', as Arendt described her situation in an article of that name of 1943, recognizing a common plight with the stateless that inspired her consciousness of the historical significance of the *Jetztzeit* she was now living through.[57] Arendt writes in 'We Refugees' that refugees, these 'Ulysses-wanderers', cannot afford the luxury of intellectual withdrawal from the world and historical time, beset by depression, confusion, and crises of identity. Arendt suggests that the meaninglessness of former distinctions among European Jewry signifies a new chapter of Jewish history that binds it to the future of humanity:

> history is no longer a closed book to them and politics no longer the privilege of gentiles . . . Refugees driven from country to country represent the vanguard of their peoples . . . For the first time Jewish history is not separate but tied up with that of all other nations.[58]

Arendt argues, in anticipation of her 1944 article, that the humane solidarity of the refugee experience reprises 'The Jew as Pariah', a 'hidden tradition' of diaspora Jewry, that of the conscious pariah, full of humanity, humour, and disinterested intelligence.[59] Where Arendt's emphasis in the early 1930s may have been on the pariah's defiant politicization of difference, in 'We Refugees' and 'The Jew as Pariah', she is primarily interested in the 'basic affinity of the pariah to the people', a tradition of Jewish poets, writers, and artists who had unabashedly claimed admission '*as Jews* to the ranks of humanity' rather than aping the gentiles or seizing the opportunity to play the parvenu.[60] In the admonitory spirit of Cohen in his essay on Heine, Arendt decries the 'reckless magnanimity' of the Jewish people in regard to 'claiming its own in the field of European arts and letters', since it has let the credit for great writers and artists go to other peoples. Those who really did most for the spiritual dignity of their people, who were 'great enough to transcend the bounds of nationality and to weave the strands of their Jewish genius into the general texture of European life', have been given only perfunctory recognition by the Jewish community.[61] Indeed, out of a highly personal vision of emancipation, evinced and expressed with passionate intensity, this 'Jewish creative genius' was able to contribute its products to the 'general spiritual life of the Western world'. Poets, writers, and schlemiels such as Heinrich Heine, Salomon Maimon, Charlie Chaplin, Bernard Lazare, and Franz Kafka had evolved the 'concept of the pariah as a human type' that was of 'supreme importance for the evaluation of mankind in our day', a concept which has 'exerted upon the gentile world' an influence which lies in strange contrast to the spiritual and political ineffectiveness which has been the fate of these men among their own brethren.[62] Arendt's *Rettungen*, her redemptive biographical interest in the fertile cultural and spiritual stream of the diasporic Jewish outsider figure under threat of historical erasure, has a much longer tradition than she perhaps knew. Nor did Arendt's wonderful conclusion – that only when a people, rather than a protesting individual, lives and functions in consort with other peoples can it contribute to the establishment upon earth of a 'commonly conditioned and commonly controlled' humanity – seriously differ from the post-Mendelssohn liberal Jewish vision of the flourishing of Judaism within a pluralist liberal-democratic framework that would enable an historical movement towards an international federation of states, the political form most congenial to our shared humanity. I would suggest that Arendt's essays of 1943–1944 affirm the significance of recent Jewish history in a fashion not dissimilar to Cassirer's liberal Jewish historical consciousness. As we have seen, while Ernst Cassirer might seem to have departed from the *Wissenschaft des Judentums* preoccupation with Judaism and Jewish history, his 'mainstream' philosophical interests and historical concerns continued to advance a robust version of German Jewish *Geistesgeschichte*, defending the Jewish contribution to a contemporary civilization normatively founded on Enlightenment era values while exemplifying the ethical virtues, the warmth, sociability, and rounded humanity of Jewish intellectuals such as Moses Mendelssohn, Hermann Cohen and Aby Warburg. In 'The Jew as Pariah', Arendt's confidence in the ethical significance of the Jewish pariah as a human type suggested a form of historical interpretation which would illuminate a variety of relational Jewish characteristics as expressive of Jewish self-formation and emancipative struggle in diaspora, while similarly imbricating recent Jewish history, the history of a stateless people, with the post-war emergence of 'humanity' as a pressing concern for historical and political thought.

Lessing: A Partisanship for the World

An essay in *Men in Dark Times*, 'On Humanity in Dark Times: Thoughts about Lessing', based on a 1959 address in Hamburg, illuminates Arendt's changed perspective on the Enlightenment and in particular the historical significance of the German *Aufklärung*. Like Cassirer some thirty years earlier, Arendt seeks to render the values of the Enlightenment, and particularly its conception of reason, visible to a German audience. In 'On Humanity in Dark Times' Arendt affirms Lessing's ethos as an 'attitude towards the world' that is neither positive nor negative but 'radically critical' and 'completely revolutionary' in respect of the public realm of his time. Arendt praises Lessing's revolutionary temper, which 'remained indebted to the world and never left the solid ground of the world', eschewing sentimental utopianism by clinging to 'concrete details'. Lessing's greatness inheres in the fact that he 'never allowed supposed objectivity' to cause him to lose sight of the real 'status in the world' of the things or people he attacked or praised.[63]

In terms which are redolent of Cassirer's interpretation of Enlightenment reason as no longer being the 'isolated substance of the intellect' but an imma- nent activity that shapes life itself, Arendt suggests that Lessing's conception of criticism takes sides for 'the world's sake', understanding and judging in terms of something's position in the world 'at any given time'. Such a mental- ity cannot give rise to a definite worldview that is then immune to further experiences. Arendt echoes Cassirer's evocation of the Enlightenment as an historical era that mocks contemporary conceptions of progress when she ruminates that 'we very much need Lessing to teach us this state of mind'. What makes learning such an ethos so difficult for us, Arendt contends, is not 'our distrust of the Enlightenment or of the eighteenth-century's belief in humanity'. Rather the obstacle is the nineteenth century. Its 'obsession with history' and commitment to ideology still looms so large in the political thinking of our times that we are inclined to regard 'entirely free thinking', which employs 'neither history nor coercive logic as crutches', as having no authority over us.[64] While we are aware that thinking calls 'not only for intelligence and profundity but above all for courage', in the contemporary world we are astonished that Lessing's 'partisanship for the world' could have gone so far as to sacrifice to it the axiom of non-contradiction, the elementary logical claim to self-consistency. In an analysis of Lessing's intellectual virtues that revises her 1932 essay, in which Lessing's *Selbsdenken* signified the repudiation of history, Arendt lauds Lessing's conviction that his ideas may be disjunctive or contradictory as long as they stir readers to 'think for themselves'.[65] Lessing never reified his own position: instead of fixing his identity in history with a 'perfectly consistent system', he scattered nothing into the world but provocations to discourse, *fermenta cognitionis*.[66] We are reminded of Cassirer's claim that Lessing's version of reason was unprecedented in that it did not exclude becoming and development, that the version of truth that Lessing endorsed, inimical to dogmatic theological and philosophical systems, and which was even foreign to his great friend Mendelssohn, seeks truth as arising provisionally, from those productive forces of doubt, confusion, and error that catalyse conversation, reflection, and analysis.[67]

Lessing's care and concern for the world was intended to avoid a dreary solitude that would 'paralyze all faculties'; sadly Lessing was unable to put right the state of the world such that individual qualities and concerns became 'visible and audible'. Although much has changed in the two centuries separating us from Lessing's lifetime, little, Arendt laments, has 'changed for the better', a complaint redolent of Cassirer's lament during the Nazi period that philosophy has lost its capacity for worldly self-disclosure. Today, Arendt avers, the 'pillars of the best known truths' are now a veritable rubble heap; outlining a radical conception of the historical task confronting us, Arendt suggests that at best this situation can promote a 'new thinking' that needs no 'pillars and props, no standards and traditions to move freely' over unfamiliar terrain.[68] In our day, Arendt warns, the 'very humanity of man' loses its vitality to the extent that we abstain from thinking and instead put our confidence in old verities or even new truths.[69]

In what was perhaps a tacit homage to Cassirer, Arendt was keen to dispel the stereotype of the Enlightenment as promulgating a thinly rationalist conception of human nature and a detached cosmopolitanism that lacked affective concern for history and tradition. The eighteenth-century Enlightenment, she observes in 'Humanity in Dark Times', was an age in which the 'public realm has been obscured and the world become so dubious' that people attempt to arrive at 'mutual understandings with their fellow men without regard for the world that lies between them'.[70] In such times a 'special kind of humanity' develops. In order to properly 'appreciate its possibilities', we 'need only think of *Nathan the Wise*', whose true theme, 'It suffices to be a man', permeates the play, and whose appeal, 'Be my friend', runs like a leitmotif.

If the spirit of the French Revolution leans upon Rousseau's egalitarian ideal of compassion, of *fraternité* as the fulfilment of humanity, Lessing, on the other hand, considered friendship, which is 'as selective as compassion is egalitarian', to be the 'central phenomenon in which alone true humanity can prove itself'.[71] Lessing's ideal of friendship, Arendt cautions, demonstrates a more worldly and durable humanism than the sentimentalized fraternal humanity of persecuted and pariah peoples, in which 'individuals feel ties of brotherhood to all men', leading to enthusiastic excesses such as the Terror.[72] Such a fraternal ideal of humanity, a combination of rationalism and sentimentalism, 'has never yet survived the hour of liberation by so much as a minute'. By contrast a proclivity towards genuine friendship, as represented by Lessing, desires a 'truly human dialogue' and is 'permeated by the pleasure in the other person and what he says'.[73]

In thinking about one's proper attitude in 'dark times', Arendt admits in this 1960 essay that she once would have considered Nathan's 'I am a man', given in response to the command 'Step closer, Jew', to be a 'grotesque and dangerous evasion of reality'. In times of defamation or persecution one can only resist 'in terms of the identity that is under attack'.[74] Thus under the conditions of the Third Reich, it could scarcely have been a sign of humaneness for the friends to have affirmed their mutual humanity; rather, such an affirmation would have been an evasion of reality, failing to resist the 'world as it was'. In keeping with a 'humanness that had not lost the solid ground of reality', those friends would have had to have said to each other, 'A German and a Jew, and friends'. Such a friendship, if it lacked false guilt complexes on the one side and complexes of superiority or inferiority on the other, would have achieved a 'bit of humanness in a world become inhuman'.[75]

Having created a rapport between an *Aufklärung* ideal of respectful friendship as a response to political oppression, and her own politicized affirmation of her Jewish identity during the Nazi era, Arendt affirms *Nathan the Wise* as a classical drama of friendship, a vision of humaneness which is 'sober and cool rather than sentimental'.[76] This great drama illustrates the fact that humanity is 'exemplified not in fraternity but friendship; that friendship is not intimately personal but makes political demands and preserves reference to the world'. Arendt argues that Nathan's warm embrace of the Templar and his attitude towards everyone he meets – 'We must, must be friends' – is obviously more important to Lessing than the play's love story.[77] Arendt notes that the love plot of *Nathan the Wise* peters out, so that the 'dramatic tension of the play lies solely in the conflict that arises between friendship and humanity with truth'. Indeed Nathan's wisdom 'consists solely in his readiness to sacrifice truth to friendship'.[78]

Lessing was content to belong to a 'race of "limited gods"', as he called human beings, believing that human society was in no way harmed by 'those who take more trouble to make clouds than to scatter them'. Seemingly reprising Cassirer's analysis, Arendt affirms that Lessing's sympathy for human striving illuminates a kind of 'tolerance' that has nothing to do with the ordinary sense of the word, but has a 'great deal to do with the gift of friendship, with openness to the world, and finally with genuine love of mankind'. Lessing's ring parable in *Nathan the Wise* illustrates his 'highly unorthodox opinions about truth', for he 'refused to accept any truths whatever'. Lessing was glad, to use his parable, that the genuine ring had been lost; he was glad for the 'sake of the infinite number of opinions that arise when men discuss the affairs of this world'.[79] Lessing's anthropological theme of 'limited gods', of the limitations of the human understanding, became the great theme of Kant's critiques.

Yet whatever the common ground between the attitudes of Kant and Lessing – and they did have much in common according to Arendt – the two thinkers 'differed on one decisive point'.[80] Kant could never have agreed that the truth, if it did exist, could be unhesitatingly sacrificed to humanity, to the 'possibility of friendship and of discourse among men'. For the 'inhumanity of Kant's moral philosophy is undeniable'. Kant's categorical ethical imperative is 'postulated as an absolute' which 'stands above men', and introduces into a human realm, which by its nature consists of relationships, a compelling power that 'runs counter to its fundamental relativity'. Kant, who so inexorably pointed out 'man's cognitive limits', could not bear to admit that in 'action too, man cannot behave like a god'.[81] Lessing's humility, his active spirit of religious toleration and sympathy for the outsider may have buttressed his belief that no doctrine, however convincingly proved, is worth the sacrifice of a single friendship between two human beings. For Lessing, no 'insight into the nature of Islam or of Judaism or of Christianity' could have prevented him from 'entering into a friendship and the discourse of a friendship with a convinced Mohammedan or a pious Jew or a believing Christian', a statement which has a decidedly Mendelssohnian ring but which is also redolent of Cohen's conception of friendship as politically significant and enabling of an ethical hermeneutics that ignores encrusted theological interpretation.[82]

Lessing did, of course, have a friendship with a 'pious Jew', Moses Mendelssohn, a friendship, moreover, of the utmost ethical and political relevance to Mendelssohn and later German Jewish historians and advocates of emancipation, including Heinrich Graetz and Abraham Geiger. They saw the promise of social and political equality in a friendship that was intellectually fertile and of epochal political significance (influencing Dohm's argument for the civil emancipation of the Jews) because, and not in spite of, the religious and cultural gulf that separated the two men. Arendt does not utter Mendelssohn's name in the essay but her interest in the theme of friendship and her prizing of the play's eponymous hero, a character inseparable from Mendelssohn in the minds of most of the play's interpreters, suggests a tacit reconciliation with the great German Jewish scholar, perhaps a confession that Lessing's epochal drama would have been unthinkable unless there had already been a respectful friendship between a German and a Jew that did not jettison their cultural, historic-philosophical, and aesthetic differences.[83]

Kant: The Prophetic Historian

As we have seen, Arendt's mature interest in Kant had little to do with either his Copernican revolution in epistemology or his explicit ethical philosophy, which she considered to be 'inhuman' in as much as it failed to take account of human plurality and the contingency of human affairs. Arendt's essay 'Truth and Politics', for example, gives short shrift to the individualistic and apolitical bias of the moral theories developed by philosophers from Socrates to Kant. Arendt complains of the 'disastrous consequences for any community that began in all earnest to follow ethical precepts derived from man in the singular'.[84] Arendt points to a different ethical tradition, that of 'teaching by example' (Arendt cites as an example Socrates' refusal to escape the death sentence by leaving Athens as the most historically influential instance of his maxim that it is 'better to suffer wrong than to do wrong'), the only way in which philosophical truth can become 'practical' and inspire action without violating the rules of the political realm, which excludes coercive metaphysical claims. It is for this reason that Arendt jettisons Kant the moral theorist *in sensu stricto* and seeks instead, as had Cassirer, to reprise the 'who' that shines forth from Kant's protean engagements with historiographical, constitutional, and political questions.

Drawing on an astute analysis by Peg Birmingham, I would argue that Arendt is interested in illustrating the affective 'principles of action' informing Kant's late critical interests, principles which mediate the private self and the citizen. These principles are not 'inherent in the self' as psychological motives nor are they prescriptive of narrowly conceived goals, but they 'inspire, as it were, from without', mapping out certain directions for activity in the public realm.[85] Arendt's pluralistic discussion of Kant in her posthumously published *Lectures on Kant's Political Philosophy* (1970) could be interpreted as exemplifying the Enlightenment 'principle' of sociability in which thought seeks to be tested (and is often expounded) by dialogue. Arendt's contextual approach to Kant might be fruitfully interpreted as an extension of Cassirer's elaboration of Kant as a multifaceted thinker who embodies, critiques, and innovates upon the historical, ethical, political, and aesthetic tendencies of his age. In her lectures on Kant, Arendt suggests that his continuing concern with the 'sociability of man', his insight that human beings are interdependent in their highest faculty, the human mind, culminated in his recognition that 'company is indispensable for the *thinker*'. This insight remained, towards the end of his life, a lingering problem from the pre-critical period, one which, Arendt suggests, helped him to articulate a hopeful and engaged, rather than dispassionate or triumphal, historical consciousness.[86]

Kant's politically suggestive theory of judgement stimulated Arendt's attempts to restore human dignity and critical autonomy in an age of mass conformism and totalizing ideologies, that is, to reprise those rational and ideational capacities of an ethical subject that had been badly vitiated by the modern 'pseudo-divinity named History'.[87] In a fashion comparable to Cassirer's critical idealism which negates the binding power of the given, Arendt argues that there is a momentous choice to be made between an approach to history that stresses the active ethical and imaginative powers of historical thought, and Hegel's sanctification of history's victors:

> Either we can say with Hegel: *Die Weltgeschichte ist das Weltgericht* [world history is the world court], leaving the ultimate judgment to Success, or we can maintain with Kant the autonomy of the minds of men and their possible independence of things as they are or as they have come into being.[88]

Continuing her disquisition on the political experiences that inform historiographical principles, Arendt notes that Kant imbibed the sense of sweeping historical change borne of a revolutionary age and absorbed the 'mentality of the Enlightenment' which loathed the arrogant pretensions of the philosophical 'Schools', since Kant affirmed that those truths that are a matter of 'general human concern' and 'within the reach of the great mass of men' are ever to be held in the 'highest esteem by us'. By contrast Hegel, of a later generation, felt that philosophy was by its nature esoteric and incapable of being understood by the 'mob'. Hegel revealed a 'relapse' into philosophy's traditional elitism, displaying a philosophical complacency and hubris which engendered in him a 'great show of indignation at the anecdote of the laughing Thracian peasant girl' who mocked the contemplative philosopher Thales for falling down a well in a state of abstraction.[89]

Kant, and the eighteenth-century context in which he wrote, offered Arendt a model for the enterprise of reclaiming a free, critical and discriminating relationship to the past which did not dwell on reified versions of philosophical 'systems'. Reprising the liberal Jewish sympathy for Kant as a prophetic thinker of humanity with manifold relationships with his age,

Arendt insists in the lectures that Kant was not a philosopher of history like Vico, Hegel, or Marx. Kant is never interested in the past; what interests him is the 'future of the species', the passage from the tutelage of nature to the attainment of culture, freedom, or sociability.[90]

We might say with Edward Said that Arendt is interested in a 'late style' Kant, a mature thinker full of dissonant reflections and passionate interests that can no longer by systematized, whose thought bespeaks not harmony and resolution but a 'nonharmonious, non serene tension', a sort of 'deliberately unproductive productiveness'.[91] It is this more uncertain Kant, more doubtful of the ethical and political implications of the division of the phenomenal and intelligible worlds, who turns to the *Critique of Judgment* for the unwitting elaboration of a genuinely political theory. In the third *Critique*, Arendt writes, Kant does not speak of 'man as an intelligible and cognitive being', while the word 'truth' barely appears. Kant speaks, rather, in the first part of the *Critique of Judgment,* of 'men in the plural, as they really are and live in societies'. The second part of the *Critique of Judgment* analyses the faculty of judgement as dealing with particulars.[92] Sadly the judgement of the particular – 'This is beautiful, this is wrong' – plays no role in Kant's conception of practical reason, since reason here is equivalent to the kind of compelling argumentation that Lessing rejected, an epiphenomenon of a (divinely conceived) will which 'lays down the law' and speaks in imperatives.[93] The Kantian faculty of judgement arises, on the other hand, from a merely contemplative pleasure or inactive delight, as a feeling of 'taste'; Kantian judgement is not the faculty of an isolated subject but indicates a concern with aesthetics that was a touchstone of his age.[94]

Arendt warns, however, against assuming that Kant's feel for the particular and contingent played no part at all in his practical philosophy. For the faculties of judgement and taste decisively influenced Kant's final position on the French Revolution, an 'event that played a central role in his old age, when he waited with great impatience every day for the newspapers'. Kant's position on the French Revolution was decided by the 'attitude of the mere spectator' who is not directly involved but who follows events with 'wishful, passionate participation'. This spectatorial attitude did not indicate, least of all for Kant, a desire to make a revolution oneself. Rather the spectator's sympathetic interest arose from a state of 'contemplative pleasure and inactive delight'.[95] Resuming Cassirer's contextual interest in Kant's politically engaged philosophy of historical spectatorship, Arendt suggests that the events of the American and then French Revolution awoke Kant from his 'political slumber' just as many years before Hume had awoken him from his dogmatic slumber and Rousseau from his moral slumber, his disregard for general human concerns.[96] Touched by these events and now unable to reconcile his moral philosophy with the constitutional demands of organizing a republican state, Kant realized that his 'moralizing' was of little use in theorizing the political; indeed Kant recognized that it was even possible for 'a bad man [to be] a good citizen in a good state'.[97] Arendt points out that Kant's highly suggestive but theoretically underdeveloped conception of politics was formed by the 'mentality of the Enlightenment'. She pays great attention to Kant's resolute opposition to belonging to a 'school of thought', and his conception of reason as 'using one's own mind' (*Selbstdenken*), a dynamic reconfiguration of reason's practical engagements which transcended dogmatic metaphysics and superficial scepticism. Echoing Cassirer's celebration of the robust independence and critical élan of Enlightenment era intellectuals, Arendt remarks that for Kant the spirit of critique meant that philosophy should never again lead to the 'positive business of system-making'.[98] She enthusiastically relates Kant's conviction that philosophy itself 'has become critical in the age of criticism and Enlightenment – the time when man had come of age'.[99]

Arendt essays that the politically engaged Kant, the spectator of human affairs, is a different persona from the moralizing Kant, who is interested in the 'individual *qua* individual'.[100] Arendt feels that Kant's actual theory of political affairs was not determined by the famous categorical imperative, which instantiates a subject of the practical will who resists sensuous and passionate inclinations. Kant's more suggestive political theory was guided, rather, by his late, more diffuse, and increasingly politicized persona. Arendt argues that the mature Kant felt the need to deploy the 'speculative use of reason', to theorize perpetual human progress and the possibility of a federated union of constitutional states, in order to give the '*idea* of mankind a political reality'.[101] She describes Kant's historical judgement of the great events of his age as being enriched by the perspective of an 'uninvolved public' of 'acclaiming spectators'. This detached but engaged spectatorial attitude made the French Revolution, in Kant's words, a 'phenomenon not to be forgotten', or, as Arendt parses it, a 'public event of world-historical significance'.[102] The events of the French Revolution inspired in Kant the regulative 'idea of progress, the hope for the future, where one judges the event according to the promise it holds for generations to come'.[103]

Having reaffirmed a neo-Kantian interpretation of Kant as a redemptive historical thinker, a critical idealist and Prophetic ethicist capable of reading events 'symbolically', as pregnant with world-historical significance, Arendt goes on to implicitly articulate a distinction between Prophetic history and Hellenic finitude which was dear to the thought of Cassirer and Cohen. Arendt stresses the degree to which Kant's notion of 'human progress' provides the standard according to which one judges. The Greek spectator finds a meaning in history that does not depend on cause or consequence but is exhausted in the story itself. For Kant, on the other hand, the story or event's importance lies precisely 'not at its end but in its opening up new horizons for the future'. It is 'the *hope* it contained for future generations that made the French Revolution such an important event'.[104]

Indeed, Arendt admits, it was also true for Hegel that the French Revolution was a world-historical event containing the seeds of the future. The difference, however, is that for Hegel it is the 'World Spirit' that reveals itself in the historical process, a terminus which the philosopher at the end of the process of historical revelation can finally interpret. For Kant, the 'subject' of world history is the human species itself', reminding us of Cassirer and Cohen's emphasis on the affinity between Kant's projective ideal of a humanity to come and the visionary ethics of the Jewish Prophets for which the regulative ideal of humanity is the subject of historical discourse and social criticism. For Kant, writes Arendt, 'progress is perpetual; there is never an end to it', and therefore no end to history. This approach is antithetical to the dialectical historicism of Hegel and Marx, who did not see the need for perpetual human striving after their respective historical goals were reached.[105] For Kant, who emphasizes the importance of culture and sociability as media of historical progress, the 'essence of man cannot be determined' and the value of existence can never be finally revealed to 'any man or generation of men'.[106] Kant's spectatorial judgement of events is not a matter of 'eschatology', Arendt assures us, for the destination of the human race towards freedom and peace, guaranteeing the free intercourse of all the nations on earth, lies in 'ideas of reason, without which the mere story of history would not make sense'.[107] Many years after Davos, Arendt seemed to revive Cassirer's humanist interpretation of Kant. As Gordon argues of the 1931 *Kantstudien* essay in which Cassirer extends his critique of Heidegger's Kant interpretation, Cassirer suggested that while Kant forsook metaphysical consolation, he retained a Platonist confidence in the pure ideas of reason; it was in the 'doctrine of the ideas' that 'Kant burst free from the circle . . . of merely-temporal existence' and opened up a fruitful tension between the 'problem of "Being" and "Ought", of "Experience" and "Idea"', in which the goal of the Kantian system was not the incorrigible finitude and temporal isolation of *Dasein* but the 'intelligible substrate of humanity'.[108]

Arendt suggests that in Kant's political philosophy and engaged conception of historical spectatorship the speculative ideas of reason which mediate the engaged spectator's historical judgement are guided by the faculty of imagination, 'the faculty of having present what is absent', as well as taste. Imagination transforms an object into something I do not have to be directly confronted with but that I have in some sense internalized such that I can now be affected by it.[109] Arendt identifies Kant's enlarged mentality as the perspective of the 'citizen of the world' in the sense of a *Weltbetrachter*, a 'world spectator' who can train their imagination 'to go visiting'. Kant himself, who never left Königsberg, taught courses in physical geography and was an eager reader of travel reports of all kinds.[110] Arendt also suggests that Kant's philosophy of history is predicated on his recognition that 'in matters of taste we must renounce ourselves in favor of others', that 'in Taste egoism is overcome'.[111] In her exuberant reconstruction of Kant's sociable and aesthetically inclined interest in worldly phenomena, Arendt seems intent on confirming Wilhelm von Humboldt's illuminating suggestion in 'The Task of the Historian' that,

> The more profoundly the historian understands mankind and its actions through intuition and study, the more humane his disposition is by nature and circumstances, and the more freely he gives rein to his humanity [*Menschlichkeit*], the more completely will he solve the problems of his profession.[112]

Arendt's reclamation of the Enlightenment era Kant is evidence of a liberal Jewish *Geistesgeschichte* resistant to canonical philosophical concerns that lack social exigency and fail to convey the nimbus of personality. Revealingly, in the holistic manner of Cassirer, Arendt foregrounds Kant's friendships with Jewish interlocutors such as Moses Mendelssohn and Kant's disciple Marcus Herz. Arendt draws attention to 'personal passages' in Kant's correspondence with Marcus Herz in the 1770s in which he talks reflexively of the need to view his judgements impartially from the standpoint of others, talks candidly of his reluctance to 'refute' reasonable objections, and discusses the relaxed conditions under which his mind can move from a 'microscopic to a general outlook'.[113] Arendt also mentions a 'curiously apologetic' letter to Mendelssohn in which Kant expresses a desire, so far unrealized, to 'popularize his thought' (which Mendelssohn had achieved magnificently in his *Phaedo*) and to render his first *Critique* comprehensible to an educated reader.[114] Elsewhere in the *Lectures on Kant* Arendt discusses a letter to Mendelssohn in which Kant expresses his abiding fear of a loss of self-approval, rejects eudemonism as a justification of existence and confesses his desire to be worthy of happiness.[115] Arendt also discusses Kant's disagreement with Mendelssohn over humanity's moral progress, Kant relying on the assumption of human progress, which is never finally broken off, to make sense of human affairs.[116]

Significant too in this analysis of Kant's intersubjective critical development is Arendt's remarks on Kant's desire for his version of philosophical critique to be a 'propaedeutic to the system' that makes it possible to evaluate all other philosophical systems. Arendt suggests that Kant's evaluative critical spirit was shaped by the eighteenth-century's 'enormous interest in aesthetics', in 'art and *art criticism*', all of which had the goal of establishing standards in the arts. While Arendt probably had Baumgarten, Herder, and Lessing's *Laocoon* in mind, she could not have been unaware of Mendelssohn's extraordinary contribution to eighteenth-century aesthetic criticism.[117]

I doubt it is a mere coincidence that in addition to her oblique discussions of the Lessing/Mendelssohn and Kant/Mendelssohn friendships, Arendt invokes other productive friendships between German and Jewish thinkers, particularly when one bears in mind her loving relationship with her German husband Heinrich Blücher and her enduring friendship with Karl Jaspers, who represented what was 'left of *humanitas* in Germany'.[118] While never explicitly recanting her earlier condemnation of Mendelssohn, Arendt's lectures on Kant subtly extend her interest in the candid, intellectually productive German Jewish friendships of the Enlightenment era. Indeed Arendt's restored confidence in the ethical importance of cross-cultural friendship, exemplified by Enlightenment sociability, may well have shaped her fractious encounter with Gershom Scholem, culminating in a dispute over their respective attitudes to Judaism and Zionism. It was an encounter which broke off their enduring friendship.

Zionism

Apart from the well-known and much-discussed context of the Eichmann controversy, there are aspects of the legendary 1963 exchange between Arendt and Scholem that remind us of Hermann Cohen's robust disagreement with Martin Buber in 1916. Like Cohen, Arendt's German inheritance and diasporic Jewish identity were put in question by a brilliant Zionist interlocutor. Before analysing Arendt's justifiably famous response to Scholem's accusations of disloyalty to the Jewish people and of having 'mocked' Zionism, it is important to trace her earlier re-appraisal of Zionism as a form of Jewish politics and interpretation of Jewish history, a re-appraisal contemporaneous with her increasing affirmation of Enlightenment thought.

Gabriel Piterberg has drawn attention to the impact of Arendt's relationship with Heinrich Blücher, whom she met in the spring of 1936 in Paris, on her attitude towards Zionism.[119] In an early exchange of letters in August 1936, when they had only known each other for a few months, Blücher had complained of Zionism as a movement of the Jewish bourgeoisie, which, rather than working with the 'Arab workers and labourers to liberate the land from the English plunderers', instead 'wants to be handed a whole country'. As Piterberg comments, Arendt had replied in 'relatively conventional Zionist mode', occluding the Arab question and couching the Jewish claim to Palestine in biblical terms, partially mediated by her Herderian analysis of Jewish identity as uniquely fortified by its relationship to its biblical history:

For whichever way you look at it, that land is unavoidably bound up with our past. Palestine is not at the centre of our national aspirations because

2,000 years ago some people lived there from whom in some sense or other we are supposed to be descended, but because for 2,000 years the craziest of peoples took pleasure in preserving the past in the present, because for them 'the ruins of Jerusalem are, as you could say, rooted in the heart of time' (Herder).[120]

Yet as Piterberg points out, within the next few years Arendt would produce not only the final chapters of *Rahel Varnhagen*, since, as she gently complains, 'Blücher and [Walter] Benjamin would not leave me in peace until I did', but also the unfinished essay 'Antisemitism'. This essay was something of a precursor to the 'Antisemitism' section of *The Origins of Totalitarianism*, though it is also a magnificent analysis in its own right, probably written, Jerome Kohn suggests, in Paris between 1938 and May 1940 while Arendt was interned for several months as an enemy alien.[121]

In 'Antisemitism', Arendt is interested in analysing the specificity of political anti-Semitism as a modern phenomenon that is capable of being understood and combatted. With this desideratum in mind, Arendt critiques both 'assimilationist' and Zionist modes of historicizing anti-Semitism. Arendt argues that upon emancipation, 'all Jewish-based critique of the non-Jewish milieu ceases entirely', because 'for assimilationists the history of the Jews coincides with the history of those nations among whom they live', inaugurating an apologetic genre of 'positive [Jewish] history' that does not recognize any difference of interest between Jews and 'any given segment of the German people'. Zionist criticism had 'finished off this absurdity' by demonstrating that assimilated Jews 'did not in fact belong to any society'. On the other hand Zionism, in treating the Jewish people as a 'nation of foreigners' in their host societies, and in opposing two abstractions to each other, that of Germans and Jews, effectively

> strips the relationship between Jews and their host nation of its historicity and reduces it to a play of forces (like those of attraction and repulsion) between two natural substances, an interaction that will be repeated everywhere Jews live.[122]

Moreover, Arendt chides, for Zionism, the 'factual assimilation' of Western European Jews, which was in reality tantamount to a 'complete transformation' of Jewish identity, is now regarded as 'extraneous to a Jewish substance that is forever the same'; regrettably Zionism regards the history of emancipation as the 'prelude to a catastrophe' that had to attend the development of national awareness. According to this view things went well for so long only because of liberal illusions and the 'individualistic biases of the Enlightenment', a position echoing her pre-war critique of German Jewish assimilation. In rejecting the naiveté of the assimilationists, and the dystopian fatalism of the Zionists, Arendt seeks a form of historical understanding that mediates between their ahistorical approaches:

> Assimilationists were never able to explain how things could ever have turned out so badly, and for Zionists there still remains the unresolved fact that things might have gone well.[123]

Significantly, where Arendt once saw in Zionism the hope of a realistic Jewish political response to anti-Semitism and the restoration of the Jewish people to their history, she is now prone to interpret political Zionism as ironically repeating the isolated posture for which she had earlier critiqued Enlightenment era Jewish emancipationists:

> The bankruptcy of the Zionist movement caused by the reality of Palestine is at the same time the bankruptcy of the illusion of autonomous, isolated Jewish politics . . . The successor to the failure of bourgeois assimilation is a failed bourgeois nationalist movement.[124]

Now warming to the acerbic historical perspective of the Jewish *schlemiel* and outsider figure, Arendt comments on Herzlian Zionism's parvenu preparedness to make any 'political concession' in support of its territorial aims by quoting Heinrich Heine in *The Rabbi of Bacharach*: '*How poorly defended Israel is! False friends stand guard outside its gates, while its guards within aare foolishness and fear*'.[125]

In her powerful essay 'Zionism Reconsidered' (1944), Arendt trenchantly critiques Zionism's undifferentiated suspicion of the innately anti-Semitic Gentile as an irrational attitude which 'cuts off Jewish history from European history and even from the rest of mankind', and 'ignores the role that European Jewry played in the construction and functioning of the national state'.[126] Zionism's monolithic lachrymose narrative of Jewish persecution throughout history will only fortify the 'dangerous, time-honored, deep-seated distrust of Jews for gentiles', transposing such an attitude to a non-European context in which it is obtuse and inappropriate.[127] Sounding very much like Cohen in 1916, Arendt cautions that Zionism's doctrine of the inevitable decline of Jewish life in *Galut*, and its interpretation of the insuperable importance of 'Palestine in the future life of the Jewish people', means that 'Zionists shut themselves off from the destiny of the Jews all over the world'.[128]

As Idith Zertal points out in an illuminating discussion of the Arendt/Scholem exchange, Arendt's report on Eichmann, the catalyst for their disagreement, criticized and even derided the notion that the Eichmann trial could serve Zionist pedagogical ends as a paradigmatic lesson about Jewish history. Arendt was critical of the 'political, educational, and propaganda nature which Ben-Gurion – the "invisible stage manager" of the trial – had imparted to the event, as he himself attested'.[129] Arendt took issue with the prosecution view of the masses in the Diaspora as 'an anonymous, passive, powerless object' lacking will or decision-making power of their own.[130] Arendt's 'provocative narrative', with its disturbing exploration of Eichmann's frightening normality, and its critical views about Israel including its laws barring inter-marriage between Jews and non-Jews, issued in a report, Zertal argues, that was 'neither a self-satisfied conclusion to an historical reckoning, nor a celebration of the new Jewish nationalism, born according to a Zionist discourse, in an inevitable, predestined, and teleological drive out of the ashes of the murdered European Jewry'.[131]

Arendt's steady disenchantment, beginning in the mid- to late 1930s, with the ideology of Zionism and with aspects of the state of Israel, which by no means prevented her celebrating its military successes in times of crisis, helps to explain the tensions which erupted in her 1963 exchange with Scholem. In their exchange, Arendt subtly implies that Scholem's embattled and coarsely ethnocentric version of Zionism ('I regard you wholly as a daughter of our people, and in no other way') has lost touch with his earlier recognition of messianic activity as sustaining Jewish diasporic existence. Arendt repudiates the notion of *Ahabath Israel* ('love of the Jewish people') and, in terms redolent of her critique of fraternal sentimentalism, affirms that she loves only her friends, that the 'only kind of love I know of and believe in is the love of persons'. Arendt then reports her conversation with Golda Meir (disguised as a prominent male political personality) who argued that while as a socialist she did not believe in God, she did 'believe in the Jewish people'. Arendt, like Cohen in 1916, Buber in 1934, and Cassirer in 1944, rejects an insular Jewish politics that retains confidence only in its own historically derived *ethnos*. She tells Scholem that at the time of her encounter with Golda Meir she should have replied that the greatness of the Jewish people was that it once believed in God in such a way that 'its trust and love towards him was greater than its fear. And now this people believes only in itself? What good can come out of that?'[132] Arendt's dismay at Israel's abandonment of its tradition of ethical monotheism was not without precedent. In her 1944 essay 'The Jew as Pariah', Arendt had celebrated Heine's Prophetic spirit, his 'traditional Jewish passion for justice'.[133] In a letter of 26 October 1953, Kurt Blumenfeld agreed with Arendt's melancholy assessment of the state of the world consequent upon the Israeli Nationality Law in March 1952 which excluded from Israeli citizenship all but ten per cent of the Palestinians living in Israel, which was followed in August by the killing of fifty-two Palestinians in the West Bank village of Kybia. Blumenfeld lamented that the 'meaning of the Ten Commandments is everywhere forgotten, in Europe and in Israel'.[134]

Some thirty years after seeking to derive Jewish identity from a Zionistic historical memory, Arendt now extols Judaism's ethical monotheism and faith in the future as an important pillar of its survival. As Zertal points out, in her dialogue with Scholem, Arendt reaffirms her belief in the role of the Jew according to the hidden tradition of the conscious pariah, in which one remains outside, a rebel and outcast by choice, so that from this singular vantage point one can, as Zertal phrases it, 'make a contribution to mankind, and . . . enter its midst as a Jew'. Perhaps Arendt assumed the role of the Jewish writer as Geiger conceived it, in which the Jewish writer, if she is to be true to her Prophetic-critical vocation of rejuvenating Judaism in its relationships with the general culture and purifying its eternal religious ideas, must communicate in a lively and penetrating manner and without compromise.[135] The Jewish writer, as Geiger describes it, looks beyond the insular 'house' of Judaism towards the 'relations of the world' and the 'needs of the time', which for Arendt included the legal recognition of genocide as a crime against humanity. Not accepted at home, Geiger's writer reaches out for a broader community of 'progressive minds', a transnational republic of letters.[136]

Responding to Scholem's claim that her Eichmann book had made a 'mockery of Zionism', Arendt complains that many Zionists can no longer listen to opinions or arguments that are not 'consonant with their ideology', although there are exceptions. What seems to confuse Scholem, who seemingly shares in this ideological obtuseness, is that she, Arendt, is truly independent, that she does not belong to an organization and speaks only for herself. Arendt informs Scholem that she has 'great confidence' in Lessing's *Selbstdenken*, for which no ideology, public opinion, or facile conviction can ever be a substitute. Thus we witness a revolution of sorts in Arendt's thinking, in which her Zionist influenced critique of the Enlightenment as an era of assimilation corrosive of Jewish politics is gradually supplanted by a liberal Jewish affirmation of the Enlightenment as a living resource for reflection on ethical and intellectual virtues; a resource which is profoundly congenial to an analysis of those sociable, politically refractory, and robustly independent diasporic Jewish characteristics that are of ongoing human significance.

Notes

1 Cassirer, *An Essay on Man*, 184.
2 Cassirer, *An Essay on Man*, 185.
3 See once more Cassirer's defence of the historical influence and continuing vitality of the natural law tradition, an address given to the Hamburg Legal Society in February 1932. Cassirer concludes the address by discussing the Dreyfus affair, which has a paradigmatic significance and 'symbolic value' (*symbolischen Wert*) as an example of

natural justice. Cassirer reminds his audience, many of whom will assume that natural law is a 'stranger and intruder' (*Fremdling und Eindringling*), to legal theory, that Lieutenant Dreyfus would never have been exonerated if his defenders had submitted to the procedural legalism of the military court in Rennes. The 'public conscience' (*öffentliche Gewissen*) can never be satisfied with written laws but must draw on other standards, those 'unwritten laws' (*ungeschriebenen Gesetzen*) which are in fact deeply rooted in the history of jurisprudence. E. Cassirer. 1932. 'Vom Wesen und Werden des Naturrechts', *Zeitschrift für Rechtsphilosophie in Lehre und Praxis* 6, 1 and 26–27. Cassirer's coded critique of German nationalist historiography and his provocative allusion to the unjust treatment of Jews surely questions Gordon's assessment that his 1928 address defending the Weimar constitution was an example of a 'private man' displaying 'rare passion' thus belying his usual political reticence and the 'tone of rational moderation' evident in his writings. See Gordon, *Continental Divide*, 24, 317.

4 Cassirer, *An Essay on Man*, 187.
5 Cassirer, *An Essay on Man*, 189.
6 Cassirer, *An Essay on Man*, 188.
7 Cassirer, *An Essay on Man*, 189.
8 Cassirer, *An Essay on Man*, 196–197.
9 Cassirer, *An Essay on Man*, 191.
10 Cassirer, *An Essay on Man*, 205.
11 The Arendt collection at Bard College library reveals that Arendt possessed copies of Cassirer's *Rousseau, Kant, Goethe: Two Essays*, the Peter Gay translation of *The Question of Jean-Jacques Rousseau*, and *An Essay on Man*, all with marginalia and underlining. See Bard College Library catalogue at http://library.bard.edu/search/Y?SEARCH= Arendt+marginalia+Cassirer&b=arend&submit=Search, accessed 20 July 2012.
12 H. Arendt. 1994. 'A Reply to Eric Voegelin' (1953), in H. Arendt, *Essays in Understanding*, New York: Schocken Books, 403.
13 Arendt, 'A Reply to Eric Voegelin', 404.
14 'The Concept of History', in H. Arendt. 1961. *Between Past and Future: Six Exercises in Political Thought*, London: Faber and Faber, 50–51.
15 D. Hammer. 2002. 'Hannah Arendt and Roman Political Thought: The Practice of Theory', *Political Theory* 30(1), 136.
16 Hammer, 'Hannah Arendt and Roman Political Thought', 126.
17 M. Canovan. 1974. *The Political Thought of Hannah Arendt*, New York: Harcourt Brace and Jovanovich, 11, cited in Hammer, 'Hannah Arendt and Roman Political Thought', 132.
18 E. Young-Bruehl. 1982. *Hannah Arendt, for Love of the World*, New Haven and London: Yale University Press, 93.
19 Young-Bruehl, *Hannah Arendt, for Love of the World*, 93.
20 Barnouw, *Visible Spaces*, 38.
21 Barnouw, *Visible Spaces*, 66–67.
22 H. Arendt. 2007 [1932]. 'The Enlightenment and the Jewish Question', in J. Kohn and R.H. Feldman (eds), *Hannah Arendt: The Jewish Writings*, New York: Schocken Books, 16.
23 Barnouw, *Visible Spaces*, 66–67.
24 Arendt, 'The Enlightenment and the Jewish Question', 16.

25 R.J. Bernstein. 1996. *Hannah Arendt and the Jewish Question*, Cambridge, Mass.: The MIT Press, 20.

26 Arendt, 'The Enlightenment and the Jewish Question', 10.

27 Arendt, 'The Enlightenment and the Jewish Question', 11.

28 Arendt, 'The Enlightenment and the Jewish Question', 11–12. On Herder's historically animated theorization of *Bildung*, see Arendt's 1931 review of Hans Weil's *The Emergence of the German Principle of Bildung* (1930), in H. Arendt, 2007 [1931]. *Reflections on Literature and Culture*, ed. Susannah Young-Ah Gottlieb, Stanford: Stanford University Press, 27.

29 Arendt, 'The Enlightenment and the Jewish Question', 12.

30 Arendt, 'The Enlightenment and the Jewish Question', 12.

31 Arendt, 'The Enlightenment and the Jewish Question', 12–13.

32 Young-Bruehl, *Hannah Arendt, for Love of the World*, 94.

33 Arendt, 'The Enlightenment and the Jewish Question', 13.

34 Arendt, 'The Enlightenment and the Jewish Question', 14.

35 Arendt, 'The Enlightenment and the Jewish Question', 16.

36 See chapter 12, 'Between Pariah and Parvenu', in which Arendt distinguishes the social climbing parvenu from the pariah whose exclusion from society is recompensed by her 'view of the whole'. H. Arendt. 1997. *Rahel Varnhagen: The Life of a Jewess*, trans. R. and C. Winston, Baltimore: The Johns Hopkins University Press, 237–249.

37 Arendt was deeply influenced by Blumenfeld's conviction that regardless of their religious, cultural, or political convictions, Jews would be perceived by non-Jews first and foremost as Jews. The goal of every Jew would be to face this fact squarely, to 'face the non-Jewish German unabashed, with an open visor', Young-Bruehl, *Hannah Arendt, for Love of the World*, 73.

38 H. Arendt. 1964. '"What Remains? The Language Remains": A Conversation with Günter Gaus', in Arendt, *Essays in Understanding*, 5.

39 Young-Bruehl, *Hannah Arendt, for Love of the World*, 161–162.

40 H. Arendt. 2007 [1948]. 'Jewish History, Revised', in Arendt, *The Jewish Writings*, 303–304.

41 Arendt, 'Jewish History, Revised', 304.

42 Arendt, 'Jewish History, Revised', 309. Arendt was probably impressed by passages like these from *The Origins of the Kabbalah*: 'This symbolism of the tree stresses an element that was to become essential in the kabbalistic doctrine of the mystical vocation of the Jew. The tree is not only kept alive and watered by the source; its flowering, growth, and prosperity, its vigor, or, alternatively, its languor, depend upon the deeds of Israel.' See G. Scholem. 1990. *Origins of the Kabbalah*, trans. A. Arkush, Princeton, NJ: The Jewish Publication Society, Princeton University Press, 79.

43 H. Arendt. 2007 [1935]. 'A Guide for Youth: Martin Buber', in Arendt, *The Jewish Writings*, 31–32.

44 Arendt, 'A Guide for Youth: Martin Buber', 32.

45 Arendt, 'A Guide for Youth: Martin Buber', 33.

46 M. Buber. 1963 [1934]. 'Teaching and Deed', in M. Buber, *Israel and the World: Essays in a Time of Crisis*, New York: Schocken Books, 154–156, 158–159.

47 G. Scholem. 1971. 'The Science of Judaism – Then and Now', in G. Scholem, *The Messianic Idea in Judaism and Other Essays*, trans. M. Meyer, New York: Schocken

Books, 305, 308. As David Biale argues, for Scholem, *Wissenschaft des Judentums* failed to include the irrational and apocalyptic elements of Jewish history in its definition of Judaism because its social context forced it into apologetics, dogmatic rationalism, and antiquarianism. Discussing Scholem's highly polemical 1945 essay, 'From Reflections on the Science of Judaism', Biale argues that Scholem interpreted nineteenth-century *Wissenschaft des Judentums* as a reformist bourgeois intellectual movement which presented a 'moribund' version of Judaism preserving the status quo; the rationalist bias of *Wissenschaft des Judentums* precluded a dialectical view of Jewish history that envisioned the possibility of future life. Biale, *Gershom Scholem,* 189 and 7.

48 Young-Bruehl, *Hannah Arendt, for Love of the World,* 94.
49 Young-Bruehl, *Hannah Arendt, for Love of the World,* 116.
50 Young-Bruehl, *Hannah Arendt, for Love of the World,* 162.
51 Young-Bruehl, *Hannah Arendt, for Love of the World,* 162.
52 H. Arendt. 1983. *Men in Dark Times,* New York: Harcourt Brace, 193.
53 Arendt, *Men in Dark Times,* 193.
54 Arendt, *Men in Dark Times,* 205–206.
55 Arendt, *Men in Dark Times,* 195.
56 Bernstein, *Hannah Arendt and the Jewish Question,* 28–29. For Arendt's discussion of Benjamin's philosophy of language see *Men in Dark Times,* 203–205. Biale compares Benjamin's theory of a divine language that underlies conventional language with Scholem's conception of the divine name as meaningless but meaning-bestowing. Biale, *Gershom Scholem,* 3, 7, 106–107.
57 H. Arendt. 2007 [1943]. 'We Refugees', in Arendt, *The Jewish Writings,* 274.
58 Arendt, 'We Refugees', 274.
59 Arendt, 'We Refugees', 274.
60 H. Arendt. 2007 [1944]. 'The Jew as Pariah: A Hidden Tradition', in Arendt, *The Jewish Writings,* 275, 279.
61 Arendt, 'The Jew as Pariah', 275.
62 Arendt, 'The Jew as Pariah', 276.
63 Arendt, *Men in Dark Times,* 5.
64 Arendt, *Men in Dark Times,* 8.
65 Arendt, *Men in Dark Times,* 8.
66 Arendt, *Men in Dark Times,* 8.
67 Cassirer, 'Die Idee der Religion bei Lessing and Mendelssohn', 34.
68 Arendt, *Men in Dark Times,* 10.
69 Arendt, *Men in Dark Times,* 11.
70 Arendt, *Men in Dark Times,* 12, 13.
71 Arendt, *Men in Dark Times,* 12.
72 Arendt, *Men in Dark Times,* 13, 16.
73 Arendt, *Men in Dark Times,* 15–16.
74 Arendt, *Men in Dark Times,* 18.
75 Arendt, *Men in Dark Times,* 23.
76 Arendt, *Men in Dark Times,* 25.
77 Arendt, *Men in Dark Times,* 25.
78 Arendt, *Men in Dark Times,* 26.
79 Arendt, *Men in Dark Times,* 26.

80 Arendt, *Men in Dark Times*, 26.
81 Arendt, *Men in Dark Times*, 27.
82 Arendt, *Men in Dark Times*, 29.
83 For an analysis of Mendelssohn and Lessing's famous epistolary disagreement as to the primacy of *Mitleid* (pity) as the dominant affect produced by tragedy, see Goetschel, *Spinoza's Modernity*, 100–118.
84 Hannah Arendt. 2003 [1967]. 'Truth and Politics', in Hannah Arendt, *The Portable Arendt*, ed. P. Baehr, New York: Penguin, 559.
85 P. Birmingham. 2006. *Hannah Arendt and Human Rights, the Predicament of Common Responsibility*, Bloomington: Indiana University Press, 14. Birmingham is drawing on Arendt's discussion of Montesquieu's analysis of republican virtue in the essay 'What is Freedom?' For Arendt's discussion of the 'who' that is disclosed by words and deeds in the public realm, see H. Arendt. 1971. *The Human Condition*, Chicago: The University of Chicago Press, 178–180.
86 H. Arendt. 1982. *Lectures on Kant's Political Philosophy*, ed. Ronald Beiner, Chicago: The University of Chicago Press, 10.
87 Arendt, *Lectures on Kant's Political Philosophy*, 5.
88 Arendt, *Lectures on Kant's Political Philosophy*, 5.
89 Arendt, *Lectures on Kant's Political Philosophy*, 35.
90 Arendt, *Lectures on Kant's Political Philosophy*, 8.
91 E.W. Said. 2006. *On Late Style*, London: Bloomsbury, 7.
92 Arendt, *Lectures on Kant's Political Philosophy*, 13.
93 Arendt, *Lectures on Kant's Political Philosophy*, 15.
94 Arendt, *Lectures on Kant's Political Philosophy*, 15.
95 Arendt, *Lectures on Kant's Political Philosophy*, 15.
96 Arendt, *Lectures on Kant's Political Philosophy*, 16–17.
97 Arendt, *Lectures on Kant's Political Philosophy*, 17.
98 Arendt, *Lectures on Kant's Political Philosophy*, 32.
99 Arendt, *Lectures on Kant's Political Philosophy*, 32.
100 Arendt, *Lectures on Kant's Political Philosophy*, 61.
101 Arendt, *Lectures on Kant's Political Philosophy*, 61.
102 Arendt, *Lectures on Kant's Political Philosophy*, 61.
103 Arendt, *Lectures on Kant's Political Philosophy*, 54.
104 Arendt, *Lectures on Kant's Political Philosophy*, 56.
105 Arendt, *Lectures on Kant's Political Philosophy*, 57.
106 Arendt, *Lectures on Kant's Political Philosophy*, 58.
107 Arendt, *Lectures on Kant's Political Philosophy*, 59.
108 Gordon, *Continental Divide*, 276–278.
109 Arendt, *Lectures on Kant's Political Philosophy*, 66–67.
110 Arendt, *Lectures on Kant's Political Philosophy*, 43–44.
111 Arendt, *Lectures on Kant's Political Philosophy*, 66–67.
112 Humboldt, 'On the Historian's Task', 59/ 'Ueber die Aufgabe des Geschichtschreibers', *Über die Sprache*, 35–36.
113 Arendt, *Lectures on Kant's Political Philosophy*, 42.
114 Arendt, *Lectures on Kant's Political Philosophy*, 38–39.
115 Arendt, *Lectures on Kant's Political Philosophy*, 20.
116 Arendt, *Lectures on Kant's Political Philosophy*, 50.

117 Arendt, *Lectures on Kant's Political Philosophy*, 32.

118 Hannah Arendt, *Men in Dark Times*, 76.

119 G. Piterberg. 2007. 'Zion's Rebel Daughter, Hannah Arendt on Palestine and Jewish Politics', *New Left Review* 48, 42–44.

120 Quoted in Piterberg, 'Zion's Rebel Daughter', 43.

121 Piterberg, 'Zion's Rebel Daughter', 43–44. See Kohn, 'Preface', *The Jewish Writings*, xix.

122 Hannah Arendt, 'Antisemitism' (1938–1939), in *The Jewish Writings*, 50–51.

123 Arendt, 'Antisemitism', 51.

124 Arendt, 'Antisemitism', 59.

125 Arendt, 'Antisemitism', 59.

126 Hannah Arendt, 'Zionism Reconsidered' (1944), in *The Jewish Writings*, 358.

127 Arendt, 'Zionism Reconsidered', 358–359.

128 Arendt, 'Zionism Reconsidered', 361.

129 I. Zertal. 2011. *Israel's Holocaust and the Politics of Nationhood*, trans. C. Galai, New York: Cambridge University Press, 145.

130 Zertal, *Israel's Holocaust*, 138.

131 Zertal, *Israel's Holocaust*, 133. For Arendt's criticism of the rabbinical law in Israel regulating the 'personal status of Jewish citizens', and her criticisms of the trial's grandiose attempts to put 'anti-Semitism throughout history' on trial, with the ironic effect that Eichmann himself was only an innocent executor of a foreordained destiny, see H. Arendt. 1994. *Eichmann in Jerusalem, A Report on the Banality of Evil*, New York: Penguin Books, 7 and 19.

132 H. Arendt. 2007 [1963]. 'A Letter to Gershom Scholem' (24 July 1963), in Arendt, *The Jewish Writings*, 467.

133 Arendt, 'The Jew as Pariah', 280.

134 'Die Bedeutung der Zehn Gebote ist überall vergessen, in Europa und in Israel'. Kurt Blumenfeld to Hannah Arendt, 26 October 1953, in 1995 [1953]. *Hannah Arendt, Kurt Blumenfeld: in keinem Besitz verwurzelt, Die Korrespondenz*, eds. Ingeborg Nordmann, Iris Pillig, Hamburg: Rotbuch Verlag, 91. See Young-Bruehl, *Hannah Arendt, for Love of the World*, 291–292.

135 Abraham Geiger, 'Die zwei verschiedenen Betrachtungsweisen: Der Schriftsteller und der Rabbiner', in *Abraham Geiger's Nachgelassene Schriften*, 495–496.

136 Koltun-Fromm, *Abraham Geiger's Liberal Judaism*, 108.

CHAPTER 8

※

Hannah Arendt
A Question of Character

'The trouble with the Nazi criminals was precisely that they renounced voluntarily all personal qualities. . . . The greatest evil perpetrated is the evil committed by nobodies, that is, by human beings who refuse to be persons.'

Hannah Arendt, 'Some Questions of Moral Philosophy'

'Philosophy constantly brings conceptual personae to life; it gives life to them.'

Deleuze and Guattari, *What is Philosophy?*

My final chapter concerns the ethical importance of 'character' or 'personality' in Hannah Arendt's political philosophy. As we discussed in the last chapter, after her caustic repudiation of Enlightenment versions of reason and *Bildung* in the late 1920s and early 1930s, Arendt became increasingly reconciled to Lessing and Kant's *Aufklärung* ethos of *Selbstdenken*, an ethos she deemed capable of expressing admirable traits of ethical independence, worldly friendship, and communicative sociability, ethical qualities resistant to the dictates of History, ideology, and social conformity. The following discussion explores Arendt's particular contribution, from a Jewish perspective, to a post-Kantian tradition of character analysis. I explore Arendt's illumination of politically relevant and ethically significant Jewish character traits that have emerged in interaction with worldly and diasporic conditions. I suggest that Arendt's mature interest in acquired character, that 'valid personality which once acquired, never leaves a man', is one of her most interesting and enduring contributions to a liberal Jewish tradition of virtue ethics.[1]

In this chapter I discuss Arendt's theorization of 'character' as a form of, in Judith Butler's words, 'rogue subjectivity', whose capacity for internal dialogue militates against fluctuating moral norms. Arendt's discussions of the ethical qualities that constitute 'character' or personality is of axiomatic importance in her attempt, after the atrocities of the Second World War, to overturn the philosophical privileging of contemplation and eidetic intuition, and to promote thinking and judgement as quintessentially worldly human activities. Arendt's interest in character reprises a liberal Jewish enthusiasm for the ethos of *Bildung*, the dialogical formation of a distinctive subject or 'personality' capable of impressing their personal style or 'character' upon the world. Arendt's analysis of moral character converses with attempts by modern Jewish thinkers to articulate and justify the social function and universal ethical validity of post-traditional diasporic Jewish characteristics, such as critical scepticism and ethical universalism. Like Arendt, Georg Simmel and Walter Benjamin placed great emphasis on resistant and refractory versions of moral character that were unburdened by the inertia and parochialism of tradition and habitual modes of thought.[2]

For Arendt, reflection on character and personality is politically and ethically important, because it enhances judgement, the consideration of particulars that cannot be subsumed under a general rule. Evoking the merits and importance of personalities who are at once exemplary characters and idiosyncratic individuals, who display luminous qualities in 'dark times' and 'borderline situations', means eschewing normative moral codes and supercessionist meta-narratives of history that stress the rise of one people, class, or idea at the expense of others. Arendt's idea, by contrast, is that political judgement requires a certain kind of cosmo-political spectatorship that journeys freely across space and time, appreciative of individual, ethically significant human qualities wherever and whenever they are displayed. Such cosmo-political spectatorship involves an equilibrium of impartial judgement of and engaged participation in human affairs that helps to ensure that the 'exemplary figures of all people are available for all people'.[3]

Let's think about the reasons why the issue of character and its exemplary ethical force and cosmopolitan possibilities assumed tremendous importance in Arendt's thought. There is a letter in the Arendt/Jaspers correspondence of 29 September 1949, in which Arendt is just coming to terms with the reality of the Holocaust and the shocking news of Heidegger's involvement with National Socialism. Responding to Jaspers' assessment of Heidegger's 'impure' character, Arendt counters that Heidegger is in fact completely lacking in character, 'in the sense that he literally has none and certainly not a particularly bad one'. She goes on to pour scorn on Heidegger's desire to crawl back into a 'mouse hole' by retreating to his hut in Todtnauberg in the Black Forest, grumbling about civilization, writing *Sein* with an archaic 'y', and only wishing to receive admiring pilgrims. Heidegger, Arendt feels, is trying to 'buy himself loose from the world', to fast-talk himself out of everything unpleasant, so he can do nothing but philosophize.[4]

Arendt's distaste for Heidegger's evasions of reality are no less evident in her published work of this period; consider her 1946 essay 'What is Existential philosophy' where she refers to Heidegger's 'obvious verbal tricks and sophistries' and where, in the second note to the original English-language version of the essay, Arendt sardonically refers to the 'comic aspect' of Heidegger's Nazi involvement. Perhaps, she reflects, Heidegger is the last of the German Romantics, someone whose 'complete lack of responsibility' stems in part from 'delusions of genius' and in part from 'despair'.[5] This is not a trite accusation when we recall Arendt's argument in 'Some Questions of Moral Philosophy' that 'all radical evil comes from despair'.[6] Nor is such a judgement merely empirical and personal, when we consider that Arendt's view of Heidegger's want of character, discrimination, and thoughtfulness ('absence of thought is not stupidity; it can be found in highly intelligent people')[7] anticipates her 'banality of evil thesis' as applied to Adolf Eichmann, where Arendt was 'struck by a manifest shallowness in the doer that made it impossible to trace the incontestable evil of his deeds to any deeper level of roots or motives'.[8]

By way of contrast to this devastating assault on Heidegger's character or lack of it, at around the same period Arendt found herself very impressed with the vigorous cosmopolitanism of the French-Algerian writer Albert Camus, whom she first met in Paris in 1946. Camus, Arendt enthuses to Jaspers, is one of those 'young men from the Resistance' who is 'absolutely honest and has great political insight'. Camus embodies a 'new type of person cropping up in all the European countries, a type that is "simply European" without any "European nationalism"'. Such a type is 'at home everywhere' even if they don't know the language very well, perhaps a reflexive allusion to Arendt's contemporaneous struggle to master English in her new homeland of the United States. Sartre, by contrast, is 'much too typically a Frenchman', too literary, 'way too talented', and too ambitious. Before the war, Arendt writes, she had barely encountered this 'European' type that Camus represents, and she muses that the experience of fascism may have forged a kind of moral quality in some people which had previously only been an 'idealistic program'.[9] We should note here, as it will become a resonant theme in Arendt's ethical and political judgement, that Camus' character type, the post-national 'European', is much more important to her than the more philosophically gifted Sartre; not for the first time Arendt expresses a preference for an intellectual with character over the *amour propre* of the professional philosopher.[10] As we shall see, Arendt's interest in Camus as a cosmopolitan outsider figure is analogous to the way she later extols Jaspers as a 'citizen of the world' and exemplary philosopher. In implicit contrast to the reclusive master philosopher Heidegger, Arendt construes Jaspers as a luminous model of engaged, communicative thinking and judgement.

When pondering Arendt's insistent preference for admirable personality over philosophical talent, it would be a mistake, I think, to claim that Arendt's search for cosmopolitan 'citizens of the world' was more politically motivated and pragmatic than philosophically relevant, responsive to the ephemeral needs of the historical moment while neglecting the enduring worth of the philosophical oeuvre. For one thing, there is an interesting genealogy of thinkers, including Kant, Nietzsche, and Erich Fromm, who were interested in the historical, philosophical, and psychological significance of 'character' or its less ambiguous synonym, 'personality'. I would suggest that Arendt is invoking and renewing this philosophical interest in character when she not only pours scorn on the empirical Heidegger's want of character but also critiques and overturns Heidegger's model of philosophical profundity, his desire to be a prophet in the wilderness, a *maître à penser* standing aloof from the decadence of his era and garnering awe-struck disciples.

Arendt's remarks on Heidegger and Camus adumbrate her feeling that philosophy must recast itself as a form of life which preserves a reference to the world by ceaselessly re-presenting itself, communicating its personae and exemplary activities. It seems to me that Arendt was well served here by another philosophical citizen of the world, Immanuel Kant, whose observations on 'the character of the person' in his *Anthropology from a Pragmatic Point of View* (1798, 1800) were an indispensable reference point.

Kant on Character: The Anthropologist as Citizen of the World

One of the most interesting aspects of Kant's analysis of the 'character of the person' in Part II of his *Anthropology from a Pragmatic Point of View* is that it is written from the perspective of the citizen of the world, providing an incomplete, provisional, and eclectic knowledge gleaned from many sources and observations.[11] As Kant comments in the preface to the published volume of his long-running lecture series on anthropology that he had given every year since 1772, a pragmatic knowledge of humanity is neither natural nor physiological; pragmatic anthropological knowledge pertains to that which man as a free agent makes, or can and should make, of himself.[12] Kantian anthropology has practical applications; it is not theoretical or definitive but a knowledge of the world that 'must come after our schooling' by dint of maturity, experience, and wider spheres of social intercourse. This kind of knowledge, Kant writes, cannot be reduced to the cognition of things in the world; it is only considered pragmatic, rather, when it is 'knowledge of man as a citizen of the world'. To orient oneself to the world of human affairs, to 'have the world' as opposed to simply having knowledge if it, Kant argues, is not a localized or empirical knowledge of 'things'; rather, to use a metaphor, it presupposes that one has not simply understood a play but 'participated in it'.[13] As Foucault argues in his introductory essay on Kant's *Anthropology*, the *Anthropology* has a kinship with Goethe's great *Bildungsroman Wilhelm Meister* to 'the extent that here, too, we find that the world is a school'.[14]

In the second part of the *Anthropology*, the 'Anthropological Characteristic', Kant turns to a consideration of moral character. In a section entitled 'The Character of the Person' (*Der Character der Person*), Kant writes that moral character is something which 'can only be one [*nur ein einziger*], or nothing at all'. As opposed to physical character, the distinguishing mark of the human being as a sensible or natural being, to have character is the distinguishing mark of the human being as a rational being endowed with freedom. The 'man of principles', from whom one knows what to expect, not from his instinct but rather from his will, 'has a character' (*hat einen Character*).[15] To say of a human being, Kant writes, that 'he has a character' is in fact 'to have said a great deal about him, but it is also to have praised him a great deal', for it is a rare phenomenon and 'inspires profound respect and admiration toward him'.[16] To have character signifies that 'property of the will by which the subject binds himself to definite practical principles that he has prescribed to himself irrevocably by his own reason'. Even if these principles might occasionally be mistaken and imperfect, the formal element of his volition in general, to act according to firm principles, has something precious and admirable about it, for it is also 'something rare'.[17] Kant critiques physiological and physiognomic conceptions of character in the work of contemporaries such as Lavater when he stresses that when it comes to character it is not a question of what nature makes of the human being, but of 'what the human being *makes of himself*'. For character is not the same as the more passive and innate concept of temperament, in that it cannot be immediately observed; rather, character is only revealed over a temporal duration and is exemplified in a variety of situations. Kant suggests here that character demands expansive narration and in its singularity provokes reflection and wonder rather than peremptory judgement.[18]

For Kant, character is unique and inimitable: it is precisely originality in one's way of thinking (*Denkungsart*). He who has character has himself tapped the spring from which he draws his conduct. He is not an eccentric, however, for he takes his stand on principles that are valid for everyone. Nevertheless, someone with character is liable to be held up as an eccentric or crank because 'he does not take part in evil once it has become public custom (fashion)'.[19] However, just so Kant's audience don't become a touch bored and think they are back in the morally pure world of the categorical imperative immune to contingency and sensuous inclination, Kant suddenly surprises us by praising a man of 'evil character', the Roman dictator Lucius Cornelius Sulla. Kant writes that although the violence of Sulla's firm maxims arouses disgust, we 'admire strength of soul generally, in comparison with goodness of soul'.[20] Indeed, Kant goes so far as to insist, as Patrick Frierson puts it, that 'character, even when evil, is better than a lack of character'. After pointing out in his lecture notes that a 'human being is truly renowned when he has a determinate character, even would this be an evil one', Kant goes on to say of Sulla, reminding us of Arendt's damning judgement of Heidegger, that 'here truly is found more excellence than with a human being that has no character, even if he already has a good heart and soul . . . Character has inner moral worth'.[21]

In the *Anthropology*, Kant makes it clear that character cannot enter into a system of equivalencies. Character is not a good or useful property of a human being that has 'a price that allows it be exchanged'; it is not a talent that has a 'market price' and is open to manipulation, nor is it an enjoyable temperament that makes a person a transiently pleasant companion. Rather character has 'an inner worth, and is beyond all price', intuitively and performatively articulating Kant's famous precept that human beings must always be regarded as ends in themselves.[22]

Soon after invoking Sulla in the *Anthropology* Kant goes on to slightly qualify the pleasure we take in unyielding, even evil character, by prosaically reiterating that 'character requires maxims that proceed from reason and morally practical principles'.[23] Still, it is clear that while Kant the moralist praises true character as bound to reason and moral principle, Kant the citizen of the world, the urbane spectator of human affairs, admires and enjoys the enigma and critical force of character as someone who challenges, provokes, and transgresses social norms, who inspires the kind of admiration that cannot be referred back to the formal imperatives of practical reason. Characters inspire a play of affects evoked in story-telling, vignette, doxography. In a note illuminating his argument for the inner moral worth of character, Kant offers the story of how the nurse who had taken care of King James I of England pleaded with him to make her son a gentleman. James answered: 'That I cannot do. I can make him an Earl, but he must make himself a gentleman'. In the same note he gives us the tale of Diogenes the Cynic, notorious for his corrosive misanthropy and public obscenities, who was captured in Crete during a voyage and put on the block in a public sale of slaves. When asked by the merchant who had put him up for auction what he could do and what he knew, Diogenes' imperious response was 'I know how to *rule*' so 'find me a buyer who needs a *master*'. The initially perplexed merchant was so impressed by this singular response that he had his own son educated, admirably, by Diogenes.[24]

Kant's examples of ornery historical characters that resist habitual social conventions and obligations leads him to deduce that the principles that have to do with character are perhaps best expounded negatively.[25] Characters resist and defy social norms of behaviour in such a way that they demand that their lives are narrated as a meaningful whole. Never a function of their class or nation, to have character is to establish an important ethical nexus between past, present, and future in the life of the individual. To have character is to refuse to break legitimate promises, which includes honouring the memory of a friendship now broken off and never abusing the former confidences of said friend; it means refraining from associating with evil-minded men, paying no attention to gossip that issues from shallow and malicious judgement, and resisting, in oneself, that natural fear which does not want to offend against prevailing fashion and opinion, always a fleeting and changeable thing.

Character has a negative or resistant quality because it proceeds from a self-reflexive act of will. A man who is conscious of having character in his way of thinking does not have it by nature; he 'must always have *acquired* it'. The act of establishing character is 'like a kind of rebirth', involving the ceremony of making a vow to oneself with a solemnity which makes it unforgettable to him that does it, 'like the beginning of a new epoch'.[26] The usual socializing processes of education, example, and instruction, Kant writes, cannot produce this firmness and steadfastness in our principles gradually, but only, as it were, by 'an explosion' that results from our being weary of the precarious and unstable state of our instincts. The act of establishing character is usually that of a mature man, who insists upon the 'absolute unity of the inner principle of conduct as such'.[27]

So how can one decide whether one has character? Kant suggests that the sole proof a man's consciousness affords him that he has character is his having made it his supreme maxim to be truthful, both in his 'confessions to himself as well as in his behaviour toward everyone else'. Since to have character is both the minimum required of a reasonable man and the maximum of inner worth or human dignity, to be a man of principles, that is, to have determinate character, 'must be possible for the most ordinary human reason and yet, according to its dignity, be superior to the greatest talent'.[28]

There are some important aspects of the Kantian description of character that resonate strongly for Arendt in her attempts to narrate and exemplify the importance of moral personality. As we shall see, Arendt responds to Kant's argument for the acquired and self-willed nature of character, the idea of character as a rebirth of the soul, arguing for exemplary intellectuals as those who has reinvented themselves in such a way that their conduct, the way they present themselves to the world, is animated by a unifying and coherent principle, an *ethos*. Arendt construes thought and consciousness in Kantian terms as forms of self-relation and self-awareness. She seizes on Kant's Enlightenment era argument that character is a potentiality of anyone capable of using their reason, deploying Kant's analysis to repeatedly critique the ways in which professional thinkers with vested interests have attempted to elevate thought and contemplation beyond the flux of phenomenal life and the diversity of human opinions. For Arendt, character is formed in the public gaze, and demands to be narrated in the tradition of philosophical doxography, that is, against a textured social and historical background in which the philosopher is one character, or *dramatis personae*, amongst others. As Arendt argues in *The Human Condition*, the disclosure of who somebody is is 'implicit in both his words and deeds', but this revelation of a unique personal identity is embedded in a social context, it 'can almost never be achieved as a wilful purpose, as though one possessed and could dispose of this "who" as one can dispose of his qualities'.[29]

Typologies of Character

In her excellent study *Mind and the Body Politic* (1989), Arendt's biographer Elisabeth Young-Bruehl argues that Arendt's great contribution to political theory is her revival of traditional discussions, from Plato to Montesquieu, of forms of government, in which Arendt attempts to add to the traditional types a new and unprecedented one, totalitarianism.[30] I think we can extend Young-Bruehl's insightful comment and reflect on whether Arendt did not also share, with Kant, an aesthetically sensitive and typologically motivated interest in the ethically robust qualities of the self-formed character and relationally articulated personality, that is, a formal, spectatorial interest in characteristic 'ways of thinking' about the world. Like Kant, Arendt was interested in those characters traversing the panorama of our melancholy history that are determinately individual and uncompromisingly resistant to the normative impositions of society and the transience of fashion and convention.

For example, in her article 'Personal Responsibility Under Dictatorship' (*The Listener* 72, 6 August 1964) Arendt argues that as character types, the rebel and the sceptic are more likely to resist totalitarian rule and the criminal 'moral' code it attempts to impose because they are habitually prone to 'doubt and think for themselves'. Arendt makes this point about the political potential of what are by no means unequivocally positive or wholesome characteristics on several occasions in her work. In her lectures at the New School University and the University of Chicago in the mid-1960s, later published as 'Some Questions of Moral Philosophy', Arendt argues in reference to the Nazi era that in Germany there was a total collapse of moral and religious standards among people who to all appearances had always firmly believed in them. She points out that those people who managed not to be 'sucked into the whirlwind' of Nazi criminality were by no means the 'moralists', people who had always upheld rules of right conduct, but on the contrary very often those who had been convinced, even before the debacle of Nazi rule, of the 'objective non-validity of these standards per se'. We hardly need experience to tell us, Arendt comments, that:

> narrow moralists who constantly appeal to high moral principles and fixed standards are usually the first to adhere to whatever fixed standard they are offered and that respectable society . . . is more liable to become very nonrespectable and even criminal than most bohemians and beatniks.[31]

In a similar vein Arendt asserts that 'morally the only reliable people when the chips are down are those who say "I can't"'.[32] Arendt associated this ethical refusal with the 'negative, marginal qualities' of Socrates, whose refusal to do wrong under any circumstances is the 'only working morality in borderline situations'.[33]

Like Kant, Arendt admires the considerable ethical and political potential inherent in nonconformist character types who may in fact be difficult, cynical, resistant to authority, and abhor their social environment. I would suggest that Arendt is also invoking Georg Simmel's classic sociological defence of 'the stranger' who, 'like the poor and sundry "inner enemies" is an element of the group itself'.[34] To be a stranger is 'naturally a very positive [form of human] relation; it is a specific form of interaction'. The stranger's 'position as a full-fledged member [of a group] involves being both outside and confronting it'.[35] For Simmel, the classic example of the 'stranger' who intrudes as a supernumerary into an established group is the 'history of European Jews' who are restricted to intermediary trade, a situation which gives the stranger the 'specific character of mobility'.[36]

Simmel lauds the 'objectivity of the stranger' who is 'not radically committed to the unique ingredients and particular tendencies of the group' and therefore possesses a certain freedom.[37] The stranger, a potential wanderer who has not quite overcome the freedom of coming and going, is 'bound by no commitments which could prejudice his perception, understanding, and evaluation of the given', nor 'tied down in his action by habit, piety, and precedent'.[38] This objectivity, Simmel stresses, does not simply involve passivity and detachment but is composed of a 'particular structure of distance and nearness, indifference and involvement'. The stranger indicates a specific form of social participation of which a typical instance is the tendency of Italian cities to call in their judges from outside so they would be free of entanglement in family and party interests.[39]

Arendt's interest in defiant and resistant characters who prove the most reliable when social norms collapse also echoes her friend Walter Benjamin's interest in the Nietzschean vitalism and historical pathos of 'the destructive character', someone whose 'need for fresh air and open space is stronger than any hatred'.[40] The destructive character, writes Benjamin:

has the consciousness of historical man, whose deepest emotion is an insuperable mistrust of the course of things and a readiness at all times to recognize that everything can go wrong. Therefore the destructive character is reliability itself.[41]

Arendt's paradoxical point, following Simmel and Benjamin's Jewish coded, anti-functional sociology, is that it is just these recalcitrant personalities who are and must remain a part of any community, regardless of their eccentricity, individuality, and sub-cultural difference from normal social values. For it is in the 'borderline' situation of a moral emergency, in which the usual moral injunctions such as 'thou shall not kill' have been completely overthrown, that people with resistant, sceptical, pessimistic, and 'strange' characteristics will demonstrate admirably independent ethical qualities. We should note Arendt's resistance to rigid code morality and normative theories of historical progress and socialization, since her thesis amounts to the suggestion that it is preferable to have a variety of personality types, with different dispositions, interests, and orientations in a society, regardless of whether they pose some threat to the commonweal, to the organic integration of a given community, the *Volksgemeinschaft*. Indeed a minority of such characters, whose existence embodies the resilience of difference and the insuperable phenomenal diversity of the world, are worth more to Arendt than millennia of normative political, educational, and theological attempts to inculcate moral codes and ethical virtues. As Arendt puts it, 'an individual's personal quality is precisely his "moral" quality'.[42]

What constitutes someone with moral personality, as far as Arendt is concerned, and here she follows Kant, is a kind of active self-relation, a dialogue of the self with the self in the process of thinking which is incessant and which avails itself of all the communicative resources of a socially constituted language and a *sensus communis*:

> In this process of thought in which I actualize the specifically human difference of speech, I explicitly constitute myself a person, and I shall remain one to the extent that I am capable of such constitution ever again and anew ... What we call personality ... has nothing to do with gifts and intelligence, it is the simple, almost automatic result of thoughtfulness.[43]

Arendt understands conscience itself as a temporally extended self-relation rather than as innate or intuitive, a dialogue with the self in which multiple perspectives are considered and debated, in which the self dramatizes its deliberations and is its own spectator. Conscience is not a faculty of knowing and judging right and wrong but is what we now call consciousness, that is, 'the faculty by which we know, are aware of, ourselves'.[44] Only the incessant

Kantian 're-birthing' of the subject in the dialogue of thinking, as catalysed by language, can guarantee ethics. As Arendt puts it, 'my conduct towards others will depend on my conduct towards myself'.[45]

Kant's precept that someone with character despises any kind of internal dishonesty or bad faith is echoed by Arendt's argument that:

> moral conduct . . . seems to depend primarily upon the intercourse of man with himself. He must not contradict himself by making an exception in his own favour, he must not place himself in a position in which he would have to despise himself... The standard is neither the love of some neighbour nor self-love, but self-respect.[46]

This dialogic process of thinking, this incessant self-renewal, enables the ethical subject to constitute themselves through remembrance, 'striking roots and thus stabilizing themselves, so as not to be swept away by whatever may occur – the Zeitgeist or History or simple temptation'. If I refuse to remember, warns Arendt, 'I am actually ready to do anything'.[47] For what we usually call a person or personality, as distinguished from a mere human being or a nobody, 'actually grows out of this root-striking process of thinking'.[48] I would suggest that Arendt's concept of moral personality as striking roots in the self-relation and self-honesty of remembrance affirms a liberal Jewish interest in *Bildung* as the formation of character through an eclectic awareness of admirably heterodox personalities and moral qualities. Arendt thereby casts an acerbic glance towards the banal, ethically void Heideggerean discourse of primordial 'rootedness' in earth, tradition, and nation.

Far from indulging a misanthropic and elitist sense of authenticity, the ethical personality is a humanist, open to the sheer variety of human and earthly phenomena; in questions of ethics and practical judgement, s/he desires to be guided by example, to be confronted with concrete, singular instances of virtue which enhance her or his common sense and relatedness to other human beings past and present: 'what we need for common-sense thinking are *examples* to illustrate our concepts'.[49] Common sense thinking dwells on the singularity of human encounters and the representative significance of what is exemplary, encouraging imaginative reflection: 'the validity of common sense grows out of . . . intercourse with people – just as we say that thought grows out of . . . intercourse with myself . . . the more people's positions I can present in my thought and hence take into account in my judgment, the more representative it will be.'[50]

A thinking and acting being who is constantly imaginatively reprising the perspectives of others, the ethical personality is never simply alone, even in their solitude they have themselves for company, they enact the unity in difference that they are: 'solitude means that though alone, I am together with some-body (myself, that is)'.[51] The ethical personality is not egoistic but a medium of plural perspectives and forces. Far from being narcissistically wrapped up in itself as if it were the whole world, the self regards itself as a citizen of the world, its *doxa* or opinion by no means automatically superior to any other, needing testing, experimentation, and perspectival enlargement.

Judith Butler, in conversation with the thought of Kant, Foucault and Arendt, has recently articulated just such a form of critical 'self-invention' that would not be 'based on an ontology of individualism' but rather presupposes that individuation is 'always, even constitutively, jeopardized by the impingements of sociality'. For Butler, the critical task of self-inventing subjectivity is not to become free of all impingement but to 'distinguish among those modes of impingement that are illegitimate and those that are not'.[52] Drawing on Arendt's interest in the political significance of civil disobedience, Butler theorizes a 'rogue subject' that refuses fluctuating norms of political rationality while retaining a 'critical relation to existing modes of intelligibility'.[53] As Butler argues in *Giving an Account of Oneself*, the subject's 'self-crafting' always takes place in relation to an imposed set of norms, such that its ethical agency is 'neither fully determined nor radically free'. The struggle of the self-forming ethical personality, its 'primary dilemma', is to 'be produced by a world, even as one must produce oneself in some way'.[54] This is an acute issue for the active Jewish personality as Arendt conceived it, who would ironize, parody and transvalue the epithets and values attributed to them by a hostile society, rather than simply hide or deny those differences which they, like Rahel Varnhagen, would not have missed for the world.

The Socratic Jaspers

In *Men in Dark Times* (1968), a series of biographical portraits which should itself be considered as an eclectic contribution to the Kantian discourse on character, Arendt situates Jaspers as a Kantian character, a subject renewed through creative volition and exposure to public affairs. Like Kant, Jaspers has more than once 'left the academic sphere and its conceptual language to address the general reading public'.[55] Jaspers concurs with Kant that a philosophy that is not susceptible to popularization is more meretricious than genuine.[56] Emulating the urbanity and ethical consistency of the Socratic personality, Jaspers articulates a 'certain cheerful recklessness' in that he 'loves to expose himself to the currents of public life, while at the same time remaining independent of all the trends and opinions that happen to be in vogue'.[57] Jaspers possesses a spirited independence because he is not even in rebellion against the conventions of his society, which are always recognized as such, hence never taken seriously as 'standards of conduct'.[58] Jaspers' confidence in the public sphere does not stem from misanthropy or elitism however, but from a 'secret trust in man', in the *humanitas* of the human race.[59]

Jaspers is a moral character in the Kantian sense because he has accepted the gift of freedom and re-invented and 'renewed' himself since the rise of Nazism and the Second World War.[60] While other intellectuals in their middle age acquiesce to temperament and habit, Jaspers has become an active political philosopher and cosmopolitan citizen of the world, a 'public figure in the full sense of the word'.[61] In the aftermath of the war he embarked on new eras of productivity, taking it upon himself to answer for his thinking before the tribunal of mankind, desiring to live in the bright light of publicity, in that 'luminosity in which oneself and everything one thinks is tested'.[62]

Jaspers also embodies the role of the philosopher as world-citizen and world-spectator, 'as linked with the world as ever and following current events with unchanging keenness and capacity for concern'.[63] A cosmopolitan thinker, Jaspers has renounced the binding authority of tradition and of his own national past, inventing a historically reflexive philosophy that speaks to the contemporary needs of a global public sphere, in which the 'great contents of the past are freely and "playfully" placed in communication with each other'.[64] Jaspers' interest in the Axial Age in *The Origins and Goal of History* (1953), in which philosophical forms of living and thinking simultaneously emerge in India, China, Palestine, and Greece, is not simply historical, but rather a means of critiquing Eurocentrism and communicating the works and deeds of great philosophical personalities (Confucius, Lao-tse, Zarathustra, Heraclitus, the Jewish Prophets) to a transnational audience.[65]

Interestingly though, when it comes to discussing the emergence of Jaspers' 'unviolable, untemptable, unswayable' personality,[66] Arendt differs from the Stoic inspired Kantian interpretation of character as emanating from a form of masculine will and pride, commensurate with the desire to display virtuosity and heroism in the public sphere while repudiating dissimulating feminized traits such as gallantry. Rather than ascribing Jaspers' character to a Stoic mastery of the will over fear and baser inclination, Arendt construes Jaspers' personality as forged through his receptiveness to sexual and cultural difference. It is due to singular good fortune, Arendt writes, that Jaspers could be isolated in the course of his life, losing his position under Nazis rule, but never driven into solitude.[67] That good fortune is due to his marriage with a German Jewish woman, Gertrud Jaspers née Meyer, who stood by his side all his life, who helped him to create a 'world' of thought, discussion, and value judgement immune to the vulgarizations of nationalism, the heady passions of mob sentiment, and the temptations of power. From this 'world in minia-ture', Jaspers learned, 'as from a model, what is essential for the whole realm of human affairs'.[68]

Within the space of this supportive and intellectually stimulating marriage, Jaspers learnt and practised an incomparable faculty for dialogue, for the art of listening, a constant readiness to give a candid account of himself, and the patience to linger over any matter under discussion.

Rosa Luxemburg

If Arendt gives the Kantian analysis of character a new wrinkle, it is precisely in the idea that steadfast and distinctive personalities actively translate arts of social intercourse that are learnt in dialogue across differences of sex, ethnicity, and milieux, into their conduct in the public sphere. This is a point that Arendt also makes in relation to the generous sociability and discerning moral taste of Rosa Luxemburg, another poignant character study in *Men in Dark Times*. It is her essay on Rosa Luxemburg that tells us more about the Jewish inspired 'world in miniature', an inspiration to robust moral conduct, that Arendt has in mind.

I would suggest that Arendt's interest, in this essay, in a diasporic Jewish social microcosm that nourished vigorous forms of cultural and political agency draws on a tradition of liberal Jewish sympathy for pluralist diasporic milieux such as Andalusian Spain and republican Amsterdam. In 'Rosa Luxemburg', Arendt evokes Luxemburg's Polish-Jewish 'peer group' as a 'highly significant and totally neglected source' of the revolutionary spirit in the twentieth century.[69] Its nucleus consisted of 'assimilated Jews from middle-class families' whose cultural background was German, whose political formation was Russian, and whose moral standards in both private and public life 'were uniquely their own'.[70] These Jews, a tiny percentage of the diaspora, 'had no conventional prejudices whatsoever'. They were formed, Arendt tells us, by a Jewish family background that 'treated one another as equals', a 'childhood world in which mutual respect and unconditional trust, a universal humanity and a genuine, almost naïve contempt for social and ethnic distinctions were taken for granted'. Members of this peer group possessed 'what can only be called moral taste', which, Arendt reminds us, is very different from so called 'moral principles'.[71] It was this milieu, and never the communist movement, which remained Rosa Luxemburg's home; a home that was 'movable up to a point', since it was 'predominantly Jewish' and did not 'coincide with any "fatherland"'.[72]

Arendt then moves on to discuss Rosa Luxemburg's obstinate critique of the nation state, which Arendt interprets ambivalently as both admirable yet lamentably unrealistic. It was Nietzsche, Arendt suggests, who first pointed out that the position and function of the Jewish people in Europe predestined them to 'become the "good Europeans"' *par excellence*, something which could be said of no other group.[73] Indeed, although the Socialist movement could not persuade the working class that they were its true fatherland, Rosa Luxemburg was by no means entirely wrong on the national question, since that small minority of Jews that could be called 'good Europeans' might well have been the only ones to have a 'presentiment of the disastrous consequences ahead'.[74] We will never know if Arendt had the prescient political thinker Ernst Cassirer in mind here; nonetheless, this remark is emblematic of her mature suspicion of the Zionist critique of Jewish life in diaspora as factitious and delusional. As we have discussed, the figure of the 'good European' as a practical ethical subject and not just an idealistic chimera was eventually fulfilled for Arendt by public-intellectuals such as Camus and Jaspers.

The Jew as Pariah

In the very practice of self-constitution, Judith Butler argues, there is a 'giving oneself over to a publicized mode of appearance', whereby a 'mode of reflexivity is stylized and maintained as a social and ethical practice'.[75] I suggest that Arendt interpreted this performative subjectivity in liberal Jewish terms, as an ethically valuable cultural-historical characteristic of Jewish diasporic existence that enabled Jews such as Nathan the Wise and Moses Mendelssohn to mediate between Jewish and non-Jewish worlds. In her lifelong struggle to give an account of herself, to constitute herself as a political philosopher, German Jewish intellectual, and representative of stateless and marginalized peoples, Arendt foregrounds, in Deleuze and Guattari's terms, a *conceptual persona*, the 'Jewish pariah'. The 'Jewish pariah' embodies the dilemma of, in Butler's terms, the self-inventing 'rogue subject' who needs to acknowledge their irreducible relation to the world while forcefully challenging social norms.[76]

The preceding discussion of Arendt's investment in the exemplary public lives of conceptual personae such as Socrates, Jaspers, and Rosa Luxemburg should encourage us to recognize that her mature account of contemporary Jewish identity is more focused on diasporic relational characteristics and socially performed arts of living, nourished by particular European Jewish milieux, than on an essentialist interpretation of Judaism. Arendt's secular interest in Jewish culture and sensibility falls very much within a liberal Jewish, post-*maskilim* focus on the social liminality and exemplary humanism of diasporic Jewish intellectuals and philosophers, many of them humble and materially impoverished outsider figures who remained marginal to mainstream Jewish communities.

Perhaps we can think about Arendt's conceptual persona of the Jewish pariah as possessing the now familiar traits of, on the one hand, the 'destructive character' who has no faith in the triumphal march of history, and the unsettling play of engagement and distance that typifies the perpetual stranger and conscientious objector in any given community, including the Jewish community. Like Judith Butler's rogue subject, the Jewish pariah is vigorously relational, choosing their mode of comportment in response to representations that seek to oppress or exclude them or the attitude and social function they represent. The Jew as pariah transmutes the stereotype of the Jew as ontologically lacking, as rootless, imitative, an actor without authentic identity, into a virtue, performing a generous humanity, a *joie de vivre* and insouciance.

Arendt is particularly interested in the poet, essayist, and political icono-clast Heinrich Heine, the 'first German prose writer really to embody the heritage of Lessing'.[77] Of all the poets of his time, Arendt writes, 'Heine was the one with the most character', which had much to do with being able to describe himself truthfully, in Arendt's terms, as 'both a German and a Jew'.[78] The Jew as pariah smiles at the hubris of ethnocentrism and has no desire to be a part of formal or respectable society, with its stiflingly repressive morality and arbitrary codes of behaviour. Drawing on a liberal Jewish tradition of religious humanism excluding clerical mediation, Arendt stresses the 'basic affinity of the pariah to the people'.[79] Of Heine, Arendt notes his sympathy for the common people, since 'sharing their social ostracism, he also shares their joys and sorrows, their pleasures and their tribulations'.[80]

Heine's pantheism, Arendt muses, smiles at human hierarchies; the bare fact that the sun shines on all alike 'affords him daily proof that men are essentially equal', an interpretation of Heine that seems to glance back at Mendelssohn's anti-colonial and egalitarian emphasis on God's providence as legible in bounteous nature rather than the exclusive Salvationist doctrines of a Revealed truth. Arendt situates Heine as a prophetic *Aufklärung* thinker when she reflects that he kept his 'passion for freedom unhampered by fetters of dogma', viewing life through a long-range telescope rather than 'through the prism of an ideology'.[81] Of Chaplin, another pariah figure, Arendt sees in him the 'entrancing charm of the little people', illustrating that the 'human ingenuity of a David can sometimes outmatch the animal strength of a Goliath'.[82] Chaplin's 'worried, careworn impudence', the kind 'so familiar to generations of Jews', represents the effrontery of the poor 'little Yid', who does not recognize the class order of the world because he sees in it neither order nor justice for himself.[83] In a footnote, Arendt casually declares that despite Chaplin's recent assertion that he is of Irish and Gypsy descent, she has selected him for discussion because, even if not a Jew, he has 'epitomized in an artistic form a character born of the Jewish pariah mentality'.[84] Arendt's inclusion of Chaplin as authentically Jewish in spirit recalls Hermann Cohen's willingness to recuperate the reviled Heine as a proud Jew in the Prophetic tradition, a gesture that looks back to Mendelssohn's embrace of the heretical Spinoza as Jewish in character if not orthodox belief. Her predilection for Chaplin and other schlemiel figures could be fruitfully compared with Cohen and Cassirer's Prophetic ethics, with its emphasis on humility and humane solidarity as the authentic characteristics of Judaism.

Arendt herself represented and performed the Jew as pariah as a self-willed and self-renewing 'character' in the Kantian tradition, someone who chooses, despite moments of weakness, grief, and anguish, to defiantly and courageously display her difference to a hostile world, exhibiting a luminous personality so as to critique and transform the public realm. Arendt's interest in character is sustained by a long liberal Jewish preoccupation with the form and function of Jewish character traits within the larger canvas of European modernity and world history. As we have seen, Arendt affirms and revitalizes a counter-historical ethos that affirms Jewish difference while arguing for the ongoing cultural-historical benefits of Jewish participation in world history.

Notes

1 Arendt, *Men in Dark Times*, 73.
2 See E. Fromm. [1942] 1963. *Fear of Freedom*, London: Routledge, 222 and *passim*, and T.W. Adorno, E. Frenkel-Brunswik, D.J. Levinson, and R.N. Sanford. 1950. *The Authoritarian Personality*, New York: Harper and Row.
3 E. Young-Bruehl. 1989. *Mind and the Body Politic*, New York: Routledge, 45.
4 Arendt to Jaspers, 29 September 1949, in L. Kohler and H. Saner (eds). 1992. *Hannah Arendt, Karl Jaspers Correspondence 1926–1969*, trans. R. and R. Kimber, New York: Harcourt Brace Jovanovich, 142.
5 H. Arendt. 1994. 'What is Existential Philosophy?' in *Essays in Understanding, 1930–1954*, New York: Schocken Books, 187, n. 2.
6 H. Arendt. 2003. 'Some Questions of Moral Philosophy', in Arendt, *Responsibility and Judgment*, ed. Jerome Kohn, New York: Schocken Books, 74.
7 H. Arendt. 1978. *The Life of the Mind, 'Thinking'*, London: Secker and Warburg, 13.
8 Arendt, *The Life of the Mind, 'Thinking'*, 13.
9 Arendt to Jaspers, 11 November 1946, in Kohler and Saner, *Hannah Arendt, Karl Jaspers Correspondence*, 66.
10 Arendt's loyalty to Camus proved very resilient; she implicitly preferred his anti-revolutionary non-violent humanism to Sartre's affirmation of anti-colonial violence, expressing her support for an increasingly embattled Camus in 1952 when she wrote him a warm and admiring letter of praise for his book *L'Homme révolté*. See N. Curthoys. 2007. 'The Refractory Legacy of Algerian Decolonization: Revisiting Arendt on Violence', in R.H. King and D. Stone (eds), *Hannah Arendt and the Uses of History: Imperialism, Nation, Race, and Genocide*, New York: Berghahn Books, 109–129.
11 All references in English are from I. Kant. 2009. *Anthropology from a Pragmatic Point of View*, R. Louden (trans. and ed.), Cambridge, UK: Cambridge University Press. All

references to the original German refer to I. Kant. 1799. *Anthropologie in pragmatischer hinsicht*, Frankfurt: Hubner.

12 Kant, *Anthropology*, 3.

13 Kant, *Anthropology*, 4.

14 M. Foucault. 2007. *Introduction to Kant's Anthropology*, trans. R. Nigro and K. Briggs, Los Angeles: Semiotext(e), 54.

15 Kant, *Anthropology*, 185.

16 Kant, *Anthropology*, 191.

17 Kant, *Anthropology*, 192.

18 Kant, *Anthropology*, 192.

19 Kant, *Anthropology*, 193.

20 Kant, *Anthropology*, 193.

21 P. Frierson. 2006. 'Character and Evil in Kant's Moral Anthropology', *Journal of the History of Philosophy* 44(4), 625–626.

22 Kant, *Anthropology*, 192.

23 Kant, *Anthropology*, 193.

24 Kant, *Anthropology*, 192.

25 Kant, *Anthropology*, 193.

26 Kant, *Anthropology*, 194.

27 Kant, *Anthropology*, 194.

28 Kant, *Anthropology*, 195.

29 Arendt, *The Human Condition*, 179.

30 Young-Bruehl, *Mind and the Body Politic*, 13.

31 Arendt, 'Some Questions of Moral Philosophy', 104.

32 Arendt, 'Some Questions of Moral Philosophy', 78.

33 Arendt, 'Some Questions of Moral Philosophy', 106.

34 Simmel, 'The Stranger', in *The Sociology of Georg Simmel*, 402.

35 Simmel, *The Sociology of Georg Simmel*, 402–403.

36 Simmel, *The Sociology of Georg Simmel*, 403.

37 Simmel, *The Sociology of Georg Simmel*, 404.

38 Simmel, *The Sociology of Georg Simmel*, 405.

39 Simmel, *The Sociology of Georg Simmel*, 404.

40 W. Benjamin. 1986. 'The Destructive Character', in P. Demetz (ed.), *Reflections*, trans. E. Jephcott, New York: Schocken Books, 301.

41 Benjamin, 'The Destructive Character', 302.

42 Arendt, 'Some Questions of Moral Philosophy', 79.

43 Arendt, 'Some Questions of Moral Philosophy', 95.

44 Arendt, 'Some Questions of Moral Philosophy', 76.

45 Arendt, 'Some Questions of Moral Philosophy', 96.

46 Arendt, 'Some Questions of Moral Philosophy', 67.

47 Arendt, 'Some Questions of Moral Philosophy', 95.

48 Arendt, 'Some Questions of Moral Philosophy', 100.

49 Arendt, *The Life of the Mind*, 'Thinking', 103.

50 Arendt, 'Some Questions of Moral Philosophy', 141.

51 Arendt, 'Some Questions of Moral Philosophy', 98.

52 J. Butler. 2009. 'Critique, Dissent, Disciplinarity', *Critical Inquiry* 35, 789, footnote 12.

53 Butler, 'Critique, Dissent, Disciplinarity', 790.
54 J. Butler. 2005. *Giving an Account of Oneself*, New York: Fordham University Press, 19.
55 Arendt, *Men in Dark Times*, 74.
56 Arendt, *Men in Dark Times*, 74.
57 Arendt, *Men in Dark Times*, 77.
58 Arendt, *Men in Dark Times*, 77.
59 Arendt, *Men in Dark Times*, 77.
60 Arendt, *Men in Dark Times*, 78.
61 Arendt, *Men in Dark Times*, 75.
62 Arendt, *Men in Dark Times*, 75.
63 Arendt, *Men in Dark Times*, 78.
64 Arendt, *Men in Dark Times*, 84.
65 Arendt, 'Karl Jaspers: Citizen of the World', 88.
66 Arendt, *Men in Dark Times*, 76.
67 Arendt, *Men in Dark Times*, 78.
68 Arendt, *Men in Dark Times*, 78.
69 Arendt, *Men in Dark Times*, 40.
70 Arendt, *Men in Dark Times*, 40.
71 Arendt, *Men in Dark Times*, 41.
72 Arendt, *Men in Dark Times*, 41.
73 Arendt, *Men in Dark Times*, 42.
74 Arendt, *Men in Dark Times*, 42–43.
75 Butler, *Giving an Account of Oneself*, 114.
76 G. Deleuze and F. Guattari. 1994. 'Conceptual Personae', in Deleuze and Guattari, *What is Philosophy?*, trans. G. Burchell and H. Tomlinson, London: Verso, 61–84.
77 Arendt, 'The Jew as Pariah: A Hidden Tradition', 275–297, on 282.
78 Arendt, 'The Jew as Pariah: A Hidden Tradition', 281–282.
79 Arendt, 'The Jew as Pariah: A Hidden Tradition', 279.
80 Arendt, 'The Jew as Pariah: A Hidden Tradition', 278.
81 Arendt, 'The Jew as Pariah: A Hidden Tradition', 281.
82 Arendt, 'The Jew as Pariah: A Hidden Tradition', 286–287.
83 Arendt, 'The Jew as Pariah: A Hidden Tradition', 288.
84 Arendt, 'The Jew as Pariah: A Hidden Tradition', note 1, 297.

Conclusion
The Legacies of Liberal Judaism

❉

The legacies of the liberal Jewish tradition in ethics, philosophy, history, and literature are many and varied. Indeed, they are too diverse and profuse to be definitively accounted for here, since 'post-Zionism' is now a rubric for a variety of scholarly tendencies encompassing revisionist Israeli historiography, denationalized versions of Jewish history, Mizrahi critiques of Zionist Eurocentrism and Ashkenazi hegemony in Israel, sociological analyses of post-national tendencies in Israel, and a growing interest in the cultural Zionism of Martin Buber and Judah Magnes.[1] The engagement with Jewish and Israeli history outside of national, religious, and ethnocentric frameworks can be situated within a liberal Jewish tradition of seeking the present reform of Jewish life through a frank, open, and creative relationship to its history.

A resurgent interest in hybridized forms of Jewish identity also recalls liberal Jewish interest in the syncretism of Jewish history. In her important 1999 essay 'Taboo Memories, Diasporic Visions: Columbus, Palestine, and Arab-Jews', the Mizrahi-Israeli intellectual Ella Shohat laments that in the wake of Israel's establishment in 1948 and the bitter conflicts attending it, Arabs and Jews have been staged as 'enemy identities'. Zionism's narrative of a monolithic Jewish experience resists parallels and overlaps with other religious and ethnic communities. The monochrome idea of a unique, transhistorical victimization of Jews 'precludes analogies' and the appreciation of linked oppressions in particular historical contexts, such as the expulsion of both Jews and Muslims from Moorish Spain in 1492.[2] Shohat's call for a relational Jewish historicity recalls Heinrich Heine's (Mendelssohnian) suggestion that the struggle for Jewish emancipation is linked with the critique of Western colonialism and the achievement of political equality for all peoples.[3]

While the critical force of liberal Jewish critique has been adapted in complex and nuanced ways to accommodate the state of Israel, post-Second World War affirmations of Jewish diasporic identity and the importance of subaltern Jewish traditions remind us of the radical hermeneutics and inclusive sympathies of liberal Jewish thought. I have in mind a *locus classicus* of post-war Jewish thought, Isaac Deutscher's memorable essay, 'The Non-Jewish Jew' (1958), based on a lecture given at the World Jewish Congress in February 1958. Struggling to overcome the conformism and polarizations of the Cold War, Deutscher reminds his Jewish audience of a *Midrash* story in which Rabbi Meir, the great saint and sage, a pillar of Mosaic orthodoxy, took lessons in theology from a heretic, Elisha ben Abiyuh, called Akher the Stranger. Recalling how Akher the heretic had prevented Rabbi Meir from breaching the ritual boundary Jews are not allowed to cross on the Sabbath, Deutscher wonders about this Jew who was both in Jewry and yet out of it, respectful of his pupil's orthodoxy, but himself 'disregarding of canon and ritual'.[4] Interested in the character of Akher, Deutscher suggests that the 'Jewish heretic who transcends Jewry belongs to a Jewish tradition'. Akher is the prototype, Deutscher argues, of great revolutionaries of modern thought such as Spinoza, Heine, Marx, Rosa Luxemburg, Trotsky, and Freud. They belong to a Jewish tradition in that they 'all went beyond the boundaries of Jewry', which they found narrow and constricting.[5] It is worth quoting at some length Deutscher's characterization of the non-Jewish Jew as a liminal figure, as it encapsulates a liberal Jewish enthusiasm for the worldly Jewish outsider figure or pariah:

> They had in themselves something of the quintessence of Jewish life and of the Jewish intellect. They were *a priori* exceptional in that as Jews they dwelt on the borderlines of various epochs. Their mind matured where the most diverse cultural influences crossed and fertilized each other. They lived on the margins or in the nooks and crannies of their respective nations. Each of them was in society and yet not in it, of it and yet not of it. It was this that enabled them to rise in thought above their societies, above their nations, above their times and generations, and to strike out mentally into wide new horizons and far into the future.[6]

The spirit of Prophetic ethics and a liberal Jewish enthusiasm for polyglot Jewish identities lives on in Deutscher's description, which attempts, like Arendt, to embrace a subaltern Jewish tradition focused on character and sensibility.

Deutscher's essay anticipates a salutary tendency in German Jewish studies itself, which in the last fifteen years has become increasingly sceptical of the assimilationist paradigm of interpretation, a paradigm very much operative in those readings of Arendt that assume that she and other Jewish intellectuals of her generation transcended the bourgeois limitations of her German Jewish background and which interprets Cassirer as a staid representative of a limited German Jewish *Weltanschauung*. In a deservedly influential revisionist appraisal of the conflicted state of German Jewish studies, Samuel Moyn invokes Jonathan and Daniel Boyarin's famous essay in defence of diaspora Judaism, 'Diaspora: Generation and the Ground of Jewish Identity', in order to rethink German Jewish history as one of diasporic innovation rather than assimilationist decline. Moyn writes:

> Paradoxically, the attempt by Zionists to isolate a Jewish essence, and to show how mixing led to its destruction, contradicted and violated the operative principle of the Jews' identity throughout their history – that of the German Jews perhaps above all.[7]

In this book I hope to have provided further confirmation of the Boyarin brothers' argument that:

> Within the conditions of Diaspora, many Jews discovered that their well-being was absolutely dependent on principles of respect for difference, indeed that, as the radical slogan goes, 'no one is free until all are free'. Absolute devotion to the maintenance of Jewish culture and the historical memory was not inconsistent with devotion to radical causes of human liberation.[8]

I also hope to have illuminated a Jewish tradition that has been repressed, if not 'hidden', a tradition that is both motivated by a rich historical archive, the ethical, literary, and philosophical sources of Judaism, while also looking forward to new, relational manifestations of Jewish culture and sensibility.

Notes

1 By revisionist Israeli historiography I refer to the 'new historical' school of Israeli history emerging in the 1980s and 1990s associated with prominent historians such as Benny Morris, Ilan Pappé, and Zeev Sternhell. For a recent critique of Zionism's account of Jewish history, see Sand, *The Invention of the Jewish People*. For a now classic critique of Zionism's Ashkenazi bias, see E. Shohat. 1988. 'Zionism from the Standpoint of its Jewish Victims', *Social Text* 19/20, 1–35. A good account of post-Zionist tendencies in Israeli and Jewish diasporic scholarship is E. Nimni (ed.). 2003. *The Challenge of Post-Zionism: Alternatives to Israeli Fundamentalist Politics*, New York: Zed Books. For a psychoanalytic analysis of the Zionist imaginary, see J. Rose. 2005. *The Question of Zion*, Melbourne: Melbourne University Press. For an excellent discussion of cultural Zionism, see chapter one, '*Bildung* in Palestine: Zionism, Binationalism, and the Strains of German-Jewish Humanism', in S.E. Aschheim. 2007. *Beyond the Border: The German-Jewish Legacy Abroad*, Princeton: Princeton University Press, 6–44.

2 E. Shohat. 2006. *Taboo Memories, Diasporic Voices*, Durham and London: Duke University Press, 201–232, esp. 214.

3 Shohat, *Taboo Memories, Diasporic Voices*, 214.

4 I. Deutscher. 1968. *The Non-Jewish Jew and other Essays*, Boston: Alyson Publications, 25–26.

5 Deutscher, *The Non-Jewish Jew,* 26.

6 Deutscher, *The Non-Jewish Jew,* 27.

7 S. Moyn. 1996. 'German Jewry and the Question of Identity: Historiography and Theory', *Leo Baeck Institute Yearbook* XLI, 304. Moyn also discusses Shulamit Volkov's influential essay 'Die Erfindung einer Tradition. Zur Entstehung des modernen Judentums in Deutschland' (*Historische Zeitschrift* 253, 1991) which sees both orthodox and reform movements in German Jewish history as part of a 'Jewish project of modernity', a collective Jewish project which did not entail the effacement of Jewish identity as maintained by the Zionist interpretation of history, but its 'creative reconfiguration' (606).

8 D. Boyarin and J. Boyarin. 1993. 'Diaspora: Generation and the Ground of Jewish Identity', *Critical Inquiry* 19(4), 720. It is a shame that I have only just become aware of Judith Butler's recent book *Parting Ways: Jewishness and the Critique of Zionism* (2012), New York: Columbia University Press. Butler's suggestion that there are 'Jewish values of cohabitation with the non-Jew that are part of the very ethical substance of diasporic Jewishness' (1) is a guiding principle of this book, though I would avoid the ontological resonance of 'substance'.

Bibliography

❊

'Abraham Geiger', in the *The Jewish Encyclopedia*. Retrieved 6 June 2012 from http://www.jewishencyclopedia.com/articles/6560–geiger-abraham.

Adorno, T.W., E. Frenkel-Brunswik, D.J. Levinson, and R.N. Sanford. 1950. *The Authoritarian Personality*, New York: Harper and Row.

Altmann, A. 1973. *Moses Mendelssohn, a Biographical Study*, London: Routledge and Kegan Paul.

Arendt, H. 1961. *Between Past and Future: Six Exercises in Political Thought*, London: Faber and Faber.

———. 1971. *The Human Condition*, Chicago: The University of Chicago Press.

———. 1973. *The Origins of Totalitarianism*, New York: Harcourt Brace Jovanovich.

———. 1978. *The Life of the Mind, 'Thinking'*, London: Secker and Warburg.

———. 1982. *Lectures on Kant's Political Philosophy*, ed. Ronald Beiner, Chicago: The University of Chicago Press.

———. 1983. *Men in Dark Times*, New York: Harcourt Brace.

———. 1994. *Eichmann in Jerusalem, A Report on the Banality of Evil*, New York: Penguin Books.

———. 1994. *Essays in Understanding, 1930–1954*, ed. Jerome Kohn, New York: Schocken Books.

———. 1997. *Rahel Varnhagen: The Life of a Jewess*, ed. L. Weissberg and trans. R. and C. Winston, Baltimore and London: The Johns Hopkins University Press.

———. 2003. *Responsibility and Judgment*, ed. Jerome Kohn, New York: Schocken Books.

———. 2007. *Hannah Arendt, the Jewish Writings*, ed. J. Kohn and R.H. Feldman, New York: Schocken Books, 275–297.

———. 2007. *Reflections on Literature and Culture*, ed. Susannah Young-Ah Gottlieb, Stanford: Stanford University Press, 24–30.

Aschheim, S. 2001. 'Introduction', in S.E. Aschheim (ed.), *Hannah Arendt in Jerusalem*, Berkeley: University of California Press, 1–15.

———. 2007. *Beyond the Border: The German-Jewish Legacy Abroad*, Princeton: Princeton University Press.

Ballan, J. 2010. 'Dialogic Monologue: Hermann Cohen's Philosophy of Prayer', *Toronto Journal of Jewish Thought* 1.

Barnouw, D. 1990. *Visible Spaces: Hannah Arendt and the German-Jewish Experience*, Baltimore and London: Johns Hopkins University Press.

Bauer, B. 1843. *Die Judenfrage*, Braunschweig.

Bauer, B. 1843. 'Die Fähigkeit der heutigen Juden und Christen, frei zu werden', in G. Herwegh (ed.), *Einundzwanzig Bogen aus der Schweiz*, Zürich und Winterthur, 56–71.

Beiner, R. (ed.). 1982. *Hannah Arendt: Lectures on Kant's Political Philosophy*, Chicago: University of Chicago Press.

Benjamin, W. 1986. 'The Destructive Character', in P. Demetz (ed.), *Reflections*, trans. E. Jephcott, New York: Schocken Books, 301–303.

Bernstein, R.J. 1996. *Hannah Arendt and the Jewish Question*, Cambridge, Mass.: MIT Press.

Bernstein-Nahar, A. 1998. 'Hermann Cohen's Teaching Concerning Modern Jewish Identity', *Leo Baeck Institute Yearbook* 43(1), 25–47.

Biale, D. 1979. *Gershom Scholem, Kabbalah and Counter-History*, Cambridge, Mass.: Harvard University Press,

Birmingham, P. 2006. *Hannah Arendt and Human Rights, the Predicament of Common Responsibility*, Bloomington: Indiana University Press.

Boyarin, D., and J. Boyarin. 1993. 'Diaspora: Generation and the Ground of Jewish Identity', *Critical Inquiry* 19(4), 693–725.

Brann, R. 2006. 'The Arabized Jews', in M.R. Menocal, R.P. Scheindlin, and M. Selis (eds), *The Literature of Al-Andalus*, Cambridge, UK: Cambridge University Press, 435–454.

Brann, R., and A. Sutcliffe. 2004. 'Introduction', in R. Brann and A. Sutcliffe (eds), *Renewing the Past, Reconfiguring Jewish Culture: From Al-Andalus to the Haskalah*, Philadelphia: University of Pennsylvania Press, 1–20.

Brenner, M. 2010. *Prophets of the Past: Interpreters of Jewish History*, trans. S. Rendall, Princeton: Princeton University Press.

Breuer, E. 1995. 'Of Miracles and Events Past: Mendelssohn on History', *Jewish History* 9(2), 27–52.

———. 1996. 'Rabbinic Law and Spirituality in Mendelssohn's "Jerusalem"', *The Jewish Quarterly Review* 86(3/4), 299–321.

Breuer, E., and D. Sorkin. 2003. 'Moses Mendelssohn's First Hebrew Publication: An Annotated Translation of the Kohelet Musar', *Leo Baeck Institute Yearbook* 48(1), 3–23.

Brody, S.H. 2010. 'Reason, Revelation, and Election: Hermann Cohen and Michael Wyschogrod', *Toronto Journal for Jewish Thought* 1, 1–20.

Bruckstein, A.S. 2004. 'Introduction', in H. Cohen, *Ethics of Maimonides*, trans. A.S. Bruckstein, Madison, Wisc.: The University of Wisconsin Press, xxi-xliii.

———. 2008. 'Practicing Intertextuality: Ernst Cassirer and Hermann Cohen on Myth and Monotheism', in J.A. Barash (ed.), *The Symbolic Construction of Reality: The Legacy of Ernst Cassirer*, Chicago: The University of Chicago Press, 174–188.

Buber, M. 1963. 'Teaching and Deed' [1934], in *Israel and the World: Essays in a Time of Crisis*, New York: Schocken Books, 154–156, 158–159.

Buber, M., and H. Cohen. 1980. 'A Debate on Zionism and Messianism', in P.R. Mendes-Flohr and J. Reinharz (eds), *The Jew in the Modern World, a Documentary History*, Oxford: Oxford University Press, 448–453.

Butler, J. 2005. *Giving an Account of Oneself*, New York: Fordham University Press.

———. 2009. 'Critique, Dissent, Disciplinarity', *Critical Inquiry* 35, 773–795.

———. 2012. *Parting Ways: Jewishness and the Critique of Zionism*, New York: Columbia University Press.

Cassirer, E. 1923. 'Der Begriff der Symbolischen Form im Aufbau der Geisteswissenschaften', in *Vorträge der Bibliothek Warburg 1921/1922*, Leipzig: B.G. Teubner.

———. 1929. 'Die Idee der Religion bei Lessing und Mendelssohn', in E. Cassirer. *Festgabe zum zehnjahrigen Bestehen der Akademie für die Wissenchaften des Judentums, 1919–1929*, Akademie Verlag, Berlin, 22–41.

———. 1929. 'Die Idee der republikanischen Verfassung. Rede zur Verfassungsfeier am 11. August 1928', in *Aufsätze und kleine Schriften* (1941–1946), ed. Birgit Recki. 2007. *Cassirer Gesammelte Werke* (24 vols), Hamburger Ausgabe (ECW), Meiner Verlag, Vol. 7, 291–307.

———. 1929. 'Die Philosophie Moses Mendelssohns', in *Aufsätze und kleine Schriften* (1927–1931), ed. Birgit Recki, Hamburg: Felix Meiner Verlag, 115–138.

———. 1932. 'Vom Wesen und Werden des Naturrechts', *Zeitschrift für Rechtsphilosophie in Lehre und Praxis* 6, 1–27.

———. 1942. 'Hegel's Theory of the State', in *Symbol, Myth, and Culture*, 108–120.

———. 1943. 'Hermann Cohen, 1842–1918', *Social Research* 10(1), 219–232.

———. 1944. *An Essay on Man*, New Haven: Yale University Press.

———. 1944. 'Judaism and the Modern Political Myths', *Contemporary Jewish Record* 7, 115–126.

———. 1946. *The Myth of the State*, New Haven: Yale University Press.

———. 1947. *Rousseau, Kant, Goethe, Two Essays*, Princeton: Princeton University Press.

———. 1955. *The Philosophy of Symbolic Forms, Volume Two: Mythical Thought*, trans. R. Manheim, New Haven: Yale University Press.

————. 1978. 'The Problem of the Symbol and its Place in the System of Philosophy', trans. J.M. Krois, *Man and World* 11(3–4), 411–428.

————. 1979 [1935]. 'The Concept of Philosophy as a Philosophical Problem', in D.P. Verene (ed.), *Symbol, Myth, and Culture: Essays and Lectures of Ernst Cassirer, 1935–1945*, New Haven and London: Yale University Press, 49–63.

————. 1981. *Kant's Life and Thought*, trans. James Haden, New Haven: Yale University Press.

————. 1989. *The Question of Jean-Jacques Rousseau,* trans. P. Gay, New Haven: Yale University Press.

————. 1995 [1932]. *Goethe und die geschichtliche Welt*, Hamburg: Felix Meiner Verlag.

————. 1996. 'Cohen's Philosophy of Religion', transcribed D. Kaegi, *Internationale Zeitschrift für Philosophie* 1, 89–104.

————. 1996. *The Philosophy of Symbolic Forms, Volume 4, the Metaphysics of Symbolic Forms*, trans. J.M. Krois, New Haven: Yale University Press.

————. 2003. *Mein Leben mit Ernst Cassirer*, Hamburg: Felix Meiner Verlag.

————. 2004. 'Hermann Cohen. Worte gesprochen an seinem Grabe am 7. April 1918 von Ernst Cassirer', in B. Recki and T. Berber (eds), *Ernst Cassirer, Aufsätze und kleine Schriften (1927–1933)*, Hamburg: Felix Meiner Verlag, 284–290.

————. 2004 [1931]. 'Kant und das Problem der Metaphysik. Bemerkungen zu Martin Heidegger's Kant-Interpretation', in B. Recki and T. Berber (eds), *Ernst Cassirer, Aufsätze und kleine Schriften (1927–1933)*, Hamburg: Felix Meiner Verlag, 221–250.

————. 2004 [1929]. 'Nachruf auf Aby Warburg', in B. Recki (ed.), *Gesammelte Werke: Hamburger Ausgabe*, Bd. 17: *Aufsätze und Kleine Schriften (1927–1931)*, Hamburg: Felix Meiner, 368–374.

————. 2009. *The Philosophy of the Enlightenment*, trans. F.C.A. Koelln, J.P. Pettegrove, Princeton: Princeton University Press.

Clifford, J. 1997. *Routes: Travel and Translation in the late Twentieth-Century*, Boston, Mass.: Harvard University Press.

Cohen, H. 1919. *Die Religion der Vernunft aus den Quellen des Judentums,* Grundriss der Gesamtwissenschaft des Judentums, Leipzig: Fock.

————. 1924 [1880]. 'Ein Bekenntnis in der Judenfrage', in Bruno Strauß (ed.), *Hermann Cohens Jüdische Schriften*, vol. 2, Berlin: C.A. Schwetschke, 73–94.

————. 1971. 'An Argument against Zionism: A Reply to Dr. Martin Buber's Letter to Hermann Cohen', in H. Cohen, *Reason and Hope: Selections from the Jewish Writings of Hermann Cohen*, trans. E. Jospe, New York: W.W. Norton and Company, 164–169.

———. 1971. *Reason and Hope: Selections from the Jewish Writings of Hermann Cohen*, trans. E. Jospe, New York: W.W. Norton and Company.

———. 1980 [1867]. 'Heinrich Heine und das Judentum', *Jüdische Schriften II*, 2–44.

———. 2004. *Ethics of Maimonides*, trans. A.S. Bruckstein, Madison, Wisc.: The University of Wisconsin Press.

———. 2004. 'The Significance of Judaism for the Religious Progress of Humanity', trans. A. Mittleman, *Modern Judaism* 24(1), 36–58.

Cohen, R.A. 2006. 'Introduction', in E. Levinas, *Humanism of the Other*, trans. N. Poller, Urbana and Chicago: University of Illinois Press, vii-xliv.

Coskun, D. 2006. 'Cassirer in Davos. An Intermezzo on Magic Mountain (1929)', *Law and Critique* 17, 1–26.

Curthoys, N. 2007. 'The Refractory Legacy of Algerian Decolonization: Revisiting Arendt on Violence', in R.H. King and D. Stone (eds), *Hannah Arendt and the Uses of History: Imperialism, Nation, Race, and Genocide*, New York: Berghahn Books, 109–129.

———. 2013. 'Redescribing the Enlightenment: The German-Jewish Adoption of Bildung as a Counter-normative Ideal', *Intellectual History Review* 23(3), forthcoming.

Deleuze, G., and F. Guattari. 1994. 'Conceptual Personae', in G. Deleuze and F. Guattari, *What is Philosophy?*, trans. G. Burchell and H. Tomlinson, London: Verso, 61–83.

Derrida, J., and M. Ron. 1991. 'Interpretations at War: Kant, the Jew, the German', *New Literary History* 22(1), 319–395.

Deutscher, I. 1968. *The Non-Jewish Jew and other Essays*, Boston, Mass.: Alyson Publications.

Docker, J. 2008. *The Origins of Violence: Religion, History, and Genocide*, Sydney: UNSW Press.

Erlin, M. 2002. 'Reluctant Modernism: Moses Mendelssohn's Philosophy of History', *Journal of the History of Ideas* 63(1), 83–104.

Feiner, S. 2004. *Haskalah and History: The Emergence of a Modern Jewish Historical Consciousness*, trans. C. Naor and S. Silverston, Oxford: The Littman Library of Jewish Civilization.

Feldman, R.H. 2010. 'The Pariah as Rebel, Hannah Arendt's Jewish Writings', in R. Berkowitz, J. Katz, and T. Keenan (eds), *Thinking in Dark Times, Hannah Arendt on Ethics and Politics*, New York: Fordham University Press, 197–205.

Foucault, M. 2007. *Introduction to Kant's Anthropology*, trans. R. Nigro and K. Briggs, Los Angeles: Semiotext(e).

Frierson, P. 2006. 'Character and Evil in Kant's Moral Anthropology', *Journal of the History of Philosophy* 44(4), 623–634.

Fromm, E. 1963 [1942]. *Fear of Freedom*, London: Routledge.

Funkenstein, A. 1993. *Perceptions of Jewish History*, Berkeley, CA: University of California Press.

Gatens, M., and G. Lloyd. 1999. *Collective Imaginings: Spinoza, Past and Present*, London: Routledge.

Geiger, A. 1942. 'Die zwei verschiedenen Betrachtungsweisen: Der Schriftsteller und der Rabbiner', in *Abraham Geiger's Nachgelassene Schriften*, vol. 1, ed. Ludwig Geiger (1885), Andover-Harvard Theological Library 1942, 492–504.

———. 1962. *Abraham Geiger and Liberal Judaism: The Challenge of the Nineteenth Century*, trans. E.J. Schlochauer, Philadelphia: The Jewish Publication Society of America.

———. 1962. 'A General Introduction to the Science of Judaism', in A. Geiger and M. Weiner, *Abraham Geiger and Liberal Judaism: the Challenge of the Nineteenth Century*, Philadelphia: The Jewish Publication Society of America, 149–169.

———. 1985. *Judaism and its History in Two Parts*, trans. C. Newburgh, Lanham, MD: University Press of America.

Gilman, S.L. 1986. *Jewish Self-Hatred, Anti-Semitism and the Hidden Language of the Jews*, Baltimore and London: The Johns Hopkins University Press.

Goetschel, W. 1999. 'Rhyming History: A Note on the "Hebrew Melodies"', *The Germanic Review* 74(4), 271–282.

———. 2000. 'Lessing, Mendelssohn, Nathan: German-Jewish Myth-Building as an Act of Emancipation', *Lessing Yearbook* XXXII, 341–360.

———. 2004. *Spinoza's Modernity: Mendelssohn, Lessing, and Heine*, Madison, Wisc.: University of Wisconsin Press.

———. 2005. 'Lessing and the Jews', in B. Fischer and T.C. Fox (eds), *A Companion to the Works of Gotthold Ephraim Lessing*, Rochester, NY: Camden House, 185–208.

———. 2007. 'Mendelssohn and the State', *Modern Language Notes* 122, 472–492.

———. 2010. 'Voices from the "Jewish Colony": Sovereignty, Power, Secularization, and the Outside Within', in R. Shilliam (ed.), *Non-Western Thought and International Relations: Retrieving the Global Context of Investigations of Modernity*, London: Routledge, 64–84.

Gordon, P.E. 2008. *Continental Divide: Heidegger, Cassirer, Davos*, Cambridge, Mass.: Harvard University Press.

———. 2008. 'Review of Thomas Meyer, *Ernst Cassirer*', *AJS Review* 32(2), 435–437.

Gottlieb, M. 2008. 'Publishing the Moses Mendelssohn *Jubiläumsausgabe* in Weimar and Nazi Germany', *Leo Baeck Institute Yearbook* 53(1), 57–75.

Graetz, H. 1894. *History of the Jews*, Philadelphia: The Jewish Publication Society of America, 6 vols.

————. 1977. 'The Diaspora, Suffering and Spirit', in N.N. Glatzer (ed.), *Modern Jewish Thought: A Source Reader*, New York: Schocken Books, 19–23.

Grossman, J.A. 2000. *The Discourse on Yiddish in Germany: From the Enlightenment to the Second Empire*, Rochester, NY: Camden House.

Habermas, J. 2002. 'The German Idealism of the Jewish Philosophers', in E. Mendieta (ed.), *Religion and Rationality: Essays on Reason, God, and Modernity*, Cambridge, Mass.: The MIT Press, 37–59.

Hammer, D. 2002. 'Hannah Arendt and Roman Political Thought: The Practice of Theory', *Political Theory* 30(1), 124–149.

'The Hannah Arendt Collection' [online] 2009. Stevenson Library, Bard College. Available at http://www.bard.edu/arendtcollection/, accessed 4 May 2011.

Hannson, J., and S. Nordin (eds). 2006. *Ernst Cassirer: The Swedish Years*, Bern: Peter Lang.

Hecht, L. 2002. '"How the Power of Thought can Develop with a Human Mind". Salomon Maimon, Peter Beer, Lazarus Bendavid: Autobiographies of *Maskilim* Written in German', *Leo Baeck Institute Yearbook* 47(1), 21–22.

Heidegger, M. 1997. *Kant and the Problem of Metaphysics*, fifth edition, trans. Richard Taft, Bloomington: Indiana University Press.

Heine, H. 1959. *Religion and Philosophy in Germany*, trans. J. Snodgrass, Boston, Mass.: Beacon Press, 69–103.

————. 1985. 'Concerning the History of Religion and Philosophy in Germany', trans. H. Mustard, in H. Heine, *The Romantic School and other Essays*, J. Hermand and R.C. Holub (eds), New York: Continuum, 128–244.

————. 1985. 'The Romantic School', trans. H. Mustard, in H. Heine, *The Romantic School and other Essays*, J. Hermand and R.C. Holub (eds), New York: Continuum, 1–127.

Hertzberg, A. 1970. 'A Reminiscence of Ernst Cassirer', *Leo Baeck Institute Yearbook* 15, 245–246.

Heschel, S. 1998. *Abraham Geiger and the Jewish Jesus*, Chicago: University of Chicago Press.

————. 2010. *The Aryan Jesus: Christian Theologians and the Bible in Nazi Germany*, Princeton: Princeton University Press, especially chapter one 'Draining Jesus of Jewishness'.

Hochman, L. 2004. 'The Other as Oneself: Mendelssohn, Diogenes, Bayle, and Spinoza', University of Florida, *Eighteenth-Century Life* 28(2), 41–60.

Horsch, S. 2004. *Rationalität und Toleranz. Lessings Auseinandersetzung mit dem Islam* (Ex Oriente Lux 5), Würzburg: Ergon.

Humboldt, W.V. 1967. 'On the Historian's Task', *History and Theory* 6(1), 57–71.

———. 2002. 'Ueber die Aufgabe des Geschichtschreibers', in *Über die Sprache, Reden vor der Akademie,* Tübingen: A. Francke Verlag, 33–51.

Israel, J.I. 2001. *Radical Enlightenment: Philosophy and the Making of Modernity, 1650–1750,* Oxford: Oxford University Press.

Jospe, E. 1971. 'Introduction, in H. Cohen, *Reason and Hope: Selections from the Jewish Writings of Hermann Cohen,* trans. E. Jospe, New York: W.W. Norton and Company, 15–39.

Kant, I. 1799. *Anthropologie in pragmatischer hinsicht,* Frankfurt: Hubner.

———. 2006. *Religion and Rational Theology,* Cambridge, UK: Cambridge University Press.

———. 2009. *Anthropology from a Pragmatic Point of View,* trans. and ed. R. Louden, Cambridge, UK: Cambridge University Press.

Kohler, L., and H. Saner (eds). 1992. *Hannah Arendt, Karl Jaspers Correspondence 1926–1969,* trans. R. and R. Kimber, New York: Harcourt Brace Jovanovich.

Kohn, J. 2010. 'Hannah Arendt's Jewish Experience: Thinking, Acting, Judging', in R. Berkowitz, J. Katz, and T. Keenan (eds), *Thinking in Dark Times, Hannah Arendt on Ethics and Politics,* New York: Fordham University Press, 179–194.

Koltun-Fromm, K. 2000. 'Historical Memory in Abraham Geiger's Account of Modern Jewish Identity', *Jewish Social Studies* 7(1), 109–126.

———. 2006. *Abraham Geiger's Liberal Judaism: Personal Meaning and Religious Authority,* Bloomington and Indianapolis: Indiana University Press.

Koselleck, R. 2002. 'The Anthropological and Semantic Structure of "Bildung"', in R. Koselleck, *The Practice of Conceptual History, Timing History, Spacing Concepts,* trans. S. Presner with others, Stanford: Stanford University Press, 170–207.

Kramer, M. 1999. *The Jewish Discovery of Islam, Studies in Honor of Bernard Lewis,* Tel Aviv: The Moshe Dayan Center for Middle Eastern and African Studies, Tel Aviv University.

Krois, J.M. 1983. 'Ernst Cassirer's Unpublished Critique of Heidegger', *Philosophy and Rhetoric* 16(3), 147–159.

———. 1987. *Cassirer: Symbolic Forms and History,* New Haven and London: Yale University Press.

———. 2006. 'Introduction', in J. Hannson and S. Nordin (eds), *Ernst Cassirer: The Swedish Years,* Bern: Peter Lang, 7–30.

Lassner, J. 1999. 'Abraham Geiger: A Nineteenth-Century Jewish Reformer on the Origins of Islam', in M. Kramer (ed.), *The Jewish Discovery of*

Islam, Studies in Honor of Bernard Lewis, Tel Aviv: The Moshe Dayan Center for Middle Eastern and African Studies, Tel Aviv University, 103–135.

Lessing, G.E. 1962. *Hamburg Dramaturgy,* trans. H. Zimmern, New York: Dover.

———. 1970–1979. 'Rettung des Hier. Cardanus', in K. Eibl and H.G. Göpfert (eds), *Theologiekritische Schiften I und II* of Lessing's *Werke,* 8 vols, Munich, vol. 7, 9–32.

———. 1994. *Nathan the Wise,* trans. S. Clenell and R. Philip, Milton Keynes: Open University Press.

———. 2000. *Nathan der Weise,* Stuttgart: Reclam.

Liebeschütz, H. 1968. 'Hermann Cohen and his Historical Background', *Leo Baeck Institute Yearbook* 13, 3–33.

López-Morillas, C. 2006. 'Language', in M.R. Menocal, R.P. Scheindlin, and M. Selis (eds), *The Literature of Al-Andalus,* Cambridge, UK: Cambridge University Press, 33–59.

Maalouf, A. 1984. *The Crusades through Arab Eyes,* trans. J. Rothschild, London: Al Saqi Books.

Mendelssohn, M. 1988 [1781]. 'To the Friends of Lessing', in G.E. Lessing, *The Spinoza Conversations between Lessing and Jacobi,* trans. G. Vallée et al., Boston, Mass.: Lanham, 127–149.

———. 1782. *Manasseh Ben Israel, Rettung der Juden. Aus dem Englischen übersetz. Nebst einer Vorrede von Moses Mendelssohn* (Friedrich Nicolai, Berlin/Stettin), reprinted in *JubA* 8, 1–25.

———. 2003. *Philosophical Writings,* trans. and ed. D.O. Dahlstrom, Cambridge, UK: Cambridge University Press.

———. 1929. *Gesammelte Schiften: Jubiläumsausgabe,* eds. Ismar Elbogen, Julius Guttmann, and Eugen Mittwoch, continued by Alexander Altmann, Berlin: Akademie Verlag, 1929–1932; Breslau; S Münzs, 1938; Stuttgart-Bad Cannstatt: F, Frommann, 1971–2011.

Mendes-Flohr, P. 1991. *Divided Passions: Jewish Intellectuals and the Experience of Modernity,* Detroit: Wayne State University Press.

———. 1999. *German Jews: A Dual Identity,* New Haven and London: Yale University Press

Mendes-Flohr, P., and J. Reinharz (eds). 1980. *The Jew in the Modern World, a Documentary History,* Oxford: Oxford University Press, 448–453.

Menocal, M.R. 2002. *The Ornament of the World: How Muslims, Jews, and Christians Created a Culture of Tolerance in Medieval Spain,* New York: Little, Brown and Company.

Meyer, M.A. 1986. 'Heinrich Graetz and Heinrich von Treitschke: A Comparison of their Historical Images of the Modern Jew', *Modern Judaism* 6(1), 1–11.

————. 1988. 'The Emergence of Jewish Historiography: Motives and Motifs', *History and Theory* 27(4), 160–175.

————. 1988. *Response to Modernity: A History of the Reform Movement in Judaism*, New York and Oxford: Oxford University Press.

————. 1989. 'Modernity as a Crisis for the Jews', *Modern Judaism* 9(2), 151–164,

————. 2006. 'German Jewish Thinkers Reflect on the Future of the Jewish Religion', *Leo Baeck Institute Yearbook* 51(1), 3–10.

Mittleman, A. 2003. 'Introduction', in '"The Jew in Christian Culture" by Hermann Cohen: An Introduction and Translation', *Modern Judaism* 23, 51–60.

Moses, A.D. 2009. 'The Contradictory Legacies of German-Jewry', *The Leo Baeck Institute Yearbook* 54, 36–43.

Mosse, G.L. 1985. 'Jewish Emancipation, Between *Bildung* and Respectability', in J. Reinharz and W. Schatzberg (eds), *The Jewish Response to German Culture*, Hanover and London: University Press of New England, 1–16.

Moyn, S. 1996. 'German Jewry and the Question of Identity: Historiography and Theory', *Leo Baeck Institute Yearbook* XLI, 291–308.

Moynahan, G.B. 2003. 'Hermann Cohen's *Das Prinzip der Infinitesimalmethode*, Ernst Cassirer, and the Politics of Science in Wilhelmine Germany', *Perspectives on Science* 11(1), 35–75.

Myers, D.N. 2001. 'Hermann Cohen and the Quest for Protestant Judaism', *Leo Baeck Institute Yearbook* 46, 195–214.

————. 2003. *Resisting History: Historicism and its Discontents in German-Jewish Thought*, Princeton: Princeton University Press.

Nadler, S. 1999. *Spinoza: A Life*, New York: Cambridge University Press.

Niehoff, M.R. 1998. 'Zunz's Concept of Haggadah as an Expression of Jewish Spirituality', *Leo Baeck Institute Yearbook* 43(1), 3–24.

Nimni, E. (ed.). 2003. *The Challenge of Post-Zionism: Alternatives to Israeli Fundamentalist Politics*, New York: Zed Books.

Novak, D. 1981. 'Universal Moral Law in the Theology of Hermann Cohen', *Modern Judaism* 1, 101–117.

————. 2005. 'Hermann Cohen on State and Nation: A Contemporary Review', in R. Munk (ed.), *Hermann Cohen's Critical Idealism*, Amsterdam: Springer, 259–282.

Piterberg, G. 2007. 'Zion's Rebel Daughter, Hannah Arendt on Palestine and Jewish Politics', *New Left Review* 48, 39–57.

Poole, B. 1998. 'Bakhtin and Cassirer: The Philosophical Origins of Bakhtin's Carnival Messianism', *South Atlantic Quarterly* 97, 537–578.

Rabinbach, A. 1985. 'Between Enlightenment and Apocalypse: Benjamin, Bloch and Modern German Jewish Messianism', *New German Critique* 34, 78–124.

Reissner, H.G. 1965. *Eduard Gans: Ein Leben im Vormaerz*, Tübingen: C.B. Mohr.

Rose, J. 2005. *The Question of Zion*, Melbourne: Melbourne University Press.

Rosen, T. 2006. 'The Muwashshah', in M.R. Menocal, R.P. Scheindlin, and M. Selis (eds), *The Literature of Al-Andalus*, Cambridge, UK: Cambridge University Press, 165–189.

Rosenzweig, F. 2000. *Cultural Writings of Franz Rosenzweig*, trans. B.E. Gall, New York: Syracuse University Press.

Said, E. 2003. *Freud and the Non-European*, New York: Verso.

———. 2006. *On Late Style*, London: Bloomsbury.

Sammons, J.L. 1999. 'Who Did Heine think He Was?', in J. Hermand and R.C. Holub (eds), *Heinrich Heine's Contested Identities: Politics, Religion and Nationalism in Nineteenth Century Germany*, New York: Peter Lang, 1–24.

Sand, S. 2010. *The Invention of the Jewish People*, trans. Y. Lotan, London: Verso.

Schatz, A. 2007. 'Returning to Sepharad: Maskilic Reflections on Hebrew in the Diaspora', in R. Fontaine, A. Schatz, and I. Zwiep (eds), *Sepharad in Ashkenaz: Medieval Knowledge and Eighteenth-Century Enlightened Jewish Discourse*, Amsterdam: Koninklijke Nederlandse Akademie van Wetenschappen, 263–277.

Schmid, P.A. 2005. 'Hermann Cohen's Theory of Virtue', in R. Munk (ed.), *Hermann Cohen's Critical Idealism*, Amsterdam: Springer, 231–258.

Scholem, G. 1971. *The Messianic Idea in Judaism and Other Essays*, trans. M. Meyer, New York: Schocken Books.

———. 1976. *On Jews and Judaism in Crisis, Selected Essays*, ed. W.J. Dannhauser, New York: Schocken Books.

———. 1990. *Origins of the Kabbalah*, trans. A. Arkush, Princeton: The Jewish Publication Society, Princeton University Press.

———. 1997. *On the Possibility of Jewish Mysticism in our Time and Other Essays*, trans. J. Chipman, Philadelphia: The Jewish Publication Society.

Schorsch, I. 1988. 'Scholarship in Service of Reform', *Leo Baeck Institute Yearbook* XXXV, 73–101.

———. 1994. *From Text to Context: The Turn to History in Modern Judaism*, Hanover and London: Brandeis University Press and University Press of New England.

Shohat, E. 1988. 'Zionism from the Standpoint of its Jewish Victims', *Social Text* 19/20, 1–35.

———. 2006. *Taboo Memories, Diasporic Voices*, Durham and London: Duke University Press.

Simmel, G. 1950. *The Sociology of Georg Simmel*, ed. and trans. K.H. Wolff, Glencoe, Ill.: The Free Press.

Skidelsky, E. 2008. *Ernst Cassirer: The Last Philosopher of Culture*, Princeton: Princeton University Press.

Sorkin, D. 1994. 'The Case for Comparison: Moses Mendelssohn and the Religious Enlightenment', *Modern Judaism* 14(2), 121–138.

———. 1995. 'Religious Reforms and Secular Trends in German-Jewish Life: An Agenda for Research', *Leo Baeck Institute Yearbook* 40(1), 169–184.

———. 1999. 'The Mendelssohn Myth and its Method', *New German Critique* 77, 7–28.

———. 2000. *The Berlin Haskalah and German Religious Thought: Orphans of Knowledge*, London-Portland: Vallentine Mitchell.

———. 2008. *The Religious Enlightenment: Protestants, Jews, and Catholics from London to Vienna*, Princeton and Oxford: Princeton University Press.

Spinoza, B. de. 1951. *A Theologico-Political Treatise*, trans. R.H.M. Elwes, New York: Dover Publications.

———. 2007. *Theological-Political Treatise*, trans. J. Israel and M. Silverthorne, Cambridge, UK: Cambridge University Press.

Strauss, L. 1947. 'Review of Ernst Cassirer's *The Myth of the State*', *Social Research* 14(1/4), 127–128.

———. 1995. 'Introduction', in H. Cohen, *Religion of Reason out of the Sources of Judaism*, Atlanta: Scholars Press, xxiii-xxxviii.

Suchoff, D. 1997. 'Gershom Scholem, Hannah Arendt, and the Scandal of Jewish Particularity', *The Germanic Review* 72(1), 57–77.

Sutcliffe, A. 2004. 'The Ambiguities of Enlightenment: Voltaire and the Jews', in A. Sutcliffe, *Judaism and Enlightenment*, Cambridge, UK: Cambridge University Press, 231–246.

———. 2004. *Judaism and Enlightenment*, Cambridge, UK: Cambridge University Press.

———. 2004. 'Quarrelling over Spinoza: Moses Mendelssohn and the Fashioning of Jewish Philosophical Heroism', in R. Brann and A. Sutcliffe (eds), *Renewing the Past, Reconfiguring Jewish Culture: From al-Andalus to the Haskalah*, Philadelphia: University of Pennsylvania Press, 167–188.

Sznaider, N. 2011. *Jewish Memory and the Cosmopolitan Order*, Cambridge, UK: Polity.

Verene, D.P. (ed.). 1979. *Symbol, Myth, and Culture: Essays and Lectures of Ernst Cassirer, 1935–1945*, New Haven and London: Yale University Press.

Weise, C. 2005. *Challenging Colonial Discourse: Jewish Studies and Protestant Theology in Wilhelmine Germany*, Leiden: Brill Publishers.

———. 2009. '"Let his Memory be Holy to Us!": Jewish Interpretations of Martin Luther from the Enlightenment to the Holocaust', *Leo Baeck Institute Year Book* 54(1), 93–126.

Westerkamp, D. 2008. 'The Philonic Distinction: German Enlightenment Historiography of Jewish Thought', *History and Theory* 47, 533–559.

Yahalom, J. 2004. 'Aesthetic Models in Conflict, Classicist versus Ornamental in Jewish Poetics', in R. Brann and A. Sutcliffe (eds), *Renewing the Past, Reconfiguring Jewish Culture: From Al-Andalus to the Haskalah*, Philadelphia: University of Pennsylvania Press, 21–30.

Young-ah Gottlieb, S. 2003. *Regions of Sorrow: Anxiety and Messianism in Hannah Arendt and W.H. Auden*, Stanford: Stanford University Press.

Young-Bruehl, E. 1982. *Hannah Arendt, for Love of the World*, New Haven and London: Yale University Press.

———. 1989. *Mind and the Body Politic*, New York: Routledge.

———. 2010. 'Hannah Arendt's Jewish Identity', in R. Berkowitz, J. Katz, and T. Keenan (eds), *Thinking in Dark Times, Hannah Arendt on Ethics and Politics*, New York: Fordham University Press, 207–212.

Zammito, J. 2002. *Kant, Herder, and the Birth of Anthropology*, Chicago: University of Chicago Press.

Zertal, I. 2011. *Israel's Holocaust and the Politics of Nationhood*, trans. C. Galai, New York: Cambridge University Press.

Zhakor, Y.H. 2005. *Jewish History and Jewish Memory*, Seattle, WA: University of Washington Press.

Zimmerman, M. 2001. 'Hannah Arendt, the Early "Post-Zionist"', in S.E. Aschheim (ed.), *Hannah Arendt in Jerusalem*, Berkeley: University of California Press, 181–193.

Index

�֍